W9-AEJ-929

THE
CORNUCOPIAN TEXT

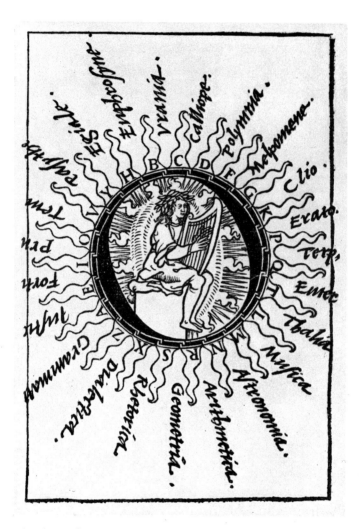

This design for the letter O (from Geoffroy Tory's *Champ fleury* of
1529) incorporates the Homeric 'golden chain', the twenty-four
letters, the rays of the sun, the nine Muses, the seven liberal arts, the
four cardinal virtues, and the three Graces. At the centre is Apollo,
representing the sun, or God, as source of all these. The figure of the
O itself signifies 'toute entiere perfection qui gist en la vraye cognoissance des bonnes lettres et Sciences' (cf. below, II. 1).

(Reproduced from a copy in the Bodleian Library)

THE CORNUCOPIAN TEXT

Problems of Writing in the French Renaissance

TERENCE CAVE

OXFORD

AT THE CLARENDON PRESS

1979

Oxford University Press, Walton Street, Oxford OX2 6DP

Oxford   New York   Toronto
Delhi   Bombay   Calcutta   Madras   Karachi
Kuala Lumpur   Singapore   Hong Kong   Tokyo
Nairobi   Dar es Salaam   Cape Town
Melbourne   Auckland
and associated companies in
Beirut   Berlin   Ibadan   Nicosia

Published in the United States by
Oxford University Press, New York

First published 1979
Bound new as paperback 1985
Reprinted 1986

British Library Cataloguing in Publication Data
Cave, Terence Christopher
The cornucopian text
1. Rhetoric – Philosophy – History
I. Title
808'.00944 PN173 78–40324
ISBN 0–19–815835–1

Printed in Great Britain by
Biddles Ltd,
Guildford and King's Lynn

CONTENTS

INTRODUCTION

*L'escrivaillerie semble estre quelque simptome d'un siecle
desbordé* (Montaigne, *Essais* III. ix, p. 946)

The sixteenth century is a period of prolific activity in both the
theory and the practice of writing. Stimulated by the success of
the printing trade, the urge to write translates itself into a spate of
manuals, tracts, dialogues, letters, fictions, and poems, which
accelerates as the century proceeds. At the same time, the problem
of how to write, together with fundamental questions concerning
the nature and status of writing, erupts not only in treatises on
rhetoric and poetics, in prologues and prefaces, but also within
the works themselves. This double characteristic—prodigality
and self-consciousness—is particularly prominent in the three
major vernacular writers of France, Rabelais, Ronsard, and Montaigne. In each case, despite obvious differences of genre, theme,
and social or political context, an initial text or group of texts is
extended, experimentally as it were, in a sequence which eventually proves itself to be open-ended. In each case, too, this
proliferation becomes a theme of the writing itself, whether explicitly or implicitly, whether in the form of metaphors or by
means of authorial intervention. Thus, in the remark quoted
above as an epigraph, Montaigne includes himself in his accusation; the *Essais* appear as a form of excess which the author cannot
bring under control: 'Qui ne voit que j'ay pris une route par
laquelle, sans cesse et sans travail, j'iray autant qu'il y aura d'ancre
et de papier au monde?' (ibid., p. 945). The problems of writing
which the present study seeks to explore all arise, in one way or
another, from this common centre of interest.

The word 'writing' is used here primarily in order to avoid
making *a priori* restrictions of material. To speak of the problems
of 'literature' in the sixteenth century would be to beg many of
the questions which the book poses, and which are posed also

by texts such as Erasmus's dialogues and the *Essais* of Montaigne. Literature can only be imagined in opposition to non-literary discourse: it is non-serious rather than serious, fictitious rather than true. Writing, on the other hand, is indifferent to these distinctions. It is constituted primarily in opposition to oral discourse, an opposition which it can itself absorb and write about, as many of the texts examined below will demonstrate.[1] It will be clear also from the use of this word that, while language in general is a major theme of this book, language is always considered in its organized form as 'discourse' (Latin *oratio*): analytical accounts of linguistic structure, such as grammatical theory, are not considered here.[2]

Since it was in Latin rather than the vernacular that the most elaborate theories of discourse were formulated in the sixteenth century, it is hardly possible to speak about such topics without bringing examples of vernacular writing into contact with Latin humanist writing. The figure of Erasmus dominates this terrain, both because of his European prestige[3] and by the quantity and variety of his theoretical reflections on writing. Indeed, far from being simply a didactic theorist, he himself wrote endlessly and obsessively, so that his theory often appears not only as a product of his activity as a writer but as a means of testing and questioning that activity. Accordingly, examples of Erasmian theory and practice play a central role in the first part of the book, although never in isolation from their classical, neo-Latin, and vernacular counterparts.

The organization of Part I gives priority to theory, in that each of the four principal chapters explores a topic belonging to

[1] It should perhaps be said here that the word 'text' will be used in this study simply to designate an instance of writing considered (more or less arbitrarily) as a unit.

[2] On this topic, see Padley, *Grammatical Theory in Western Europe 1500–1700*.

[3] The direct influence of Erasmus after his death in 1536 is hard to trace in France, since he is scarcely ever named by those who may be his debtors; most of the evidence is circumstantial, although some verifiable textual borrowings may be located (see for example Margaret Mann Phillips, 'Erasmus in France' and 'From the *Ciceronianus* to Montaigne'). This difficulty is only of marginal importance for the present study where, as will be indicated below, the determining of precise historical connections and influences is not the primary aim.

the theory of discourse. The first raises the question of writing and its status through the Erasmian notion of *copia*.[4] By placing rhetoric under the aegis of this (essentially figurative) notion in his enormously popular handbook *De duplici copia verborum ac rerum*, Erasmus adumbrates a theory of writing as an activity at once productive and open-ended, escaping the limits which formal treatises of rhetoric and dialectic attempt to impose on it. Prescription is reduced, even undermined, in favour of *exercitatio* or *experientia*: practice is already gaining the upper hand over codified theory. At the same time, in an important section of the manual, a complementary theory of 'imitation' is sketched out. Writing is acknowledged to be dependent on what has been written before (particularly in classical antiquity); according to Erasmus, the writer must assert his independence by both multiplying and fragmenting his models so that he is not trapped by the prestige of a single author. Accordingly chapter 2 investigates the problem of imitation, chiefly through an analysis of two key texts, Erasmus's *Ciceronianus* (1528) and Du Bellay's *Deffence et illustration* (1549).

Chapter 1 had also raised the question of the classical opposition between *verba* and *res*. The simplicity of these terms—which might be approximately and provisionally rendered as 'style' and 'subject-matter'—proves to be deceptive: their sense shifts with the context in which they appear, and their duality is never fully symmetrical. For the present, it is enough to indicate that the opposition is central also to imitation theory, which turns on the possibility of transposing 'meaning' from one text (verbal surface) to another. The problem of meaning is then isolated and restated in a series of different contexts—Latin and vernacular, sacred and profane—by chapter 3. Here, Erasmus's strictures on allegory and his elaboration of more flexible interpretative models are juxtaposed with Rabelais's sophisticated and elusive fictions of interpretation.

The twin topics of chapter 4, improvisation and inspiration, do not follow in any logical sequence from the previous three

---

[4] On the range of meanings of this virtually untranslatable word, see below, I.1.

chapters, but are germane to them all. Indeed, they serve to clarify the nature and limits of 'writing theory' in that, as theoretical models, they attempt to impose on writing the supposed authenticity of oral utterance. Both improvisation and inspiration are concepts which seek to erase the wealth of preexisting written materials and represent discourse as arising immediately from the mind, breath, or voice of the speaker. Erasmian dialogue, Rabelais's quasi-oral narrative, the poetics of Ronsard, and the extempore mode of the *Essais* develop in their various ways this set of possibilities.

It must be emphasized at this point that the treatment of all these topics is highly selective and is not designed as a general historical survey. Certain questions and texts have been given prominence in an attempt to illustrate the problems of writing as posed by some of the more complex sixteenth-century accounts. Hence the *De copia*, the *Ciceronianus*, the *Ratio verae theologiae*, and the *Convivium religiosum* of Erasmus are considered primarily as theoretical paradigms, rather than as historically influential works. The same could be said of Quintilian's *Institutiones oratoriae*, which provides significant formulations of the notion of *copia* and of the theories of imitation and improvisation; except that, in this case, its interest necessarily has a historical aspect, since there would be little point in citing it in a study on the sixteenth century unless it were persistently echoed by sixteenth-century texts.

Chapter 5 of Part I and chapter 1 of Part II form a bridge between the two parts. The first briefly rephrases certain of the problems raised in the earlier chapters in terms of contemporary preoccupations with specious discourse and with the fundamentally devious nature of language: it points towards the possibility of a discourse (literature?) which accepts and takes advantage of such deviousness. The second, by contrast, sketches some of the ways in which sixteenth-century writers imagined the possibility of an ideal text: here, a utopian fiction or scripture emerges as a counterpart—and even as a threat—to their own desire to write.

The three central chapters of Part II, unlike those of the first part, carry as their titles the names of three authors. In each case, a corpus with its own generic characteristics is explored for evidence of how the problems of writing erupt in 'practice'. This is not meant to suggest that Part II simply provides examples of how the theories of Part I were consciously applied to the composition of literary texts. Any reader who looks for such one-to-one relationships will be disappointed and, no doubt, confused. Each chapter is an essay which gives priority to the idiosyncrasies of a given text or set of texts. The theoretical issues— both as sixteenth-century commonplaces and as topics of the text itself—are allowed to emerge from writing in action. This is perhaps particularly the case with Rabelais and Ronsard. Montaigne, whose writing is not expressly fictional, provides a context in which theory and practice are in a more explicit and continuous relationship with one another; but the difference is not a fundamental one.

Once again, the approach is deliberately selective. In order to suggest interconnections between the writers and to impose a certain coherence on material which is often centrifugal and digressive, a group of figurative themes has been chosen as emblems of how the texts manifest their own problems. These are the figures of abundance: cornucopia, natural or seasonal productivity, gold and other forms of material affluence, sexual fertility, eating and drinking. In some cases, the figures are directly related within the text to the activity of the writer; elsewhere, there is no such relationship. I have no wish to argue that the first category predetermines the reading of the second. Throughout, any allegorization of the text which may be explicit or implicit in my argument has a purely provisional status: it could hardly be otherwise in a book so centrally concerned with the relatively indeterminate character of all interpretation. But precisely because interpretation is indeterminate, one may legitimately indicate and play on possibilities of meaning, particularly where those possibilities are so frequently provoked by the texts themselves (in the sense that the reader is constantly being lured into discovering them). For example, the juxtaposition of the 'cornucopian text' metaphor of the Prologue to Rabelais's *Tiers*

Livre with the 'cornucopian codpiece' of *Gargantua* 8 and Panurge's praise of the codpiece in the *Tiers Livre* is a device designed
to uncover ways in which Rabelais's text operates by mimicking
the very fictional licence which is at the heart of his writing.

The book thus falls with apparent neatness into its two parts,
the first concerned with theory, the second with practice. But
its structure is not primarily that of a study in intellectual or
literary history; as already indicated, the two parts are not related
as cause to effect. The categories 'theory' and 'practice' are undermined from the outset, on the one hand by the tendency of
Erasmian theory to enact (or perform) the very principles it
enunciates, and on the other by the reflexive character of the
literary texts.[5] The theory I am interested in is characteristically
a self-eliminating one, a kind of anti-theory designed to release
the movement of discourse rather than to master it and circumscribe it pedagogically; and the practice—the writing of fictions,
poems, essays—constantly adumbrates the possibility of a theoretical formulation, while necessarily preventing any such formulation from crystallizing fully.

I have encouraged this reciprocity between theory and practice
by introducing vernacular texts into Part I at various focal points.
These examples are partly intended to suggest analogies of a
relatively straightforward kind (as, for example, between the
imitation theory of the *Ciceronianus* and that of the *Deffence et
illustration*). More centrally, however, they have the function of
developing in Part I itself that movement from theory to practice
which is implicit in the theories.

The reciprocal structure of the book may also be indicated by
taking *copia* and cornucopia respectively as the emblems of the
two parts. A sixteenth-century text already associates these two

[5] I use the word 'reflexive'—spelt thus to distinguish it from 'reflective'—in the
now widely accepted sense of 'reflecting its own operations': reflexive writing
comments on itself (explicitly or implicitly), displays and mirrors its own characteristics, presents itself as a topic. For a recent discussion of reflexivity in narrative
writing, see Dällenbach, *Le Récit spéculaire*. I have preferred, here and elsewhere
in this study, to adopt the convention of speaking of the text as in some sense
autonomous: hence phrases like 'Erasmian theory' or 'the Erasmian text', and the
tendency to make the text itself (rather than the author) the active subject of a
sentence.

figures with one another: Melanchthon, introducing an edition of
the *De copia*, alludes to the popularity of the work, its productive
concision, and hence its cornucopian character:

Here is Erasmus's treatise on *copia*, whose utility I should like to be as
clearly perceived by the public as the title is everywhere known.
For although the work seems small in appearance (*in speciem*), yet if
you inspect it more closely, you may find it truly to be what they
call a cornucopia. For since it sets out and represents all the figures
for enriching and embellishing discourse (*figuras omnes locupletandae
illustrandaeque orationis*), it contains an uncommon store (*thesaurum*) of
eloquence.[6]

I have thus used the double figure of *copia* and cornucopia as a
thread which may be followed through the labyrinth of sixteenth-
century writing, connecting many domains which have hitherto
been treated separately, or at most related by means of strictly
historical methods. In addition, many other secondary figures
recur as leitmotivs of the book—the Erasmian (and Ciceronian)
metaphor of the lattice (*transenna*), the 'paroles mouvantes'
attributed by Aristotle to Homer, the story of Babel—while
certain of the metaphors of abundance characteristic of Part II
appear already in Part I.

It will be clear by now that this study is a composite one. I
have deliberately brought together in the space of a single book
materials and methods which are usually kept separate. To
divide it into a study in intellectual history and a set of literary
essays would be to endorse that hygienic separation of two
supposedly opposite forms of discourse which I should like to
call in question. It also seems particularly appropriate to aim at
such a synthesis when speaking of a period in which writers
refused compartmentalization, in which the theory and practice
of writing flowed across the boundary between 'systematic'
and 'imaginative' approaches.

Thus, on the one hand, my treatment is by no means anti-
historical. I have referred specifically to historical questions,
sketched in the evolution of certain topics, indicated direct

---

[6] Melanchthon, *In Erasmi Rot. Libellum de duplici copia*, fol. [c6 v°].

textual borrowing, and in general attempted to define a configuration which is significantly different from what one might find in the fifteenth or the seventeenth centuries (the word 'century' is here used only as the crudest of yardsticks). On the other hand, anyone who is acquainted with the concerns of what may loosely be called *la nouvelle critique* will already have noticed, in the foregoing summary, signs of an interest in certain aspects of structuralism and its aftermath. This interest developed for a number of reasons. In the first place, the rapidly shifting methodology and terminology of the Parisian scene invites a *prima facie* analogy—albeit a distant one—with the situation of the 1520s and 1530s, when the rapid acceleration of conceptual shifts gave rise to deep anxieties and bitter polemical confrontations. More specifically, the problems of reading and writing formulated in, or implied by, sixteenth-century texts are often remarkably similar to those faced by a modern writer or critic. The consequences of Babel, the uncertainties of the 'logocentric' model (according to which language is presumed to have a natural and, ultimately, a supernatural grounding), were as pervasive then as now.[7] Thus my concern with theories of discourse and with reflexive texts may be seen as the result of a convergence between an attempt to deal with the empirical evidence of sixteenth-century writing and an attempt to grasp important aspects of modern critical reflection.

Here again, I should like to insist on the reciprocity, the conciliation of different possibilities, which such an approach implies. I have not adopted any specific model of analysis—structuralist, Lacanian, Derridian—since to do so would have been to reduce the sixteenth-century texts to the status of local illustrations of a modern theory. Even if, strictly speaking, this predicament can never be wholly avoided, it can in practice be mitigated by the refusal of any single, rigorously delimited model. Thus I have chosen rather to borrow *topoi*, figures, and devices from

---

[7] For a concise account of sixteenth-century views on language, see Dubois, *Mythe et langage*. On a broader level, George Steiner's *After Babel* provides a (somewhat erratic) survey of the history and recent development of certain of the topics which are raised in the present study.

various forms of *nouvelle critique*, and to juxtapose them with those of more traditional methods, and with themes and figures drawn from sixteenth-century texts. At the broadest possible level, it may be said that the language of the earlier chapters is predominantly traditional; responding to the character of the topics, it becomes increasingly adventurous towards the end of Part I and in the more 'poetic' contexts of Part II.[8] But this movement, once again, implies a continuous interchange between different registers of discourse: from the opening of the first chapter, with its semi-literary play on the etymologies of *copia*, theoretical and historical analysis is always open to a degree of poetic licence.

The four principal writers discussed here all play with language in various ways. Likewise, a good deal of recent theoretical writing reveals by means of typographical and other devices the accidents, absurdities, and etymological conditioning to which any use of language is subject, and which are liable to undermine any attempt to achieve full mastery of one's discourse.[9] In Erasmus, as in Barthes or Derrida, the use of certain rhetorical procedures indicates a high degree of self-consciousness; what appears to be (and indeed is) a highly technical discourse is pervaded by the surreptitious movement of figures. Metaphor, metonymy, catachresis, and other tropes, refusing to be tied down to a purely accessory function, govern the development of apparently conceptual arguments, while figures involving word-play—*annominatio* or *paronomasia*—repeatedly draw the reader's

[8] The extent to which one or the other register is seen to predominate will necessarily depend also on the perspective of the reader. I am aware that those who prefer the traditional methods of literary and intellectual history may find much of the argument unorthodox, while those who are engaged in current debates on theory will consider my approach cautious if not wholly conservative. This predicament illustrates rather aptly a central problem of reading and writing, one which also lies behind Rabelais's anecdote, in the Prologue to the *Tiers Livre*, about the parti-coloured slave riding a black camel: namely, the pressure on the writer to adopt a reassuringly uniform set of conventions.

[9] Barthes and Derrida provide the most striking and the richest examples of such procedures. The difficulty here, of course, is that word-play—like other signs of authorial self-consciousness—may become too prominent and thus, instead of multiplying the possibilities of meaning, have a reductive effect on the argument.

attention to the autonomy of language. The humanists' use of Greek words and phrases might also be quoted here as an example of the high degree of linguistic eclecticism and allusiveness which characterizes their writing. My own intermittent use of such devices (tropes, puns, etymological allusions, Latinisms, Gallicisms, and the like) is similarly meant to have the function of emphasizing the ways in which any argument is subject to a non-logic inherent in the singularities of language itself. Rather than pretending that they do not exist, or that careful definition of terms and use of syntax can somehow eliminate them, it seemed preferable to bring them to the surface and exploit them.

Such a procedure has the further advantage of permitting a certain degree of exuberance and rhetorical colouring in a book whose topics are often markedly festive. Indeed, the opening chapter culminates in the discussion of a phenomenon similar to what Barthes calls the 'pleasure of the text': advertising its autonomy and licence, writing escapes the constraints which dialectical and even rhetorical method seeks to impose on it. Thus, whereas the title of Erasmus's *De duplici copia verborum ac rerum* seems to indicate a reassuring duality in which words reflect reality, and are in consequence subordinate to it, it will be seen that this duality may easily become a duplicity. Users of language are duped by deeply ingrained linguistic habits into supposing that discourse mirrors, represents, or mimes reality, and tend to underestimate its congenital inclination to deviate from the 'things' it purports to represent. Or, to make the same point from another angle, words reconstitute things in their own mould (lexical, syntactical, phonological), asserting their domination over what they were supposed to serve. Hence language is both deviant (deviating from its 'origin' in reality) and devious (concealing its duplicity, undermining the assurance with which it is commonly used). The duplicity may be partially unmasked, though never eliminated, by means of a reflexive rhetoric which exploits the devices of word-play, and by associating the operations of language with themes of pleasure.

The use of certain verbal motifs may consequently be added to the group of recurrent metaphors mentioned earlier (*copia*, cornucopia, and their progeny) in so far as they play a similar part in the structure and argument of this study. They are instances of *annominatio* in that they form a set of variations on a given semantic or lexical theme. One is the notion of the *topos* or *locus* as a fragment of discourse which is constantly rewritten in order to produce new texts. *Topos* (a place or commonplace) is cognate with 'topic' and 'topical'; *locus* with 'locate' and 'dislocate'; 'place' with 'replace' and 'displace'. The repetition of the *topos* in successive texts causes a replacement or displacement of the meanings produced by that same *topos* in other contexts. The consideration of the *topos* as a fragment in its own right dislocates the text in which it is sited, loosens the apparent coherence and unity which a contextual reading would seek to impose. A particularly important kind of displacement occurs where a theoretical *topos* occurs in a non-theoretical text (as in the Prologue to Rabelais's *Gargantua* or in Ronsard's *La Lyre*): this creates what is sometimes called a 'fold' in the text (echoing Mallarmé's metaphor of the *pli* and more recent exploitations of the same image). In these reflexive instances of discourse, the fold is an unresolvable convolution: the theory cannot simply be taken out and used to explain the practice, since it is already contaminated by that practice, of which it is also a constitutive part. On some occasions, however, I have used 'fold' in a somewhat simpler sense in order to make explicit the etymology of 'explicit', 'explication', 'implicit', 'implication', even 'deployment', words which suggest in various ways the folding and unfolding of discourse (the interdependence of *copia* and *brevitas*, for example). 'Duplicity' naturally has a part to play in this series. Hence the metaphor of the fold provides a further example of *annominatio* as a device used for linking a group of textual phenomena.

It may be helpful at this point to comment on one or two other words which I have used in a sense other than that provided by standard dictionaries, although such uses are now widely acknowledged, if not accepted, in the context of literary theory. Like the examples given above, they are not strictly speaking 'terms' (building blocks in a conceptual system), since they all have a metaphorical character; their value lies in their flexibility and semantic resonance, qualities which are denied to precisely defined terms.

I have chosen on many occasions to use the word 'performance' instead of 'practice' (i.e. as the antonym of 'theory'). It usefully evokes the notion of an enactment (this word is used, too), of a mime taking place in language: classical oratory, humanist dialogue, and Rabelais's fictions all have their theatrical aspects. It is not identical to the linguists' term (antonym of 'competence'), nor to Dr. Jonathan Culler's transposition of it to the context of a structuralist poetics; but it may at times move very close to those uses. I have adopted 'performative' as its adjectival form, without meaning to invoke—except perhaps distantly—echoes of Austin. In so far as the two words have a special sense, they refer to a 'practice' (*exercitatio*) which is close to theory, which often carries fragments of theory in its folds, and which is thus a kind of demonstration. They also suggest the exuberance of a discourse in action, exploring its own liberties. Performance is the primary manifestation of the figures of abundance, which are often personifications (Panurge, Bacchus, Montaigne) acting out a celebration of textual productivity.

The notion of 'plurality' is used to denote the character of a discourse which resists interpretative integration, not because it is obscure, or because it has several levels of meaning, but because it is set up in such a way as to block normal interpretative procedures. *Jacques le fataliste* or the novels of Alain Robbe-Grillet are examples of plural discourse in this sense; so too, it may be argued, are the writings of the three major vernacular authors considered in this study.[10]

'Presence' may have either a spatial or a temporal sense, or both: it is the attribute of that which is present. It is a particularly important word in that it is contained also in the notion of language (or literature, as in Aristotle's theory of *mimesis*) as representation, as a copy which necessarily displaces the original.

[10] The doublet 'monologic'–'dialogic', introduced by Julia Kristeva on the basis of Bakhtin's study of Rabelais and Dostoyevsky, similarly opposes a linear, univocal text to a multiple, discontinuous one.

One variation on this theme is contained in Pascal's admirably concise formula, 'Figure porte absence et présence' (*Pensées*, Lafuma no. 265). The notion has also been repeatedly exploited by Derrida, especially with regard to the supposed coincidence of sound and sense in oral utterance, and to the relationship of oral discourse to writing.[11] On one or two occasions, I allude to other Derridian notions such as 'supplement', 'difference', and 'deconstruction'. In particular, the word 'deferment', as used in I. 3 below, is a transposition (and very much a dilution, it must be said) of Derrida's invented word *différance* (*sic*), which associates the ordinary sense of 'difference' with a temporal one, much as in the case of 'presence'. 'Supplement' comes from *suppléer*, 'to supply', 'to fulfil a need', but also 'to take the place of', 'displace'. The notions of necessity and excess are both present here: language is a 'supplement' in that it is both unavoidable and superfluous, as the first meeting between Pantagruel and Panurge demonstrates.[12] The etymology of the word suggests an over-filling, a superabundance, which I have located rather in the figure of cornucopia. This example is in fact a central one, since I have in the main attempted to avoid using the terminology of recent theoretical speculation, transposing it into distinctively sixteenth-century words and figures—and thereby, of course, displacing it.

The recourse to such procedures—the construction of an eclectic and intrinsically unstable critical vocabulary—is a consequence of the hypothesis that sixteenth-century texts make their problems evident in similar ways. Yet it should be stressed that, however great their lucidity, such texts also, necessarily, disguise or partially ignore them. Here, the advantage of a modern perspective, with its strategies for exploding logocentrism, is that it enables one to

[11] See in particular Derrida's *La Voix et le phénomène*, and his elaboration of similar problems in *De la grammatologie*. I touch on this issue primarily in I.4 below.

[12] See below, p. 115. Cf. Derrida's essay 'La différance' in *Marges de la philosophie*. The notion of the 'supplement' is developed, once again, in *De la grammatologie*. Mention should also be made here of 'La pharmacie de Platon' (in *La Dissémination*), Derrida's colourful variation on themes drawn from Plato's *Phaedrus*: my interest in Erasmian topics such as the curing of the *logos* by the *logos*, or the adage *ubi uber, ibi tuber*, was encouraged by this essay.

place maximum pressure on a given text and thus to display its structure ('deconstruct' it). This does not imply that any of the methodologies of our own day is in a privileged position from which it can denounce errors in other texts. Indeed, it might be preferable to invert the terms of the relationship and to consider the sixteenth-century text as challenging and deconstructing that critical language which attempts to master it: the host-text may easily come to appear as a parasite, and vice versa. Error is a property of all discursive language; the problems of writing (and of reading) can never be solved.

While the footnotes of this study contain references to secondary materials which seemed of particular relevance to the point concerned, no attempt has been made to be comprehensive, or to engage consistently in scholarly debate, whether on historical or theoretical issues. In consequence, similarities between my argument and that of previous writers have not always been indicated; I should therefore like to make a preliminary acknowledgement of the principal debts I am conscious of having incurred.

In recent times, attention has increasingly been given to the ways in which Latin humanist theories of discourse are related both to vernacular theories and to vernacular literature. In particular, Professor J.-C. Margolin has indicated Erasmus's concern with the problems of writing in his articles 'Érasme et le verbe: de la rhétorique à l'herméneutique' and 'Érasme et la vérité' (in *Recherches érasmiennes*). Likewise, Dr. Margaret Mann Phillips, following a line of inquiry opened up by Dr. Bolgar, has probed the points of contact between Erasmus and vernacular literature, using the *De copia* as a key text.[13] Three studies of a wide-ranging character—Walter Kaiser's *Praisers of Folly*, Rosalie Colie's *Paradoxia Epidemica*, and Barbara Bowen's *The Age of Bluff*—have provided me with insights into key Renaissance writing strategies such as the paradox and the mock encomium. The discussion of Renaissance dialectic and rhetoric by Professors Ong, Vasoli, and Griffin have informed my re-

[13] See 'Erasmus and the art of writing', 'Érasme et Montaigne', and 'From the *Ciceronianus* to Montaigne'.

flections on the theoretical topics of Part I, while Dr. Grahame Castor's *Pléiade Poetics* provided a lucid analysis of similar terminology. More recently—indeed, during the composition of the book—a conference at the University of Edinburgh on French Renaissance humanism clarified a number of central issues, in particular the sixteenth-century notion of the 'encyclopedia'; the conference papers were subsequently edited by Dr. Peter Sharratt and published under the title *French Renaissance Studies 1540–70*.

My discussions with George Kerferd and Philip O'Prey, and my reading of their as yet unpublished graduate work, drew my attention to the importance of texts like Erasmus's *Lingua*, and helped me to verify certain of my own hypotheses as well as suggesting new ones. What I owe to them both could not adequately be expressed in the form of simple footnote references.

Michel Foucault's *Les Mots et les choses*, while disappointing in its treatment of the Renaissance, was valuable to me from a methodological point of view; moreover, certain remarks on pages 55–6 (for example, 'Le langage a en lui-même son principe intérieur de prolifération') are germane to my own preoccupations. The most fruitful modern critical studies on this period have however undoubtedly been those on Rabelais. Encouraged by the translation into French and English of Bakhtin's seminal study of Rabelais's popular themes and dialogic form, theorists of fiction have drawn attention to the complexities of his writing and the ways in which it anticipates certain modern concerns. In particular, Jean Paris's *Rabelais au futur* and Michel Beaujour's *Le Jeu de Rabelais* heralded a spate of books and articles of which I can mention here only a handful, of particular relevance to my own topics. François Rigolot, in his *Les Langages de Rabelais*, and more recently in his article 'Cratylisme et Pantagruélisme', has investigated many key areas of Rabelais's interest in language and its mechanisms, while Floyd Gray's *Rabelais et l'écriture* deals comprehensively with Rabelaisian problems of writing. In certain respects, Professor Gray's study rephrases in a different terminology the preoccupations of Alfred Glauser's *Rabelais créateur*, where Rabelais's themes and rhetorical procedures are persuasively shown to have a kind of poetic autonomy, irrespective of their historical context. Likewise, Dorothy Coleman's *Rabelais* must claim priority both as a comprehensive 'literary' study of Rabelais, and in particular for its productive application to his work of the notion of the authorial persona. Mention should also be made here of Raymond C. La Charité's two articles 'The unity of Rabelais's *Pantagruel*' and '*Mundus inversus*: the fictional world of Rabelais's *Pantagruel*', which raise the problem of the apparent incoherence of Rabelais's narrative, and move towards the solution of proposing disruption or non-integration itself as an interpretative theme.

I owe a good deal to these studies, although some of them were not available to me when I drafted my Rabelais chapter. On the other hand, I feel no less indebted to those whose patient and exacting investigation of Rabelais's historical, intellectual, and textual environment has clarified so many difficulties and corrected so many errors and anachronisms. Chief among these is Professor Screech, whose articles, books, and editions of *Gargantua* and the *Tiers Livre* have constantly accompanied my reading of Rabelais; the work of Professor Marichal on the *Quart Livre* has likewise been of great value.

In the earlier stages of my work on Ronsard, I learnt a great deal from the colleagues who collaborated with me on *Ronsard the Poet*; from Professor Gilbert Gadoffre; and from the writings of Marcel Raymond, whose reflection on baroque and mannerist characteristics of Ronsard's poetry converged with my own interest in the inbred nature of his aesthetic. From a quite different point of view, the Ronsard chapter owes a certain number of its themes to Jacques Derrida's 'La mythologie blanche' (in *Marges de la philosophie*) and to Marcel Detienne's *Les Jardins d'Adonis*.

Studies on Montaigne are gradually beginning to rival the attention paid to Rabelais by modern critics. Among those I have found most penetrating and relevant to my own concerns, I will mention here only Glauser's *Montaigne paradoxal*, Margaret McGowan's *Montaigne's Deceits*, Jean-Yves Pouilloux's *Lire les 'Essais' de Montaigne*, and Anthony Wilden's article 'Par divers moyens on arrive à pareille fin'. *O un amy!*, a collection of essays on Montaigne edited by Raymond C. La Charité and dedicated to Donald Frame, appeared too late for me to be able to take it into account in my own chapter. Like any other reader of Montaigne, I have made constant reference to the studies of Villey and of Friedrich. However, I should here like to pay special tribute to *The Essays of Montaigne* by the late Richard Sayce, which must surely rank as one of the most balanced, judicious, and sensitive studies of any major French writer. It has provided me with an invaluable means of checking my own observations and renewing acquaintance with areas of Montaigne's writing which I had forgotten or neglected.

Where my argument touches on issues raised by modern literary theorists, I have avoided making specific reference to their works, primarily because it would have been impossible to do justice to the complexity of their reflections without seriously disrupting my own discussion. I have tried to make good this deficiency, not only by sketching out some of the key questions above, but also by including in the Bibliography a highly selective list of texts which I have found particularly valuable.

I am deeply grateful to Ian McFarlane, Grahame Castor, Nicholas Mann, and Michel Jeanneret, all of whom read my manuscript in something approaching its final form and gave invaluable advice and encouragement. They bear responsibility neither for any errors which may still remain in the text, nor for those idiosyncrasies of method and style which I decided not to remove.

The friends and colleagues who read (or heard) fragments of the book at various stages of its composition and made constructive criticisms, who have stimulated my interest in sixteenth-century literature and humanism, or given me the benefits of their knowledge of other fields, are too numerous to mention here: their contributions are none the less warmly appreciated.

I am grateful to Edinburgh University Press and Dr. Peter Sharratt for permission to reproduce here parts of my article 'Copia and cornucopia', and to the editors of *L'Esprit créateur* and Mrs. Barbara Bowen for similar permission in respect of my article *'Enargeia*: Erasmus and the rhetoric of presence in the sixteenth century'.

The earliest stages of my research for this study were generously supported by the University of Warwick; since then, the Board of the Faculty of Medieval and Modern Languages at Oxford has likewise provided me with grants for research travel and attendance at conferences. St. John's College, by granting me sabbatical leave on two occasions, has enabled me to finish a project which might otherwise have languished indefinitely. I am grateful to the Warden and Fellows of All Souls College for electing me to a Visiting Fellowship in 1971: the hospitality and the facilities they provided allowed me to carry out an important part of my preliminary work. Similarly, my colleagues and students at the University of California, Santa Barbara, where I held a visiting post in 1976, nourished my reflections on many of the topics discussed here.

Finally, I should like to thank my wife Helen for showing tolerance and giving support beyond the call even of marital duty.

T.C.C.

September 1977

NOTE ON REFERENCES AND ABBREVIATIONS

References in the text and notes are given in the briefest possible form. Full details of all works mentioned are provided in the Bibliography. Where page numbers only are given for a quotation, they always refer to the work most recently mentioned, in the edition listed in the Bibliography (unless otherwise indicated). Where Latin passages are quoted in translation, the page numbers refer to the Latin text, not to any published translation (except in the case of Margaret Mann Phillips's version of the *Sileni Alcibiades*). For classical and patristic works, standard forms of reference have been used.

In the case of Erasmus, reference is made to those volumes of the new Amsterdam edition (Am.) which have so far appeared. Texts which appear in P. S. Allen's edition of Erasmus's letters are indicated thus: Allen 107, the number being that assigned by Allen (the same numbering system is being adopted in the Toronto edition of Erasmus's letters in English translation). Elsewhere, I have used the Froben edition of 1540 (Fr.), but I have also supplied references to the more widely available Leyden edition (LB), omitting the volume number, which is in every case the same as in the Froben edition.

Rabelais is quoted according to the Demerson edition; all page numbers refer to that edition. This seemed more convenient than using the still incomplete Lefranc edition as a basis for reference, although I have of course consulted it and other editions listed in the Bibliography. Passages in Rabelais can readily be identified in most instances by using chapter numbers, which I have supplied. I have used the abbreviations *TL*, *QL*, and *CL* for the *Tiers Livre*, *Quart Livre*, and *Cinquième Livre* respectively.

Ronsard is quoted according to the Laumonier edition (*L*).

In the chapter on Ronsard (II. 3), line numbers only are given where a single poem is analysed at length.

Montaigne is quoted according to the edition by Villey and Saulnier, and page numbers refer to that edition.

All these editions are listed in the Bibliography.

I have used the same spelling conventions as the editions used, except that in the case of sixteenth-century texts I resolve abbreviations and distinguish between 'i' and 'j' (in French), 'u' and 'v' (in French and Latin). Greek words have usually been transliterated in order to permit identification by readers unfamiliar with the Greek alphabet; in one or two instances where transliteration seemed superfluous or confusing, I have retained the Greek form. Latin (and Greek) quotations have been given in English translation, although I have always based my own work on the original texts. Key Latin words and phrases are provided in parenthesis. Translations of post-classical Latin texts are usually my own unless otherwise indicated, and are intended to be literal rather than elegant. For individual works of Erasmus, I have also consulted and made some use of the versions of Rix and King, Thompson, Mann Phillips, Mesnard, and Radice listed in the Bibliography. Translations of classical texts are taken from the versions in the Loeb Classical Library, although I have sometimes found it necessary to modify these in accordance with my argument. On translations from French into English, see below, p. 335.

I

ubi uber, ibi tuber
(Latin proverb, quoted in Erasmus's *Lingua*)

1

Copia

THE etymologies of *copia* touch on many central aspects of Latin culture and its European legacy. They originate in a spectacularly successful outgrowth, via [*co-ops*]—*copis*, from the parent form *ops*, which already embraces the domains of material riches, natural plenty (personified as the goddess Ops), and figurative abundance.[1] Although [*ops*]—*opes* continues to be common, it is hardly comparable in frequency and range of usage with *copia*, which draws into its semantic net connotations of military strength (pl. *copiae*, 'forces') and above all of eloquent speech (*copia dicendi*), while retaining its connection with riches and a broad range of more general notions—abundance, plenty, variety, satiety, resources. Furthermore, it is commonly (though not exclusively) used in an affirmative sense: it confidently asserts the values of affluence, military power, and rhetorical fluency. That such a word was brought into prominence might indeed be taken in itself as an indicator of the social and economic priorities of Rome. It is as if the instruments of power—money, armies— were aligned with that linguistic facility which assumed the role of resolving both political and private tensions in the *quaestiones civiles* of forensic oratory. Thus in many of its senses, *copia* implies the notion of mastery, whether social or linguistic. One might also evoke here, as a parallel to Cicero's forensic *copia*, the settings of his dialogues, where a group of well-born, affluent gentlemen meet in a country house or its gardens to discuss

---

[1] Likewise, the myths of the horn of plenty (*copiae cornu*) are linked both with natural abundance and with wealth (as in the widespread folk-motif of the magic pouch or purse which refills as soon as it is emptied). For the etymologies and meanings cited here, see *Oxford Latin Dictionary*, articles 'copia', 'copis', and 'ops'; Lewis and Short, article 'ops'. Lewis and Short also comment on the frequency of the word *copia* in all periods of Latin antiquity and in all types of writing.

ethics, metaphysics, and indeed rhetoric itself. Images of plenty
abound in such settings, and in Renaissance versions of the same
topos.[2]

By contrast, medieval Latin will develop a wholly new branch
of meaning which rapidly passes into the vernaculars: owing to a
productive accident of usage, *copia* comes to mean a 'copy',
accompanied by its cognates *copiare* and *copista*.[3] Hundreds of
years of manuscript copying have, indeed, preserved the written
materials of the Latin world while converting one of its most
fertile concepts from a context of dynamically deployed energies
(rooted in *oral* discourse) to one of endless repetition. Accelerating
the same process, the advent of printing, followed by the other
technologies of mass production, has assured the triumph of the
word 'copy' and its modern range of meanings.[4] The semantic
force of this deflection is such that, despite some medieval and
Renaissance vernacular continuations of earlier senses,[5] it has now

[2] See below, pp. 102 ff. In the garden of his country house at Arpinum, Cicero
built a shrine to Amaltheia, the nymph of the cornucopia, in imitation of the one
built by his friend Atticus; see *Ad Atticum* I.16 (end), II. 1 (end); also *De leg.* II.
iii. 7, where reference is made both to Amaltheia and to the delights of the
dialogue setting.

[3] It is not clear how this shift occurred. It may have arisen 'out of such Latin
phrases as . . . *facere copiam describendi* to give the power of transcription, to allow
a transcript to be made' (Murray, *New English Dictionary*); if so, the change of
meaning bears no relation to the notion of abundance. Bloch and Wartburg suggest that *copiare* was coined first, in the sense 'to multiply', hence 'to make copies';
Skeat proposes a similar derivation. A third possibility is that, since *copia* was also
used to denote an original document or collection of documents, such as a legal
dossier (see Du Cange, article 'copia'), the modern sense may have arisen by
metonymy, the reproduction ('copy') taking the name of the original. The
English 'copy' continued for some time to denote the thing copied as well as the
reproduction: cf. 'Be copy now to men of grosser blood' (*Henry V*, III. i), and
OED, article 'copy'. A trace of this usage remains in journalism and printing
(to provide 'copy' for a newspaper).

[4] While *copia* has primarily positive connotations, 'copy' is often used pejora-
tively, as if it were a fallen *copia*. One might add that the Latin words for 'copy'
(noun or verb) either stress the importance of the model (*exemplar, imitari*) or
the act of rewriting (*describere, exscribere, transcribere*). The two senses converge in
descriptio, which is both a 'written copy' and, in a much broader sense, a 'representation'; in rhetorical contexts, one normally associates *descriptio* with
mimesis, but its etymological connection with writing should not be forgotten.

[5] See Godefroy, Huguet, and Cotgrave. Godefroy cites this colourful variant:

wholly taken over the noun-form proper in both French and English; in English it is still possible to revert, via the adjective, to 'copiousness', but in French even that expedient is absent, so that only the adjective remains.

Thus the original shift from *ops* to the various senses of classical *copia* is a peculiarly Latin phenomenon. There is no equivalent in Greek, and modern English translators are forced to use a variety of approximate equivalents even in the segment of usage concerned with oratory. Here, the theoretical writings of Cicero and Quintilian provide an exhaustive set of examples of how the word could be used, and a brief account of these is necessary as a prelude to an examination of Renaissance *copia*.

The phrase *copia dicendi*, or even *copia* alone, is a ubiquitous synonym for eloquence.[6] Coupled with other words from the same semantic domain (*abundantia, ubertas, opes, varietas, divitiae, vis, facultas, facilitas*), it suggests a rich, many faceted discourse springing from a fertile mind and powerfully affecting its recipient. At this level, its value lies precisely in the broadness of its figurative register: it transcends specific techniques and materials, pointing towards an ideal of 'articulate energy', of speech in action. It has two kinds of negative counterpart: *inopia*, poverty of diction, is its antithesis; empty prolixity (*loquacitas*), *copia* without *varietas*, or Asiatic over-elaboration are its inversions.[7]

Both Cicero and Quintilian use the term in the context of the still more fundamental duality of 'things' (*res*) and 'words' (*verba*). *Res* may provisionally be paraphrased as 'subject-matter',

'Compains, il te fault laisser ceste fille, car j'en veuil aussi bien avoir copie comme tu l'en as'; Huguet provides some similar examples from the sixteenth century. *Copie* appears first in the sense of 'copy' and then in the sense of 'abundance' in Rabelais, *Pant.* 8 (title: 'letres ... et la copie d'icelles'; '. . . n'avoys copie de telz precepteurs comme tu as eu').

6 For the analysis which follows, use has been made of word-lists such as the Abbott–Oldfather–Canter *Index verborum in Ciceronis Rhetorica*, and the lexicon of the Spalding edition of Quintilian, vol. VI. On Ciceronian rhetoric in general, see A. Michel, *Rhétorique et philosophie chez Cicéron.*

7 Cf. Cicero, *Brutus* xiii. 51; *Orator* lxix. 231; *De opt. gen. orat.* iii–iv; Quintilian, *Institutiones oratoriae* II. iv. 4; VIII. ii. 17; X. i. 62, iii. 2, v. 22.

and is particularized in phrases like *copia argumentorum*, *copia exemplorum*, *copia sententiarum*; *res* are generated by the *ratio disserendi* (dialectic or topical logic), which in classical rhetoric is subsumed under the heading *inventio*. *Verba* include not simply lexical units such as synonyms, but also tropes and other verbal figures: *elocutio* is their domain. Although *copia rerum* and *copia verborum* are often referred to separately, their integration in an ideally abundant discourse is always recommended, as is the priority of *res*:

for a full supply (*copia*) of facts (*rerum*) begets a full supply of words, and if the subjects (*rebus*) discussed are themselves of an elevated character, this produces a spontaneous (*naturalis*) brilliance in the language (*verbis*).[8]

According to this theory (a commonplace since the ancient Greek debates on rhetoric), true *copia*—as opposed to *vitiosa abundantia* or *loquacitas*—is assured where *res* inform or guarantee *verba*.

As the division of *copia dicendi* into *rerum* and *verborum* already implies, the semantic field of *copia* includes not only the notion of abundance itself but also the place where abundance is to be found, or, more strictly, the place and its contents: one of the particular senses of *copia* is 'treasure-chest', 'hoard', or 'store' (*thesaurus*). By an inverse movement, *locuples* ('rich in lands', 'opulent'), a synonym for *copiosus*, is derived from *locus* and *plenus*. In this sense, *copia* is especially appropriate to topical logic, which constitutes a set of places (*topoi*, *loci*) in which arguments may be 'found', *inventio* being the finding or generation of propositions. Thus *copia argumentorum*, for example, means not so much a 'quantity' as a 'store' of arguments. This is true of many of the contexts in which Cicero and Quintilian use the word: the orator is to acquire a hoard or treasure-house of *res* and *verba*. Hence *copia* subsumes all the techniques of collecting materials (wide reading, translation, paraphrase, imitation)

---

[8] Cicero, *De oratore* III. xxi. 125. Cf. *De inventione* I. i. 1, and Cicero's definition of eloquence as a 'wisdom speaking copiously' ('copiose loquens sapientia') (*De partitione oratoria* xxiii. 79). However, the function of *res* in the ideal alignment *sapientia–res–verba* may be equivocal, as the analysis of Erasmus's *De copia* in the present chapter will seek to show.

which are elaborated most fully by Quintilian in Book X of the *Institutiones oratoriae*; furthermore, it becomes associated with the art of memory, whose function is to fix *res* and *verba* clearly in the mind as in a storehouse. At the same time, *copia* is not—or ought not to be, according to Quintilian—a store of inert goods:

> although it is essential to bring with us into court a supply of eloquence which has been prepared in advance in the study (*paratam dicendi copiam*) and on which we can confidently rely, there is no greater folly than the rejection of the gifts of the moment (*temporis munera*). (X. vi. 6)

A potential *copia* (*facultas*, i.e. capacity which has yet to be deployed) is actualized in the speech act, or by extension the act of writing, where it becomes the *vis* or *facilitas* of a discourse committed to time, to the *ex tempore* mode: *Institutiones* X. vii develops the theme of spontaneous eloquence (see below, I. 4). It is only by this dynamic process that the copious metamorphoses of rhetoric may achieve their aim by activating parallel changes in the mind of the recipient.

It must be stressed that *copia* was never, in classical antiquity, a fully technical term. If Cicero uses it to characterize elevated style, a *locus* transmitted to the Middle Ages by Macrobius,[9] he neither gives it the status of a theoretical rubric nor restricts its scope to that particular style. Quintilian seems to found a method for acquiring *copia rerum et verborum* in *Institutiones* X. i. 5–15; but he dismisses *res* as particular to given 'causes', and his treatment of *verba* is brief and relatively unsystematic. He has, after all, treated *inventio* and *elocutio* at length in earlier books; once again, the figurative vocabulary of abundance and 'force' of eloquence flows across the barriers set up by pedagogical categorization.

As far as I am aware, *copia* is not much in evidence in medieval handbooks of rhetoric, although 'humanists' like John of Salisbury would have been conscious of some of its uses by Cicero and

---

[9] Cicero, *Orator* xxviii. 97 ff.; Macrobius, *Saturnalia* V. i. 7 ff., distinguishes between four styles, of which the first is the 'copious', exemplified above all by Cicero.

perhaps Quintilian.[10] Yet, under other names, the various modes
of compiling materials and extending discourse have moved to
the centre of attention. Following Pliny and other compilers of
late antiquity, encyclopedism flourished throughout the Middle
Ages, constituting a wide-ranging store of *res*. Similarly, if Dr.
Bolgar is right,[11] Agricola borrowed his mode of classifying the
materials to be deployed in eloquent discourse from medieval
arts of preaching. Still more important perhaps, particularly for
elocutio, is the evolution of the term *amplificatio*. For the classical
theorists, *amplificatio* had been a device used in judicial and
demonstrative rhetoric to give weight and substance to an
argument or to praise a person or an act: it is the cause which is
amplified, rather than the style itself (although of course the
device has stylistic implications). Medieval rhetoric shifted it
eventually to a specifically 'generative' sense: it became a comprehensive label for the various ways of saying more about a
topic, of extending or spinning out a discourse.[12] Used thus, it
was indeed one of the central principles of medieval rhetoric.
The humanist rhetoricians of the Renaissance restore the term to
its classical sense, so that it is regularly treated under the rubric
of *inventio* rather than of *elocutio*; and, as Professor Ong has
pointed out, *copia* takes the place of medieval *amplificatio*.[13]
Melanchthon and others will continue to use *amplificatio* from
time to time as a synonym for *copia*; but the shift from medieval
amplificatio to Renaissance *copia* is nevertheless a major one. A
term used to denote a set of formal procedures which can be
learnt and deployed systematically by virtually any writer is
replaced by a concept which, while including many of the same

[10] James Murphy's *Rhetoric in the Middle Ages* makes no reference to the use of
the word *copia*, but testifies to the familiarity of twelfth-century scholars with some
of the principal classical treatises on rhetoric (chapter III). As far as the vernacular
is concerned, Godefroy lists no examples of *copie* in its rhetorical applications
before the sixteenth century, whereas they become frequent thereafter (cf. also
Huguet). See below, note 14.

[11] *The Classical Heritage*, p. 272. See also Engelhardt, 'Medieval vestiges in the
rhetoric of Erasmus'.

[12] See Arbusow, *Colores rhetorici*, pp. 21 ff.; also Lausberg, *Handbuch*, references
listed on p. 645, col. 2.

[13] Cf. Ong, *Ramus: Method*, pp. 211, 213.

procedures, allows figurative associations of a wholly different
order to insert themselves into literary aesthetics. This is by no
means to belittle the varied and sophisticated arts of writing of
the Middle Ages, of which this study can take no account; the
techniques of *dilatatio* not only provide a rich counterpoint to the
vast structures of late medieval prose and verse, they must also be
presumed to have prepared the ground for an exploration of
copia which went far beyond what Cicero and Quintilian had
imagined, and which represents the last great flowering in Europe
of *copia*-abundance as opposed to *copia*-copy.

A study of Renaissance *copia* necessarily presupposes the intrinsic interest and the broad diffusion of Erasmus's handbook
De duplici copia verborum ac rerum.[14] Were it not for this elementary
textbook on how to write copiously in Latin, one could no doubt
still explore the aesthetics of abundance in French vernacular
literature and its immediate humanist environment, but the
orientation of the inquiry would be quite different. Erasmus here
succeeded in setting out, lucidly and succinctly, a particular
approach to the problem of writing Latin in a cultural and social
environment radically different from that of Cicero and Quintilian; and it so happened that this approach was disseminated
among a whole generation of European students precisely at a
moment when the potentialities of the vernacular were being

---

[14] Cf. Bolgar, op. cit., pp. 272–5, 297–8, 320 ff.; Mann Phillips, 'Erasmus and
the art of writing'; Vallese, 'Érasme et le *De duplici copia*'; Rix, 'The editions of
Erasmus's *De copia*'; also Mann Phillips, 'Érasme et Montaigne: II'. While the
popularity of the handbook is easily established (see also below, pp. 17–18), there
is little direct evidence of its impact on vernacular theory and practice in France.
However, the circumstantial evidence is considerable; in addition to the sugges-
tions of Bolgar and Mann Phillips, see my remarks in 'Copia and cornucopia',
and in 'Ronsard's mythological universe', pp. 168 ff. It seems reasonable to
attribute in large measure to the *De copia* the frequent rhetorical applications of
the word *copie* in the mid sixteenth century, as in Du Bellay's *Deffence et illustration* (I. iii, v, vii, ix, x; II. vi); in Sebillet's *Art poétique* (p. 32) (translation of good
authors contributes to the 'copie du futur Pöéte'); and in Rabelais, *CL* 19 ('la
copie melliflue de Platon', here cited as inadequate to describe a sumptuous
banquet; a reference to Amaltheia occurs in the same passage). Comparable uses
of the adjectival and adverbial forms of the word are also widespread; one finds
them, once again, in Pléiade theory, and for example in Telin's *Brief sommaire*
of 1533 (o.s.).

vigorously defended and explored. The priority of the *De copia*
in Erasmus's own work is symbolized by the fact that, in the
Basle edition of 1540, it is printed at the beginning of the first
volume, a position to which he had already assigned it in a
much earlier project for a complete edition. It is both an early
work, conceived against the background of Colet's experiment
at St. Paul's and completed in the first version by 1512, and a
point of departure for Erasmus's meditations on pedagogical
method, on the lessons of antiquity, and on the nature of human
discourse.

In a historical perspective, the conception of the *De copia* is
prepared, made possible, in many different ways. A detailed
reading of Cicero and Quintilian, and in particular of *Institutiones*
X, may be taken for granted. But when one turns to the
humanists who preceded Erasmus, the situation is a little more
complicated. In his dedicatory letter to Colet, Erasmus claims
originality for his project:

I believe I may credit myself with having been the first to contrive and
make known this topic.   (Fr. I, p. 1; LB 1–2)

A group of possible claimants to priority are rejected with a
gesture of contempt. They include the *Onomasticon* of the late
Greek writer Julius Pollux and the *Etymologiae* of Isidore of Seville,
the pseudo-Ciceronian *Synonyma*, and the *Sentenciarum varia-
tiones sive synonima* of Stephanus Fliscus ('Philiscus'). Of these,
the first two are massive compilations based on lexical classification and speculative etymology; the others, often published
together,[15] comprise lists of synonyms. The pseudo-Cicero
uses an alphabetical classification, while Fliscus groups his synonyms under the headings *prudentia, iustitia, fortitudo, temperantia*,
each of these virtues being subdivided grammatically (nouns,
adjectives, verbs) and antithetically according to the epideictic
categories 'in laudem et bonum' and 'ad vituperandum malum'.
Pollux is rejected by Erasmus for heaping up synonyms and
'neighbouring terms' ('synonyma quaedam ac finitima'), while

---

[15] There were many editions of Fliscus's synonyms up to 1525; some of them
were edited by Josse Clichtove, together with Gasparino Barzizza's popular
treatise *De eloquentia*.

copia is 'so foreign to Isidore and Fliscus that they cannot even once express in Latin what they think' ('homines in tantum alienos a copia, ut ne semel quidem quae sentiunt Latine possint efferre'); the pseudo-Cicero consists of a 'scanty, hastily assembled collection of words' ('tumultuariam paucarum vocum congeriem'). Erasmus claims, by contrast, to set forth the principles or sources of *copia* ('formulas quasdam copie, ceu fontes'), proceeding from the general to the particular. Thus a crucial distinction is made in this prefatory letter between, on the one hand, static collections of materials governed by more or less arbitrary classification systems, and, on the other, a dynamic method rooted in generative principles.

Bearing these remarks of Erasmus in mind—and not taking too literally his claim to originality—one may turn to other theoretical works which anticipated aspects of the *De copia*. The *Artis rhetoricae praecepta* of Aeneas Sylvius Piccolomini (Pius II) is undoubtedly such a text. Its purpose is essentially to enumerate ways of composing elegant sentences (that is, the art of *compositio* or *concinnitas*); the exploitation of grammatical, syntactical, lexical, and stylistic devices for extending simple propositions is prescribed, not so much by detailed theoretical analysis as by example. One suspects that Erasmus would have been scornful of Piccolomini's lengthy and often random lists of examples; on the other hand, the first *Tractatus* ends by stressing that, once the central point has been grasped in each instance, further examples are superfluous since the student may then generate his own. The second *Tractatus* begins by recalling that, in the first, the author had attempted to show 'by what method, in what form, and in what order an apt, adequate, and euphonious discourse may be woven together'; now, he says,

it has come into my mind that it would be useful also to set out for [the reader] some of the synonymous variations on propositions which have been furnished by the distinguished orators Fliscus and Barzizza. (*Opera*, p. 1016)

These 'variation exercises' are classified in terms of the six parts of discourse (*exordium, narratio, divisio, confirmatio, confutatio, conclusio*). Once again, Piccolomini is inclined simply to accumulate useful formulas, to present the student with a set of predigested materials. On the other hand, it looks as if Erasmus found here the idea for one of the more celebrated developments in the *De copia*, namely the two variation exercises of Book I, chapter 33. One of Piccolomini's examples (designed for use in the *exordium*) is the set phrase 'thank you for your letter' (literally, 'your letter has pleased me') which Erasmus will adopt, and certain of his variations anticipate those of the *De copia*, as for example 'your most affectionate letter has brought me a great store of joy' ('Amantissimae tuae literae amplum mihi gaudii cumulum attulerunt').[16]

It is no doubt significant that Piccolomini's treatise makes no use of the term *copia*. He certainly aims at injecting abundance and variety into the student's discourse, but offers no central focus which might release his categories and examples from an essentially static schematization. Of far more immediate relevance to Erasmus is Rudolph Agricola, who must count as one of the principal scholars through whose agency the aims and methods of Italian humanists such as Valla—and indeed Piccolomini himself—were transmitted into the cultural climate of northern Europe towards the end of the fifteenth century. Bolgar has pointed out that Agricola's letter *De formando studio* (dated 1484, printed posthumously, and still popular in the seventeenth century) retailed to a wide northern audience a succinct account of the 'notebook' method of imitation, that is to say the systematic assimilation and classification of the materials of classical literature, which Bolgar takes to be the central principle of Erasmus's text. It is certainly true that Agricola's suggested rubrics indicate a far more sophisticated and flexible approach than do those of, say, Fliscus; characteristically, it is left to the student to devise his own categories and assemble his own material, while the 'fruition' or production of knowledge by constant practice (*exercitatio*), and the invention of new 'things' on the basis of what is known, are given high priority. Thus Agricola envisages a

---

[16] p. 1017. Such variation exercises had also been performed by medieval rhetoricians: Alberic of Monte Cassino varies the phrase 'Have you eaten?' in his *De dictamine* (I owe this example to Lanham, *Motives of Eloquence*, p. 24).

constant process of absorption and creative re-production; to a much greater extent than that of Piccolomini, his method is fluid and open-ended. On the other hand, the only really significant use of the word *copia* itself occurs in the context, not of the classification method, but of the dialectical analysis of a line from Virgil:

If anyone extends these [i.e. the constituents of the line] broadly through all the dialectical places, in so far as the nature of each is appropriate to them, a great abundance of resources both for discourse and for invention (*ingens . . . copia et ad dicendum, et ad inveniendum*) will become manifest. (fol. Bi vº)

Thus for Agricola, the key to abundant discourse is provided by dialectical method, on which—as he indicates in his letter—he had himself written an important treatise first published in 1515, three years after Erasmus composed his prefatory letter to Colet.

The *De inventione dialectica*, as its name suggests, is restricted to *inventio*, the generation of propositions; the second 'part' of dialectic, namely *iudicium* ('judgement', the consideration of which propositions are relevant and persuasive in a given context), is postponed to a later treatise which appears to have remained unwritten. Book I is concerned with an analysis of the 'places' of invention, and of the categories into which they may be systematically divided; Book II principally with the art of drawing *copia dicendi* from them; and Book III, which includes a chapter on *copia* and *brevitas*, with the techniques which may be used for 'moving the affections' of the audience and compelling assent. In exploiting the term *copia* in the context of topical logic, Agricola is developing a classical commonplace represented, for example, by the phrase *copia argumentorum*, or by the image of an all-embracing river ('universum flumen') with which Cicero introduces his summary of topics in *De oratore* II. 162. On the other hand, a comparison between the *De inventione* and its closest humanist counterpart, the *Dialecticae disputationes* of Lorenzo Valla, reveals that Agricola's exploitation of *copia* as denoting the aim of dialectical method creates a wholly new emphasis: the word is virtually absent from Valla, whereas in

Agricola it recurs in key positions.[17] The climax of the work is located in II. 18–21, a section placed under the general heading *De locorum usu, deque paranda ex locis copia*. Here Agricola affirms central principles, in particular the monopolization of *inventio* by dialectic, the restriction of rhetoric to *elocutio*, and the consequent claim that there is no difference between dialectical and rhetorical *loci*. Here, too, *descriptio* is redefined as a global aspect of dialectical method. It is in this context that the release of *copia* from the 'places' of dialectic is given full prominence. Chapter 19 puts firmly in the centre of attention the objective of gathering from the places 'a complete supply and store of arguments' ('omnis argumentorum facultas et copia'), and, like Quintilian, exploits the notion of a *thesaurus* which the speaker will always have at his finger-tips ('copia quaedam et thesaurus paratur, qui semper nobis in promptu sit') (pp. 327–8). Likewise, the concluding sentence of chapter 21 emphasizes the universality of the method:

Such indeed are the foundations of all invention: once they have been correctly and firmly established, very little work will need to be done on the remainder; all the material of discourse is provided by them. Whatever can build up the resources of the future speaker (*dicturi copiam*) is gathered together by this method.   (p. 350)

Dialectical invention is thus characterized as an art of *copia*; in consequence, the word begins to acquire a technical status which it had lacked in Cicero and even Quintilian. Conversely, copious discourse is to be produced, according to Agricola, by a method designed to guarantee intellectual stringency. Thus, while certain *loci* are cited in passing as being particularly 'copious', Agricola is cautious about that kind of loose *copia* which will only convince the ignorant. *Comparatio* and *similitudo* have precisely this low status: 'these two places are copious' ('copiosi sunt hi duo loci'), he says,

and particularly suitable for common opinion and attitudes . . . For dull minds, which cannot penetrate into the heart of the matter itself (*in ipsas res*) . . . may be most easily led by the image and figure of other

---

[17] A detailed account of the place of Valla and Agricola in Renaissance dialectic is given in Vasoli's *La dialettica e la retorica*.

better-known things into that which we wish to show. Sharper minds,
like clear-sighted men, follow their eyes; dull ones, by contrast,
like blind men, have to grope their way along by touch.   (p. 119)

The same reservation is carried over into III. 5. *Copia* here
appears as a device for 'moving the affections' and thus has a
somewhat different aspect from that implied by its use in Book II.
The dialectical *loci* are now invoked as an aid to the art of emo-
tively extending and compressing discourse, a strange reversal
of the situation in the earlier books. The fact is that Agricola is
drawing into his discussion categories of *res*, which in II. 20
he had excluded from dialectic on the grounds that subject-
matter belongs to the realm of 'common sense', not to the art of
finding arguments. In III. 5, by contrast, his initial equations for
fertility of speech (*orationis ubertas*) clearly embrace the realm of
res, in spite of the initial claim that this chapter legitimately
belongs to *inventio*:

Since by abundance and brevity of discourse, more than by any other
means, we delight or offend, and since moreover they are consistent
with the art of invention, it appears relevant to our purpose to say a
little about them. Fertility of speech arises either where we express a
few topics in many words; or where, although we say little about each,
we pile up many topics and stretch our speech not with the size but
with the sheer quantity of things (*rerum*); or, most copiously of all
(*quod affluentissimum est*), where we say much about many things.
(p. 378)

The examples which follow show that the complete dialectical
model of how to 'lead' a subject (*res*) systematically through the
loci, which assigned only a nominal value to *res*, has now been
fragmented so that *res* may proliferate. None of the relations have
been changed; the system has simply been turned inside out. It is
significant that the first example of 'saying many things', which is
placed under the heading of *expositio* (roughly equivalent to
narratio), is a demonstration of how a paraphrase of the first
book of the *Aeneid* may be extended by the inclusion of more and
more narrative details or explanations; the commentary on a
line from Virgil in the *De formando studio* is clearly an echo of this

development. Agricola designates an intermediate stage at which 'poetic ornamentation' is excluded:

The history of Troy depicted in a painting in the temple has no relevance to the order of things (*ad ordinem rerum*); nor has the beauty of Dido, or the description of the appearance of the temple; nor have many other items which lend great weight to the ornamentation of things (*ornandis rebus*) but none to their understanding. (p. 379)

But the logic of Agricola's argument points towards an increasing proliferation of concrete and decorative detail, to which he has in fact already given licence in the preceding chapters (see below, pp. 32–3). The subject has taken over and multiplies itself well beyond the rigorous pathways of dialectic. Inevitably, the same movement carries Agricola close to the domain of *elocutio*, or *copia verborum*; indeed, he touches at one point on the multiple repetition of a 'thing' in different words, only to reject this as irrelevant:

There is also another way of speaking copiously, which arises when we say the same thing again and again in so many words ... But this belongs to the rules of diction (*eloquendi*), not of invention, and thus is remote from our purpose. (p. 382)

The tension between Agricola's preference for disciplined argument and his orientation of dialectic in Book III towards affective modes of discourse becomes increasingly evident in the later part of chapter 5. He hesitates at first between the rival attractions of *copia* and *brevitas*, and of the authors who incarnate them (Cicero and Demosthenes respectively).[18] Inevitably, he recommends moderation, with a slight preference for *copia* ('minus quidem erit mea sententia culpandus, qui in id quod plus, quam quod minus est, deflexerit') (p. 386); it is better to demonstrate superfluously than inadequately. But when he comes to considering the requirements of different audiences, a strong moral and intellectual colouring emerges: grave and learned

---

[18] 'for some will prefer a full discourse, carried away as it were by the impetus of abundance; others like an eloquence which is concise and witty, and valued more for its sinews than its flesh' (p. 386).

men will prefer *brevitas*, but the mob requires a more ostentatious manner:

The people and all the common crowd must be flattered with great abundance (*copia*), force, and magnificence of discourse. Therefore all the fertile resources (*sinus*) of eloquence must be poured out over them. (p. 388)

Ironically enough, the situation is reversed where the faculties of the speaker himself are concerned:

The ignorant have no source from which they may procure abundance (*copiam*) . . . By contrast, fertility (*ubertas*) is more to be pursued by the humble, the calm, the prudent, and the learned.

This oscillation is no doubt intimately connected with Agricola's attempt to mediate between dialectical and rhetorical functions; it is also polarized by the very fact that his manner of exposition is based on his own method of division and analysis, with its mechanical, almost computer-like enumeration of all possibilities. The closing passage of the chapter resolves it (or rather leaves it suspended) by the subordination of precept to utility ('utilitati nimirum cedent praecepta'): the needs of the moment must impose their own rule. A surprising statement, perhaps, given that Agricola's method is apparently designed to provide precepts for all situations; but it is provoked by the temptations of a *copia* which, by undermining the constraints of dialectic, has laid bare a fundamental ambiguity in his project of generating discourse.

Agricola's commentator Ioannes Matthaeus Phrissemius concludes his remarks on this chapter by referring the reader to Erasmus: 'for the exact understanding of the whole of this chapter', he says, 'Erasmus's books on *copia* contribute much that is of importance'.[19] By the time his commentary was written, Erasmus had made the topic his own; so much so, indeed, that a rhetorical theorist like Melanchthon feels it both essential to include *copia* in his analysis and superfluous to deal with it in detail, since Erasmus's text is so widely known ('omnibus in manu sunt Erasmi

[19] This commentary accompanies the treatise in the edition I have used (see Bibliography); the remark quoted appears on p. 391.

libelli').[20] Whether or not Agricola influenced Erasmus indirectly
by his teaching, there is no doubt that his work contains much
that is germane to the *De copia*, though subordinated to Agricola's
predominantly dialectical concerns.[21] The classification system of
the *De formando studio*, for example, is not mentioned in the
final chapter on reading and imitation in the *De inventione*,
whereas Erasmus will bring both topics together in a celebrated
section of his work; and the discrepancy between the supposedly
guaranteed *copia* which is the objective of dialectic and the ambivalent *copia* of Book III, chapter 5, will in Erasmus be absorbed
by that crucial shift of perspective which regroups all the techniques of discourse under the sign of *copia* itself.

As already indicated, it can be misleading to assume that the
relationship between *res* and *verba* is exactly parallel to that
between *inventio* and *elocutio*. If Erasmus's *copia verborum*, being
concerned almost exclusively with verbal tropes, would certainly
have been classified by any contemporary theorist as belonging
to the domain of *elocutio*, his second book places *res* in the fore-
front of attention at the expense of *inventio* as 'method'. Only
vestigial aspects of dialectical invention in the Agricolan manner
remain, as for example in II. 10 and 11, where Erasmus deals
with *propositiones*, *probationes*, and *loci communes* in a legal context.

[20] Melanchthon, *Elementorum rhetorices* (1532), fol. 45 v°.
[21] Ong comments: 'Book III [of the *De inventione*] . . . changes the whole
climate of dialectic as represented by Peter of Spain, and assimilates the art of
dialectic to that of rhetoric in many of its aspects. Erasmus's rhetorical interests
in the same subject will grow out of Agricola's concern with "copie of words"
here in dialectic' (op. cit., p. 100). This assertion requires modification. In the
first place, the relationship between dialectic and rhetoric was already a very
fluid one in the Middle Ages, in spite of the late medieval 'triumph of logic' (see
McKeon, 'Rhetoric in the Middle Ages'). Secondly, Agricola is not concerned
with 'copie of words', even in Book III (see the quotation from p. 382, above,
p. 16). And thirdly, the extent of Erasmus's debt to Agricola is very unclear. In
a letter to Budé (1516), Erasmus expresses regret that Agricola's *De inventione*
was not available to him when he wrote the *De copia* (La Garanderie, *La Correspondance d'Érasme*, p. 74; Allen 480). However, even if this remark is taken at
face value, thus excluding any possible influence of the *De inventione* on the
De copia, it shows that Erasmus was aware of the central role played by *copia* in
Agricola's work.

His orientation is made quite plain by the fact that he refers the reader to the 'topical' masters Aristotle, Boethius, Cicero, Quintilian, and Hermogenes; and while conceding that the *loci* of dialectic may provide a source of eloquence, excludes them from further discussion as irrelevant to his purpose. He is above all concerned with *res* as 'subject-matter': that is to say, as discourse at a level of organization which prepares, yet also defers, the ordered articulation of 'ideas'. To render *res* itself as 'idea' would be to confuse, or rather over-simplify the issue. In some contexts, it is true, *res* could be defined as the extra-linguistic reality apprehended by the mind and reproduced in the form of *verba*; in this sense, according to the classic mimetic model, words copy or represent the objects of thought. But in the *De copia*, as the remainder of this chapter will argue, this reassuring hierarchy is disturbed, if not inverted. *Res* do not emerge from the mind as spontaneous 'ideas'; they are already there, embedded in language, forming the materials of a writing exercise. Erasmus is exploiting Quintilian's notion of a 'treasure-house of things': hence the prevalence of borrowed fragments of discourse such as *exempla* in Book II of the *De copia*. It is no accident that the discussion of *copia rerum* culminates in a method for 'imitation' (*ratio colligendi exempla*), where it is not reality that is imitated, but other writers; not ideas, but texts.[22]

Hence rhetoric (or something like it: for Erasmus avoids the term, preferring *copia*) has reconquered the terrain of *inventio*, emphasizing the materials to be produced rather than the rigorous

[22] *Res* is rendered as 'idea' (or 'thought') by Rix and King in their translation of the *De copia*, with the approval of Margolin ('Érasme et le verbe', p. 93) and Mann Phillips ('Erasmus and the art of writing', p. 342); cf. also Vallese, art. cit., p. 235. Rhetorically speaking, the transfer of *res* from one sense (object-thing) to another (word-thing) is an example of catachresis, the 'improper' use of a word, usually where a 'proper' term is lacking. This trope is essential to the self-generating powers of language; here it both delimits and disguises the crucial space between words and things. By identifying words with a primary reality, the apparent sameness of the word *res* effaces the very difference which constitutes language (in this respect, it resembles *logos*: see below, I. 5). Conversely, when the duplicity is unmasked, *res* provides a paradigm of this difference: the meaning of the word 'thing', the thing it represents, is radically unstable, so that *a fortiori* all the *copia* of things is contaminated with the same versatility.

constraints of the system which is to produce them.[23] Where
Agricola touches on *copia verborum* only to turn back to his primary
concern, Erasmus's passing reference to dialectic equally defines the
limits of his project. There is of course an overlap, a crucial one
to which it will be necessary to return; but the perspectives, the
avenues of approach, of the two authors are clearly different.

In his *De ratione studii*, Erasmus will establish the principle
'words come first, but subject-matter is more important'.[24]
In a sense, the *De copia* already adopts this balance. The discussion
of 'words' is placed first, but only after repeated warnings that
'empty' verbal *copia* is pernicious. The opening chapters raise
immediately and significantly the relationship between *copia* and
brevitas. Although extension and compression of language had not
always been treated as antithetical and mutually exclusive techniques in rhetorical theory, Erasmus's insistence that they are
complementary is of particular interest. A writer who has a
talent for one is likely to have a talent for the other, he says,
and Quintilian cites Homer as a supreme master of both.[25]
This observation is related to Erasmus's keen awareness of the
dangers of empty loquacity, on which he was to write his essay
Lingua and for which antecedents may be found in classical
rhetorical theory, in Plutarch, and in Petrarch;[26] the first chapter

---

[23] Melanchthon's theory of *loci* provides a parallel for this manœuvre, which is
of central importance for humanist theories of discourse. See Breen, 'The subordination to rhetoric' and 'The terms "loci communes" and "loci" '.

[24] Am. I–2, p. 113: 'Principio duplex omnino videtur cognitio rerum ac
verborum. Verborum prior, rerum potior'. It is important to note that, in predominantly ethical contexts, the relationship of words to things may appear to be
less problematic than in linguistic or rhetorical contexts: things are identified as
empirically observable behaviour, which may or may not correspond with verbal
utterance. This is the case, for example, in Erasmus's dialogue *De rebus et vocabulis*
(Am. I–3, pp. 566 ff.). However, the linguistic problem is liable to erupt in the
moral domain also; the questions are not ultimately separable (see for example
below, I. 5).

[25] Fr. I, p. 2 (LB 4) (Book I, ch. 3). Cf. p. 3 (LB 5) (I. 5): 'no author will com-
press his discourse with greater art than the one who is skilful in enriching it with
the most varied store of materials (*quam qui calleat eandem quam maxime varia
supellectile locupletare*).'

[26] See above, note 7; Plutarch, *De garrulitate*; Petrarch, *De remediis* I. ix, 'De
eloquentia'.

of the *De copia*, indeed, is entitled 'Periculosam esse Copiae affectationem'. The importance of the balance between *copia* and *brevitas* is that it enables Erasmus to suggest that true plenitude of language is to be found not in simple extension, but in inventive and imaginative richness. The *Adagia*, which Erasmus was beginning to elaborate at this time, provide a striking example of the marriage of *copia* and *brevitas*. Elsewhere in the *De copia*, this emphasis on textual productivity is exemplified by Erasmus's concern to provide 'significant' examples, that is to say ones with moral or evangelical implications, rather than purely arbitrary formulae.[27]

Ideally, then, true linguistic plenitude is attained when *verba*, coalescing into *res*, point towards a *sententia* ('idea'); but conversely, the movement of the treatise, asserting the priority (if not the primacy) of words, reveals that 'things' can only become apparent by virtue of language. *Res* are neither prior to words as their 'origin', nor are they a productive residue which remains after the words cease. *Res* and *verba* slide together to become 'word-things'; the notion of a single domain (language) having a double aspect replaces that of two distinct domains, language and thought.

The word *copia* may thus be seen to provide a unifying frame which overrides the duality of words and things, while avoiding the sense of classifying method evoked by the term 'rhetoric'. In I. 7 Erasmus refers, indeed, to the artificial, pedagogical nature of the distinction between the two parts of his work, and the same point is made in another way by his characteristic adoption of the 'self-deprecation' or 'humility' *topos*. In the prefatory letter, he speaks of not having had the time to perfect his work; referring to incorrect pirated editions, he maintains that he has chosen the lesser evil of publishing the text as it stands. The tactic is like that adopted in the liminary epistle of the *Praise of Folly*, dated 'from the country', and claiming that the text was written to while away the tedium of a journey.[28]

[27] See Sowards, 'Erasmus and the apologetic textbook'. At such points, the moral criterion referred to above, note 24, may provisionally intervene; but it is contaminated by the priority given to the practice of writing.

[28] Cf. the account of the composition of the *Praise of Folly* given in the letter to Martin Dorp of 1515, regularly printed with the *Folly* from 1516.

Similarly, the epilogue of the *De copia* evokes the spirit of laughter and play, affirming the right to licence when 'practising' for more serious concerns ('Sed in exercendo detur venia, si luxuriet adolescens . . .').[29] Thus this text already exploits a territory in which rules may be suspended and formal categories dislocated in the interests of pedagogical *exercitatio*; it manifests Erasmus's distaste for systematization and his preference for a mobile, open-ended treatment of topics, features which will become an integral part of the Rabelaisian and the Montaignian manner.

It is true that Erasmus itemizes verbal figures in the first book in much the same way as other teachers of rhetoric: the categories and the terminology are traditional, and the brevity of the treatment is no doubt due, in part at least, to the elementary character of the textbook. Later editions even reveal the 'incompleteness' of the initial version by adding a vast outgrowth of further chapters to Book I. Nevertheless, there is a marked indeterminacy in Erasmus's account of the modes of *copia*, and one soon becomes aware that a demonstration is taking place by means of an interplay between the expository level—the giving of precepts—and the exploitation of certain thematic or figurative motifs which are germane to the notion of *copia*. A key factor in this demonstration is the distinction between dull repetition or extension on the one hand and fruitful variation (*varietas*) on the other. Thus, in I. 8, the profusion of the natural world becomes the model for *copia* in discourse. Nature proliferates without repeating itself:

Variety has everywhere such great force that there is nothing at all, however polished it may be, which does not seem uncouth without its support. Nature herself rejoices particularly in variety, for there is nothing anywhere in the immense multitude of things which she has left unpainted with the wonderful art of variety (*varietatis artificio*). (Fr. I, p. 4; LB 6)

One might remark in passing that Erasmus has inserted into his

---

[29] p. 95 (LB 110). In an exchange of letters with Budé in 1516, Erasmus defended the *De copia* (with some irony) against Budé's contention that it was a frivolous work (see La Garanderie, *La Correspondance d'Érasme*, pp. 51 ff., especially p. 67 and pp. 72 ff.; Allen 435 and 480).

'natural' model a figure of 'art', so that a figurative bridge is built here between *copia* in the realm of writing (which necessarily belongs to the domain of art), and the authentic productivity of nature. A sentence or two later, a further image is introduced to clarify the principle of *copia* as *varietas*:

And so this great evil [sc. repetition without variation] may easily be avoided by anyone who has acquired the facility of changing the same thought (*sententiam*) into more forms than Proteus himself is said to have transformed himself.[30]

The same image occurs at the beginning of I. 33 to characterize the ensuing set of variations. And the section entitled *Ratio colligendi exempla* in Book II contains an extraordinary inventory of transformation *exempla*, an indication that the sign of Proteus is not simply a pedagogical marker, but a generative principle with wide-ranging functions.

In the specific context of rhetoric, the notion of transformation is of course immediately—and etymologically—present in the category of tropes which forms the substance of Book I. According to Quintilian's classic definition, 'a trope is the effective changing of a word or phrase from its proper meaning to another' ('tropus est verbi vel sermonis a propria significatione in aliam cum virtute mutatio') (*Inst. orat.* VIII. vi. 1):[31] the etymology of 'trope' is disclosed, and its metaphorical (tropical) force renewed, by the Latin *mutatio*. Erasmus's insistence on the modes of verbal transformation is designed to preclude the notion of listing, or of random synonymy. Thus, at the outset (I. 11), synonyms are classified stylistically rather than thematically, and emphasis is laid on the ultimate particularity of each word and its meaning, beyond the appearance of sameness. The analysis then moves on to the most common tropes—enallage, antonomasia, metaphor, allegory, catachresis, and so on. In defining them, Erasmus reverts throughout to the notion of change, mutation,

---

[30] Loc. cit. This image is further connected with the cultivation of extempore fluency, thus stressing the notion of an intuitive and spontaneous mode of discourse which can adapt itself to the needs of the moment (cf. below, I. 4).

[31] The phrase 'cum virtute' might also be rendered as 'productive'; 'mutatio' as 'alteration' or 'mutation'.

permutation, so that his own analytic discourse reveals itself as figurative, caught in the tropical movement; the terminology of rhetoric is thereby subordinated to a sense of the virtually infinite possibilities of displacement inherent in a natural language (here, of course, the Latin language). The underlying theme of the analysis is recapitulated thus at the end of chapter 32:

Hitherto I have indicated briefly almost all the ways in which discourse may be transformed (*commutatur*) while the thought remains the same (*manente sententia*).

Synonymy as a kind of generative rhetoric rather than as lexical accumulation is then exemplified at the level of *exercitatio* or *experientia* ('Nunc experiamur') in the celebrated double set of 'variation exercises' of chapter 33. These conclude Book I, in the earlier editions at least, with a virtuoso display which has provoked comparison with Queneau's *Exercices de style*.[32] Unlike Piccolomini's variations, those of Erasmus are dynamic and imaginative. The first in particular, based on the epistolary 'gratitude' formula ('tuae literae me magnopere delectarunt'), becomes more and more exuberant as it proceeds, each version of the sentence being richer than the one before; and the sense of *crescendo* includes also a development by association, so that the figures of rhetorical transformation become linked in a generative series. Thus, towards the end of the sequence, the sense of pleasure contained in embryo in the formula of thanks is explored through a series of metaphors involving drinking and feasting, so that a kind of 'symposium' atmosphere, a verbal *festivitas*, is conjured up:

I would give no nectar preference over your writing. Do you think I would compare any Attic honey with your most cherished letter? Sugar is not sugar, if it is placed beside your letter. The lotus has not such a sweet taste for any mortal as the relish I find in your letter. What wine is to a thirsty man, so is your letter to me . . . When I received your eagerly awaited letter, you would have said that Erasmus was quite drunk with joy. When your letter was delivered to me, immediately you would have seen me as it were intoxicated with great

[32] Margolin, 'Érasme et le verbe', p. 95.

delight . . . No delicacies so caress the palate as your letter soothes my mind. No sweetmeats stimulate the palate more delightfully than your writing stimulates my mind . . .   (Fr. I, p. 20; LB 25)

The sequence closes with a strong stress on imagery of abundance: 'your letters are a wagon full of pleasures', 'a well of pleasures', 'a sea of joys'; and Erasmus's verbal excitement is further indicated by his use of Greek words and phrases to carry these images.[33] Having abandoned *doctrina* for *experientia*, Erasmus has created a sequence which celebrates abundance of language as a form of positive intoxication, as a feast of the mind. The movement towards plenitude is apparent both in the compressed richness of each variation and in the dynamic expansion of the sequence as a whole; it is not a product of any schematic conjunction of *verba* and *res*, still less of a thought-producing mechanism like Agricola's. Furthermore, *copia* is envisaged not as a quantitative, linear process but as a manifestation of the desire to write, releasing and bringing to life, as in poetry, the potential nuances of a single bare statement.[34] Indeed, as if Erasmus has

[33] The final variation ('Your letter was to me exactly what "the brain of Zeus" was to the Persians, as the Greeks say') is explained by *Adages* I. vi. 60: the Greek phrase 'brain of Zeus' is a metaphor for especially delicious and sumptuous food. One might cautiously read this image of supreme gastronomic delight as also implying a sense of superior wisdom, bearing in mind the birth of Pallas Athene from the brain of Zeus.

[34] The 'variation' or 'transformation' exercise is closely related to word-for-word paraphrase or translation (*interpretatio*) and thence to free paraphrase (*imitatio*) (see below, I. 2 *passim*). It will be clear from the Erasmian example that metaphor (*translatio*) is one of its most productive resources. The vocabulary involved here is suggestive: the shifts from *interpretatio* to 'interpretation' and from *translatio* to 'translation' are not necessarily direct or causal, but they nevertheless indicate important ways in which rhetoric, imitation, and interpretation are interrelated, and constitute a key motif of the first three chapters of the present study. *Copia*, copying, and explicating are generically the same activity. One might, in order to open a central perspective, cite here an article from Montaigne's educational programme:

Qu'il [sc. the teacher] ne luy [sc. the pupil] demande pas seulement compte des mots de sa leçon, mais du sens et de la substance, et qu'il juge du profit qu'il aura fait, non par le tesmoignage de sa memoire, mais de sa vie. Que ce qu'il viendra d'apprendre, il le lui face mettre en cent visages et accommoder à autant de divers subjets, pour voir s'il l'a encore bien pris et bien faict sien . . . (*Essais* I. xxvi, p. 151).

'Experience' (*experientia, exercitatio*) appears here as a principle of transformation;

become aware retrospectively of the poetic implications of the sequence he has just composed, he immediately adds the following adjustment:

Moreover, if some of these examples seem to be of a kind which might be thought scarcely tolerable in prose, it should be borne in mind that this exercise may also be adapted to the composition of poetry.[35]

It was, then, with this movement towards a place of celebration that Book I originally ended. The later addition of a hundred-odd new chapters suggests a retrospective anxiety about the insufficiency of Erasmus's first sketch of *copia verborum* and institutes a characteristically Erasmian tension. In terms of the classical pedagogical triad *natura–doctrina–exercitatio*, Erasmus was inclined to give relatively low priority to exactness of *doctrina*, which must not be allowed to efface its grounding in *natura* nor to hinder its realization in *exercitatio*. In other words, the primary impulse to write, and the act of writing itself, assert their domination over the mediation of technique. *Copia* cannot be instituted except under such conditions. Yet a contrary desire to add more and more pedagogical detail, to clarify and make explicit, reveals itself in the gradual sedimentation of Erasmus's production over the years. It is apparent in his work on the New Testament, and above all in the movement which begins in the *Paraclesis* and unfolds through the expanding versions of the *Ratio verae theologiae* to reach its most evident realization in the *Ecclesiastes*. Few will think of this last treatise as representative of the characteristic Erasmian manner; but it reveals precisely an underlying desire for security in the proliferation of precept, an escape, via another mode of copiousness, from the perilous freedom of *copia* on the one hand and of irony on the other.

Book II of the *De copia* is more centrifugal than Book I: necessarily, since it opens up the limitless domain of *res*. The sections are fewer in number, but far longer, and the text is rich

the appropriation of the 'sens' of a reading ('leçon') is manifest in the pupil's ability to perform a kind of multiple tropology.

[35] p. 21 (LB 26). In I. 8, p. 4 (LB 6), Erasmus claims that *copia* is also useful for the composition of verse.

in Erasmian inventions, particularly in the list of *exempla*—a virtuoso demonstration which could well be juxtaposed with the variation exercises as another instance of composition by free association (such association always being in reality far from free, in that it brings into play a characteristic set of obsessive figures and analogies, as the 'Proteus' development shows). The book moves towards Erasmus's exposition of the 'notebook' method, probably derived via Agricola from the imitation techniques of Italian humanists on the one hand and, on the other, from late medieval sermon rhetoric. The method is expanded so that it draws on the whole corpus of classical writing, and involves the intermediate 'processing' technique of thematic and dialectical classification which will be exemplified in the index of the *Adages*. Here *copia* takes on the sense of 'storehouse', although the store is always envisaged in terms of release mechanisms which will allow the processed materials to flow back into the stream of writing. Bolgar takes it for granted that this is the core of Erasmus's *copia* method, and it is certainly arguable that the re-statement of an already familiar principle in what was to become an all-pervasive text-book assured the success of an aesthetic of abundance grounded in an eclectic imitation theory.

It is important, however, to stress the orientation which is given to *copia* as the notebook method by *copia* as the practice of writing. A central example—and a test-case for the relation-ship between *verba* and *res*—is provided by the extended treat-ment, in the second book, of the figure *enargeia*. Medieval rhetoric makes much of *descriptio*, and the term continues to be used in the sixteenth century. But the increasing taste for Greek terminology —and no doubt other, more profound, factors[36]—brings into prominence a somewhat different range of terms: in particular *enargeia*, which may be initially defined as the evocation of a visual scene, in all its details and colours, as if the reader were

[36] I am thinking here of the link between 'ways of seeing' and shifts in rhetori-cal terminology analysed by Baxandall, *Giotto and the Orators*; Baxandall's account of the figure ecphrasis (pp. 85–7, 90–6) is especially relevant. *Enargeia* and related figures must be carefully distinguished from the Ramist notion of the visual representation of concepts, which tends to be formal and schematic. Ramist rhetorics do not dwell much on the rendering of sense-impressions.

present as a spectator.[37] Its Latin equivalents are *evidentia* and *illustratio*, which are often used synonymously by rhetorical theorists. *Illustratio* is etymologically the more exact rendering, since the root *arg* carries the sense of 'bright', 'shining'.[38] But of course the metaphor is an essentially visual one. Argus has a hundred eyes, some of which are always open. Hence *e-videntia* is germane to *enargeia-illustratio*.[39]

If *res*, as the counterpart of *verbum*, moves towards the domain of 'thought' (*sententia*), it also includes the whole domain of physical objects conceived of as materials for rhetorical elaboration: in other words, one of the functions of *copia rerum* is the unfolding of object-things within language. The *quinta ratio locupletandi* of the second part of Erasmus's treatise explores at length precisely that verbal landscape of object-things which is classed as *enargeia*, rendered in Latin as *evidentia* ('quam evidentiam vertunt'). Erasmus gives the following definition:

We use [*enargeia*] whenever . . . we do not explain a thing simply,

[37] The whole range of terminology for 'vivid representation' is analysed in detail in Lausberg, *Handbuch*, paras. 810 ff.

[38] It is perhaps not irrelevant that the title of Du Bellay's *Deffence* contains a synonym for *enargeia*. No doubt the word is meant to have a wider resonance than that of a rhetorical category, but Du Bellay's indications within the treatise of the kind of 'illustration' he is thinking of announce a poetics of ornamentation: it is as if each line of poetry were a surface to be decorated (cf. *Deffence*, pp. 40, 114). The figure is conjoined with 'abundance' in the following example of a vernacular variant on *evidentia*, provided by Geoffroy Tory: 'Ovide, fontaine de fluantes et doulces parolles latines et poeticques, descript la susdicte Fable tresabundamment et evidamment en ses Metamorphoses' (*Champ fleury*, fol. ix r°).

[39] A further etymological peculiarity of *enargeia* arises from its similarity to the (Aristotelian) term *energeia*. Phrissemius's 'scholia' on Agricola's *De inventione* III. 3 include a note distinguishing between *energeia* (rendered as *efficacia*) and *enargeia* (*evidentia*) (p. 370). But in Weltkirchius's commentary on the *De copia*, *energeia* replaces *enargeia*, as if one were simply a variant spelling of the other. The confusion is still more evident in the vernacular: cf. Du Bellay's *Deffence*, p. 35 (and Chamard's note; 'energie' occurs again on p. 40). Sebillet uses 'enargie', Peletier 'eficace', and Du Bellay 'energie' in almost identical contexts (see below, pp. 57–8, 61, 63, 69). Thus *enargeia* becomes linked with the Aristotelian notion of dynamism or 'actuality' in the domain of metaphor. Cf. Aristotle, *Rhetoric* III. xi. 2–4: 'Homer often, by making use of metaphor, speaks of inanimate things as if they were animate; and it is to creating actuality (*energeian*) in all cases that his popularity is due . . . for he gives movement and life to all, and actuality is movement (*kinesis*).'

but display it to be looked at as if it were expressed in colour in a
picture, so that it may seem that we have painted, not narrated, and
that the reader has seen, not read. (Fr. I, p. 66; LB 77)

The etymological sense of *evidentia* is echoed soon after by the
adjective 'evidens' (doubled by 'perspicua'), while the parallel
of the roots *arg* and *lustr* is recalled by the verb 'lustremus'.[40]
Yet the visualization is of course quite explicitly metaphorical—
'*ceu* coloribus', '*veluti* faciem'—and ironically, another metaphorical verb of seeing ('videatur') undercuts the transference
of things seen into words, so that the act of seeing is deflected
into one of seeming.

Thus a theme begins to take shape: the presence or 'evidence'
of *res* in a verbal surface. It belongs to an ancient rhetorical
tradition, one which carries within it all the key assumptions and
problems of rhetoric as an art: namely the theory of the representation of reality. The reduplication of terms for this 'device'
—mimesis, hypotyposis, ecphrasis, *enargeia*, *evidentia*, *illustratio*,
demonstratio, *descriptio*—echoes both the fascination and the
futility of the attempt to display the world in language. Because
of their etymological shading and the different contexts in which
they are used and reused, they continually open up new perspectives on the ways in which we appear to see the world through
the lattices of language; they modulate the senses in which
'things' (in the present instance, physical objects) are presumed to
inhabit words. Yet, like metaphor, which displaces the 'proper'
term, mimesis necessarily entails the absence of that which it
purports to represent: the word 're-presentation' itself implies a
secondary or feigned presence. Likewise, although the group of
terms for detailed mimesis which cluster around *enargeia* all carry
in their etymology a presupposition that verbal vision is possible,
it is self-evident that words (whether as written or oral signs)
always interpose their opacity between the reader-listener and
any conceivable experience of things seen. The speech-act here
disguises its intermediary function as a mode of communication

---

40 'We shall succeed in this, if we first mentally survey (*lustremus*) the whole
nature of the thing, all its circumstances and, as it were, its aspect (*faciem*). Then
we must represent (*effingamus*) it with suitable words and figures, so that it becomes as evident and clear (*evidens perspicuaque*) as possible for the reader.'

and poses as an event: hence the characteristic emphasis, in rhetorical theory, on the apparent *disappearance* of language ('so that it may seem that . . . the reader has seen, not read').[41] At the same time, the impossibility of escaping from verbal appearances (from what might be called the 'fallacy of presence') does not eradicate the impulse to stabilize them, to anchor them in a referent located outside their domain.[42]

To speak of a 'verbal surface' is itself another metaphor within the tradition which makes linguistic representation seem to be a visual act. It is perhaps with the constraints of such a metaphor in mind that one should read the passage where Erasmus, elaborating his theme, refers to the depiction not only of primary or 'real' objects and events but also of decorated surfaces: tapestries, sculptures, paintings, the shields of Achilles and Aeneas (pp. 67–8; LB 79). Here a further potential ambiguity emerges: *copia* in the form of *enargeia* overrides the distinction between 'true' and 'false' representation. The linguistic surface renders with equal colour and evidence the face of real things and of imaginary things. Speaking of tragic *récits*, Erasmus says: 'It is not relevant for this purpose whether they are true or false.' Potential as well as actual occurrences may become the material of *enargeia*: the possible future, no less than the historical past, may become present in language. The duality recurs in a passage on how to contrive a *simulacrum* of different modes of life, not only by *ars* and *ingenium*, but also by practical observation; for this procedure is followed by its inverse: 'There are also fabulous descriptions of things, which nevertheless allude to true ones.' In one instance, physical observation leads to the contrivance of a surrogate: in the other, an imaginary seeing refers back to a world of 'true' things.[43] No doubt Erasmus implies a hierarchy of values, a priority of true over false, and elsewhere he will explore the possibility of such a distinction.[44] But here, for the most part,

---

[41] See also Quintilian, *Inst. orat.* IV. ii. 32; IX. ii. 40; and below, p. 32.

[42] Hence this whole question is germane to the problems raised in I. 3. ii below, where the figures of 'evidence' and of the 'lattice' will reappear.

[43] The same ambiguity arises in the passage on *loci descriptio* (p. 70; LB 82).

[44] For example, in the *Convivium religiosum*; see the analysis below, I. 3. ii; also above, note 24.

the real and the imaginary are allowed to slide together and con-
taminate one another; the things which appear in the verbal
surface have discarded the signs of their provenance and are
happy to masquerade as words. Moreover, in some mysterious
way, a rupture has taken place within the texture of language
(a lattice or window has been opened), and through it passes an
endless succession of word-things:

But if you open up those things which were included in a single word,
there will appear flames pouring through houses and temples . . .
[etc.].[45]

It is not perhaps entirely by chance that the ensuing section (the
sexta ratio locupletandi) will be *egressio* or *digressio*: terms which
both carry etymologically the sense of an excursion or deflection.
In such instances, *res* seem to be less the source of production than
a by-product; they are revealed by the autonomous proliferation
of language.

Just as, in the first variation exercise, the activity of writing
asserts itself as a kind of hedonism, so also the *enargeia* section
stresses the pleasures of unconstrained 'evidence':

But when the whole thing concerns pleasure, as is usually the case in
poetry, and in *apodeixeis*, which are treated for the sake of exercising
and displaying one's talent, it is permissible to indulge more freely in
fictions of this kind. To this category belong Homer's descriptions,
as when he arms his gods or heroes, or describes a banquet, a battle, a
retreat, a council.[46]

The feast of copious words or things takes place under the sign of

[45] p. 66 (LB 78). The single word is 'expugnatam' ('stormed'), the reference
being to the storming of a city. Erasmus is here overtly quoting a standard example
provided by Quintilian (*Inst. orat.* VIII. iii. 68): *enargeia* is illustrated by the
rewriting of a *topos*.

[46] p. 67 (LB 78–9). It may be noted that, in quoting from Quintilian (see
above, note 45), Erasmus also reproduces Quintilian's description—borrowed
from Cicero—of a 'convivium luxuriosum' (*Inst. orat.* VIII. iii. 66). On *apodeixis*
(*evidens probatio*) as a rhetorical figure, see Lausberg, paras. 357 and 372. It is
clearly germane to the Latin term *demonstratio* as a synonym for *evidentia*. *Enargeia*
might indeed be seen as a rhetorical usurpation of the apodeictic function of logic.
It purports to demonstrate by linguistic immediacy and presence; it asserts a
tautology or self-evidence.—Pierre Fabri uses the term *demonstrance* for the same
figure (*Le Grant et vray art*, fol. ciiii r°).

fiction and of licence. In the third book of Agricola's *De inventione*, this same notion had found its way to the surface in spite of the constraints which the dialectical method was intended to impose. In III. 4, having treated *enargeia* in the preceding chapter as one of the most powerful devices for moving the affections, Agricola develops at considerable length the different types of pleasure (*voluptas*) which may arise from discourse, beginning with a distinction between the sensual, located in stylistic register ('ex orationis genere'), and the mental, generated by the subject-matter ('ex rebus de quibus disseritur') (op. cit., p. 372). This hierarchical duality quickly gives way to a profusion of colourful examples in the sensual rather than the mental mode: Agricola is already being seduced by the movement of his own discourse. He speaks of digressions and transitions which give unity to a diversified *oratio*, while adding that the licence to digress ('digrediendi . . . libertas') is particularly given to poets.[47] And then he returns to a topic which Erasmus treats under the heading of *enargeia*, namely *prosopopeia* (or the sub-topic *sermocinatio* or *dialogismos*): if the dialogue is properly animated and speeches appropriately attributed, the topic will seem not to be said but to be enacted ('ut non dici sed agi videatur res'). At this point, he remarks that this is done by the power of discourse, not by the nature of the subject-matter, and thus should rightly be attributed to *oratio*, the sensuous surface ('id quoniam fit orationis virtute, non rerum natura, idcirco est etiam orationi iure tribuendum') (p. 376). Poems, he adds, are particularly capable of manifesting this 'grace'. The point is summarized in two key sentences:

For the style (*oratio*) does not follow the subject-matter (*rem*), but the subject-matter is adapted to the pleasure of the style (*voluptati orationis*), and everything is devised (*finguntur*) in order to please as much as possible; for this reason it [the poem] has the greatest liberty in style for grasping this beauty. History (*historia*) comes next, though stricter

[47] The self-consciousness of Agricola in this key chapter is indicated at this point in his argument by a sentence relating the licence of his own discourse to the topic of digression: 'since we have been induced to digress by a discussion of digression (*quia digrediendi ratione sumus adducti, ut digrederemur*), let us now return to our main purpose.'

and with a more solemn brow, since its play must leave truth unharmed (*ut quam illaesa veritate ludere oporteat*).

Thus Agricola makes quite explicit the degree to which, in devices like *enargeia*, the pleasing surface of the discourse is the operative factor, *res* only becoming apparent, once again, through *verba*.[48] This is a realm in which the licence of *oratio* goes furthest in search of *voluptas*, leaving behind it nature and truth: the shift back to a more austere tone in the sentence about *historia* reveals that the game had hitherto depended on the generation of fictions.

Towards the end of the *De copia*, Erasmus devotes considerable space both to fables and to fictions.[49] Lucian and comedy indicate the type of fiction he is thinking of: these, he says, 'please not by imitation of reality, but by allusions and allegories'; and earlier, he had put the point still more clearly:

The farther they [sc. those fictions devised for the sake of humour] are from truth, the more they delight the spirit, provided that they don't resemble the absurdities of old women, and can by erudite allusions capture the attention of the learned.   (Fr. I, p. 86; LB 99)

The centrifugal movement which constantly asserts and reasserts itself throughout the *De copia* and its prolific successors, that same movement of discourse towards pleasure, towards a place of celebration which is also a place of fiction, triumphs in spite of Erasmus's cautions. Allegories and erudite allusions, scattered as *res* on the colourful surface of *verba*, point back towards a supposed *sententia* or *sensus* whose hidden presence would give plenitude to *copia*. Whether this guarantee is effective or not must be left to a later discussion, although the fact that the problem of allegory arises already in this context is worth attention; but in the *De copia*, there is no doubt that the licence which Erasmus had given himself (for the sake of teaching and for the sake of

---

48 One may here recall Agricola's analysis in *De inventione* II. 20 of dialectical *descriptio* as a system for producing a *copia* of places independently of the *verba* or *res* which might fill them; in Book III, by contrast, rhetorical *descriptio* (*enargeia*) has the function of displaying *res* through *verba*, as concretely and attractively as possible.

49 In the sections entitled *De exemplo fabuloso*, *De parabola*, *De apologis*, *De somnio*, *De fictis narrationibus*.

youth) releases *res* from the constraints of a predetermined *sententia* so that they may flow with the devious, Protean current of *verba*. Things, once again, are neither more nor less than configurations of those verbal figures treated in Book I. They are, indeed, 'word-things', all of them, and as such they monopolize the landscape of discourse, endlessly deferring the realization of sense. The Erasmian text, by its very movement from *verba* towards *res*, uncovers the essential duplicity of *copia*.[50]

[50] It should perhaps be made clear that the word 'duplici', in the title of Erasmus's handbook, means simply 'twofold', and has itself no connotation of 'duplicity'. However, the proposed duality is clearly a problematic one: *res* as subject-matter can only appear qualitatively different from *verba* by means of the catachresis (or abuse) indicated above, note 22. The possibility of a distinction between 'full' and 'empty' *copia* is thus placed in perpetual suspension; duplicity emerges as the versatile, unstable twin of duality.

2

Imitation

IN that it associates the practice of writing with an exhaustive programme of reading, the *De copia* already constitutes a major episode in the history of imitation theory. In imitation, indeed, the activities of reading and writing become virtually identified. A text is read in view of its transcription as part of another text; conversely, the writer as imitator concedes that he cannot entirely escape the constraints of what he has read. In this respect, imitation is also germane to interpretation, since the interpretative act can only become visible in a second discourse which claims to be a reconstitution of the first; the meanings of *interpretatio* include translation, synonymy, and interpretation. Questions concerning the relationship of *verba* to *res* continue to be of fundamental importance here: can *res* be separated from *verba*? if so, which should the imitator attempt to transcribe? what is the distinctive quality of a text consecrated by tradition? can this elusive factor be captured and resuscitated? Such questions are raised by all the texts discussed in this chapter: by Erasmus's *Ciceronianus* of 1528 and Dolet's counter-attack of 1535, the *De imitatione ciceroniana*; and by the French theorists of the 1540s and 1550s who attempted to find a formula for the displacement of classical materials into the vernacular.

Among the central themes which emerge from these texts is the desire to appropriate or naturalize an alien discourse: Erasmian theory may for example be seen to anticipate Montaigne's development of the self-portrait as a reaction against the pressure of what has already been written. If the writer is to achieve *copia*, his imitation must not appear to be a mere copy. At the same time, it is worth emphasizing that the two major episodes discussed here—the Erasmus–Dolet debate and Du

Bellay's defence of vernacular imitation—are both polemical in character. This fact would be significant even if it only served to show that, within the arbitrary and unstable set of conceptual counters available at a given moment of history, what seem to be purely tactical manœuvres may open up new ways of playing fruitful games with language. But it also reflects the essential character of imitation, which could be defined as a kind of inter-textual dialogue or conflict (compare Quintilian's definition of paraphrase as *certamen* or *aemulatio*, quoted below). In Du Bellay's textual borrowings and the commentary of the *Quintil horatian*, no less than in the explicitly dialogic form adopted by Erasmus and Dolet, imitation theory is itself manifestly rendered as a plurality of voices, each seeking to differentiate itself within a prescribed textual space.

In the tenth book of Quintilian's *Institutiones*, imitation is recom-mended as an important step in the acquisition of *copia*, providing a transition between the rhetorical precept of the earlier books and the ultimate ideal of performance: it is indeed the principal mode of extended *exercitatio*. Since Renaissance imitation theory exploits *topoi* derived from Quintilian's discussion, it will be convenient to indicate some of these at this point as a prelude to the analysis of sixteenth-century texts.

The imitator, says Quintilian, must first read and meditate on complete works, and not make abstractions; context is essential: 'nor must we study a text merely in parts, but must read it through in its entirety and then read it afresh (*perlectus liber utique ex integro resumendus*)' (X. i. 20). The definition of paraphrase in a later section provides a complementary theoretical principle which elaborates Cicero's rejection of word-for-word translation: 'But I would not have paraphrase restrict itself to the bare transposition (*interpretationem*) of the model: its function is rather to rival and vie with the original in the expression of the same meaning (*circa eosdem sensus certamen atque aemulationem*).'[1]

---

[1] X. v. 5. Cf. Cicero, *De finibus* I. ii. 6; also *De oratore* I. xxxiv. 154–5; *De opt. gen. orat.* iv. 14. See also Horace, *Epistula ad Pisones*, lines 133–4. These theoretical *loci* and their impact in the French Renaissance are helpfully discussed by Norton,

Out of these two passages arises the notion that the 'integrity' or wholeness of a model-text cannot be regenerated by linear repetition in the mode of 'translation' (*interpretatio*). The identity (sameness) of the sense or senses may be preserved by a 'circular' movement ('circa eosdem sensus') which is also a kind of dialectic or rivalry, asserting the necessity of difference. One might well recall, in this context, Erasmus's experiment in transforming 'words' while the *sententia* remains the same.

In the paragraph preceding the first of the above two quotations, the use of memory is represented by an image of digestion or 'innutrition' which will become a *topos* of Renaissance theory:

We must return to (*repetamus*) what we have read and reconsider it with care, while, just as we do not swallow our food till we have chewed it and reduced it almost to a state of liquefaction to assist the process of digestion, so what we read must not be committed to the memory for subsequent imitation while it is still in a crude state, but must be softened and, if I may use the phrase, reduced to a pulp by frequent re-perusal.   (X. i. 19)

This notion of incorporation or consubstantiality transfers to language the possibility of a process by which alien, external materials may be transformed so that they may re-emerge as a function of 'nature', and more specifically of the speaker's nature. The same operation is indicated, in Quintilian's account of improvisation, by the virtually untranslatable terms 'pectus' and 'vis mentis': 'Pectus est enim, quod disertos facit, et vis mentis' (X. vii. 15). The immediate context of this sentence connects 'pectus' with the affections (*adfectus*), 'vis mentis' with clarity and immediacy of thought (as in *enargeia*),[2] so that a translation might read: 'It is feeling which makes men eloquent, and clarity of conception.' The word *pectus*, however, has a range of meanings which embraces cognitive as well as affective modes of awareness, and should not be equated with 'emotion' in the Romantic sense. The twin poles of *pectus* and *vis mentis* together indicate the total active engagement of the speaker as the 'subject'

'Translation theory in Renaissance France: Étienne Dolet'; Norton also lists the principal earlier studies of the subject (see especially note 1).

[2] The context will be discussed at greater length below, pp. 130, 134, 141–2.

of his utterance. Although Quintilian is not here discussing imitation, it is presumably by means of some such intuitive process that a *sensus* may ideally be transferred from one speaker or text to another without losing its identity or immobilizing the dynamics of copious discourse.[3]

In order to complete this configuration of theoretical *topoi* from the *Institutiones*, one may quote another passage which associates nature with an ineradicable but productive difference, a passage exploited, not only by Erasmus, but also by Du Bellay and Montaigne:

> there is nothing harder than to produce an exact likeness, and nature herself has so far failed in this endeavour that there is always some difference which enables us to distinguish even the things which seem most like and most equal to one another. (X. ii. 10)

Quintilian is here, once again, urging emulation rather than slavish imitation. The copy is necessarily inferior to its model ('quidquid alteri simile est, necesse est minus sit eo') as art is to nature (X. ii. 11). Thus, in Book X as a whole, there is a precarious balance between art and nature. Imitation is already closer to nature (and to *exercitatio*) than is the precept of earlier books, and it attracts the concepts and metaphors of nature (digestion, *pectus*, etc.). Yet it is still an art, a secondary representation: it mediates between art and nature at the risk of inverting their proper relationship.

In 1531, Robert Estienne, quoting Quintilian X. v. 5 in the article *paraphrasis* of his *Dictionarium*, adds his own definition: the paraphrast is one who 'does not transfer letter from letter, but sense from sense, as if he were speaking alongside his model' ('non literam ex litera, sed sensum e sensu transfert, quasi iuxta

---

[3] It will be apparent that the problem sketched out here involves two senses of the word 'identity': (i) that which is inalienable from ('proper to') the individual, which constitutes him as an individual; (ii) the likeness or 'sameness' (*identitas*) of one thing (or text) to another. The notion that language must become different in order to preserve this double identity initiates a deconstruction of identity: discourse must either fall into 'empty' verbal repetition (a copy) or embark on an open-ended series of transformations which may be only nominally identified by the signature of a given writer, and which defer indefinitely the production of an identical *sensus*.

loquens').[4] This rephrasing (one might well say 'paraphrase') of Quintilian adds a striking new image for the identity-difference crux. The transference of sense takes place, not by a reworking of the surface, but by a regeneration of the same sense, the phrase 'sensum e sensu' mirroring this reproductive act. Two voices are heard, each authentic, each grounded in the same *sensus*. Erasmus, in a preface to his paraphrase of St. Matthew's Gospel, had made the same kind of point in terms of a problem to be surmounted: whereas the commentator may legitimately confess that he cannot explain a difficult passage, the paraphrast must attempt to resolve obscurities (Allen 1255, p. 6). It is the central purpose of Erasmus's enterprise that paraphrase should speak clearly to a modern reader; it must therefore re-create, as lucidly as possible, and in language appropriate to a new audience, the sense of the original. This preface leads into the heart of his view of interpretation theory in a scriptural context; thus it indicates precisely the proximity of the domains of interpretation and imitation, which should be borne in mind as one probes more deeply, via the question of Ciceronianism, into imitation theory proper.

The quasi-polemical situation of the Ciceronian debate is internalized in Erasmus's *Ciceronianus* as dialogue: Nosoponus, the 'Ciceronian' man of straw, is the pretext for the lengthy and often repetitious theoretical discourse ascribed mainly to the 'Erasmian' Bulephorus. From this dialogue will emerge detailed formulations of the relationship between the writer as model and the writer as reader, a relationship which will turn, once again, on the key problem of identity and difference. This crux is already present in the well-known passage, early in the dialogue, where Bulephorus coaxes Nosoponus to admit that his desire to re-enact Ciceronian discourse leads him to exclude not only all words, but also any morphological variant, not used by Cicero himself (Am. I-2, pp. 610-11). Identity—and thus authenticity—is here asserting itself as a rearrangement of a given set of *verba*; and in due course, Nosoponus will develop his view of the priority

---

[4] See Norton, art. cit., note 26.

of *verba* over *res* (taken here, it seems, as virtually interchangeable with *sententia* and *sensus*). Scandal erupts at the point where he maintains that the function of 'art' is to discover appropriate senses for verbal ornaments which have been pre-selected from Ciceronian 'voces', 'tropos', 'formulas', 'numeros', and 'flosculos' ('Hoc enim iam artis est, sensus ad haec verborum ornamenta invenire'). Hypologus, Bulephorus's auxiliary, counters with an image designed to expose the inauthenticity of any such discourse:

It is as if some outstanding craftsman (*artifex*) prepared a beautiful garment, added a great number of necklaces, rings, and jewels, and then devised (*affingat*) a wax statue to which he might fit these ornaments, or rather which he might adapt (*conflectat*) to the ornaments. (p. 614)

What is of importance in Erasmus's text here—as elsewhere—may well be, not what he openly accepts or rejects, but what he is able to envisage. Hypologus's statue image, which might be seen as a variant of the Pygmalion myth, conveys a striking insight into the reversibility of surface and intention in discourse: once again, a duplicity is revealed within the traditional alignment of *verba* and *res*, undoing from the outset precisely that guarantee of authenticity which Bulephorus will seek to impose. At all events, the language of both Hypologus and Bulephorus reveals a profound fear of Nosoponus's distortion. The verb *affingere*, which recurs in Erasmus's strictures on allegory, denotes the gratuitous way in which, according to Hypologus's formula, a *sensus* which ought to have been origin and grounding is 'invented'[5] so that it becomes an alien and rootless growth in the culture of words. The potential malignancy of this inverted perspective will be indicated elsewhere in the *Ciceronianus* (see below, p. 44).

The elaboration of a counter-theory exploits many approaches:

[5] Nosoponus, in the preceding remark quoted above, inverts the classic relationship of *inventio* and *elocutio* and thus relegates *inventio* to the status of a secondary art, instead of aligning it with nature (i.e. with *ratio* defined as an innate faculty of the mind). On *fingere* and its compounds in the context of allegorical theory, see below, pp. 87–8.

Bulephorus stresses the importance of poetry, which Nosoponus had excluded (given Cicero's lack of talent in that genre) (p. 623); and, inevitably, he quotes Horace's 'bee' image in support of selective and multiple imitation.[6] But the argument proper begins to gather momentum at the point where Bulephorus realigns the *verba–(res)–sententia* equation in favour of *sententia* ('Verbis itaque non vincimur, imo vincimus potius: sententia longe superamus') (p. 628). The central strategy involves a repeated stress on the ineradicable difference of Cicero's text, a difference which is in the first instance a consequence of the passage of time: the world has changed since Cicero's day; we speak of things he never dreamed of (p. 629). Thus Ciceronian discourse is authentic, according to Bulephorus, only when understood as the property of the living person who was Cicero. Its verbal surface, anchored in that distant origin, cannot be manipulated at will; the movement from author to text is irreversible. Furthermore, since the identity of Cicero is (was) unique, any attempt to repeat it can only result in a lifeless, fictive 'simulacrum'; here Bulephorus's metaphor recalls Hypologus's 'statue' image:

If the portrait (*simulacrum*) in which we represent (*effingimus*) Cicero lacks life, movement, feeling, sinews, and bones, what will be colder than our imitation?[7]

The antithesis of this dead copy is then characterized in an important speech by Bulephorus through a set of terms for

---

[6] p. 625; cf. p. 652, where this image is developed in detail, and p. 703.

[7] p. 630. The analogy here is with painting: Erasmus echoes the *topos* according to which man's inner nature cannot be imitated by the painter ('quae sunt hominis praecipua, pictori sunt inimitabilia'). The point is subsequently clarified by a *reductio ad absurdum* of the painting analogy: the painter who aims at total realism will paint hairs on his model's chin before he has shaved, and remove them afterwards; he will paint him first awake, then asleep, and so on *ad infinitum*: 'if he could express the true and innate form of man, he would not take refuge in these secondary details.' The painter's art is trapped in the world of external appearances, and is thus condemned to be eternally unfinished; Ciceronian imitation is likewise, according to Erasmus, a wild goose chase. The insistent recurrence in the *Ciceronianus* of analogies with painting, which draws an unfavourable comment from Mesnard (Am. I–2, pp. 594–5), reveals Erasmus's desire to clarify the problem of writing as a mimetic activity.

inalienable (living) identity: *genius, pectus, vis, arcana energia*—
terms which all carry the notion of an inscrutable dynamism
deployed in language (and, one should note in passing, only
apparent to the reader *through* language). The whole of Cicero's
rhetorical technique (*inventio, dispositio*, and so on) is seen as the
manifestation of such a *genius*: the sense of a 'mind breathing even
now in the written word' ('mens illa spirans etiamnum in scriptis')
cannot be copied, and Bulephorus stresses the peril of playing with
this almost supernaturally charged discourse ('Periculosae plenum
opus aleae est, divinam illam et humana natura superiorem
exprimere linguam') (pp. 631–2).

Erasmus's particularly insistent reversion to the question of difference, besides opening the way for his preference for inclusive
imitation, leads directly to a solution based precisely on the
irreversibility of the author–text relationship: one must attempt
to re-enact the process by which the self, as author, generates and
authenticates its own text. The would-be writer must first ascer-
tain the kind of eloquence (*dicendi genus*) for which nature has
created him; true eloquence must be grounded in intrinsic, natural
gifts:

If you want to express Cicero totally, you cannot express yourself.
If you do not express yourself, your discourse will be a lying mirror.
(p. 649)

It is important, of course, not to attach to the phrase 'si teipsum
non exprimis' the connotations which 'self-expression' acquires
as the focus of a Romantic insistence on intensity of emotional
experience. Nevertheless, it is a formulation virtually absent
from classical and medieval rhetoric,[8] and marks a shift the magni-
tude of which it is hard to measure. In the first place, it may be

---

[8] I have only been able to find one example of a reflexive use of *exprimere*
(cited in the *Thesaurus linguae latinae*). It appears in the fourth-century *Rhetoric*
of Marius Victorinus (II. 47): 'for neither the speech of men nor any writing fully
expresses itself or enunciates the will' ('quod neque sermo hominum neque
scriptum aliquod plane se exprimat aut eloquatur voluntatem') ('voluntatem'
might also be translated as 'desire' or 'intention'). This interestingly negative
instance makes discourse itself the subject of (imperfect) self-expression. There are
of course many classical and medieval uses of the ordinary transitive *exprimere*
denoting the expression of thought, meaning, desires, and so on.

seen to extend the movement, illustrated by *Institutiones* X, from dependence on formal precept to an intuitive grasp of the potentialities of discourse: significant utterance is now said to arise from, and to be guaranteed by, a subjective 'self'. But the specific character of the shift is defined by the conjunction of deictic pronoun and reflexive verb: self-identity is thereby enacted syntactically as both the origin and the object of discourse. Classical accounts of affective speech (like Quintilian's 'Pectus est, quod disertos facit') are phrased in the third person. Likewise, 'personal' discourse—in prose at least—had traditionally been restricted to informal genres like the letter.[9] Erasmus places it at the centre of the problem of rhetoric, thus renewing the ancient debate on the relationship between rhetoric and truth in terms of a new and potent grammar of identity and an intensified textual self-consciousness.

The debate—and the problem—are resumed in the metaphor of speech as a 'lying mirror'. Many years before, through the mouth of Folly (with all that that implies in terms of a dislocation of formalism), Erasmus had called speech ('oratio') the least deceptive mirror of the mind ('minime mendax animi speculum').[10] The point is made rather differently in the *Ciceronianus*,

[9] Cf. e.g. Demetrius, *De elocutione* 227 ('it may be said that everybody writes images of his own soul in his letters'). The epistolary genre was of course enormously popular in the sixteenth century. Erasmus's own published letters no doubt encouraged the use of first-person discourse of an informal kind. Although his treatise *De conscribendis epistolis* contains no specific reference to 'self-expression', an early letter to Colet (Allen 107) speaks of Colet's image as reflected in the letter he had sent to Erasmus.

[10] Fr. IV, p. 354 (LB 408). Cf. the sentence immediately following: 'I don't use cosmetics, nor do I say one thing with my face while concealing another in my breast (*pectore*).' Folly also insists on her own self-evident right to self-expression: 'For who can better express me than I myself? unless by chance someone else knows me better than I know myself' ('Quis enim me melius exprimat quam ipsa me? nisi si cui forte notior sim, quam egomet sum mihi') (loc. cit.; LB 406). The link between the Socratic *topos* of self-knowledge and the notion of self-expression is here clearly (and ironically) visible. The notion of *oratio speculum animi* also occurs in Erasmus's *Apophthegmata* III (Fr. IV, p. 148; LB 162) and in the *Lingua* (Am. IV–1, p. 296). It recalls traditional uses of the word *speculum*, in titles, to denote the text itself (as in *Speculum sapientiae*, or Marguerite de Navarre's *Miroir de l'âme pécheresse*), and the equally commonplace formulations *oratio index animi* (or *mentis*), *vultus index mentis*, etc. The most striking and richly

but it is fundamentally the same one. Discourse should be a direct counterpart of the inner self; those who try to make it something else—a false mask—indirectly reflect their own mendacity. Nosoponus, and the Ciceronians in general, are morally flawed; their intolerance, their paganism, and their elegant, factitious phrasing are profoundly interconnected; they are sick, and will not speak well until they are cured.[11] In other words, they have become alienated, through language, from their authentic nature. The mirror image itself recalls the humanist *topos* of the ideal consonance of *ratio* and *oratio*, which Erasmus himself exploits and which points towards the still more central duality of the word *logos*, denoting—simultaneously as it were—speech and reason grounded finally in the Christian Logos. But it is necessary to make a careful distinction here. *Ratio*, in humanist theory, is most often considered as transcending individual identity: the dialectical systems of Agricola or Ramus have little to do with self-expression. Or again, the mirror image as embodied in the term 'speculative grammarians' carries the notion, common to late medieval analysis of language, that the structures of language in some way mirror those of the world. Indeed, whatever the differences between scholastics and humanists, such theories recall the paradigm outlined at the beginning of Aristotle's *De interpretatione*, with its harmoniously superimposed layers of writing, oral discourse, mind, and world. Erasmus's development of the theme in contexts such as that of imitation realigns this

developed instance in the earlier sixteenth century outside the works of Erasmus is to be found in Luther's preface to his translation of the Psalms, published in 1528, the same year as the *Ciceronianus* (a contemporary French translation of the Latin text is given in Rice, *Prefatory Epistles*, no. 149): the emphasis here on affectivity as the sign of inwardness recalls a long-standing devotional tradition; but the mirror image, together with the notion of an absent individual (David) recovered through writing, confers a special status on language as something like 'self-expression' in the Erasmian sense.

[11] On the paganism of the Ciceronians, see Am. I-2, pp. 694 and 709; their aesthetic is associated by Erasmus with dreams of nationalistic power, exemplified by the cities of Rome and Jerusalem. The name 'Nosoponus' is a Greek coinage meaning 'suffering from a sickness'; the metaphor is exploited from the beginning of the dialogue, and recurs in relation to the possibility of a cure towards the end. On both points, see also below, pp. 158-60.

model on a different axis, in that it stresses the first-person singularity of the speaker, his difference, his unrepeatable identity. Here alone is the *locus* of plenitude, the origin of fruitfully copious discourse.

Bulephorus develops these arguments, first through a paradox or 'enigma' which turns on the equation of identity with difference, and then through a series of metaphors of consubstantiality. The speech which moves the listener must arise from the most intimate fabric of the body ('Ex intimis enim vaenis') and not from the skin ('in cute'); it will be 'vivid' if it is born in the heart, not the lips (p. 651); and therefore all that one reads must be properly digested:

You must digest what you have consumed (*devoraris*) in varied and prolonged reading, and transfer it by reflection (*meditatione*) into the veins of the mind (*in vaenas animi*), rather than into your memory or your notebook (*indicem*). Thus your natural talent (*ingenium*), gorged on all kinds of foods, will of itself beget a discourse (*ex sese gignat orationem*) which will be redolent, not of any particular flower, leaf, or herb, but of the character and feelings of your own heart (*indolem affectusque pectoris tui*), so that whoever reads your work will not recognize fragments excerpted from Cicero, but the image of a mind replete with every kind of learning.   (p. 652)

If this passage is compared with Quintilian's digestion simile (above, p. 37), one is struck first of all by the extent to which, while 'imitating' Quintilian (repeating his *topos*), Erasmus has elaborated the rhetorical surface in terms of metaphor (*translatio*) rather than simile (*comparatio*): the act of converting other people's books into one's own *oratio* is here made wholly interchangeable with the processes of digestion, nourishment, and rebirth. Furthermore, while Quintilian is making a relatively simple point about the advantages of reading over listening to speeches as a means of forming the judgement, Erasmus is in these pages of the *Ciceronianus* probing the core of his imitation theory. The notions of personal differentiation and of *oratio* as an image of the mind are interwoven here with a no less fundamental theory of transference, or transformation. The reader must devour his models, destroying their alien substance so that they may be regenerated in his living utterance as a product of his own essential nature.[12]

Towards the end of the dialogue, Bulephorus returns to the mirror image, linking it with the concept of nature ('natura . . . voluit orationem esse speculum animi'). He continues as follows:

and the first thing which delights the reader is to recognize in a text (*oratione*) the affections, image, intention (*sensum*) and mind (*ingenium*) of the writer, no less than if you had spent several years in his company. (p. 703)

The author–reader differentiation and analogy—the twin voices of Estienne's 'quasi iuxta loquens'—are now presented as a dialogue: not, it is clear, a formal debate on questions of style, or ethics, or metaphysics, but a perfect intersubjective contact between the self as reader and the authentic personality of his long-dead model, mysteriously preserved in the text. Bulephorus (and Erasmus?) illustrates this contact through his own avowed affinity with Horace, which he describes as a certain arcane affinity of souls ('geniorum arcanam quandam affinitatem') which is recognized in those dumb letters ('quae in mutis illis literis agnoscitur'). Each reader should likewise seek out the author who is closest to his own temperament, even where this involves estimating oneself at a lower level than one might like: ugly men, if they are honest, will not try to put on the mask ('persona') of someone outstandingly beautiful.[13] And now Bulephorus-Erasmus appeals to that visceral attachment to one's own identity which, he implies, is at the core of everyone's personality: 'nemo velit alius esse quam est . . .' (p. 704). It is in this context that, for the last time, after yet another application of the mirror image, the principles of true imitation are restated, characterizing 'self-expression' through a rich orchestration of

---

[12] The same metaphor is central to Erasmian interpretation theory: see below, pp. 85–6.

[13] Loc. cit. This is a highly specific (and ethically loaded) development of Quintilian's general advice that each student should 'consult his own powers' in selecting materials for imitation (*Inst. orat.* X. ii. 19 ff.). Cf. also Am. I–2, p. 648. Bulephorus goes on to say that it is a kind of imposture not to express oneself but to place before the eyes of men the illusion (*praestigium*) of an alien form (*alienae formae*) (p. 704).

metaphors: digestion, generation, and the notion of *oratio* as the breathing image of *pectus*.[14]

The obsessive repetition of Erasmus's metaphors deserves special attention, since he is clearly not engaged in a purely conceptual exposition of a neutral problem (if such a thing is possible), but rather in a compulsive attempt to justify his own commitment to writing against potential detractors or enemies. In this respect, his position is not unlike Rousseau's. Having left the monastic environment of Deventer, with its strong stress on inward values, Erasmus embarks on a career as writer in order to disseminate a profound mistrust of 'externals', whether in the ethics of a 'Judaizing' Church or the histrionics of the so-called Ciceronians. As he writes, he constructs a public persona, defined in contradistinction to those whom he discerns as opponents. The name or pseudonym of Erasmus (Desiderius, the loved one) figures in many of his writings—the *Praise of Folly*, the *Ichthyophagia*—as an ironically paraded self, a special instance of that mirror-image which, according to the theory of *oratio* as *speculum animi*, is to be composed by the text.[15] The letters, spanning the whole of his lifetime, would deserve detailed analysis, not only as the diary of a humanist at a significant moment in European history, but as the construction of such a persona: the ostensibly 'private' nature of the epistolary genre lends itself ideally to that inversion by which the face seen in the mirror is advertised to the public at large. The movement of his writing towards *autrui*, whether the addressees of his letters or his polemical adversaries, is an act of self-definition which carries a deep ambiguity. For his whole value-system, based as it is on interiority, on *pectus*, on the plenitude of self, is compromised by the public, exterior nature of writing.

[14] This whole passage (pp. 703–5: 'Iam si in hoc . . . propius exprimit') would deserve to be quoted in full, were it not for its length. It contains virtually all the essential articles of Erasmus's imitation theory.

[15] The cratylist desire for a 'proper' name which will reflect the self is balanced here against a Socratic irony which recognizes the discontinuity between name and self. A similar tension is apparent in Montaigne's *De la gloire* (*Essais* II. xvi) and elsewhere in the *Essais*, although in this case there is no play on etymology, and no coining of a pseudonym. See Margolin, 'Érasme et le verbe', p. 97; for another passage in which Erasmus discusses the value and limits of cratylism, see Am. IV–1, p. 82.

Erasmus purports to write as an evangelical humanist; but the compulsion endlessly to extend his writing reveals, with increasing evidence, the desire to recognize himself (see his face in the mirror) and be recognized.[16] He must become an alien surface in order to constitute himself as an identity, an *apparent* nature, grafted (perhaps) only on the culture of discourse. The Erasmian *sensus* or *sententia*, issuing supposedly from a unique identity, translates itself into words, and thus inevitably betrays itself.

That the notions of identity, recognition, the mirror, differentiation, and the obsessive absorption of *other* texts should recur so insistently in the *Ciceronianus* is particularly revealing given that the dialogue deliberately and even arbitrarily revives what was virtually a dead issue; Erasmus, towards the end of his life, in increasing solitude, sets in motion a factitious polemic in an attempt to reveal the authentic locus of copious discourse. Dolet's counter-attack on behalf of Ciceronianism clarifies this point by what looks like a strange inversion of Erasmus's dialogue *qua* dialogue. On the one hand, the hard-pressed, negative Nosoponus is resurrected as the confidently eloquent Villanovus (a surrogate

[16] In 1519 Erasmus had a medal struck bearing his portrait, by Quentin Matsys. Two inscriptions accompany the image: one, in Latin, declares that it is a living representation ('imago ad vivam effigiem expressa'); the other, in Greek, that the best portrait of Erasmus is to be found in his writings (see Pope-Hennessy, *The Portrait in the Renaissance*, pp. 92–3). On the superior status of writing as a means of portraiture, see above, note 7; for the same theme in an evangelical context, cf. the *Paraclesis* (Fr. V, p. 121; LB 144); see also the anecdote recounted in the *Apophthegmata* and the *Lingua* (loc. cit. above, note 10) in connection with the notion of speech as the mirror of the mind: a handsome young man is brought to Socrates so that his character may be inferred from his appearance (*ut ex aspectu colligeret indolem*); but Socrates says, 'Speak so that I may see you (*loquere ut te videam*).' In the *Ciceronianus*, Erasmus places an ironically unflattering portrait of himself in the mouth of Nosoponus (Am. I–2, pp. 680–1): he is accused of being a sterile 'polygraph', writing on the spur of the moment. Later in the dialogue, he refers to the *Colloquies* as being at once frivolous and widely read (p. 697). Such passages make it clear that Erasmus's theory of self-expression accompanies a practice which is both reflexive and ironical, drawing attention to itself and to its ambiguous status (the representation, from inside a fictional dialogue, of an 'Erasmus' who is outside the dialogue, is a device which necessarily makes the persona of the writer unstable). On the question of the self in Erasmus, see Telle's *Avant-propos* to his edition of Dolet's *De imitatione*, pp. 11–13; on the notion of personal identity in the period as a whole, see Richmond, 'Personal identity and literary personae'.

for Simon de Neufville, the Ciceronian scholar who had taught Dolet and who had died in 1530). On the other, rather than inventing a pseudonymous target, Dolet makes Erasmus's old friend More the mouthpiece for the views he wishes to ridicule; indeed, 'More' repeats verbatim virtually all the key passages of the *Ciceronianus*. In an initial note, Dolet publicizes the fact in case the reader should think that he is 'unlike himself' in writing in a style 'now inflated, now flaccid':[17] Dolet is engaging very specifically in a contest of styles as well as of theoretical arguments. Nor is More simply an antithetical springboard for the exposition of Dolet's position. Two sharply contrasted voices, styles, and ways of understanding the nature of discourse are juxtaposed within a single text.[18]

One of the consequences of this is that little is gained by asking whether or not Dolet is successful in refuting Erasmus: the two voices are talking on different levels, or at a tangent to one another (the antithesis of 'iuxta loquens'); and the tone is often one of invective rather than of rational debate, on Villanovus's side at least. Both texts are in any case heavily dependent on metaphor, and on argument from analogy. Once again, the topic of the debate (what kind of Latin one should write) is of minimal interest in itself. But what does emerge, and often quite explicitly in Villanovus's speeches, is the precarious reversibility of the Erasmian arguments. Countering the accusation that 'Ciceronian' discourse is a sterile and pernicious alienation, the wearing of a rhetorical mask, Villanovus asks what kind of a mask ('persona') Erasmus wears:

A double one (*duplici*), indeed, and doubly misshapen and ugly, not to

[17] *De imitatione ciceroniana* (in *L'Erasmianus sive Ciceronianus d'Étienne Dolet*), ed. Telle, p. 8 (the page numbers given here are those of the original 1535 edition, reproduced by Telle in facsimile).

[18] The diametrical opposition of attitudes is apparent also in a strange disjunction which Dolet imposes on Erasmus's text. Villanovus invites More to take him systematically through the arguments of the *Ciceronianus*; but More begins with Erasmus's later arguments and then shifts back quite explicitly (p. 95) to an earlier stage; thus some of Erasmus's most powerful points are disposed of less than half-way through the *De imitatione*, whereas at the end the interlocutors give the impression of clearing up whatever scraps of defence More may still have to offer (cf. e.g. pp. 188, 191).

be tolerated among learned men. He has forged (*confecit*) for himself a verbal persona (if this expression is permissible, although novel and inelegant) out of Horatian tags, filthy language from Apuleius, and the adages of Beroaldus; and after long and worthless labours his style has become impure like the face of a leper, repulsive and wretchedly disfigured with pallid, rotten sores full of foul matter. And where has he got his *sententia*-mask from—here again I beg you to excuse the expression [sc. *sententiarum Larvam*]—if not from Lucian, that most scurrilous and immoral of all authors, an expert on religion but ignorant of God. (pp. 89–90)

In a satirical reference to the *De duplici copia*, duplicity is thus attributed to Erasmian *verba* and *sententiae* in that they are in-authentically borrowed from imperfect and indeed pernicious authors. The theme of duplicity, together with words like *larva* denoting a false mask, recurs frequently in this dialogue (cf. pp. III, 158, 185); here it follows an ironic summary of Erasmus's theory of self-expression and identity. By turning the tables on Erasmus, by looking from the outside at his tenacious assertion of personal authenticity, Dolet reveals all the ambiguities of his opponent's attempt to ground discourse in the self. When it becomes public ('in publicum venit'), it inevitably appears as a *larva* or *persona*, and it only remains to ask whether the verbal shell is harmonious and aesthetically pleasing, or grotesque and deformed.

For where can one be sure of finding true *sensus*, *pectus*, *genius* beyond that surface? In Dolet's dialogue, Erasmus himself, repeated and travestied as (a repeated and travestied) More, becomes a grotesquely inflated word-thing. And significantly enough, the most insistent leitmotiv of Dolet's invective is that Erasmus is garrulous: the dialogue is full of *ad hominem* attacks on the 'inane babblings' of this 'toothless and malicious' old man. Erasmian *copia*, as a product of Erasmian identity, has now been exactly inverted to become that *loquacitas* which he himself so often condemned. Losing its origin in the plenitude of the mind present to itself, the mirror-image moves away centrifugally; discourse is emptied out and becomes mere extension, deviation, an incurable sickness.[19]

[19] Cf. Villanovus's reversal of Erasmus's contention that Ciceronianism is a sickness or madness (pp. 53–5).

Although Dolet has here unmasked a deep problem in Erasmus's theory, he does so only in order to discredit a view of
aesthetics which he finds distasteful and, no doubt, disquieting.
His own theory is in fact highly logocentric. Erasmus's appre-
hension of the profound changes reflected in the evolution of
customs and fashions is dismissed in favour of an aesthetic absolute
on the one hand, and, on the other, a fundamental unity in
human experience (see pp. 171 ff.); likewise, the passages of the
Ciceronianus in which Erasmus probes the differentiation of identity and its implications for imitation theory are countered by an
insistence on the homogeneity and permanence of nature. Dolet's
prevailing vision of a unified, centripetal universe of discourse is
most clearly illustrated by his reaction to Erasmus's claim that
Cicero's identity is inaccessible and inimitable.[20] Cicero's eloquence is seen perfectly to embody that segment of nature which
comprises the *ars dicendi* and which is embryonically present in
all minds ('ars tota dicendi, imago quaedam est et similitudo in
ingeniis omnium insita'); if we seek to bring nature to perfection
in our own discourse, we cannot do better than strive to imitate
this ideal model. What Dolet envisages is a pure, self-sufficient
domain of language, whether potential (in all men) or actual (in
Cicero) and generated by a universal nature; and this supra-
personal vision is defended with extraordinary energy against
Erasmus's corrosive view of a centrifugal nature dispersing itself in
an infinite number of irreducible personal identities. Dolet is prepared to allow, marginally, for the notion of self-expression, but
only within the Ciceronian canon.[21] No account is taken of those
varieties and nuances of sensibility of which Erasmus is so acutely
aware.

If we are to unravel the knot of this particular Ciceronian
debate, it is not adequate to say that it was a non-event, that
Ciceronianism was already a dead or dying cause, and that the

[20] See pp. 163–4 ('Quid nos . . . nihil corrigendum'), a passage which summarizes with particular clarity Dolet's position, and thus appears as the antithesis of
the Erasmus passage referred to above, note 14. It is likewise too long to be quoted
here in full.

[21] See pp. 88–9; on the question of 'expressing Cicero' (with or without his
'vices'), see p. 146.

aggressive Dolet, whether wilfully or not, misunderstood Erasmus.[22] The interrelation of the two texts is at once more complex
and more intimate than such an account would suggest. Erasmus
and Dolet disagree in terms of strategy and, more profoundly, of
aesthetic vision. Yet, if the apparatus of polemical debate were
dismantled, they would also be seen to agree at many significant
points. When Villanovus sets out the procedures for moving
through a study of *verba* to a proper grasp of *sententiae*, his insistence on the proper awareness of the contexts, modes, and
registers of a given word is wholly in accord with the methods
of preliminary textual analysis prevalent in humanist—and not
least Erasmian—scholarship: the *sensus* or *sententia* is approached
by a series of checks and cautions designed to filter out arbitrariness of interpretation (p. 65). Both texts agree on the ideal of
encyclopedic knowledge, properly assimilated, as a foundation
for eloquence, and Dolet's centripetal principle does not prevent
him from allowing this knowledge to be drawn from outside the
Ciceronian canon (pp. 77–8, 114–15). Dolet's argument that
Cicero's moral insights are very close to those of Christian ethics
(although weakened by his separation elsewhere of morals from
eloquence) would likewise have been endorsed by Erasmus, who,
notoriously, liked to envisage the possibility of Cicero's salvation.[23] The list of convergences could be extended without
difficulty, particularly if one were to register systematically the
appearance in each writer of the *topoi* of classical rhetorical theory.
But, more centrally, both conceptions of eloquence share a
preoccupation with the conditions of the author–reader (author–

[22] Such approaches are countered by Telle in his *Avant-propos*, pp. 9–10.
Mesnard, in his introduction to the *Ciceronianus*, estimates that at most half of
Erasmus's dialogue is devoted to the polemical issue of Ciceronianism (Am. I–2,
p. 593). For a more general account of the relations between Dolet and Erasmus,
see Telle, 'Dolet et Érasme'.

[23] pp. 78 ff. The separation of morals from eloquence is argued on pp. 106 ff.
The two points of view are linked by a disjunction of 'letter' and 'spirit': Dolet
points out that Christian language is not a guarantee of Christian morals, and
conversely that 'pagan' language may be used in a Christian spirit (see especially
pp. 157–8, 177 ff.).—There is no reference to the sanctity of pagans in the
Ciceronianus itself; the classic example occurs in the *Convivium religiosum* (Am.
I–3, p. 251); cf. Béné, *Érasme et saint Augustin*, pp. 345 ff.

model) relationship, and the ways in which it can be authenticated, 'brought to life'. Erasmus's exploration in depth of Quintilian's digestion image meets with the approval of Villanovus (pp. 90–1), although he of course restricts the range of materials to be digested; and elsewhere, Dolet attempts to convey a sense of ideal identity with Cicero by a series of images of self-abandonment, of corporal and mental presence, of festive pleasure, and of intense mental penetration of the Ciceronian text: 'quam [sc. orationem] tota mente atque omni animo intueamur'.[24] Dolet's hand-to-hand struggle with Erasmus exactly inverts, in one sense, his conception of Ciceronian imitation: the presence of Erasmus is repudiated in proportion as the presence of Cicero is embraced.[25] Yet the *Ciceronianus* is irreducibly, *textually* present at the heart of the *De imitatione*; the two texts circle around one another, vie with one another, as mirror-images of their common (and absent) centre which is the intuitively perceived evidence of an authentic discourse.

So powerful is this desire for authenticity that each tries to underpin it in his own way, with reference to the currently available criteria of nature and faith. Such conceptual guarantees cannot but be drawn into the web of what they are supposed to underpin: they are, in the end, 'simply' words in a text which can thus never be fully mastered and guaranteed. Yet the search demonstrates its fruitfulness by incessantly reappearing as the theme of major texts. The appropriation of authentic discourse— a moment of presence to be discovered amid fragments of the textual past—will be the goal of theories and fictions, poetry and prose, throughout the sixteenth century. The remainder of this chapter will be concerned with one relatively limited segment of that itinerary, namely with theories of imitation and transla- tion in the French vernacular between 1540 and 1555. But the

[24] p. 77. Cf. pp. 63, 73, 75. The images in these passages include the notions of swimming, or riding, or being swept along in the river (torrent) of Cicero's eloquence; of riches and blessedness; of Bacchic fury ('debacchamur'); of Cicero's text as pure food and delicious wine; of joking and playing.

[25] This emerges explicitly from Dolet's contention that Erasmus wants his readers to abandon Cicero and adopt an Erasmian style (pp. 61, 79, 143), as well as from the pervasive *ad hominem* invective.

manœuvres performed by Sebillet, Peletier, and Du Bellay, however parochial, illustrate problems which later chapters will show to be endemic in the practice of Ronsard and Montaigne.

Erasmus's stylistic eclecticism is characterized by Dolet as a kind of rootless and aimless wandering;[26] the same accusation is levelled at his detachment from any national affiliation, at his habit of living successively in different countries, which becomes the image of his 'inability to speak any language properly' (p. 92). Here, too, Dolet is centripetal: he uses nationalistic Roman exclusiveness as an illustration of the purity of discourse he seeks (p. 93); and he ends the dialogue proper with a eulogy of Budé and the French, of whom, he says, Erasmus always speaks ill. If Cicero's Rome no doubt continued to be the symbol of Dolet's stylistic purism, the French vernacular was none the less not neglected. The short treatise *La Maniere de bien traduire d'une langue en autre* (1540) was to have been part of *L'Orateur françoys*, a work which was never published (although it was posthumously advertised by Du Bellay at the end of the first book of the *Deffence et illustration*), but which clearly ran parallel, at a secondary level, to Dolet's Ciceronian publications.[27]

The theory of translation outlined in the 1540 treatise contains little that is new: it repeatedly emphasizes that the *sens, sentences,* or *intention* of the author must have priority, and that the translator must not limit himself to a word-for-word rendering.[28] This is precisely the contrary of that wrong-headed subordination of *res* or *sententiae* to *verba* which Erasmus attributed to Nosopo-

[26] See p. 141: 'should we flutter about [like bees], wandering indiscriminately from one author to another?' ('an per omnes generatim volitandum et vagandum?'); cf. p. 192.

[27] See Norton, art. cit., p. 2. Dolet produced a bilingual (Latin and French) version of Cicero's *Familiares*, first published in 1542. Also relevant to the remainder of the present chapter is Norton's article 'Translation theory in Renaissance France: the poetic controversy'; Higman's 'Calvin and the art of translation' provides an interesting example of contemporary practice.

[28] That this theory had long since been absorbed by French humanists is demonstrated, not only by Estienne's definition of *paraphrasis*, but also by the second preface to Lefèvre d'Étaples's paraphrases of Aristotle's *Physics* (1492) (*Prefatory Epistles*, ed. Rice, no. 3, p. 11), although here the reference is to the rendering of Greek into Latin.

nus; more importantly, it might seem to modify the view of Villanovus that elegant Ciceronian words and phrases should be preserved even in Christian contexts. But of course the situation is quite different: the translator *must* use a different language, and Dolet makes it a condition of good translation that the preservation of the author's intention go hand in hand with respect for the 'propriété de l'une et l'aultre langue' (*La Maniere*, p. 15). This grafting of a new linguistic apparatus on to a presumed intention is presented as a conjunction, or at least a matching, of two 'natures'; it corresponds exactly, not only to Quintilian's definition of paraphrase, but also to Erasmus's claim that, if Cicero were to be alive in our times, he would speak in our terms. Erasmus's theory of imitation, if extended logically, would indeed imply the use of the vernacular, whereas Dolet's cult of Ciceronianism might seem to exclude the vernacular as incapable of achieving Ciceronian perfection. Yet, ironically, it is Dolet who seeks to *illustrer* the vernacular, no doubt because his humanism is culturally based in a nation where propaganda for the national language has been gathering way for many years, while Erasmus remains eternally a *peregrinus*.

Peletier's preface to his translation of Horace's *Epistula ad Pisones* (1544), while emphasizing much more strongly than Dolet the potentialities of the vernacular, nevertheless reveals a fundamentally similar set of preoccupations. The first two-thirds of the preface are hardly concerned with poetry at all, except as part of a broader concern with the value of the French language. Furthermore, the prestige of the writers of antiquity is given firm priority; Peletier contends that it is impossible to speak or write French correctly without a knowledge of Latin, if not of Greek (Du Bellay will make the same point in almost precisely the same words),[29] and quotes Petrarch, Boccaccio, Dante, and Sannazaro as writers who distinguished themselves in both Latin and the vernacular. Cicero himself boasted of his exemplary transposition of Greek thought ('Philosophie') into the more

[29] Peletier's preface is reproduced in an appendix to Boulanger's edition of his *Art poëtique*. The point in question is made on p. 227. See Du Bellay, *Deffence* I. xi, pp. 74–5.

copious medium of Latin (p. 228). But in this instance, the example
is designed to prove that naturalized materials can indeed surpass
the original,[30] and forms part of a wider argument based on an
opposition between foreign ('peregrine') and native ('domestique') languages. The argument culminates in an appeal to
nature:

quand a ceux qui totalement se vouent et adonnent a une langue
peregrine (j'entens peregrine pour le respect de la domestique) il me
semble qu'il ne leur est possible d'atteindre a cette naïve perfection
des anciens non plus qu'a l'art d'exprimer Nature, quelque ressemblance
qu'il i pretende.   (pp. 228–9)

We thus return to the principle of two analogous but essentially
different manifestations of nature, that of the original writer and
his language, and that of the contemporary writer; any attempt
to suppress the difference is an effect of contrivance ('art'), and
falls short of the perfection which only nature can guarantee.
Peletier's remarks on his own translation should be read in the
light of this assertion:

j'ai translaté cetui livre intitulé l'Art Poetique, et l'ai voulu approprier
a icelle notre Poesie Francoise entant qu'ai peu sauver l'integrite du
sens.   (p. 229)

The adaptation of Horace's text to the character of French poetry
is thus made conditional on the preservation of the wholeness
or authenticity ('integrite') of its 'sens'; although Peletier does not
specifically speak of *verba* as distinct from *sensus*, his alignment
with Cicero and Quintilian via Estienne's 'quasi iuxta loquens'
and Dolet's 'gardant curieusement la propriété de l'une et l'aultre
langue' is quite clear.[31]

   Peletier would no doubt have been aware that Cicero's depre-

---

[30] Cf. Quintilian, *Inst. orat.* X. ii. 4 ff.; X. v. 5. Dolet, in the *De imitatione*,
speaks of his own contemporaries as surpassing Cicero's oratory, whereas Erasmus
is suspicious of perfectionism in the rhetorical sphere. Cf. Telle, *L'Erasmianus*,
Introduction, pp. 52–3, 57. Peletier later predicts that the French language will
outstrip Spanish and Italian (op. cit., p. 229).

[31] The word 'approprier' used here by Peletier recalls Dolet's 'propriété'; since
proprietas and *natura* are closely related concepts, Peletier's 'appropriation' may
be said to be a form of 'naturalization'.

cation of word-for-word translation is echoed in the *Ars poetica* itself, and the same *topos* recurs in Sebillet's *Art poétique françoys* of 1548:

ne jure tant superstitieusement aus mos de ton autheur, que iceus delaissés [here the text gives the reference 'Horace en l'art poét.'] pour retenir la sentence, tu ne serves de plus pres a la phrase et propriété de ta langue, qu'a la diction de l'estrangére. La dignité toutesfois de l'auteur, et l'enargie de son oraison tant curieusement exprimée, que puis qu'il n'est possible de réprésenter son mesme visage, autant en montre ton oeuvre, qu'en représenteroit le miroir . . .[32]

The mirror image (even if, as Gaiffe suggests, it seems to imply too perfect a reduplication) is yet another attempt to convey the joint notions of identity and difference, and demonstrates that Sebillet is aligning himself with a well-established theory. Sebillet's reservation is, however, potentially a crucial one: the translator is to aim at recasting, not only the *sentence*, but also, in so far as it is possible, the style of the original, the special vividness ('enargie') of the author's discourse; as we shall see shortly, this is precisely the basis for Du Bellay's theory of imitation, translation being reserved by him for the transposition of *res* alone. And one should also note that, in the following sentence, Sebillet claims that 'la version n'est rien qu'une imitation': a serious confusion, no doubt, from Du Bellay's point of view, but also a reminder that translation theory was effectively only an outgrowth of imitation theory.

Peletier's 1555 *Art poëtique* assigns separate chapters to imitation and to translation; but the opening of the translation chapter preserves their essential interconnection:

La plus vreę especę d'Imitacion, c'ęt dę traduirę: Car imiter n'ęt autrę chosę quę vouloęr ferę cę quę fęt un autrę: Einsi quę fęt lę Traducteur qui s'asseruìt non seulęmant a l'Inuantion d'autrui, męs aussi a la Disposicion: e ancor a l'Elocucion tant qu'il peùt, e tant quę lui pęrmęt lę naturęl dę la Languę tranlatiuę: par cę quę l'eficacę d'un Ecrit, bien souuant consistę an la propriete des moz e locucions: laquelę omisę, otę la gracę, e defraudę lę sans dę l'Auteur.   (I. vi, p. 105)

---

[32] I. xiv, pp. 189–90. On the word 'enargie', see above, p. 28, note 39.

Sebillet's inclusion of *elocutio* in the domain of translation is retained here also: the word 'eficace' seems to echo Sebillet's
'enargie' as a means of conveying the sense of an inherent quality
in a given style, its impact. Significantly, however, Peletier
points out that any neglect of *élocution* will distort the 'sans de
l'Auteur': form and content, *verba* and *res* cannot be separated
with impunity. Again, Peletier claims that

l¢ Traducteur pourra fer¢ Françoęs¢ un¢ bęl¢ locucion Latin¢ ou
Grecqu¢: e aporter an sa Cite, avęc l¢ poęs des santanc¢s, la majeste
des claus¢s e eleganc¢s d¢ la langu¢ etranger¢ . . . (pp. 106–7)

Since he is prepared to acknowledge the constraints traditionally
imposed on translation (the need to respect the 'naturęl d¢ la
Langu¢ tranlativ¢', the rejection of word-for-word translation), he
is in this chapter walking a theoretical tightrope, as the concluding
passage clearly shows:

les Traduccions d¢ mot a mot n'ont pas grac¢: non qu'ęl¢s sǫęt contr¢
la lǫę d¢ Traduccion: męs seul¢mant pour ręson qu¢ deus langu¢s
n¢ sont jamęs uniform¢s en fras¢s. Les concepcions sont comun¢s
aus antand¢mans d¢ tous homm¢s: męs les moz e manier¢s d¢ parler
sont particuliers aus nacions. E qu'on n¢ m¢ vien¢ point aleguer
Ciceron: l¢quel n¢ lou¢ pas l¢ Traducteur consciancieus. Car aussi
n¢ fęj¢. E n¢ l'antàn point autr¢mant, sinon qu¢ l¢ Tranlateur dǫęue
garder la propriete e l¢ naïf d¢ la Langu¢ an laquęl¢ il tranlat¢: Męs
cęrt¢s j¢ dì qu'an c¢ qu¢ les deux Langu¢s simbolis¢ront: il n¢ dǫęt
rien pęrdr¢ des locucions, ni mém¢s d¢ la priuaute des moz d¢ l'Auteur,
duquel l'esprit e la sutilite souuant consist¢ an c¢la. E qui pourrǫęt
traduir¢ tout Virgil¢ an vęrs Francoęs, fras¢ pour fras¢, e mot pour mot:
c¢ s¢rǫęt un¢ louang¢ inestimabl¢. Car un Traducteur, commant saurǫęt
il mieus fęr¢ son d¢uǫęr, sinon an aprochant tousjours l¢ plus pręs
qu'il serǫęt possibl¢ d¢ l'Auteur auquel il ęt sugęt? Puis, pansèz quel¢
grandeur c¢ serǫęt d¢ voęr un¢ s¢cond¢ Langu¢ repondr¢ a tout¢
l'eleganc¢ d¢ la pr¢mier¢: e ancor auoęr la sienn¢ propr¢. Męs, comm¢
j'è dìt, il n¢ s¢ peùt fęr¢. (pp. 110–11)

This fine adjustment of opposing theories, culminating in a
Utopian vision of equivalence between the translation and its
model, echoes the predicament of the conjectural Ciceronian. In

endlessly attempting to recreate, in Latin, a discourse authenticated by the paradigm of Cicero's prose, the Ciceronian is clearly vulnerable to the Erasmian inquisition, and in particular to the *reductio ad absurdum* that one must either repeat what Cicero said or, necessarily, institute a different discourse. The Ciceronian as translator (whether it be Cicero himself, one of Cicero's translators, or Dolet)[33] is still more committed to difference, and accepts it as a condition of writing. Thus he must inevitably move closer to the position adopted by Erasmus on the basis of historical change and personal identity. But there still remains the problem of achieving equivalence. The miraculously living, yet alien, language of the ancients offers a model of (almost) perfect discourse which demands emulation; to sever oneself from it is to commit oneself to a fragile and obscure present, but to attempt to repeat it in the vernacular is to incur the risk of falsity and emptiness. If only repetition and plenitude could be combined, if only the dead substitution of word for word could be replaced by a harmonious mirroring of two texts, perfectly identical and equally authentic, then Cicero, Homer, Virgil, Ovid, would speak again in French. 'Mę̧s...il nę sę peùt fęrę.' It is only when the irreducibility of this problem has been fully clarified that it becomes possible for the writer to understand what it means to speak with another voice ('his own'), to arrive at the proposition that any new and valid discourse must arise from an enactment within the author of the primary linguistic impulse exploited by the great writers of antiquity. Erasmus had elaborated an extensive theory of imitation in order to arrive at precisely this insight; some twenty years after the publication of the *Ciceronianus*, Du Bellay was to outline a theory less rich and penetrating, no doubt, but in certain important respects similar.[34]

[33] See above, note 27, on Dolet as translator; translations of Cicero's orations (e.g. by Antoine Macault, Étienne Le Blanc, and Jean Colin) flourished in the 1530s.

[34] The *Deffence* was published some six years before Peletier's *Art poëtique*; I have preferred to show how Peletier develops the translation problem posed by Sebillet, rather than interposing Du Bellay's significantly different treatment. Telle, in the *Introduction* to his edition of Dolet's *De imitatione*, comments briefly on the relevance of Erasmus's *Ciceronianus* to the *Deffence* (pp. 93–4).

The core of Du Bellay's general theory of *illustration* of the vernacular is to be found in *La Deffence et illustration* I. iv–viii, similar
themes being developed in II. i–iii. It begins with a cautious but
positive *praise* of translation. François Ier has

> premierement restitué tous le bons Ars et Sciences en leur ancienne
> dignité: et si a nostre Langaige, au paravant scabreux et mal poly,
> rendu elegant, et si non tant copieux qu'il poura bien estre, pour le
> moins fidele interprete de tous les autres. Et qu'ainsi soit, philosophes,
> historiens, medicins, poëtes, orateurs Grecz et Latins ont apris à
> parler Francois. Que diray-je des Hebreux? Les Saintes Lettres donnent
> ample temoingnaige de ce que je dy.   (I. iv, pp. 30–1)

The inclusion of poets in the list of those who have 'learnt to
speak French' does not necessarily indicate that Du Bellay wants
to stress the value of verse translation *per se*: what he has in mind
here is the transposition into French of the materials (*res*) of the
humanist encyclopedia, as is shown by the composition and
ordering of the list, by his reference to the 'Ars et Sciences' and to
the three languages, and, a little later, by the claim that 'toutes
Sciences se peuvent fidelement et copieusement traicter en icelle'.
The distinction between this domain and that of poetry is clarified
at the beginning of I. x:

> Tout ce que j'ay dict pour la defence et illustration de notre Langue,
> apartient principalement à ceux qui font profession de bien dire,
> comme les poëtes et les orateurs. Quand aux autres parties de Literature,
> et ce rond de Sciences que les Grecz ont nommé *Encyclopedie*, j'en
> ay touché au commencement une partie de ce que m'en semble:
> c'est que l'industrie des fideles traducteurs est en cet endroict fort utile
> et necessaire . . .   (pp. 58–9)

It is true that, although the notion of 'fidelity' is again stressed
here, and although the context indicates a clear priority of *res* over
verba, Du Bellay allows marginally for the special properties of
the vernacular by inserting the 'paraphrase' *topos*:

> Encores seroy' je bien d'opinion que le scavant translateur fist plus
> tost l'office de paraphraste que de traducteur, s'efforceant donner a
> toutes les Sciences qu'il voudra traiter l'ornement et lumiere de sa
> Langue, comme Ciceron se vante d'avoir fait en la phylosophie . . .
> (p. 60)

However, the reference is brief, and Du Bellay maintains, throughout, the strategic separation between translation as a means of domesticating the encyclopedia of *res*, which he accepts, and as a means of 'perfecting' the French language, which he rejects.[35] Equally, no overlap is allowed between translation (from which concern for *elocutio* is virtually excluded) and imitation, to which *elocutio* is fundamental. The distinction is found again, in a slightly different form, in I. v, where the attack on translation begins. Quoting Cicero's *De oratore*, Du Bellay defines eloquence as essentially consisting of *inventio* coupled with *elocutio*. But *inventio* must be nourished by 'l'intelligence parfaite des Sciences', which requires either a knowledge of Greek and Latin or recourse to the work of 'les fideles traducteurs'. Thus *inventio* is concerned with *res* and does not exclude translation. But, says Du Bellay,

Mais quand à l'eloquution, partie certes la plus difficile, et sans la quelle toutes autres choses restent comme inutiles et semblables à un glayve encores couvert de sa gayne: eloquution (dy je) par la quelle principalement un orateur est jugé plus excellent, et un genre de dire meilleur que l'autre: comme celle dont est apellée la mesme eloquence: et dont la vertu gist aux motz propres, usitez, et non aliénés du commun usaige de parler, aux metaphores, alegories, comparaisons, similitudes, energies, et tant d'autres figures et ornemens, sans les quelz tout oraison et poëme sont nudz, manques et debiles: je ne croyray jamais qu'on puisse bien apprendre tout cela des traducteurs, pour ce qu'il est impossible de le rendre avecques la mesme grace dont l'autheur en a usé: d'autant que chacune Langue a je ne scay quoy propre seulement à elle, dont si vous efforcez exprimer le naif en une autre Langue, observant la loy de traduyre, qui est n'espacier point hors des limites de l'aucteur, vostre diction sera contrainte, froide, et de mauvaise grace.[36]

Thus the difficulty from which Peletier will conjure up an impossible dream of perfect translation is here seen unambiguously

[35] Cf. I. v, pp. 38–9, where Cicero's translations are referred to concessively; the classical Latin writers only practised translation 'pour leur etude et profit particulier', not 'pour le publier à l'amplification de leur Langue'. Public acclaim ('gloire') is a prerequisite for successful 'illustration'.

[36] pp. 34–6. The *topos* of the sword in its sheath—*res* being hidden until displayed by *elocutio*—is derived from Quintilian, *Inst. orat.* VIII. Pr. 15.

as an impasse. *Elocutio* is the stumbling-block of translation, the domain in which the essential difference of languages asserts itself intransigently. The encyclopedia, understood as a collection of materials which can be rendered indifferently by any language, remains static unless it is unfolded in this privileged apparatus of style. To convey a sense of its richness, Du Bellay compresses into a few lines the wealth of rhetorical categories enumerated by Cicero and Quintilian and their successors, and anchors the word *elocutio* in *eloquentia* itself: it is not simply the name for a set of procedures (a rhetoric), but rather an intrinsically distinct mode of language, imbued with its own motive power ('vertu', a term germane to Sebillet's 'enargie' and Peletier's 'eficace'). This characteristic is for Du Bellay linked to the special property (the 'je ne scay quoy propre seulement à elle', the 'naif') of each language. Consequently, the translation theory of Dolet and the rest, which rejected literalness as inconsistent with the *propriété* of the vernacular, is here given a new direction: paraphrase-translation (directed towards *sententiae* rather than *verba*) has been relegated to a kind of propaedeutic function, and *elocutio* begins to be explored as the domain of positive difference, within which imitation will deploy itself centrifugally.

At this point in his analysis, Du Bellay introduces the notion of the reader's affective response as a criterion for *elocutio-eloquentia*:

vostre diction sera contrainte, froide, et de mauvaise grace. Et qu'ainsi soit, qu'on me lyse un Demosthene et Homere Latins, un Ciceron et Vergile Francoys, pour voir s'ilz vous engendreront telles affections, voyre ainsi qu'un Prothée vous transformeront en diverses sortes, comme vous sentez, lysant ces aucteurs en leurs Langues. Ils vous semblera passer de l'ardente montaigne d'Aethne sur le froid sommet de Caucase. (pp. 36–7)

The images of constraint and coldness invoke their antithesis, the fires of Etna and a Protean liberation from constraint. This figure of transformation, of an open-ended series of metamorphoses, is a key *topos*, recalling much that is essential to Erasmian theories of interpretation and imitation. In this context, where it recalls the *topos* of rhetoric as a means of releasing affectivity,[37] it also reveals a deep awareness of the difference of languages. Of course the Protean variety of the affections is not seen as a product of the variety of languages: it is important for Du Bellay that a similar result might be arrived at in French, for a French reader. Nevertheless, the two kinds of difference are linked. Reading is the commutation of one nature into another; the reader becomes, in the moment of reading, identified with the text; and that text is perceived to be grounded in the authenticity of an author intuitively exploiting the properties of his own language. For this authenticity to be preserved, it is essential that the difference (of language, author, text) is not effaced.

The following chapter (I. vi) begins with another attack on bad translators (Marot?), who are ignorant of the languages—Hebrew and Greek—which they attempt to translate. But Du Bellay rapidly returns to the question of *elocutio*: these translators

se prennent aux poëtes, genre d'aucteurs certes auquel, si je scavoy' ou vouloy' traduyre, je m'adroisseroy' aussi peu à cause de ceste divinité d'invention qu'ilz ont plus que les autres, de ceste grandeur de style, magnificence de motz, gravité de sentences, audace et varieté de figures, et mil' autres lumieres de poesie: bref ceste energie, et ne scay quel esprit, qui est en leurs ecriz, que les Latins appelleroient *genius*. Toutes les quelles choses se peuvent autant exprimer en traduisant, comme un peintre peut representer l'ame avecques le cors de celuy qu'il entreprent tyrer apres le naturel. (pp. 40–1)

Poetry, the supreme and most problematic form of *elocutio-eloquentia*, is now specifically the focus of attention, and prompts a restatement of the principles sketched in chapter v. Again, an ideal *inventio* is intrinsically present in the panoply of *elocutio*: the apparent separation of 'invention' and 'style' is effaced by the recapitulation ('bref . . .') which defines both, and the nature of poetry itself, in terms of a single generating force. 'Vertu' in the earlier passage is here echoed by 'energie', the 'je ne scay quoy propre . . .' by 'ne scay quel esprit . . .'. This inward source of textual energy, which is beyond exact description or analysis, is of

[37] Cf. the important passage in II. xi on the affective impact of poetry as 'la vraye pierre de touche, ou il fault que tu epreuves tous poëmes, et en toute Langues' (pp. 179–80). These passages have celebrated antecedents in classical rhetorical theory.

a quasi-supernatural order, as the use of the word *genius* suggests,[38] and has the same relationship to the text as soul has to body: a *topos*, once again, which takes on specific resonances in its context. Any duality which it might seem to establish is implicitly overruled: the authentic text is one in which an 'esprit' is intrinsic to the configurations of style (*elocutio*); and in so far as the *âme–corps* opposition recalls a relationship between *sensus* and *verba*, *genius* becomes the active deployment of 'sense' in every articulation of (poetic) language. The painting simile which gives rise to the *âme–corps* opposition adds yet another dimension to this theoretical model of the ideal text. It repeats briefly but precisely the example elaborated by Erasmus to demonstrate the impossibility of arriving at a true representation on the basis of externals. In fact, Du Bellay's attack on translation is analogous to Erasmus's attack on Ciceronianism. Both reject formalism and encourage awareness of that inaccessible intuitive centre (*genius*) from which a great text arises; both take as a fundamental premise of their arguments the essentially different identities of individuals and their languages.

The outline of imitation theory proper in the following two chapters embroiders on these same themes. Du Bellay invokes the well-established example of Latins imitating Greeks:

par quelz moyens donques ont ils [sc. les Romains] peu ainsi enrichir leur Langue, voyre jusques à l'egaller quasi à la Greque? Immitant les meilleurs aucteurs Grecz, se transformant en eux, les devorant, et apres les avoir bien digerez, les convertissant en sang et nouriture, se proposant, chacun selon son naturel et l'argument qu'il vouloit elire, le meilleur aucteur, dont ilz observoint diligemment toutes les plus rares et exquises vertuz, et icelles comme grephes, ainsi que j'ay dict devant, entoint et apliquoint à leur Langue. Cela faisant . . . les Romains ont baty tous ces beaux ecriz, que nous louons et admirons si fort . . . (I. vii, pp. 42–3).

The dual act of reading and writing is here represented as a reciprocal process of incorporation or consubstantiation: the reader is transformed into what he reads (which Du Bellay refers

---

[38] Du Bellay's analysis here converges with the theories of inspiration considered below, pp. 141 f.

to as the author rather than the text); at the same time, he converts it into his own substance (author again being equated with text). This image of corporal exchange, which implies both destruction and reconstitution, renders as immediate perception what is then explained in the ensuing literal exposition. Like Quintilian and Erasmus, Du Bellay stresses the importance of choosing one's model correctly, the essential criterion being the convergence of the *naturel* and topical situation of the author with those of his model: once again, true imitation reverts to the *source* of eloquence and envisages a concordance of identities as the basis for two discourses, parallel but necessarily and authentically different. Hence Cicero's imitation of Plato, Demosthenes, and Isocrates; or Virgil imitating Homer, Hesiod, and Theocritus (pp. 43–4). The corresponding passage in I. viii sounds like a *redite*; but it must be quoted, if only to demonstrate that such configurations of image and theory are not casual or accidental in Du Bellay's discourse:

entende celuy qui voudra immiter, que ce n'est chose facile de bien suyvre les *vertuz* d'un bon aucteur, et quasi comme se *transformer* en luy, veu que la Nature mesmes aux choses qui paroissent tressemblables, n'a sceu tant faire, que par quelque notte et *difference* elles ne puissent estre discernées. Je dy cecy, pour ce qu'il y en a beaucoup en toutes Langues, qui sans *penetrer aux plus cachées et interieures parties de l'aucteur* qu'ilz se sont proposé, s'adaptent seulement au premier regard, et s'amusant à la beauté des *motz*, perdent la force des *choses*. (p. 46, my italics)

Once again, the *res–verba* opposition should not be taken as a devaluation of words in favour of things (which would take us back to the art of the 'fideles interpretes' of the encyclopedia), but as a plea for their reunification, the *res–inventio–sensus* aspect of a text serving as an intrinsic guarantee for the authenticity of *verba–elocutio*. And the quotations from Quintilian, while establishing a clear line of affiliation with the principal source of humanist imitation theory, may be considered as products of a text which, according to its own principles, selects, meditates on, and reworks its materials. For example, the quotation from

Quintilian of the key *topos* of the irreducible difference inherent in nature arises directly in Du Bellay's discourse, by a process of association, from a recapitulation of the transformation image, so that the profound linking of the two becomes evident. Likewise, Quintilian's censure of those who address themselves to the outward aspect of a text ('primum . . . adspectum orationis') rather than engaging in a thorough examination of its 'virtues' ('non introspectis penitus virtutibus') is rephrased in terms of a penetration into the hidden centre of an author, a metaphor which picks up and prolongs the resonance of both 'transformation' and 'difference'. Thus Du Bellay's text, mirroring its own prescription, inserts itself surreptitiously into the heart of Quintilian's and re-emerges with its difference intact.[39]

The *Deffence* has no theory of self-expression and only an embryonic version of the identity problem, so that one should be cautious of suggesting any direct influence of the *Ciceronianus*. Nevertheless, Du Bellay's liking for transformation and digestion imagery, and his awareness of the Protean character of the author–reader–writer relationships, recall important themes in Erasmus. It is significant, too, that he deploys arguments characteristic of anti-Ciceronianism, both in his attack on translation and, later, in a rejection—following Peletier—of the value of neo-Latin composition (I. xi). In this latter instance, he even makes an oblique allusion to Erasmus, quoting the onslaught on Longueil's inappropriate use of Roman terminology in a speech at the Papal curia.[40] Indeed, both Du Bellay and Erasmus appear to be in similar strategic positions: both caricature their adversaries (translators and Marotics in one case, Ciceronians and Longueil in the other), and appear to reject indiscriminately techniques which they themselves are quite capable of using and may not always

[39] The quotations from Quintilian come from *Inst. orat.* X. ii. 10 and 16. A further example is provided by the ensuing rejection of imitation within the same language (p. 47): recalling Cicero's remarks in the *De finibus*, as well as Quintilian, it takes on an entirely new colouring in the light of Du Bellay's strategic attack on Sebillet and the Marotic school, and demonstrates again the crucial importance of linguistic and cultural differentiation in Du Bellay's theory.

[40] pp. 77–8. Erasmus is referred to simply as 'quelqu'un', but the passage in question is taken directly from the *Ciceronianus* (Am. I–2, p. 695).

consider in such a pejorative light; both use their targets as a sounding-board for their own positive and fertile theoretical meditations.

The tone of optimism which pervades Du Bellay's investigation of the principles of *imitatio* and his polemical gestures of innovation must, however, be reassessed in the light of the more general theory of language(s) sketched out in *Deffence* I. i and I. ix–xi, which form a framework for the chapters considered so far. The *Deffence* opens with a development of the Tower of Babel *topos* and of the associated notion that languages are conventional rather than natural.[41] Nature is single, continuous, universal, as is that other 'universe' which ideally reflects it, the encyclopedia of knowledge; by contrast, the plurality of languages arises from the differentiated *vouloir* or *fantasie* of men, and all— potentially at least—are neutral and equivalent. This theme, which recurs in I. x, institutes what appears to be a clear-cut distinction between nature and art (things and words). It provides a platform on which Du Bellay can argue against translation, since the dream of the translator as embodied in Sebillet's mirror image is made impossible by that irremediable exile from nature of which Babel is the symbol. Equally, the nature–art distinction allows Du Bellay to support the view that the French language is not *per se* ('naturally') less valid than Greek or Latin, and that its *illustration* depends on human will. This apparently optimistic view must carry with it an assertion of the value of 'art', since language is seen as being wholly on the side of art: the same theme reappears in II. iii, where Du Bellay stresses the inadequacy of nature alone in the achievement of greatness.

It remains true that the Tower of Babel image hardly seems to

---

[41] I. i, pp. 12–13. The currency of this notion in the earlier sixteenth century is indicated by its appearance in Du Bellay's immediate source, Speroni's *Dialogo delle lingue* (1542), in the *Liber de differentia* of Bovillus (1533), chapters lii–liii, and in Rabelais, *TL* 19. Cf. also the quotations from St. Augustine, below, pp. 80–2, and Montaigne, *Essais* II. xii. 553 (on the Tower of Babel). On Panurge as a 'Tower of Babel', see below, pp. 111 ff. A detailed account of the ways in which these themes were treated in the sixteenth century is given in Borst, *Der Turmbau von Babel*, IV. 2: 'Humanismus und Reformation'. See also Dubois, *Mythe et langage*.

inaugurate a mood of total optimism. There are moments, for
example, when Du Bellay yearns for a single, natural language:

> Las et combien seroit meilleur qu'il y eust au monde un seul langaige
> naturel, que d'employer tant d'années pour apprendre des motz!
> (I. x, pp. 64–5)

Likewise, an assumption of the priority of *natura-res* over mere
verba ('art') surfaces again and again, as in this passage, which
leads directly to the one just quoted:

> Les ecritures et langaiges ont été trouvez, non pour la conservation de la
> Nature, la quelle (comme divine qu'elle est) n'a mestier de nostre
> ayde: mais seulement à nostre bien et utilité: affin que presens, absens,
> vyfz et mors, manifestans l'un à l'autre le secret de notz cœurs, plus
> facilement parvenions à notre propre felicité, qui gist en l'intelligence
> des Sciences, non point au son des paroles . . .[42]

The prevailing distinction between thought (the encyclopedia)
and poetry does, it is true, give a grounding to the depreciation
of words in one domain and the endorsement of *elocutio* in the
other, as does the anchoring of *elocutio* in the *naturel* of the poet-
orator. But there is a fundamental unease in the *Deffence* which
such distinctions cannot quite overcome. It re-emerges, for
example, in I. xi, where Du Bellay argues against neo-Latin
composition in the shadow of Erasmus's anti-Ciceronianism. The
ancient languages are equated with a ruined edifice; the neo-
Latins (or neo-Greeks) pick up a few stones here and there and
attempt to piece them together, but have no hope of success:

> si vous esperez . . . que par ces fragmentz recuilliz [les langues Greque et
> Latine] puyssent estre resuscitées, vous vous abusez, ne pensant point
> qu'à la cheute de si superbes edifices conjointe à la ruyne fatale de ces
> deux puissantes monarchies, une partie devint poudre, et l'autre doit
> estre en beaucoup de pieces, les queles vouloir reduire en un seroit
> chose impossible: outre que beaucoup d'autres parties sont demeurées
> aux fondementz des vieilles murailles, ou egarées par le long cours des
> siecles ne se peuvent trouver d'aucun. Parquoy venant à redifier cete
> fabrique, vous serez bien loing de luy restituer sa premiere grandeur,
> quand, ou souloit estre la sale, vous ferez paravanture les chambres,

---

[42] p. 64; cf. p. 73, and the passage quoted above, p. 65.

les etables ou la cuysine, confundant les portes et les fenestres, bref changeant toute la forme de l'edifice.   (pp. 79–80)

This powerful image of the death of antique cultures is based on an important humanist *topos*.[43] In this context, it echoes both the Babel image and the repeated allusion to the 'paroles mortes' of antiquity in I. x (pp. 70, 73); it also anticipates a strange shift of perspective towards the end of I. xi, where Du Bellay imagines the French language 'comme la Greque et Latine pery et mis en reliquaire de livres . . .' in order to stress once again its potential equivalence with Latin and Greek.[44] All this is linked to the nature–art opposition, as is shown by the conclusion of the 'ruined edifice' image:

Finablement j'estimeroy' l'Art pouvoir exprimer la vive energie de la Nature, si vous pouviez rendre cete fabrique renouvelée semblable à l'antique, etant manque l'Idée de la quele faudroit tyrer l'exemple pour la redifier.   (pp. 80–1)

Art is here equated with the artificiality of neo-Latin composition, and is seen as a dead surrogate by contrast with the 'vive energie de la Nature'. Just as, in the painting *topos*, the soul is inaccessible to the painter's art, so too in this instance, contact with an original source and principle of unity (the 'Idée') has been lost.

It is true that the relegation of art to a realm of decay and senseless repetition is tempered in this passage, as in those on imitation, by the notion of a valid art proceeding from nature, and not simply attempting to copy or reconstruct nature independently of it:

les Anciens usoint des Langues, qu'ilz avoint succées avecques le laict de la nourice, et aussi bien parloint les indoctes comme les doctes,

---

[43] As variations on the same theme, one might cite the *Songe de Poliphile*, fol. 4; Rabelais, *QL* 25 (see below, p. 207); and Du Bellay's own *Antiquitez* and *Songe*. The notion of irreparable fragmentation, and of the sterile pursuit of reintegration, is present in the second dialogue of Bonaventure Des Périers's *Cymbalum mundi*, where the 'pierre philosophale' has been reduced to dust. Cf. Goebel, 'Zwei Versuche zur Architekturbeschreibung', and Mortier, *La Poétique des ruines*.

[44] p. 82. Chamard (note 4) quotes a parallel image ('sepultures de literature') from Budé's *Institution du Prince*, xv.

si non que ceux cy aprenoint les disciplines et l'art de bien dire, se rendant par ce moyen plus eloquens que les autres.[45]

The vernacular thus appears in this perspective as a 'natural' language, guaranteeing the authenticity of an 'art de bien dire' constructed with its native materials.[46] Moreover, this exercise of conceiving of the ancients as speaking a *vernacular* tongue releases a crucial insight for the French poet, who must be made to conceive of culture as residing not in the past but in an imminent future; as a discourse which he is about to utter in his own 'domestic' language.

Nevertheless, the exercise is double-edged, as the subsequent inversion of the strategy by Du Bellay himself demonstrates. French culture, and the French language, will one day be consigned to the tomb of books. The presence of the living vernacular, of those 'paroles . . . qui sont vives et volent ordinairement par les bouches des hommes', is a precarious moment, surrounded by past and future deaths, and not sure of its own fruition.[47] Du Bellay's text is located between a living but unconsecrated language and a consecrated but dead culture. An earlier passage had already sketched out a theory of the evolution of cultures, rejecting the inferiority of modern times by reference to the 'printing and gunpowder' *topos* (itself intrinsically ambiguous) and grounding the possibility of perfecting the French language in a cyclic conception of history:

Mais que par longue et diligente immitation de ceux qui ont occupé les premiers ce que Nature n'ha pourtant denié aux autres, nous ne

[45] I. xi, p. 81. The same affirmative note, associated with a metaphor of common experience, reappears at the end of the chapter, where Du Bellay contrasts the evaluation of ancient and modern languages in the following terms: 'la curiosité humaine admire trop plus les choses rares et difficiles à trouver, bien qu'elles ne soint si commodes pour l'usaige de la vie, comme les odeurs et les gemmes, que les communes et necessaires, comme le pain et le vin' (p. 83).

[46] Cf. Peletier, *Art poëtique*, I. ii, p. 73, on 'natural artifice': 'an cetɇ façon l'artificɇ mɇ̂mɇ aura sa naturɇ: Commɇ quand on dìt l'ordrɇ naturɇl e lɇ parler naturɇl.'

[47] See I. x, p. 70. Cf. also the quotation given above, p. 68 ('presens, absens, vyfz et mors, manifestans l'un à l'autre le secret de notz coeurs'); and I. iii, p. 24: 'nostre Langue, qui commence encores à fleurir sans fructifier, ou plus tost, comme une plante et vergette, n'a point encores fleury, tant se fault qu'elle ait apporté tout le fruict qu'elle pouroit bien produyre.'

puissions leur succeder aussi bien en cela que nous avons deja fait en la plus grand' part de leurs ars mecaniques, et quelquefois en leur monarchie, je ne le diray pas: car telle injure ne s'etendroit seulement contre les espris des hommes, mais contre Dieu, qui a donné pour loy inviolable à toute chose crée de ne durer perpetuellement, mais passer sans fin d'un etat en l'autre, etant la fin et corruption de l'un, le commencement et generation de l'autre.   (I. ix, pp. 56–7)

Although Du Bellay concludes the chapter by speculating that French culture will last all the longer because it has taken so long to mature, it is clear that a sense of change and decay is deeply inscribed in his defence of the French language.

If Du Bellay had looked on translation as a means of making the encyclopedia directly accessible and thus of avoiding the erosion of life itself which results from the need to learn the ancient languages (pp. 65 ff.), the poet cannot thus free himself from the burden of antiquity. The dead must be devoured and digested before new life can ensue: culture is a form of cannibalism. Indeed, the creation of a discourse which will, ideally, consecrate the living qualities of the vernacular and achieve 'immortality' demands of the poet a kind of death, a removal at least from the celebration of life:

Qui veut voler par les mains et bouches des hommes, doit longuement demeurer en sa chambre: et qui desire vivre en la memoire de la posterité, doit comme mort en soymesmes suer et trembler maintesfois, et autant que notz poëtes courtizans boyvent, mangent et dorment à leur oyse, endurer de faim, de soif et de longues vigiles. Ce sont les esles dont les ecriz des hommes volent au ciel.   (II. iii, pp. 105–6)

Thus the absence or death of the poet in the act of writing parallels the conditions to which the greatness of classical culture is subject. The living (and hence authentic) quality of nature can only be transferred to art by a process which will eventually eliminate the living presence of the poet, his vernacular, and his culture: *exegi monumentum*.

The principal theme of the first book of the *Deffence* could be said to be not so much 'nature versus art' as the transference of

characteristics between nature and art, or the shifting of perspectives in order to surmount their antinomy. Thus, in spite of the
initial (and repeated) assertion of the conventionality of languages,
Du Bellay refers again and again to the *naturel* of given languages;
in spite of the attribution (following Quintilian) of imitation to
the domain of *artifice (ars)*,[48] true imitation is none the less held
to incorporate nature into *elocutio*. Seen externally, or in retrospect, language always belongs to art; in this sense, it is an object,
inert although infinitely malleable. Seen from within, as an actual
or potential presence, it has its own nature, and is aligned with
the nature of a subject (a present speaker or writer). In order to
'voler par les mains et les bouches des hommes' (or 'au ciel'),
it must move from 'natural' subject to 'artificial' object; and Du
Bellay attempts to overcome the problematic nature of this shift
by presenting it as a transition from the status of natural art
(the vernacular) to that of art authenticated by nature (*elocutio*).

   In accordance with this duality, the prevalent imagery of the
first book oscillates between the organic (growing, flowering,
fruition) and the architectural. The organic metaphors are
presented within the purview of culture: it is man who must
cultivate the plants of language, avoid a sterile flowering, and
bring them in due time to fruition. Above all, he must improve the
quality of his produce by a process of 'naturalization', of 'pruning'
and 'grafting':

Mais eux [sc. les anciens Romains], en guise de bons agriculteurs, . . .
ont premierement transmuée [leur Langue] d'un lieu sauvaige en un
domestique: puis affin que plus tost et mieux elle peust fructifier,
coupant à l'entour les inutiles rameaux, l'ont pour echange d'iceux
restaurée de rameaux francz et domestiques, magistralement tirez de la
Langue Greque, les quelz soudainement se sont si bien entez et faiz

---

   [48] 'Car il n'y a point de doute que la plus grand' part de l'artifice ne soit
contenue en l'immitation' (I. viii, p. 45); cf. *Inst. orat.* X. ii. 1: 'Neque enim
dubitari potest quin artis pars magna contineatur imitatione.' It should be noted,
however, that this formulation modifies *ars* also, shifting the balance from precept
to example; cf. also Du Bellay's frequent references to intuitive judgement as
a substitute for precept (e.g. I. v, p. 33). On these issues, see also Peletier, *Art
poëtique*, I. ii, where imitation is attributed to art, and where the limitations of
precept are emphasized (Quintilian's excessively detailed and lengthy *ars* being
here condemned).

semblables à leur tronc, que desormais n'apparoissent plus adoptifz, mais naturelz. De la sont nées en la Langue Latine ces fleurs, et ces fruictz colorez de cete grande eloquence, avecques ces nombres et cete lyaison si artificielle, toutes les quelles choses, non tant de sa propre nature que par artifice, toute Langue a coutume de produyre.[49]

The metaphor creates an ideal reciprocity between nature and art; the poet-orator is here imaginatively installed in a fertile garden where death is absorbed into an endlessly renewed fruition. Du Bellay consciously recalls the image in I. vii (see above, p. 64), coupling it with metaphors of digestion and of building. The *Quintil horatian* mocks the 'translation [metaphors] vicieuse et inconsequente' of this later passage.[50] But in the transition from a human-organic metaphor (involving destruction and re-creation) via an image of nature induced by art (fragments of quasi-dead material being resuscitated by conjunction with a living stock) to that of a beautiful edifice which we retrospectively praise and admire, the text enacts virtually all the central problems and conciliations of Du Bellay's theory. The cycle is completed by the image, in chapter ix, of the crumbling architecture of antiquity, and of the futile attempt, by means of art alone, to reconstruct it from the remaining dead fragments.

The foregoing may be restated in terms of a schematic model. In the interstices of Du Bellay's shifting text, two conceptual

[49] pp. 25–6. The ambivalent status of the new nature thus produced is indicated in particular by the word 'apparoissent', and by the movement of the final sentence from a trope of nature ('sont nées . . . ces fleurs') to the tropical flowering of artifice in *elocutio* ('artificielle'; 'non tant de sa propre nature que par artifice'). The comment of the *Quintil horatian* (Du Bellay's anonymous critic) deconstructs this metaphor, and shows that what Du Bellay grounds in nature falls wholly in the domain of art (p. 26, note 2).

[50] p. 43, note 2: 'Tout le commencement du chapitre est de translation vicieuse et inconsequente, commençant par *manger*, moyennant par *planter*, et finissant par *bastir*, en parlant tousjours de mesmes choses. Auquel vice tombent coutumierement ceux qui tousjours veulent metaphoriser ou il n'est besoing, et appliquer figures ou proprieté seroit mieux convenante, estimans l'oraison par tout figurée estre plus belle que la simple et egale et rarement entremeslée de telz ornemens' (the *Quintil* here adds a simile of his own, presumably as an example of appropriate figuration). Such comments reveal the extent to which Du Bellay's discourse is not a rational exposition of theory, but a performance, enacting rather than analysing the problems of imitation theory.

series appear to be adumbrated, one positive, the other negative. The positive series moves from a pure undivided nature via natural language to a superior and authentic *ars dicendi* guaranteed by an intuition itself located in nature. The negative series begins with a nature irremediably fragmented in and by the art of language; envisages languages in their inert, undeveloped state as embodying a merely arbitrary differentiation; and culminates in the notion of an art-language (neo-Latin) wholly dissociated from nature, of which it offers a dead simulacrum. According to the first series, nature is at the origin of art, which thus becomes virtually a second nature; the decay of a culture, the consumption and digestion of a dead author, are the prelude to life grasped and lived out in the substance of language itself. According to the second, art penetrates and deforms nature from its very origin; the 'Idée', the pure natural language of undivided humanity are lost; the moment of intuitive presence is always either past or yet to come; and discourse is a place of alienation, decay, and death. These series (which seem distantly to echo the antithesis between a Pelagian optimism and an Augustinian pessimism) are not only inextricably linked: they are simultaneous and inter-dependent, each requiring the other's existence, each existing at the expense of the other. For, unlike Erasmus, Du Bellay cannot or will not appeal to a Christian Logos or any other fully super-natural agent as a means of stabilizing the fluctuations of discourse. Whether it is nature or art that is proteiform (and the ambiguity here is central), whether the difference of languages is an obstacle or a source of renewed vitality, whether the positive or the negative pole predominates at a given moment, Du Bellay commits the poet to the licence ('arbitre') of his own discourse. The transformations cannot be contained within a closed system; the cycles of cultural generation are not perfectly self-repeating; the centrifugal impulse of the writer can be given no term.

At this point, a well-known textual fact must be taken into consideration: much of the material analysed above as 'Du Bellay's' text is directly derived—at times *translated*—from Sperone Speroni's *Dialogo delle lingue* of 1542. More specifically, Du Bellay is indebted to Speroni in the passages on the Tower of

Babel and the conventionality of languages, on the 'cultivation' of the vernacular and the careful grafting of foreign materials, on the ruins of antiquity, and on the self-sacrifice of the poet.[51] In other words, the general theory of language, with its mingled pessimism and optimism and its images of conciliation between nature and art, is for the most part borrowed as a framework for a theory of imitation which freely adaps a set of different sources (Cicero, Quintilian, Erasmus, Peletier, perhaps Dolet). The Speroni materials are thus redistributed: their order has in several instances been transposed, other materials have been inserted, and new emphases created by the repetition of a theme at a distance of several chapters. Hence Du Bellay's own grafting of Speroni's arguments is clearly not random, and close examination of it would doubtless reveal further modulations. Furthermore, one may well argue that in this instance, as so often in the sixteenth century, the publication of a particular point of view at a particular moment has an importance which bears little relationship to its originality (or lack of it) when seen in a wider context.[52] It is the text that matters, not the putative qualities of the author's mind.

Indeed, precisely in so far as it *is* a mosaic of *topoi*, the *Deffence* enacts the tactics of defence and aggression of a writer enmeshed in one of the fundamental ambiguities of language, which one might phrase in terms of the contrast (or equivalence) between *copia* as plenitude and *copia* as copy. The voice of the author as he pleads for the distinctive and authentic character of his language and for his own right to authorship is caught repeating the words of other men, until the echoes and counter-echoes prevail and one is tempted to hear the text as a set of empty common-places. Thus its aggressions may seem an oddly misplaced piece of

[51] The relevant passages from Speroni are quoted by Chamard in his annotations on the *Deffence*.

[52] In his comment on Du Bellay's dedicatory epistle, the *Quintil horatian* says that he will not accuse Du Bellay of borrowing excessively from Horace ('ton œuvre quasi total estre rapiecé d'iceluy decousu de son ordre'): 'car telles usurpations bien appropriées en leur lieu sont tresbonnes et louables.' But he objects to Du Bellay's prohibition of the translation of poetry, while he himself translates Horace (p. 4, note). The reference here, however, is primarily to the poetry published together with the *Deffence* in 1549. The *Quintil* treats the text of the *Deffence* itself as if it were Du Bellay's.

shadow-boxing which proves the superiority of no one.[53] Yet the text admits this necessity of decay and emptiness; its 'author' foresees the ultimate distancing of his text from an immediate, living context. If this is self-evidently the condition of a polemical manifesto, the awareness of temporality will take on a richer resonance in the *Antiquitez* and the *Regrets*; there, the ruin of Rome and the ideal landscape of a renounced poetic ambition serve as twin counterpoints for an ironic cultivation of the local and contingent, of an untransfigured personal 'nature'.

The problems which sixteenth-century theorists discuss under the heading of 'imitation' reappear, in literary historical method, as the study of sources, influences, or traditions. But the establishing of sources has usually been the prelude to a definition of the 'originality' of an author as the residue which remains when the source-materials have been subtracted from his text. Any such residue is thus seen as having its source or origin in the author's mind, as being produced by an act of creation (virtually *ex nihilo*). Imitation theory is more complex in that it recognizes the extent to which the production of any discourse is conditioned by pre-existing instances of discourse; the writer is always a rewriter, the problem then being to differentiate and authenticate the re-writing. This is executed not by the addition of something wholly new, but by the dismembering and reconstruction of what has already been written. Figures of nature appear in this perspective as the sign and confirmation of authentic rewriting, but always elusively and always within the margins of an art of writing. Recent critical theory has coined the term 'intertextuality' to describe the interplay of texts without fabricating the image of an author who creatively determines the nature of his own text. In this respect it differs from imitation theory no less

[53] See the *Préambule* of the *Quintil horatian* (*Deffence*, p. xi): 'danger y a que quelqu'un ne te impose le surnom, que baille Barptolemy Scale Florentin à l'Ange Politian, l'appellant *Hercules factitius*, qui se forge luy mesme des monstres faits tout à propos, tels qu'il les puisse aisément defaire.' The *Quintil* himself becomes a participant in this intertextual struggle, since his own nominal adversary 'Du Bellay' is a Protean figure whose identity is dispersed by the repetition of other texts.

than from literary historical method. Nevertheless, the three principal texts examined in this chapter—the Erasmian *Ciceronianus*, Dolet's *De imitatione*, and the *Deffence*—all provide clear examples of intertextuality in their rewriting of *imitatio*; and none more overtly than the *De imitatione*, where the *Ciceronianus* is repeated in a fragmented and reordered form as a springboard for a 'different' text, both being also rewritings of classical *topoi*. Of course, such repetitions engender important shifts of perspective: in particular, the Erasmian constitution of a subject expressing itself deictically in language opens up a possibility of far-reaching developments. But it is striking that this theme of textual self-portraiture is a direct product of the problem of imitation as a form of intertextuality. Rewriting betrays its own anxiety by personifying itself as the product of an author; it imprints on itself—one might even say *forges*—an identity. Hence the lack of any radically 'new' discourse is supplemented or compensated for by the grammar and topics of personal identity (or, elsewhere, of nature or corporal identity). This process will dominate the text of the *Essais*, where imitation is one of the most pervasive themes and is closely linked to the topic of self-portraiture. But the pressure of what has already been written may manifest itself in other forms: in Rabelais's comic and ironic transcriptions, for example, or in Ronsard's elaboration of a poetic persona which both re-enacts the achievements of earlier poets and contests their superiority. These questions, which manifest what Harold Bloom has called the 'anxiety of influence', will be considered again in Part II. For the present, it is sufficient to have drawn attention to the involutions of a theoretical discourse which seeks to circumscribe the constraints of intertextuality while being itself subject to those very constraints.

3

Interpretation

THE ramifications of interpretation theory in the early sixteenth century are of such range and complexity that an analysis of theories of discourse in that period could easily take hermeneutics as its point of departure, and indeed as its central model. Histories of 'allegory', both profane and sacred, from the late classical period to the Renaissance, are now available, together with assessments of the mutations which this set of theories underwent, whether in the context of humanist classical scholarship, neoplatonist thought, or scriptural exegesis.[1] From this vast terrain, the Erasmian approach to biblical interpretation has been selected as the focus of the present chapter, partly in order to facilitate analogies with other chapters; partly also because Erasmus's reflections are among the most sophisticated and flexible ones to emerge in a period when scriptural reading became a central problem. But above all, perhaps, the scriptural model poses the allegorical question in a context where there is maximum pressure to ensure that the products of exegesis—gloss, commentary, paraphrase—are germane to the source-text; in this domain, failure to recover the true sense is the most dangerous of deviations. Hence any centrifugal movement which asserts itself here will be greatly multiplied when a similar model is applied to

[1] Seznec's *Survival of the Pagan Gods* and de Lubac's *Exégèse médiévale* remain the foundation studies for mythological and biblical interpretation theory respectively. On late antiquity, see Buffière, *Les Mythes d'Homère*, and Pépin, *Mythe et allégorie*; on medieval Biblical interpretation, see Smalley, *The Study of the Bible in the Middle Ages*; on neoplatonist allegory in the French Renaissance, see Walker, *The Ancient Theology*, ch. III; on Renaissance hermetism, see the earlier chapters of Yates, *Giordano Bruno*. A useful summary of allegorical theories in the sixteenth century is provided by Cameron Allen, *Mysteriously Meant*. On Erasmus's interpretation of Scripture, see the important article of Payne, 'Towards the hermeneutics of Erasmus'.

profane texts; still more where new texts are concerned, where the act of writing is not subject to pre-established limits.

The present chapter is designed to imitate, in some measure, this centrifugal itinerary. It is divided into two parts. The first outlines the Erasmian theory of a 'self-allegorizing' Scripture in which an authentic sense (*sensus germanus*) is immanent, and then proceeds to a comparison of prefatory texts drawn from secular works, classical and modern (notably the Prologue to *Gargantua*). The second part begins by examining Erasmus's *Convivium religiosum* as an enactment of problems of interpretation. Here, particular stress is laid on the ways in which the fruition of sense (the moment of full understanding) is seen to be perpetually deferred; subsequently, the deferment problem is traced through the fictions of Rabelais, including the Fifth Book. Erasmus and Rabelais thus appear in this chapter as the figures of a hermeneutic displacement: the desire to conserve some original sense (ideally, that enunciated by God) initiates an endless series of rewritings—paraphrases, allegorizations, linguistic and other glosses—and an infinite regression of meaning.

i. *Allegory without allegories*

The problem of scriptural exegesis rests on much the same basis as the problem of imitation. The recovery of *sensus* from a verbal surface is still the central issue; but now the *verba* are not only obscure at times, but also multilingual: the presupposed unity of the divine text is manifestly split by the difference of languages, by that second fall of which the emblem is the Tower of Babel. Thus the problem of reading is polarized: on the one hand, the unique identity of the divine 'author' guarantees the *sensus* absolutely, making the authenticity of even the greatest pagan writers seem equivocal; on the other, the reader finds himself distanced from the text by the labours of language-learning, textual emendation, and—especially in the Old Testament—alien structures of society and thought. How then is that transcendent identity to be reached through such a proliferation of differences, linguistic and cultural? Furthermore, the reader may not in this instance envisage himself as a writer, as he does in the imitation debate; but for Erasmus—or, say, Jacques Lefèvre d'Étaples—the authentic reading of the Bible demands the subsequent attempt to disseminate its *sensus* by means of commentary, paraphrase, translation, or preaching: a new discourse will be generated by the reading act, so that in effect 'interpretation' becomes a special mode of 'imitation'. Here, the problem will be to release the plenitude of Scripture into a different language which cannot but extend itself indefinitely, but which must nevertheless attempt to keep intact the precious self-identity of its model.

The *topos* of scriptural obscurity was powerfully formulated, in the context of a Christian theory of rhetoric, by Augustine in the *De doctrina christiana*. This work was known throughout the Middle Ages, but the key notion of the fall and difference of languages was to be renewed with considerable force in the earlier sixteenth century.[2] The focal passage occurs in Book II, which opens with a distinction between 'natural' and 'conventional' (or 'given') signs. Augustine concerns himself only with the latter, and in particular with written language as a set of more or less obscure signs to be interpreted only with difficulty. After an allusion to the Tower of Babel and the resulting 'dissonance of voices' (or of words: the Latin has 'vocum'), he proceeds as follows:

The result was this. Although Sacred Scripture, which heals such grave maladies of human hearts (*voluntatum*), began from one language, by which it could be spread abroad (*disseminari*) through the whole world at the proper time, it was scattered far and wide by the various languages of translators (*interpretum*), and only thus became known to the nations for their salvation. (II. 5 (6))

The original language of Scripture is Hebrew; and the juxtaposition of this passage with the reference to the Tower of Babel suggests the priority of Hebrew as the language closest to a prelapsarian state. But the dissemination of the Scriptures necessarily entails a diffusion in which the plurality of post-Babel languages

---

[2] See above, p. 67 and note 41. On Babel and the plurality of languages in Augustine, see Borst, *Der Turmbau* III. 1: 'Lateinische Kirchenväter', pp. 391–404.

will assert itself. Augustine then outlines an intentional theory which is dependent on this situation:

> In reading it, men are desirous only of discovering the thoughts and intentions (*cogitationes voluntatemque*) of those by whom it was written, and through these the will of God (*voluntatem dei*) according to which we believe such men spoke.

Thus the desire to penetrate to the will of God (which will cure the sickness of human wills) necessitates a movement through human intentions; an opacity, which is directly consequent upon the difference of language, inserts itself between the desire and its *telos*. The degree of uncertainty, or of 'deferment' of a presupposed original intention, is underscored by the word 'credimus': an initial act of faith is required in order to believe that these men spoke according to the will of God. Thus the authenticating intention of the divine author, mediated by the plural wills of men, invites a corresponding disposition of goodwill on the part of the reader.[3]

The problems of this theory of communication are elaborated by Augustine in the following passage. An inherent opacity and plurality is compounded by a reading whose indiscreet boldness (echoing the pride of the inhabitants of Babel) is a source of deception:

> Those who read indiscreetly (*temere*) are deceived by numerous and various instances of obscurity and ambiguity, supposing one meaning instead of another (*aliud pro alio sentientes*). In some passages they do not find anything to surmise even erroneously, so thoroughly do certain texts draw around them the most impenetrable obscurity. (II. 6 (7))

For such readers, the pursuit of sense is blocked, perhaps irremediably. Yet the very conditions in which fallen man and fallen language seem to lead one another into deeper and deeper darkness may also provoke a providentially designed movement towards truth and salvation:

> I am convinced that this whole situation was ordained by God in order

---

[3] Augustine's intentional theory is elaborated in greater detail in the *De utilitate credendi* IV and V; this analysis includes a catalogue of various forms of misreading, productive and otherwise.

to overcome pride by work and restrain from haughtiness our minds which usually disdain anything they have learned easily.

The diseases of fallen language—plurality, ambiguity, obscurity—are themselves an antidote for the 'sickness of human wills' and in particular for pride. This principle is developed a little later as follows:

Those who do not find what they are seeking are afflicted with hunger, but those who do not seek, because they have it in their possession, often waste away in their pride. Yet, in both cases, we must guard against discouragement. The Holy Ghost, therefore, has generously and advantageously planned Holy Scripture in such a way that in the easier passages he relieves our hunger; in the ones that are harder to understand he drives away our pride. Practically nothing is dug out from those unintelligible texts which is not discovered to be said very plainly in another place.[4]

Between the polarities of hunger and possession, the movement towards an authentic understanding is indicated. The deferment of an ultimate revelation is essential to the proper working of human cognition: tension is inherent in the reading process.[5] Augustine's analysis, moreover, reveals that Scripture is in some sense 'reflexive'. 'Clear places' provide a key to obscure ones: the Biblical text decodes itself, allegorizes itself. Once this central principle (and its corollaries, which the *De doctrina* seeks to clarify) has been understood, the reader will need no intermediate interpreter to lay open what is obscure: he will arrive at the hidden meaning for himself.[6]

This text has been selected in order to illustrate a commonplace rather than as a source of later theory. However, it is now established that Erasmus valued the *De doctrina* throughout his career,

[4] The translation quoted here is that of J. J. Gavigan, in *Writings of St. Augustine*, vol. IV. For an account of Augustine's theory of language in general, see Colish, *The Mirror of Language*, I.

[5] One might add that an awareness of the temporal constraints of reading is implied here: understanding is committed to movement, to a constant *devenir*. Cf. Augustine's use of the reading of a Psalm-text as an illustration of temporal consciousness in *Confessions* XI. 28.

[6] See *De doctrina*, Prol. 9. This rather optimistic statement is elsewhere counterbalanced, if not undermined, by Augustine's acute awareness of the errors into which the reader of Scripture may fall.

and drew on it increasingly for his exegetical theory from the *Ratio verae theologiae* onwards; this process was to reach its culminating point in the *Ecclesiastes* of 1535.[7] Since his New Testament prefaces and the *Ratio* arose in the context of his concern for philological elucidation and for the notion of a Christian eloquence, it is not surprising to find him drawing on those sections of the *De doctrina* where Augustine recommends knowledge of the three languages and of classical rhetoric.[8] These two areas of linguistic preoccupation converge in the central problem of the figurative nature of the Bible, to which Erasmus returns again and again. Like Augustine, he stresses the advantages of presenting truths in a covered form; and he lays down comparable principles for deciding whether a scriptural passage is to be read figuratively or not.[9] The most frequently reiterated principle of interpretation is the collation of obscure passages with clear ones:

Often the collation of places undoes the knot of difficulty, since what in one place is said darkly, is elsewhere expounded most lucidly.

[7] See Béné, *Érasme et saint Augustin*, *passim*. It may be contended that Erasmus's dependence on Augustine was less extensive, and above all less exclusive, than Béné suggests: Erasmus himself frequently acknowledges his debt to Origen and other Church Fathers. However, there is plenty of textual evidence, implicit and explicit, that he knew and exploited the *De doctrina*.

[8] These questions were of course highly controversial in the earlier sixteenth century. Béné points out that in the polemic between Erasmus and his scholastic adversaries the *De doctrina* was used as an authority by both parties: as always in this period, slight shifts of tone and emphasis can make all the difference between a 'scholastic' and a 'humanist' viewpoint.

[9] On the advantages of allegory, see *Ratio verae theologiae*, Fr. V, p. 99 (LB 117–18). This passage is one of the many in the *Ratio* which Erasmus expanded at considerable length in the later editions of the text. The rules for distinguishing between literal and figurative passages of Scripture include the notion that, without allegory, many readings are absurd, pernicious, or futile (ibid., p. 105, LB 124; see below, quotation on p. 87; cf. Pépin, 'A propos de l'histoire de l'exégèse allégorique: l'absurdité, signe de l'allégorie'). Both of these aspects of allegorical theory are developed in the celebrated and influential adage *Sileni Alcibiadis* (*Adages* III. iii. 1, translated in Mann Phillips, *The Adages of Erasmus*). Erasmus also recommends 'playing' for a while with poetic allegories as a prelude to the reading of Scripture ('in poeticis allegoriis per aetatem praelusisse'), and learning how to draw similes from every area of experience ('ab omni genere rerum'); here (*Ratio*, p. 105; LB 125) he refers to his own text on this subject, the *Parabolae sive similia*.

Not only for Origen, but also for Augustine, the best method of inter-
preting the divine text (*literas*) is to make evident (*illustrem*) an obscure
place by collation with other places, so that the mystic explains mystic
scripture, and the sacred explains the sacred (*mysticam scripturam,
mystica; sacra sacram exponat*).[10]

Erasmus is here very close to Augustine's formula in the *De
doctrina*.[11] Yet the second of these passages, by means of an elegant
chiasmus, makes much more explicit the self-allegorizing nature
of the Bible, expressing the collation principle precisely in a
reflexive form. The same notion underlies Erasmus's frequent
appeal to the *orbs doctrinae Christianae* as a matrix within which a
particular *sensus* may be verified: the scriptural text describes an
ideal circle, producing meaning according to a principle of perfect
adequation.[12]

While exploiting the *De doctrina*, Erasmus shows a greater
preoccupation with the problem of a hidden sense, using the
term 'allegory' again and again, not simply to denote a figure of
speech, but to indicate the whole scale of possibilities from the
reading of simple tropes to the comprehensive use of the 'fourfold sense' method of interpretation.[13] What emerges from his

[10] Fr. V, pp. 72, 110 (LB 85, 131). This second passage follows a recommendation to prepare an inventory of biblical *loci* in the manner outlined in the *De
copia*: thus collation—or rather collocation—for interpretative purposes is
facilitated.

[11] See also Rice, *Prefatory Epistles*, nos. 147 and 152, where the same commonplace formula appears. It is exploited, with a rather different emphasis, by Luther:
see for example the polemical tract *Auf das überchristlich . . . Buch Bocks Emsers
Antwort* (1521) in *Werke* VII, p. 639; for a comparison of Erasmus and Luther on
the notion of *claritas scripturae*, see Augustijn, '*Hyperaspistes I*'. It should be noted
that Erasmus cites Origen as well as Augustine as an authority for this rule.

[12] On the *orbs doctrinae*, see *Ratio*, p. 108 (LB 128); on Christ as the 'perfect
circle' and the primacy of the New Testament, see pp. 74–7 (LB 88–92); on
contextual reading, see p. 107 (LB 127–8). It will no doubt be apparent that the
notion of a 'self-allegorizing' text cannot exclude the intervention of a reader,
who has to perform the necessary collation; but, as will shortly be indicated, such
theories point towards the ideal possibility that mediation may be eliminated,
the 'reader' becoming identified with a text which itself performs the reading
operation so that no opacity of 'human will' may cloud its sense.

[13] Augustine uses the word 'allegory' rarely, and restricts its status to that of
one trope among many (cf. *De doctrina* III. 11 (17), 29 (40)). While it is of course
necessary to distinguish between the various uses of the word in different contexts,

exploration of this terrain is the inadequacy of any system to measure up to the productivity of the scriptural text, and the need for the reader to develop his own criterion, his own 'sense of meaning'. Still more forcefully than Augustine, he demands the independence of the reader from intermediaries:

But the sage rightly warns that you should drink water from your own cistern; that it is not necessary to seek help from elsewhere, but rather to divert water from your spring into others (*ut tu potius de tuo fonte derives in alios*). Therefore, leaving aside those confused and petty rules, and the impure waters of standard compendia (*summulariorum*), make your own heart (*pectus*) the library of Christ himself. Like the provident father of a family, draw out from him as from a store-room either new or old materials as the situation demands (*seu nova, seu vetera, utcunque postulabit res*). What you produce from your heart (*e tuo pectore*) like living things (*ceu viva*) will penetrate the minds of your listeners far more vividly than what is stolen from a hotch-potch of other people's writings (*quae ex aliorum farragine subleguntur*). (p. 111; LB 132)

In this passage, with its fusion of the wisdom of Solomon and Quintilian's rhetorical theory, Erasmus constructs the model of a dynamic imitation or reproduction of Scripture. The text is to be wholly absorbed by the reader and located in the *pectus*, that intuitive focus of the self which is presumed to guarantee profound understanding and *living* expression.[14] In other words, the scriptural text is made consubstantial with the reader and is then re-uttered in a speech-act grounded in the living presence of the speaker, a process which achieves its end in that vivid penetration of the listener's mind which is in itself a mark of

its rhetorical grounding nevertheless reminds one of the close relationship between allegorical reading and the rhetorical analysis of discourse. On the 'fourfold sense' in Erasmus, see for example *Ratio*, p. 107 (LB 127); also *Ecclesiastes*, Fr. V, pp. 862 ff. (LB 1034 ff.).

[14] On the absorption of the text by means of constant re-reading and even memorization, see p. 111 (LB 131–2). The way in which, according to this theory, a reader may 'naturalize' the biblical text by immersing himself in it ('in naturam ibit, quod usu perpetuo fuerit infixum'), once again recalls passages in *Institutiones* X. Cf. the notion of the reader being transformed by (or into) Scripture, which recurs in the *Paraclesis* (Fr. V, pp. 116, 119 (twice), 120–1; LB 138, 141, 142, 144).

authenticity. The imagery of submissiveness is particularly central here. Instead of himself penetrating the text in an attempt to extract meaning, or imposing alien senses on it, the reader is penetrated by it, transformed into it; the same process is then repeated in the *auditores*. Between these two submissions, the reader acts as a container, or store-keeper, harbouring and handing on the infinite principle of life with which he has become imbued: he is himself a place of plenitude, the place where the virtual productivity of Scripture becomes actual. Furthermore, the 'difference' which intervenes between the identities of author and reader in secular imitation theory is now, ideally, effaced. Christ as a library (an encyclopedia) achieves presence by virtue of the contingent humanity of the reader-reproducer. One may note in passing that this is, self-evidently, an ideal; it depends on the total transparency of the self, the elimination of the congenital obscurity or opacity of fallen man and fallen language. The problem is by no means ignored by Erasmus; what is interesting is the conceptual and figurative adjustments which he makes in order to give licence to the unfolding of the divine Logos in human discourse.[15]

This model for the transmission of *sensus* may be complemented by the quotation of a passage in which Erasmus attempts to define the boundary between an authentic and an inauthentic representation of biblical sense in the domain of allegory. If he refers caustically to the shortcomings of even the most venerable of the Fathers,[16] his greatest distrust is reserved for the invented allegorizations of modern commentators:

[15] Cf. his notorious rendering of *logos* as *sermo* in his translation of St. John. If Christ is *sermo*, he is not so much the once-and-for-all utterance of God (*verbum*) as a divinely present discourse, a living utterance which includes Christ's recorded (written) words yet is infinitely renewed in their re-utterance by readers of subsequent ages. Thus the translation of *logos* as *sermo* consecrates human discourse; but at the same time it destroys the unity of the original utterance and initiates a movement beyond the scriptural circle into the fallen language of man. See Margolin, 'Érasme et le Verbe', pp. 107 f., and Erasmus's *Apologia de in principio erat sermo* (Fr. IX, pp. 95–104; LB 111–22).

[16] He says, for example, that the Fathers were only human, that they were ignorant of certain things, that they were sometimes deluded (*hallucinati sunt*) and sometimes nodded (*dormitarunt*), that they were often governed by polemical concerns (Fr. V, p. 112; LB 133). Thus they were capable of doing violence to the text (cf. p. 108; LB 129). In the preface of the St. Matthew paraphrase,

Some people despise all allegories as arbitrary and dream-like. I strongly disagree with these; for I perceive that without allegory many senses (*sensus*) are either absurd, or pernicious, or futile, ground-less, and frigid, and it is well-known that Christ used allegories, and that Paul sometimes interpreted passages (*locos*) of the Old Testament allegorically. Yet I cannot but disapprove of the inept allegorizing of certain commentators who invent (*fingunt*) something which they can then explain allegorically. A weary traveller sits on the back of a huge dragon, thinking it is a tree-trunk; the dragon, waking up, devours the wretch. The traveller is man, the dragon the world, which destroys those who depend on it. It is sufficient to adapt to an allegorical reading what we find in Scripture, if circumstances demand it, so that we invent nothing supplementary to it (*ut ipsi nihil affingamus*). I have heard a certain Parisian theologian who dragged out the parable of the Prodigal Son for forty days . . .   (p. 106; LB 126)

The delicacy of the balance is striking. The extreme view which discounts all allegories is rejected on both rational and evangelical grounds. On the other hand, this positive acceptance of allegory, defined in an explicit movement away from negation, is syntac-tically directed (by an 'ut . . . ita . . .' correlative, and by parallel 'cum' clauses with their attendant subjunctives) towards a new negation: in other words, the defence of allegory is presented here in what amounts to a concessive clause. Thus the domain of valid and necessary allegory is shown to be perilously balanced between two modes of inauthenticity. In the third, attacking phase of this argument, the realm of the 'arbitrary and dream-like' is exposed with unreserved contempt. The example of the traveller and the dragon embodies an extreme of gratuitousness: as a fiction, it is doubly alien from the scriptural text, a doubly devalued copy. The second example, falling within the range of Scripture itself, reveals more clearly the margin of illicit supple-mentation. The fiction of the Prodigal Son is authorized by Christ himself; it is the endless 'affictions' of the Paris theologian which make it deviate into the realm of the arbitrary and the absurd. He 'draws out' of the parable an empty sequence of details,

he claims that they sometimes seem to him to be playing (*ludere*), a phrase which brought down on his head the wrath of the Sorbonne (see Fr. IX pp. 447 ff., LB 453, where he defends his remark).

inventing (*affingens*) the journey of the son as he sets out and returns, as if he now eats in the tavern a pudding made of tongues, now passes by a water-mill, now does this, that or the other; to such confected fairy-tales (*confictas naenias*) the theologian deflected (*detorquebat*) the words of the prophets and Gospels.[17]

It is no doubt in reaction to such prodigal deviations that Erasmus experimented in the early 1520s with paraphrase, the mode of 'speaking alongside'. At precisely this time also, he coined the phrase *sensus germanus* as an index of authenticity in biblical reading. It is absent from the *Ratio verae theologiae*, but occurs in the *Convivium religiosum* (1522) and immediately afterwards in the preface to the paraphrase of St. John's Gospel. Above all, it recurs again and again in the *Ecclesiastes* of 1535: once he had discovered it, Erasmus clearly found it particularly expressive.[18] *Germanus* already has the sense of 'genuine' in classical Latin: Cicero was fond of it, and the Fathers also used it regularly, often in affective contexts.[19] But Erasmus applies the word to a new and sensitive context. The phrase *sensus germanus* does not appear to have been used by patristic and medieval commentators as indicating the genuine sense of Scripture; it is indeed absent from all the standard compilations of his own day as well as of ours. At the same time, there were plenty of adjectives which *were*

[17] Loc. cit. Helgerson's *The Elizabethan Prodigals* discusses English variants of the Prodigal Son narrative, drawing attention to the ambivalence of a fiction which enacts in its own structure a deviant 'prodigality' in order to fulfil its narrative destiny of a triumphant conversion and homecoming. In the context of the Erasmian discussion of the limits of allegory, the parable reveals the difficulty of distinguishing between internal and external, authentic and inauthentic, serious and non-serious, true and fictive: Christ's own discourse includes and indeed depends on tropes and fictions which invite the reader to embark on interpretative detours. See below, p. 93; also the preface to the paraphrase of St. Matthew, on Christ speaking as if he did not wish to be understood (Allen 1255, p. 6.)

[18] For the instance in the *Convivium religiosum*, see Am. I–3, p. 251. The preface to the St. John paraphrase (quoted below) is dated 5 January 1523; the same date is given to the dedicatory epistle to Erasmus's edition of the works of Hilary (Allen 1334), in which the phrase 'germana scriptura' appears in the context of interpretation. Similar uses of the word *germanus* in the *Ecclesiastes* are to be found in Fr. V, pp. 849, 854, 861, 868, 873 (LB 1019, 1026, 1033, 1041, 1048).

[19] I have consulted the *Oxford Latin Dictionary*, the *Thesaurus linguae latinae*, and Blaise for examples of its use.

currently (and traditionally) used to define Scriptural meaning: *sensus allegoricus, anagogicus, evangelicus, litteralis, moralis, mysticus, spiritualis, tropologicus,* and so on.[20] Hence it is reasonable to infer that Erasmus felt the need to innovate, to define in his own way the notion of a true, intrinsic meaning. It was at much the same time that Luther expressed dissatisfaction with traditional categories of allegory; and the fact that one of Erasmus's opponents satirized him by taking the phrase as meaning 'German sense' indicates that it was indeed both novel and provocative.[21]

An early example of how he uses it will reveal its principal connotations. Dedicating his paraphrase of St. John's Gospel to Archduke Ferdinand, he cautiously defends his own orthodoxy while claiming the right to independence:

I wish the reader to be advised that I have in this work followed the most reliable doctors of the Church: but not indiscriminately, nor on all matters, in so much as even they not infrequently disagree among themselves. However, I always offer in good faith what seemed to me to be the genuine sense (*quod mihi germani sensus esse videbatur*), when I observe that certain things have been violently distorted by the ancient authors in their struggle against the opinions of heretics. (Allen 1333, p. 172)

The strategy will by now be familiar. The need to establish a *sensus germanus* is rendered legitimate, indeed imposed, by the conflict of existing interpretations; and it is further defined in opposition to the distortion of sense by those with extrinsic concerns: Erasmus has already used the phrase *sensus alienus* for such instances in the *Ratio* (p. 108; LB 128–9), and *sensus germanus* now appears as its natural antonym. This 'authentic sense' does not arise exclusively from allegorical reading, since Erasmus goes on to express caution about over-indulgence in allegory and claims the right to use his own judgement in determining how

---

[20] Rice, *Prefatory Epistles*, provides many examples of early sixteenth-century usage (see *Index of Latin words*, article 'sensus').

[21] The most detailed account of Luther's interpretation theory (though with reference primarily to the New Testament) is given by Ebeling, *Evangelische Evangelienauslegung* (especially pp. 44–89). I have mislaid the reference to Erasmus's 'German sense'; in a letter of 1523, Erasmus himself plays on the double sense of *germanus* (Allen 1353).

much to allegorize.[22] On the other hand, it is equally clear that it cannot be separated from allegorical procedures: paraphrase requires the resolution of certain tropes and figures, so that the desire always to offer the *sensus germanus* necessarily implicates the paraphrast in that process of 'translation' or transformation which institutes allegory (see above, pp. 38–9). All the Erasmian precautions of philological and rhetorical preparation, moderation, and reference to the 'self-allegorizing' model are thus unable to repress a certain centrifugality. In so far as the phrase *sensus germanus* represents an attempt to express a global notion of how a text may authentically signify, it betrays a precarious optimism with regard to the reading process and its reproduction in paraphrase (or preaching, as in the *Ecclesiastes*). Once again, it appears, Erasmus is in the domain of that concessive clause which circumscribed within a double negation the possibility of authentic reading.

Germanus denotes close relationship, consanguinity, and a consequent affective reciprocity. It replaces the publicly authorized systems of allegorical commentary with a private, inwardly experienced bond between reader and text: an androgynous union, as it were, revivifying the dead fragments of a Scripture turned inside out. Furthermore, the bond is renewed as the reader-author turns towards his own readers: 'semper *bona fide* profero, quod mihi germani sensus esse videbatur.' The phrase *sensus germanus* is thus a *figure* of authenticity (rather than a precise theoretical concept), by means of which Erasmus attempts to close the fissure between the text and what it signifies, or—more problematically—between the discourse of Scripture and a new discourse seeking to reproduce its sense. At this point, a duplicity becomes apparent. Erasmus uses a trope (which, together with his other tropes for authentic reading—the store-keeper, the father-reproducer, and the like—constitutes something like an allegory)

---

[22] 'As for allegories, in which I perceive that certain of the early commentators (*veterum*) were zealous to the point of superstition, I have touched on them sparingly and have not gone further than I thought necessary' (Preface, loc. cit.). In the *Ecclesiastes*, the phrase is used with relation to the understanding of a passage in terms of its context: 'ex iis quae precedunt, quaeque sequuntur, germanum scripturae sensum rimetur' (Fr. V, p. 845; LB 1026).

to restore the unity of a text fragmented by its tropical involutions: he sets a thief to catch a thief, a figure to domesticate disconcerting and alien figures. The movement towards the true centre of Scripture, towards its intrinsic properties, conceals and depends on a deviant counter-movement. Paraphrase is only the more protracted writing-out of that duplicity. The voice which seeks to erase the arbitrary proliferation of readings (allegories, glosses) by the singularity of its enunciation cannot but assert its own freedom from formal constraints. The paraphrase model is in fact very close to Erasmus's celebration of Christian charity as relieving man of the burden of 'Judaism': according to the Erasmian evangelical ethic, rules and laws fall away in favour of a directly grasped unifying truth, in accord with man's intrinsic nature (and hence his deepest psychological needs). The arbitrary multiplication of rules under the old dispensation is replaced by a Christian liberty. Similarly, the formalistic grid imposed on the biblical text by the Fathers in their wilder moments, and more perniciously by later scholastic commentators, is seen as the source of a plurality of interpretative transgressions; the new liberty of the reader, delimited by the circularity of a Christocentric Scripture,[23] should ideally lead to unity and authenticity. Yet this liberty—to a far greater extent, perhaps, in the interpretative than in the ethical domain—acts as a solvent, breaking down the carefully elaborated structure of orthodox external constraints, and thus opening up the possibility of an infinite series of 'authentic' readings, or rewritings. To put it in another way, interpretation becomes in paraphrase a mode of imitation, and is thus subject to Quintilian's law of 'difference'. Once again, in proposing the interchangeability of a hermeneutic model and a rhetorical model, the text of Erasmus discloses the ineradicable element of licence which is germane to his theory and its figures.

[23] Cf. once again the notion of the *orbs doctrinae Christianae* (above, note 12). This central rule is aligned with a principle of natural judgement (*aequitas naturalis*), which for Erasmus would no doubt be clarified by a properly directed education. Elsewhere, stress is laid on the affective disposition of the reader: love of the author of Scripture will guarantee fruitful reading (cf. *Ecclesiastes*, Fr. V, p. 885, LB 1062, where Augustine's exposition of this fundamental affective principle is alluded to).

Shifted into the domain of secular letters (more particularly in the vernacular), the freedom of the reader-writer to produce an endless series of new authenticities according to such a principle would of course be still more overtly unconstrained. The preacher, novelist, or poet, released from the margins of Scripture and thus from the scandal of 'affiction', could then allow his prodigal fictions to multiply indefinitely. At this point, one may invoke an essential respect in which Erasmus's perspective differs from Augustine's. When, in the *Enchiridion*, he claimed to prefer an allegorical reading of pagan poetry to a literal reading of Scripture, he was perhaps being deliberately provocative. Nevertheless, he was doubtless aware at that stage of the passage in the *De doctrina* where Augustine, quoting a few lines of poetry by an unknown author, speaks of the shell or husk ('siliqua') of the poem as a pleasant covering ('dulce tectorium') containing only pebbles ('lapillos'); on the following page, he uses Augustine's image in the context of biblical interpretation, inverting its sense by placing a nourishing marrow ('medullam') in the husk.[24] This shift reflects a crucial contrast between Augustine's emphasis on the fallen nature of language and the consequent emptiness of profane letters on the one hand, and the Erasmian attempt to rehabilitate nature and language (encouraged no doubt by neo-platonist theories of 'poetic theology') on the other. The extent of the deviation can be measured again, some twenty years later, by the fact that, in his polemic with Latomus, Erasmus is forced to quote a tag from Augustine's early *De ordine* as an authority for his defence of poetry, there being no favourable reference in the *De doctrina*.[25]

[24] Augustine, *De doctrina* III. 7 (11); Erasmus, *Enchiridion* (section entitled 'De armis militiae christianae'), Fr. V, pp. 8 and 9 (LB 7, 8). The relevant sentences from the *Enchiridion* are as follows: 'Sed uti divina scriptura non multum habet fructus, si in litera persistas haereasque: Ita non parum utilis est Homerica Vergilianaque poesis, si memineris eam totam esse allegoricam' (p. 8); 'Magis sapiet, magis pascet, unius versiculi meditatio, si rupta siliqua medullam erueris, quam universum Psalterium ad literam tantum decantatum' (p. 9). See Béné, op. cit., p. 268. The metaphor of the marrow and its covering is in itself a commonplace of exegetical theory (see also below, note 30).

[25] See Béné, pp. 245, 295–6, 319–20; Augustine, *De ordine* I. 8 (23–4). Cf. *De doctrina* II. 17–18 (27–8), where Augustine speaks deprecatingly of pagan mythology.

Erasmus's enthusiasm for pagan verse is not without major reservations. In his more austere works, such as the *Ratio verae theologiae*, the interpretation of pagan fables is in most instances seen as a preliminary training for scriptural reading, and must not be dwelt on too long. In these contexts, allegory is usually treated systematically and pedagogically, and does not provoke any reflection on the problem of authenticity: the examples given provide reductive tropologies for mythological figures isolated from any context.[26] Yet, in the opening pages of the *Ratio*, Erasmus reorientates Augustine's defence of rhetorical study by placing a much stronger emphasis on the figurative or poetic language of the Bible:

The writings (*litterae*) of the prophets abound everywhere in poetic figures and tropes; Christ clothed (*convestivit*) almost all his sayings in parables, a procedure which is peculiar to poets.   (p. 69; LB 82)

Just before this passage, he had contrasted the Fathers with contemporary theologians; he now goes on to make a still more damning distinction between the *style* of the prophets and Christ on the one hand, and that of the followers of Thomas and Scotus on the other. Finally, he transfers to this anti-scholastic and 'literary' context Augustine's argument that platonist thought is the nearest equivalent in antiquity to the teaching of Christ.[27] Such a juxtaposition of poetic ornamentation, Christian eloquence, and pagan insights, with its polemical overtones, is characteristically Erasmian; it reminds one that, although the strictly biblical concerns of the *Ratio* allow relatively low priority to pagan culture, the provocative optimism of the *Convivium*

[26] See, for example, *Ratio*, p. 106 (LB 126): 'not without reason does Jerome mock those who twist (*detorquent*) the myths of the poets to make them apply to Christ, except where a particular case may be suitably adapted (*deflectetur*) to a moral reading, as for example the myth of Proteus to denote inconstancy, Phaëthon rashness . . . Ixion and the Danaides those who labour in vain' (this passage immediately follows the development on inauthentic allegory quoted above, pp. 87–8). Cf. above, note 9 (on poetic allegories); also *Ratio*, p. 67 (LB 80) ('Nec illud opinor, inutile fuerit, si Theologiae destinatus adolescens . . . praeludat in fabulis ad allegoriam explicandis, praesertim iis quae ad mores bonos pertinent').

[27] Loc. cit. Cf. Augustine, *De doctrina* II. 40 (60)–42 (63).

religiosum (in which the phrase *sensus germanus* emerges from a discussion of both pagan and Christian texts), or the exploitation of platonist fable in the adage *Sileni Alcibiadis*, offer an alternative perspective.[28]

This shift towards an extra-scriptural domain (defined thus because the proximity of the scriptural model remains apparent) may be further explored by means of a brief examination of two prefaces to fictional works published in French in the early 1530s. Here, the desire to recover a systematic 'sense' under the auspices of some controlling principle may be seen to yield to the licence of the reader (or writer); and if the adjustment appears in one instance—the prefaces of the *Grand Olympe*—to be of limited scope, in another, the Prologue of *Gargantua*, it will reveal a scandal: the impossibility of theory *qua* theory, and thus the need to replace, or displace, theoretical discourse altogether.

Before we come to these texts, their status may be more clearly defined by referring to certain counter-examples which are somewhat earlier in date and which (although not necessarily for that reason) bear the marks of a 'conservative' approach to the problem of interpretation. The first of these is a French translation of Erasmus's *Praise of Folly*, published in 1520. It is of interest because

[28] The *Sileni* opens with a list of 'wise fools', in which Christ appears as the paradigm after a number of pagan sages (Socrates, Antisthenes, Diogenes, Epictetus). An important reference to Scripture as a Silenus is interposed a little later, forging a link between ethical *exempla* and interpretation theory which will be elaborated in the Prologue to *Gargantua*: 'If you remain on the surface, a thing may sometimes appear absurd; if you pierce through to the spiritual meaning, you will adore the divine wisdom' (Mann Phillips, *Adages*, p. 275). The stories of the Old Testament resemble Homeric fables, the parables of the Gospel seem naïve when taken at face value: 'And yet if you crack the nut, you find inside that profound wisdom, truly divine, a touch of something which is clearly like Christ himself' (p. 276). In so far as the adage itself exploits a mythological figure, it may thus be read as an allegory of allegory, even if this reflexive aspect of the text is limited (as it is not in Rabelais) by the relatively simple, non-ironic treatment of the 'appearance and reality' commonplace. The concluding passage refers to the digressive or deviant nature of the text, to that interplay between intoxication and sobriety which gives licence to the 'flow of words': 'it was the drunken Alcibiades with his Sileni which drew us into this very sober discussion' (p. 296).

it puts to the test of transcription a mode of writing developed in order to resist schematic interpretation. Erasmus's ironies and ambiguities may of course be mimed in another language; but the difficulty for any translator of reproducing his allusive word-play and figures, or the strategies of his self-parody, reveals the character of *Folly* as a 'plural' text, that is to say one in which it is strictly impossible to homologize the levels of significance and, in consequence, the meaning it produces. The sixteenth-century French translator, responding no doubt to the pressure of a moralizing tradition embedded in fifteenth-century French scholarship, attempts to eliminate this plurality by glossing (or glossing over) the text as he translates, systematically restricting the production of meaning and turning the piece into a didactic tract.[29] This is similar to the technique applied to Ovid by the various versions of the *Ovide moralisé*, which continue to proliferate in the early sixteenth century. A series of editions of the Latin text of Bersuire had been printed by Badius Ascensius between 1509 and 1523, while as late as 1531, the conservative printer Philippe Le Noir published the French *Bible des Poetes* (attributed to Thomas Walleys) in Gothic characters, and with the preface dedicated by the translator to Charles VIII. In the same group of conservative editions one might also place the moralized version of the *Roman de la Rose* attributed to Marot, which appeared in the late 1520s: in this instance, it is a vernacular fiction which is rendered harmless and regularized by the allegorical glosses.[30] Despite the differences of situation, the model of interpretation offered by these texts moves towards the articulation of a 'hidden sense' not simply in the margins of the original text but in its place: Erasmus, Ovid, and Jean de Meun are systematically displaced by their allegorizers,

[29] See Rechtien, 'A 1520 French translation of the *Moriae Encomium*'.

[30] The prologue of this edition provides a particularly explicit example of the 'marrow' *topos* applied to a vernacular secular work, but used in such a way as to evoke the methods of scriptural exegesis. Having quoted the biblical passage in which the image of bark and marrow appears (Ezek. 17: 3), the editor continues: 'Semblablement si nous ne creusions plus avant que lescorce du sens litteral nous naurions que le plaisir des fables et histoires sans obtenir le singulier proffit de la mouelle neupmaticque / cest assavoir venant par linspiration du sainct esprit quant a lintelligence moralle' (fol. iii r⁰). Cf. Gilson, 'Rabelais franciscain', in *Les Idées et les lettres*, p. 201.

while at the same time the range of their signification is trapped
in what is essentially a monologic discourse.

An alternative solution is adumbrated by a new presentation
of Ovid's *Metamorphoses* which first appeared in 1532 under the
title *Le Grand Olympe des Hystoires Poetiques*, quite possibly as a
direct challenge to the 1531 folio of the *Bible des Poetes*. It is a prose
translation by an anonymous author, and seems to have been
favourably received, since new editions were published in 1537,
1539, and later (until 1586). Each of its three parts (which are
paginated separately) comprises five books of the *Metamorphoses*
and is accompanied by a prefatory note. These notes are brief and
relatively modest, but they have a clearly defined character. The
first begins with a double *exemplum*:

> Le divin philosophe Plato estant malade / et voyant les limites de sa vie:
> commanda luy estre faict oreillier du livre de Sophron poete mimo-
> graphe / estimant poesie estre profonde philosophie couverte du
> rideau de infatigable delectation et ayant la congnoissance de la vie de
> Lhomme / que nest que une fable / voulut mourir sur icelluy. A ce
> mesmes exemple Alexandre le grand souloit prendre sommeil sur sa
> Iliade Dhomere: laquelle lesmouvoit a chevallerie et hautz faictz.
> (I, fol. i v°)

Neither the allusions nor the notion of allegory which they convey
are strikingly novel in a text of 1532. Yet the priority given to
Plato as a 'divin philosophe' echoes Erasmian *loci* like the *Sileni
Alcibiadis* rather than the *Ovide moralisé*, and although the phrase
'chevallerie et hautz faictz' recalls an earlier native ethic, the
Alexander story itself had been recounted by Erasmus in the
Apophthegmata.[31] More centrally, the first prefatory note claims
that the French language is 'digne que tel livre soit par icelle leu
selon le naturel du livre sans allegories'. The defence of the
vernacular here turns on the ability of French to embody the
'naturel' of the original rather than being limited to a set of
didactic commentaries. The possibilities of imitation are thus
deeply linked with the exegetical perspective: an authentic
rewriting has as its corollary the disappearance of allegorical

---

[31] *Apophthegmata* VIII (Fr. IV, p. 343; LB 370). The story of Plato using
Sophron's works as a pillow is recounted in Valerius Maximus VIII. 7. *ext.* 3.

accretions. No allegories are in fact provided, the work being a straightforward translation of the *Metamorphoses*.[32] Yet the phrase 'sans allegories' is not the end of the sentence: the author adds 'lesquelles mieulx que ailleurs sont traictees par Fulgence en ses Mithologies / lequel avec celeste faveur au premier jour parlera Francoys. Et par ainsi a chascun autheur sa louenge sera gardee.' 'Fulgence' is presumably Fulgentius Planciades, who in his *Mythologiae* gives a succinct account of the moral and physical significance attributable to the principal classical deities.[33] Moreover, the reference in the opening sentence to the 'profound philosophy' hidden beneath the 'curtain of pleasure' indicates clearly enough the translator's readiness to accept an inherent duality in his text. The implication seems to be that the reader will consult Fulgentius and, with his interpretations in mind, read the *Metamorphoses* for himself; the 'philosophie profonde', which is the authentic sense ('le naturel') of the text, will then become apparent without intermediaries.

Precisely the same notion of an 'allegory without allegories' is present in the second prefatory note:

Poesie mere de subtile et joyeuse invention soubz une couverte de Fable elegante a si vrayement exprime la doctrine morale et humaine / que si lentement du liseur nest du tout efface par ignorance / il en tirera honnestes enseignemens et maniere de bien vivre: car ce nest que pure philosophie latente / . . . (II, fol. i v°)

The translator now limits the 'philosophie latente' explictly to ethics ('doctrine morale et humaine'), presumably in order to exclude those Christian theological interpretations which are characteristic of the *Ovide moralisé* tradition: a manœuvre of which

---

[32] Except that the episode of the wedding of Peleus and Thetis is interposed in the eleventh book ('faisant digression pour enchainer les matieres', III, fol. viii v°) in accordance with the *Ovide moralisé* tradition. The fact that this is a prose rather than a verse translation does not necessarily indicate a pedantic failure to grasp the poetic character of Ovid's work. Quintilian (X. v. 4) had advised prose paraphrase of verse as a means of enriching one's style with the special qualities of poetry; this suggestion, which follows a discussion of paraphrase from one language to another, may have been known to the translator of the *Grand Olympe*.

[33] See Seznec, op. cit., pp. 89, 226, 306. It is possible that the author of the preface may be referring to the so-called *Fulgentius metaforalis*, a fifteenth-century text by John Ridewall (see Seznec, p. 94).

Erasmus would have approved. Again, the 'pleasure and profit' *topos* introduces the notion of an authentic reading accessible to any reader of ordinary intelligence. In this instance, however, the authority cited is not Plato, but Augustine:

ce nest que pure philosophie latente / a laquelle sainct Augustin au ii. de sa doctrine Chrestienne / prohibe faire allegories / comme assez delle mesmes allegorisant. Parquoy en ce grand Olympe sont obmises en gardant le naturel de Lautheur tant que faire cest peu / ainsi que chascun est tenu.   (loc. cit.)

Augustine makes no such prohibition in the second book or any other part of the *De doctrina*. In the first place, Augustine is exclusively interested in the understanding of Scripture; as has been shown, his rare allusions to classical mythology are contemptuous. Secondly, although he says much about the difficulties and obscurities of Scripture, he does not, in the *De doctrina*, use the term 'allegory' to designate them (see above, note 13). It seems likely that the translator is alluding *grosso modo* to the group of theories analysed above: the notion of a self-allegorizing Scripture, the removal of intermediaries, and the attempt to suppress any *sensus alienus* or 'affiction'. Indeed, the phrase 'le naturel' has connotations not unlike those of *sensus germanus*. Augustine is invoked, as fountainhead and unassailable authority, in a phraseology and in a context which are not at all Augustinian, although they are arguably Erasmian. Thus a powerfully redirected allegorical theory is transferred to the reading of a secular fiction while retaining the sign of its scriptural provenance.[34]

Even in its own right, the *Grand Olympe* was not without its importance: through its successive editions (each carrying the same prefaces), it helped to disseminate in France a strong claim for the autonomy of the text and consequently for the liberty of the reader. But the fact that it first appeared, like *Pantagruel*, in Lyons in 1532, and that the *Gargantua* with its celebrated and enigmatic prologue appeared some two years later, allows one to

---

[34] It should perhaps be added that this translation also falls within the general humanist project of a return to pure classical sources (*fontes*), bypassing medieval commentary.

trace the notion of what one might call a self-eliminating theory of allegory to its most complex formulation. Rabelais, too, begins by citing Plato (and Socrates, with his 'entendement plus que humain') as supreme authority for the hiding of profound truths beneath a delightful surface, although here of course the allusion to the *Sileni Alcibiadis* is unmistakable; Rabelais, too, to the confusion of many of his commentators, appears both to recommend allegorical reading and to reject it as a falsification of what the author intended. The *Grand Olympe* prefaces do not explicate the folds of Rabelais's text; but they offer a kind of control sample, a manifestly non-comic variant of the allegorical dilemma as it was posed in the early 1530s. They clarify a polemical situation (the reaction against the method of the *Bible des Poetes* and, more indirectly, of late medieval biblical commentary), and reveal a simple strategy for combining the mirage of 'depth' in privileged texts (the notion of 'surface' and 'content') with a preservation of their Protean mobility.

In such a perspective, it is difficult to revert to the view defended most vigorously by Spitzer that Rabelais is here mocking any form of serious interpretation and presenting his work as 'purely' comic.[35] But it is equally misleading to use this conclusion as an excuse for treating the comedy as mere surface, as a brilliant but in the end secondary sugaring of the pill. For the Janus-faced character of this prologue controverts any attempt to extract a theoretical model which may then be used to 'explicate' the book as a whole. This is not simply because Rabelais tells his readers to look for a 'substantificque mouelle' and then warns them not to allegorize his text: the second movement may plausibly be taken as a restriction rather than a reversal. Partly, it is because the

---

[35] See Spitzer, 'Rabelais et les "rabelaisants"' and 'Ancora sul prologo al *Gargantua*'. The bibliography of commentaries on this prologue is too extensive to be summarized here. Raible, 'Der Prolog zu *Gargantua*', lists the principal contributions up to 1966 at the end of his article. Screech (ed. *Gargantua*, pp. 9–16, notes) provides central references, and makes the important suggestion, which seems to have escaped most other commentators, that the opposition on which the prologue turns may be that between 'good' and 'bad' allegorization, rather than between a pro- and an anti-allegorical view (see also Mallary Masters, *Rabelaisian Dialectic*, pp. 16–17). Among more recent discussions, Coleman, *Rabelais*, chapter 3, and Rigolot, *Les Langages de Rabelais*, I, should be mentioned.

language of the prologue, being comic, ruins its own game if it crystallizes at any point into a *discours du savoir* (straight theory); like certain passages of the *Praise of Folly*, it has an inbuilt reversibility which evades systematization. But what is most crucial here is the convergence of this comic deviousness with the theory of self-allegorization. The questioning of imposed meanings points the reader back towards the comic surface, with all its transgressions and incoherences, as the place where the potential productivity of the text is located. The fiction is strictly irreplaceable; it can of course be subjected to any mode of exegesis, but continually reasserts itself. Its plurality, in other words, is always in excess of any gloss, any analytic discourse which may be added to it.

The point may be clarified by recalling the radical difference of situation between Rabelais's work and the instances considered earlier. The *Metamorphoses* and *a fortiori* the Bible may be regarded by reverent readers as self-allegorizing because long traditions have placed their productivity beyond doubt. But *Gargantua* has no such guarantee. It purports to prolong a mode of fiction (the Gargantuan chronicles) which is far more difficult to domesticate, morally speaking, than even the *Roman de la Rose*; and yet, at a liminary moment before it is written (or read), it performs a pantomime of its own autonomy and productivity. This prologue is not a piece of theory added to an existing, consecrated text; it is itself part of the text, part of the performance. The fiction begins with the first page of the prologue, not with chapter one. Thus Rabelais displaces the whole of the allegorical question as formulated in the early 1530s by making it a topic of the comic fiction, an ineradicable fold in its surface.[36] In consequence, the impasse of allegorical theory, as pure theory, is overcome. By undercutting the reader's right to systematize its meaning, the text gives full licence to its prodigal surface. Deviation, evasion, the blocking of the reader's desire for coherence, are the means by which

---

[36] The problem of interpretation is a recurrent theme of *Gargantua* (the *Fanfreluches antidotées*, the discussion of the significance of the colours blue and white, the *Énigme en prophétie*), and reappears at the heart of Panurge's inquiry in the *Tiers Livre*.

a fallen text asserts its 'authenticity' and the proliferation of its 'significance'.

When, in the liminary poem 'Aux lecteurs', Rabelais claims that 'rire est le propre de l'homme', he invokes a long-standing *topos* according to which laughter (like language itself in other accounts) is a distinguishing and indeed a constitutive feature of man.[37] Thus the grotesque and risible surfaces of the Silenes or apothecary's boxes (the *figure* with which the prologue opens) appear, by extension, as the domain of man's *proprietas*, the ground of his authenticity. This displacement governs all the subsequent allusions to the traditional distinction between a figurative exterior and a hidden, non-figurative interior (*proprietas*), which is also that between body and soul.[38] Man is exiled on the surface, in a world of figures or of comic impropriety which has become his only 'property'; he can designate but never articulate the absent place in which his dislocations would be fully resolved. If the Bible and the *Metamorphoses* owe much if not all of their productivity to the density of their figuration, the writer of new fictions must accept the centrifugal movement already inscribed in the notion of a figure. If the sense of Scripture and of Ovid often appears absurd and pernicious, to generate the absurd and the pernicious cannot but be his task. Meanwhile, and from the very threshold, the reader's desire for sense must be excited, but its satisfaction deferred *sine die*.

ii. *The pursuit of sense*

Erasmus's logocentric optimism—his conviction that there *is* a *sensus germanus*—is always balanced against an awareness of the problematic nature of the pursuit of sense. His analysis of biblical exegesis provides a paradigm both of that desire for plenitude and presence which only a uniquely guaranteed text might eventually fulfil, and of the obstacles which frustrate its fulfilment: namely, the distortions, deflections, and fossilized mediations endemic in

[37] See Screech, ed. *Gargantua*, pp. 6–7, note.
[38] Cf. the parallel between Silenus, Socrates, and Scripture in the *Sileni Alcibiadis*, where the relationship between exterior and interior is only marginally disrupted by irony (see above, note 28).

the proliferation of human discourse outside the scriptural circle. Empty repetition—the copying of glosses, for example—forestalls the achievement of a positive identity, the arrival at a place of abundance where difference is effaced and the same rejoins the same. It would be wrong, however, to polarize this dialectic (essentially that between the 'clear' and the 'obscure') into a naïve positive–negative antithesis. As Augustine had shown, the opacity and ambiguity of fallen language are not simply an inert barrier: they are the means by which desire is aroused, appetite provoked, and the pursuit set in motion. Self-evidence is stasis: a premature arrival at an empty place. It is only through the awareness of not-having, of not-seeing, that the movement towards possession and insight (true evidence) may be released.

If the emergence of the phrase *sensus germanus* is undoubtedly connected with the theory and practice of paraphrase, it is still more deeply embedded in the movement of a dialogue—the *Convivium religiosum*—which enacts, precisely and explicitly, the pursuit of sense in terms of the dynamics of appetite. The dialogue begins with a brief prelude: through the fiction of a projected lunch-party at the country house of one 'Eusebius',[39] a tissue of key themes is introduced. *Voluptas* and abundance preside over the scene: the riches of nature will supply the materials of the meal. But at the same time, a dichotomy emerges between the values of *urbs* and *rus*. The city is at first rejected as a place of material cupidity and of not-seeing: it is symbolized by the figure of 'a certain blind beggar who liked to be hemmed in by the human throng, saying that the right place for begging (*quaestum*) was amid the crowd (*populus*).'[40] Philosophers, says the host Eusebius,

[39] On the names of the characters in the dialogue and their significance as personifications of evangelical and humanist values, see the introduction to the *Convivium religiosum* in *Colloquies*, trans. Thompson, pp. 46–7. My discussion in the following pages was originally published in a more extended form as part of my article '*Enargeia*: Erasmus and the rhetoric of presence'; the argument of the article—that *enargeia* is a key figure of the *Convivium*—is of relevance to the present chapter, and may be reconstructed by recalling the remarks made above, pp. 27 ff., while reading this section. My use in this and other contexts of the word 'evidence' (also 'evident'), in a sense broadened to include rhetorical *evidentia* and the French *évidence*, is intended to indicate the interconnection of these concerns.

[40] Am. I–3, p. 231. A further set of cross-references is adumbrated by the

have nothing to do with such blind beggars and their false
'quest'. But then Timotheus evokes Socrates, with his preference
for *urbs* over *rus*: 'And the philosopher Socrates preferred towns
to fields because he was desirous of learning (*quod esset discendi
cupidus*).' The opposition between true and false desire is thus
established on the basis of a mediation between nature and culture:
an allusion is made to the *Phaedrus*, where Socrates himself leaves
the city for a while to teach and learn; and the image of the
country house and its gardens constitutes an ideal place in which a
harmonious equilibrium may be reached between the rustic and
the urban(e). In this way, authenticity of desire—of the 'appetite'
or 'hunger' ('famem') which the guests are told to bring to the
feast—is located in a figurative place where the needs of human
communication may be met while the perils of a city (which might
easily be Babel) are eliminated. For the hunger that conjures up
a fictional feast is also an appetite for talk, or, more strictly, for
the dialogue-text which is about to be written or read.

The dialogue proper has a ternary structure. The host begins
by conducting his guests through the gardens and painted galleries
of his house; but before the tour is over, he breaks it off in order
to take them in for lunch, telling them that he is leaving more for
later:

For the present I shall not allow you to look at anything more, so that
there shall be something to call you back afterwards as to a new
spectacle. After lunch I shall show you the rest.   (Am. I–3, p. 240)

The second section consists of the lunch-party itself, and the discussion of biblical texts and moral themes which takes place during it; the third (comparatively brief) section reverts, as promised,
to the gardens, courtyards, library, and chapel of the house. The
whole itinerary of the outer sections is a visual one, a feast for the
eyes ('Haec pascunt oculos'): verbs of seeing and showing, nouns
like *species* and *spectaculum*, recur constantly. Furthermore, the
evidence of the décor embraces both natural and artificial elements, since the real garden is paralleled by a realistically painted

beggar: the mendicant orders are habitually associated by Erasmus with luxurious
living (see for example the reference in the same dialogue, pp. 257–8, to the
costly building programmes of 'those who live by begging').

garden; such devices draw the reader's attention to the mimetic fiction of the dialogue itself.

The distinction which this ternary structure appears to establish between a physical setting and an intellectual debate, between décor and enactment, between surface and content, is eroded by an interchange which takes place throughout the dialogue between the poles of this conventional duality. The visible gardens are full of signs, emblems, and mottoes. An image of St. Peter is painted on the gate; further on, Christ himself confers upon the scene a supernatural presence:

And look: the opening immediately to the right reveals a most elegant little chapel. On the altar, Jesus Christ looks up towards heaven, whence the Father and the Holy Ghost look out, and he points to heaven with his right hand, while with his left he invites, as it were, and entices the passer-by.   (p. 234)

The interlocutors observe, read the mottoes, draw moral and evangelical conclusions. A fountain appears as a symbol of spiritual thirst, whereas a stream, polluted by kitchen waste, warns of the dangers of corrupting the pure source of Scripture. In the concluding section, the subjects of the paintings include the Last Supper, Herod's feast, Dives and Lazarus, Cleopatra eating her pearl: emblems of spiritual abundance and poverty which echo the convivial theme. An image of Christ dominates the library, and his life is depicted in the frescoes of a gallery, thus closing the sequence as it began: the house and gardens are Christocentric. Conversely, a frugally domesticated nature penetrates the religious colloquy in the most literal sense: remarks about food and drink are juxtaposed with comments on scriptural meaning in such a way that a continuity and even an equivalence is established between them. The food is integral to the discussion; evangelical points are constantly being made through metaphors of tasting.[41] Christ has no chair at the table, but he mingles with the food and

[41] When one of the guests has made a 'point', Eusebius says: 'rem (ni fallor) non acu, quod aiunt, sed lingua tetigisti' (p. 245). Erasmus's play on the set phrase 'rem acu tangere' refers no doubt primarily to the speech-act in which the tongue 'touches the thing'; but in this context the other activity in which the tongue is engaged can hardly be ignored.

drink, 'so that everything shall taste of him' (p. 241). If the speech of the interlocutors is to be authentic, it must mingle with and be made wholesome by the frugal meal; for the dinner is explicitly a sacramental one, a celebration of Christ's presence (cf. pp. 240, 242).

Hence the décor and the banquet reflect one another, establishing an equilibrium (or reversible transference) between art and nature, body and soul, human and divine, and ensuring that the linguistic surface, with its copious provision of sights and savours, is not divorced from true plenitude. Ideally, in this dialogue, words become present through things, and things through words.

But it must be observed at once that, however great the sense of confidence and of *festivitas*, such an epiphany is not without its problems. The discussion of biblical texts at lunch is an attempt to resolve difficulties: the Bible, even the New Testament, seem sometimes to speak obliquely. Thus, although the speakers end in each case by arriving at a 'consensus' with regard to the sense of each text, the clarification of meaning is both gradual and open-ended. On one particularly thorny point, Theophilus says:

My mind is dreaming up and bringing to birth something, I know not what, and if you command me to do so, I shall bring it before you, whatever it is, so that you will be dream-interpreters, or mid-wives. (p. 259)

This 'labour'—the deferment or mediation of a coming-into-significance—is for Erasmus undoubtedly connected with those limitations of human understanding and language which Augustine liked to emphasize. *Sensus* is never immediately perceived, never fully present; the blind philosopher gropes forward in his mediate *quaestus*, and only the (invisible) presence of Christ guarantees that his provisional interpretations are spiritually fertile.

Likewise, the objects in the garden—the statues, the herbs, the fountains, the painted surfaces—all 'speak', but for the most part indirectly. Beneath the image of St. Peter, something is seen to be written in three languages; but, for it to be seen clearly, the host has to lend his guests a magnifying glass. The sense comes closer, begins to articulate itself on the visible surface. With the aid of the glass, Timotheus is able to read or 'see' the Latin ('Latina video'). He is also able to see the Greek, but this time the seeing is empty, unreciprocated by the text, so that he is obliged to hand the glass to Theophilus, who can read Greek;[42] similarly, the third inscription, in Hebrew, has to be read out by another interlocutor. It might be said that the guests end by possessing the sense: the Latin texts are 'transparent', since Latin is the language of the colloquy, and although the Greek and Hebrew texts are not translated, they are *paraphrased* by Eusebius. Yet a residue of opacity remains. In the first place, the mottoes are not paraphrased in the order in which they are read out, so that the *sensus germanus* (assuming that Eusebius has located it correctly) is reworked contextually and to that extent at least alienated from its textual origin. Secondly, a similar set of trilingual mottoes beneath the image of Christ is neither translated nor paraphrased. And finally, for the reader of the *Convivium*—unless he himself reads Greek and Hebrew—the alien characters which he sees on the printed page cannot even be vocalized, let alone deciphered.

Elsewhere, and notably in the tour of the house and gardens, the same ambivalence is manifested. Sometimes the surface becomes transparent and reveals a hidden meaning (as with the fountain and the polluted stream); but not always. The painted gardens contain enigmas—the open-mouthed chameleon and the fig-tree, the dancing camel and the piping monkey—which are not explained: literal seeing has to suffice, and the host comments that, for the moment, it will be enough to have seen these emblems as if through a lattice ('nunc satis erit veluti per transennam vidisse') (p. 237). Such a remark recalls the Pauline notion of seeing through a glass darkly, as well as the contemporary fashion for hieroglyphs, emblems, and enigmas, which one finds in works such as the *Hypnerotomachia* and which Erasmus himself cultivated (in particular in the *Adages*). But within the thematic structure of the *Convivium religiosum*, the figure of the lattice has a special suggestiveness. For the house and the gardens constitute a place where, as the guests walk, perspectives are constantly shifting; there are

---

[42] 'I see the Greek, but it doesn't see me' (p. 233).

gateways, courtyards, gardens within gardens, galleries, layer upon layer of moving surfaces endlessly pointing towards new and unexpected significations. In the concluding section, the host refers to the opening and shutting of windows in different seasons so as to create differing views, different spaces and places. The house of dialogue has an intrinsic elusiveness which is never fully dispelled: the host interrupts the tour at lunchtime, deferring further reflection on the emblems, and, at the end, leaves the guests to enjoy the house as they will.

In this dialogue, then, the dynamics of the pursuit of sense are enacted in terms of metaphors which are at once spatial and temporal. The *transenna*, which—like Robbe-Grillet's *jalousie*—constitutes a figure for the entire fictional house, encodes visually the pattern of obscure and clear places; while the labyrinthine character of the décor, always suggesting further possibilities of exploration, provides a model for the endless differentiation of a sense which is (supposedly) grounded in a single, Christocentric principle. This *sensus*, precisely because it is conceived of as germane to the signs which carry it, slides with and across the surface of the décor, sometimes approaching, sometimes receding. In the passage on the trilingual inscriptions, indeed, it approaches and recedes simultaneously: the guests move nearer and nearer to the texts, and then to their sense, but the same movement draws them ever deeper into the opacity of the Hebrew, which is at once the closest surviving approximation to the original, pre-Babel tongue and the most alien and difficult language for the guests, symbolizing the obscurity of the Old Testament as opposed to the clarity of the New. Likewise, the emblems and paintings, while inviting the spectator to consider them as signs and thus to penetrate them in search of their meaning, also assert themselves as pure decoration; their presence entails the absence of what, eventually, they might signify. The epiphany of the *sensus germanus* is never complete; it is always trapped in the spatio-temporal movement of mediation; its passage into and through the 'mind' (i.e. the words) of Theophilus is charted as a vector of appetite closing on an ever-elusive *telos*. The house of Eusebius is an ideal place, a place of plenitude; but the unfolding of abundance reveals its necessary dependence on duplicity and deferment.[43]

The *Convivium* may thus be read as a highly sophisticated elaboration of the Augustinian model of scriptural reading. Some years later, in the *Ecclesiastes*, Erasmus suggestively (if more simply) rephrased Augustine's principle in terms of pedagogical method:

In the *De doctrina christiana*, Augustine elegantly explains (*explicat*) why God wished Scripture to be enveloped with this kind of covering (*involucris . . . opertam et involutam*) and with other obscurities. We neglect whatever is close to hand (*in promptu*) . . . We are greedier for hidden and remote things (*recondita semotaque*); and just as what is bought dearly gives more pleasure, so the things we have pursued arduously are dearer to us than those which happen of their own accord. Moreover, as many things shine forth more attractively through glass or amber, so truth also is more delightful when it shines through allegory . . . Prophetic discourse has the character of foreshadowing a thing by means of a sign (*Propheticum est prius signo rem adumbrare*) rather than narrating it openly (*quam aperte narretur*) . . . Gregory Nazianzene shows that the most convenient method for teaching divine philosophy is to avoid embarking on the central issue straight away (*si non statim aperiantur summa*), and to lead the audience by stages towards perfect knowledge (*per gradus quosdam, auditores deducantur ad perfectam cognitionem*). (Fr. V, pp. 872–3; LB 1047)

This passage, which links the notion of the arousing of appetite through difficulty with images of mediation recalling the *transenna*, initiates a heuristic movement from obscurity towards the light of perfect knowledge. As the ensuing passage makes clear, this movement is enacted by the Bible, with its transition from the 'types' and enigmas of the Old Testament to the speech of Christ, still covered with parables and ambiguities, but pointing towards an eventual recognition of Christ's divinity. But the attainment of the goal of truth, however optimistically anticipated here, is nevertheless made subject to the intervention of the Holy

[43] In order to substantiate the reference to duplicity here, it is necessary to refer again to my more detailed analysis in '*Enargeia*' of the shifting relationships enacted in the *Convivium* between appearance and reality.

Spirit: 'But all these things are perceived as in a dream, until that fiery spirit comes to dissipate the dream and to lead us to the whole truth' (p. 873). An immediate insight, supernaturally guaranteed, is thus envisaged; but its intervention is always a future possibility, and the lesson of the *Convivium* would suggest that deferment is intrinsic to human experience and human language: appetite is never quite satisfied, lest the pursuit be abandoned.[44]

This development forms part of a defence of allegory against the charge of 'uselessness', which in turn arises from Erasmus's rejection of the notion that allegory may be used to prove articles of faith. The function of allegory is different from that of a *discours du savoir*; its epistemological value is of another order, and is defined by the process sketched out above. But meanwhile, Erasmus is led by his argument to deal with a specific, and crucial, point. If allegory has no apodeictic powers, does it not point towards an unconstrained and arbitrary multiplication of biblical sense? Erasmus first appeals to the inscrutability of the divine intention in a negative counter-argument: 'if it is not certain that the Holy Spirit meant (*sensisse*) what the interpreter of the allegory

[44] Passages such as this have clear neoplatonist affinities (for example in the notion of the progressive revealing of mysteries, the 'steps to perfect knowledge', and the theme of inspiration); Erasmus is no doubt endorsing and developing the platonist elements already present in his patristic sources. A particularly clear example of such themes expressed in a secular vernacular context, and with overt reference to neoplatonist theory, is provided by Aneau's introduction to a translation of the *Metamorphoses* (1556): 'L'ame de lhomme procedée de l'infini, est aussi infinie en ces deux propres actes de volunté, et de intelligence. Tellement que par nul povoir, et avoir, tant ample soit, ne peut estre plenement acomply le desir voluntaire, qu'il ne luy reste quelque chose à plus vouloir: et par ouyr et apprendre ne peut tant parfaictement estre assouvy l'entendement qu'il ne luy vienne au devant de l'esprit plus à entendre et savoir, qu'il n'a jamais sceu, ne entendu . . . Laquelle Ame estant infinie en ces deux puissances et actes, ne se contente de la simple et nue declaration des choses: mais oultre ce a voulu y cercher aultre sens plus secret, et attaindre à plus hault entendre: ou elle cognoissoit icelluy estre abscons, et elevé: ou bien si tel n'y sembloit estre, le y a voulu adapter' (fol. a4 r°–v°). There follows a reference to *enthousiasme*, to Ovid's 'est deus in nobis', and to the covering of religious or moral truth beneath 'une fiction miraculeuse, et non vray-semblable narration de fables elegantes, et joyeuses'; the word used here for 'cover' is *adombrer* (cf. 'adumbrare' in the passage quoted from the *Ecclesiastes*).

suggests, it is nevertheless not certain that the Holy Spirit did not
mean it' (p. 872). This argument in effect rephrases Augustine's
notion of a mediated divine will or intention; but it rephrases it in
such a way as to give licence to a degree of plurality (or 'probabi-
lism') in interpretation: 'Rather, it is most probable that he did
mean it, if only what is proposed is in accord with the articles of
a healthy faith and with other scriptural places.' The plurality
becomes wholly explicit at the end of the development:

It is not absurd to believe that the Holy Ghost also desired Scripture
at times to generate various senses (*varios gignat sensus*), to suit the
disposition of each reader, just as manna tasted as each one wished it to.
Nor is this to be attributed to the uncertainty of Scripture, but rather
to its fertility (*Nec haec est scripturarum incertitudo, sed foecunditas*).[45]

The *sensus germanus*, while subject to the rule of faith and the
control of the *orbs doctrinae Christianae*, is thus revealed to be
intrinsically multiple, and its multiplicity a manifestation of the
fertility or plenitude of Scripture. This is the pregnant text which
was 'delivered' by Theophilus and his friends as by midwives; it
is also the language of the Protean Christ, endlessly transmutable
into salvific senses.[46] But Erasmus's affirmation that this fecundity
excludes uncertainty cannot arrest the essentially centrifugal
movement of the scriptural text; this is demonstrated, in what one
might think of as a direct inversion of Erasmian dialogue, by the
second part of Bonaventure Des Périers's *Cymbalum mundi*, with

[45] Loc. cit. Cf. Augustine's analysis of divine intentionality and of the relative
indeterminacy of biblical sense, *De doctrina* III. 27–8 (38–9) (see also above, note
3). This question had been raised in an exchange of letters between Erasmus and
Colet in 1499, reissued as the *Disputatio de taedio et pavore Christi* of 1504 (Fr. V,
pp. 1057–81; LB 1265–94); Erasmus asserts the multiplicity of senses inherent in
Scripture, Colet insists on its fundamental unity of sense, associating fertility
with frugality and multiplicity (abundance) with sterility.

[46] See *Ratio*, Fr. V, p. 79 (LB 94): 'While nothing is simpler than our Christ,
nevertheless, according to some mysterious purpose, he represents a kind of
Proteus in the variety of his life and teaching' (the context stresses the different
types of discourse, plain and obscure, used by Christ). Cf. Budé, *De transitu*, in
Omnia opera, I, p. 239: 'The speech of God (*sermo dei*) is truly (*proprie*) a Proteus,
transforming itself into all kinds of marvellous things.' Such images, of course,
represent ideals of fruitful discourse, guaranteed by a supernatural principle. But
Proteus (like Apollo) is a figure of elusive as well as of prophetic utterance.

its *mise en scène* of a shifty, Protean Mercury and of a group of bickering biblical scholars.[47]

Hence Erasmus's hermeneutics are subject to the same reversibility as his theories of *copia* and imitation. Indeed, the perpetual deferment of sense encourages—even constitutes—*copia*, defined as the ability of language to generate detours and deflections. Textual abundance (the extension of the surface) opens up in its turn an indefinite plurality of possible senses. The intention (will, *sententia*) which was supposed to inform the origin of a text and to guarantee the ultimate resolution of its *sensus* remains for ever suspended, or submerged, in the flow of words. ·

The same problem is represented emblematically by the prologue of *Gargantua* which, as suggested above, institutes a perpetual suspension of judgement on the allegorical question: that is to say, it presents allegory *as* a question endemic in the whole work, rather than imposing a liminary formula according to which the text may be decoded. If 'allegory' is thus parenthesized, the pursuit of sense is deprived *ab initio* of any definitive point of arrival. '*Ab initio*' is, however, hardly the appropriate expression: *Gargantua* is already the second book, in order of publication, and *Pantagruel* had already opened a comparable parenthesis.

At the beginning of *Pantagruel* 9, Pantagruel and his friends see a figure approaching; he is 'beau de stature et élégant en tous linéamens du corps, mais pitoyablement navré en divers lieux . . .'. As he comes nearer, Pantagruel himself rephrases the description:

Voyez-vous cest homme qui vient par le chemin du pont Charanton? Par ma foy, il n'est pauvre que par fortune, car je vous asseure que, à sa physionomie, Nature l'a produict de riche et noble lignée, mais

---

[47] The group includes, apparently, Erasmus himself, disguised under the pseudonym 'Drarig'. Des Périers assisted Dolet in the preparation of his *Commentarii linguae latinae* in the mid-1530s, and their anti-Erasmian dialogues could profitably be compared, although the *Cymbalum* is far more oblique—indeed enigmatic—than the *De imitatione*. The important question here is the deconstruction of one dialogue by another (see also below, pp. 138–41): for example, the décor of Des Périers's second dialogue is a dry, arid *arena* where the textual scholars hunt for fragments of a (non-existent) 'real' stone amid the specious sand—a far cry from the setting of the *Convivium religiosum*.

les adventures des gens curieulx le ont réduict en telle pénurie et
indigence.   (p. 249)

Thus, at his first appearance, Panurge presents himself as a paradigm of fallen nature, the fall being associated with, if not ascribed
to, a desire for knowledge (*curiosité*).[48] He is also marked by
poverty: his need for alms puts him in the posture of a beggar.
Rather than responding directly to this tacit *quaestus* or *quaestio*
(which, as the text makes clear, he recognizes), Pantagruel poses
a series of questions: 'Qui estes-vous? Dont venez-vous? Où
allez-vous? Que quérez-vous? Et quel est vostre nom?' Such
questions inaugurate fictions from the questioning of strangers in
Homeric epic to the ironic opening strategy of *Jacques le fataliste*.
They echo the reader's interrogation of the text, its origins, and
its *telos*: the theme of its quest ('Où allez-vous? Que quérez-
vous?'). They also initiate, in this instance, a dialogue which will
be continued throughout *Pantagruel* and, after a hiatus, provide
the structure of the later books. Immediacy of response is deferred
by their productive intervention (productive because they release
the book's chances of perpetuation), and thus by a deflection into
the language of *curiosité*.

Or better, the *curiosité* of language. For Panurge responds in
kind by unfolding a dazzling display of linguistic skills. The range
of languages is such that it has suggested to more than one
commentator the image of the Tower of Babel.[49] The resemblance is far from fortuitous. Not only is the *topos* a current one in
this period; its fundamental structure—the fall of a natural,
universal language—is already apparent in the initial descriptions
of Panurge. Given these indications, it seems to follow that
Pantagruel's phrase 'les adventures des gens curieulx' is a specific
reference to the curiosity of the people of Babel, who built the

[48] I am here assuming that Rabelais is using 'curieulx' in the sense of 'desirous
of knowledge'. As Foulet points out (' "Les adventures des gens curieulx" '), this
sense was rare in the sixteenth century, although the noun *curiosité* had long had
the sense of 'inquisitiveness', 'desire for knowledge'. But the usual sixteenth-
century sense of 'curieulx' ('careful', 'diligent') is clearly inappropriate here, and
if, as Foulet suggests, 'curieulx' is a misprint for 'curiaulx' ('courtly'), one wonders
why it was not corrected in subsequent editions. See also below, note 50.

[49] Rigolot, *Les Langages de Rabelais*, p. 36; Berry, 'Rabelais: Homo Logos'.

tower in a Promethean attempt to penetrate the secrets of heaven.[50] If this is so, then Panurge is indeed a walking Babel, and his intervention in Rabelais's first-published book, immediately after the 'optimistic' educational programme of Gargantua's letter (*Pantagruel* 8), is crucial.

The sequence of languages proffered by Panurge begins with nine modern tongues (two being invented ones), which are incomprehensible to the fictional listeners. This is the synchronic plurality of alien vernacular languages which split Babel and continues to divide nations. In losing its immediate grounding in nature, language becomes conventional and arbitrary; the gratuitousness of Panurge's variation exercise is manifest.[51] But the perspective shifts in the last four languages, which form a diachronic scheme: Panurge uses the ancient languages Hebrew, Greek, and Latin, together with another invented language ('Utopian'). We are now in the domain of the biblical and classical languages recommended in Gargantua's letter, and immediately the mood of incomprehension begins to disperse:

A quoy respondit Épistémon: 'A ceste heure ay-je bien entendu: car c'est langue Hébraïcque bien rhétoricquement pronuncée.' (p. 254)

—Quoy! dist Carpalim, lacquays de Pantagruel, c'est Grec, je l'ay entendu. Et comment? as-tu demouré en Grece? (p. 255)

Yet Panurge's speeches are not translated, and the reiterated verb *entendre* remains ambiguous: it might mean 'I hear', that is to say 'I recognize that this is Hebrew, Greek, etc.', or 'I understand'. Erasmus had played on the precisely similar ambiguity of *video* in the *Convivium*. This uncertainty becomes critical in Pantagruel's reference to Utopian, which breaks the sequence of the three ancient languages:

—J'entends, se me semble (dist Pantagruel), car ou c'est langaige

---

[50] Commentators have generally taken this phrase to mean 'the adventures that befall inquisitive people', thus turning it into a moral comment on the character of Panurge. Panurge is, no doubt, to be included among the 'gens curieulx', but he is also their archetype. *Curiositas* is the mark of original sin (see Blaise for examples of its pejorative connotations).

[51] Pantagruel will allude specifically to the conventional nature of language in *TL* 19, p. 438.

de mon pays de Utopie, ou bien luy ressemble quant au son. (loc. cit.)

Presumably, the language of Utopia might be a privileged one, not too far removed from the original prelapsarian language of nature. If so, Panurge's Utopian seems to be not immediately comprehensible to Pantagruel, who hears or recognizes only its sound, its audible surface. The listeners, the pursuers of sense, are here tantalizingly close to a linguistic origin, but it still eludes them.

The character of the whole development is by now apparent. As in the *Convivium*, the sense begins to approach the surface in the consecrated languages of antiquity, although in the reverse order: the movement now is towards the present. The emphasis, here too, is on the dynamic aspect of this process as much as on its product: in the case of the Utopian speech, language has become nearly transparent, but not quite.[52] It is followed by Latin, which presumably all of Pantagruel's companions and most of Rabelais's readers can understand. No one even bothers to say 'J'entends': the character of the language and what it signifies are presumably self-evident. But there is still no translation, and the use of Latin rather than French still appears as a deflection or deferment,[53] since Pantagruel at this point finally asks Panurge if he cannot speak French:

—Si faictz très bien, Seigneur, respondit le compaignon, Dieu mercy. C'est ma langue naturelle et maternelle, car je suis né et ay esté nourry jeune au jardin de France: c'est Touraine.

The tension is at last broken, communication is restored, as Panurge returns to a 'natural' language, to his own linguistic property, from his alien places of exile. The vernacular of the

---

[52] Paradoxically, the near-transparency of the speech for Pantagruel is accompanied by its almost total impenetrability for the reader—'almost', since a sense can be reconstructed (this being a variation exercise) by reference to the speeches in known languages; see Pons, 'Les "jargons" de Panurge', on the decoding of Rabelais's invented languages.

[53] The Latin speech *interrupts* Pantagruel's nascent gloss on the Utopian speech: 'Et, comme il vouloit commencer quelque propos, le compaignon dist . . .'. On interruption as a structural principle of the *QL*, see below, pp. 206 ff.

speaker, although not natural like the pre-Babel language, is grounded in his own nature, as Du Bellay's imitation theory also implies. Thus the text of Rabelais opposes an arbitrary plurality to a quasi-natural mode of exchange and communication.

At this point, it is necessary to take into account the fact that the 'message' of the speeches—a broadly evangelical injunction to replace curiosity by charity—may be decoded by a reader who knows some or all of the languages of Panurge. Thus the episode operates on two converging levels, the moral and the linguistic. The message was, in a sense, apparent to Pantagruel from the outset, since he recognized at once that Panurge needed 'charity'. But instead of acting according to this ethic of immediacy, he allowed himself to be deflected into language. In other words, his initial insight is neglected or deferred. Panurge uses language and its inherent characteristic of deferment in order to instruct Pantagruel that the linguistic excursion should not have been necessary at all. The inaugural dialogue between Pantagruel and Panurge is a self-erasing one, a colourful proliferation of linguistic surface as (almost) pure excess; its function is to make evident what had been merely, and fruitlessly, obvious.[54]

In the *Tiers* and *Quart Livre*, the same structure emerges; but now the Pantagruel–Panurge relationship is reversed. Panurge's question about marriage is answered from the outset, yet he persists in questioning the oracles, the representatives of the Faculties, the fool, and so on, in the pursuit of an answer. They reply in their technical languages or codes, each embodying the same message which, just like Panurge's own speeches in *Pantagruel* 9, sends the interrogator back to his point of departure. Only in this instance Panurge incessantly refuses the insight which Pantagruel had tacitly accepted, so that the quest and the questions

---

[54] This theme is particularly clear in Panurge's Greek speech: 'All lovers of learning (*philologi*) are agreed, however, that speeches and words are superfluous when the facts are clear to all. Speeches are only necessary when the facts under discussion are not wholly evident (*epiphenete*)'. There is an irony here in the juxtaposition of 'philologi' (literally 'lovers of words') with the theme of the superfluous character of language (Panurge plays on the word *logos*). In such situations, the evidence of language supplements and thus displaces the evidence of the phenomenal world.

continue indefinitely. One might add that the repetition of this situation is also a repetition of the question of allegory or interpretation, since in every instance the 'language', when interrogated, reveals a double aspect and thus undermines the possibility of a stabilization of sense.

Towards the end of the *Quart Livre*, the fiction refracts these problems in a particularly elaborate and striking way. The episode of the 'parolles dégelées' (*QL* 55–6) enacts once more the self-presentation of language:

[Pantagruel] nous dist: 'Compaignons, oyez-vous rien? Me semble que je oy quelques gens parlans en l'air, je n'y voy toutesfoys personne. Escoutez!' A son commandement nous feusmes attentifz, et à pleines aureilles humions l'air comme belles huytres en escalle pour entendre si voix ou son aulcun y seroit espart . . . Ce néantmoins protestions voix quelconques n'entendre.

Pantagruel continuoit affermant ouyr voix diverses en l'air tant de homes comme de femmes, quand nous feut advis, ou que nous les oyons pareillement, ou que les aureilles nous cornoient. Plus persévérions escoutans, plus discernions les voix, jusques à entendre motz entiers.   (p. 729)

The figures here are aural rather than visual, but the gradual movement towards the surface is none the less directly comparable to that in the *Convivium* and in *Pantagruel* 9. It subsequently reappears in two *topoi* cited by Pantagruel. The first is derived from Plutarch's famous essay on the cessation of oracles, and points to an ideal realm, 'le manoir de Vérité', which is inhabited by 'les Parolles, les Idées, les Exemplaires et protraictz de toutes choses passées et futures' (p. 730). From this realm, which is marked by the absence of any present time, words occasionally fall to earth; these, one might say, achieve a dubious presence as sensible phenomena. The remainder is 'réservée pour l'advenir, jusques à la consommation du Siècle': their deferment is thus only resolved by the ultimate transcendent *telos*.

The second *topos* evokes the death and dismemberment of Orpheus:

Nous serions bien esbahiz si c'estoient les teste et lyre de Orpheus. Car, après que les femmes Thréisses eurent Orpheus mis en pièces, elles jectèrent sa teste et sa lyre dedans le fleuve Hebrus; icelles par ce fleuve descendirent en la mer Pontiq, jusques en l'isle de Lesbos tousjours ensemble sus mer naigeantes. Et de la teste continuellement sortoyt un chant lugubre, comme lamentant la mort de Orpheus; la lyre, à l'impulsion des vents mouvens les chordes, accordoit harmonieusement avecques le chant. Reguardons si les voirons cy autour. (p. 731)

These parallel *topoi* are clearly figures of the fall of language from an ideal origin. The movement into the realm of human experience is a movement into imperfection, fragmentation, even gratuitousness as figured by the random blowing of the wind which animates the lyre.[55] Thus it is not surprising to find that, subsequently, Panurge wants to *see* the sounds or voices:

Mais en pourrions-nous veoir quelqu'une? Me soubvient avoir leu que, l'orée de la montaigne en laquelle Moses receut la loy des Juifz, le peuple voyoit les voix sensiblement.[56]

Pantagruel, like Moses, is far closer to the metaphysical origin of language; Panurge is concerned only with its sensible surface.[57] But of course this is precisely the situation which makes the dynamics of language problematic. The epiphany of sense in the

[55] On wind imagery, see below, pp. 146–7 and 212 ff.; on the *topos* concerning Homeric language, cited by Pantagruel together with the Orpheus story, see p. 144, note 24.

[56] In connection with the visualization of language, cf. the recurrent references to *bezicles* or *lunettes* in association with seeing the truth, or seeing the reader, at the beginning of the prologues of both the *TL* and the *QL* (cf. Gray, *Rabelais et l'écriture*, pp. 32 ff.), and in *Gargantua* 1, where the author is summoned to read the giants' genealogy 'à grand renfort de bezicles, practicant l'art dont on peut lire lettres non apparentes' (p. 43); at the end of this genealogy is the 'petit traicté intitulé: *les Fanfreluches antidotées*', a corrupt and obscure text. Thus, from an early stage in Rabelais's fiction, the theme of decipherment or interpretation is related to a visual image of 'bringing the sense nearer'. Cf. also *TL* 15 ('I can see you, but I can't hear you'), and the Socratic 'Speak, so that I may see you', quoted by Erasmus (see above, p. 48, note 16).

[57] The opposition may also be phrased as that between the spirit of the Law (as received by Moses by direct inspiration) and the letter of the Law, as understood by the Jews, an opposition elaborated in St. Paul's distinction between flesh and spirit and exploited by the Church Fathers and Erasmus. See Jeanneret, 'Les paroles dégelées', where these themes are probed in depth and the 'paroles gelées' chapters related to surrounding episodes.

visible or audible text is both a movement towards understanding and a deviation from 'la parole pure' (whether conceived of as a truth existing prior to language, or as a prelapsarian language coterminous with truth). Pantagruel can, after all, only exhibit his superiority by citing learned glosses, which ironically defer the crystallization (or rather 'thawing out') in the text of the colours and sounds of language.

Panurge's quest remains flamboyantly unresolved at the indeterminate end of the *Quart Livre*. Some might say, however, that the resolution occurs at the end of the *Cinquième Livre*, and that the consonance of this conclusion with the thematic structure of the earlier books is an indication of its authenticity.[58] The link in such a hypothesis between the desire for full closure and the nostalgia for authenticity and legitimacy might, however, suggest the need for caution. An analysis of thematic structures can never reconstitute the identity of an author whose supposed unity of intention would then explain the coherence of the work. Conversely—and more pertinently—the discovery of a manuscript of the complete Fifth Book signed 'François Rabelais' would not allow one to assume that this book is anything more than the supplement it appears to be; that some system of thought (platonic-hermetic or other) is triumphantly brought to a conclusion in Panurge's consultation of the *dive bouteille*; or that this conclusion stabilizes the sense of the preceding books. The very doubts which surround the authenticity of the *Cinquième Livre* indicate that discontinuity and plurality are endemic in Rabelais's work, and cannot be erased by the fiction of a conclusion.

The point may be demonstrated more specifically by a brief analysis of the 'final' chapters. Panurge is looking for a word, the 'mot de la dive bouteille'. Prompted by the priestess Bacbuc, he sings a ritual chant to induce the bottle to proffer it:

> O Bouteille
> Pleine toute

---

[58] This is the central hypothesis of Mallary Masters, *Rabelaisian Dialectic*, endorsed by F. Weinberg, *The Wine and the Will*, chapter 3. Arguments for the non-authentic character of the Fifth Book are developed in Glauser, *Le Faux Rabelais*.

De mistères,
D'une aureille
Je t'escoute:
Ne diffères,
Et le mot profères
Auquel pend mon cœur.
(CL 44, p. 906)

The theme of deferment becomes explicit in the refrain, which is repeated at the end, so that 'Ne diffères' is the last phrase. Panurge, who is a past master of the art of deferment, is at last within reach of his *telos*: the full presence to his consciousness of the word and its sense. The bottle speaks: the word 'Trinch' is heard. But this moment passes without immediate understanding. Panurge thinks the sound was that of the bottle cracking, a simple aural pheno-menon without depth (except perhaps for the possibility of a disaster glimpsed in the *fracturing* of the sacred vessel). Bacbuc must now lead him on to yet another stage, that of the *glose*. This is physically swallowed by Panurge in the form of wine, so that the sense which is added to the word has the maximum degree of immediacy. But this is still not the 'word', but a gloss: a supplement. And although Panurge is predictably delighted with it, he is quite clearly not filled with immediate certainty:

'Voicy', dist Panurge, 'un notable chapitre, et glose fort autentique: est-ce tout ce que vouloit prétendre·le mot de la Bouteille trimégiste? J'en suis bien, vrayement.'   (CL 45, p. 908)

He is still asking questions, and his affirmation of authenticity has an inescapable, and singularly appropriate, tone of irony. The over-filling (supplementation) of this liquid gloss will soon be-come apparent in his dithyrambic recitation. Meanwhile, Bacbuc provides a learned gloss on the ultimate *glose* on the would-be transcendent *mot* (as Montaigne will say, 'Nous ne faisons que nous entregloser'). She speaks of the universal currency of the word 'Trinch', comparing it to 'sac', and thus evoking the image of Babel: when the people of Babel were dispersed, each took with him his own bag, so that this word echoes the original, universal language.[59] She also associates 'sac' with poverty ('tous humains naissent un sac au col, souffreteux par nature et mandians l'un de l'autre'). Despite the supernatural aura of the scene, the fall and the consequent beginning of quest and questions are still very much in the centre of the stage. Moreover, the retrospective (or retrogressive) movement of these remarks is paralleled by Bacbuc's final referral of Panurge back to his own insight: 'soyez vous mesmes interprètes de vostre entreprinse.' And Pantagruel echoes her: 'Autant vous en di-je, lors que première-ment m'en parlastes' (p. 909). During the quest, the 'sense' is always ahead; at the end, it is discovered to have been at the beginning, in the past. There is no moment of presence, when the desire for sense is fully satisfied; either the question, which is the sign of desire (*curiosité*), is never posed, or its answer is subject to endless deferment.

This dilemma is profoundly connected with the ineradicable gap between the word and its sense, 'Trinch' and the gloss (and *its* glosses, *ad infinitum*). If the sense is not immediately present in the word, its authenticity is diminished; more words become necessary in order to establish the sense, but then of course a principle of infinite regression (supplementation, excess) has been established. The sense is simply *more words*, not some hidden essence. One could argue that Bacbuc and Pantagruel transcend this problem by referring to an insight which bypasses (or precedes) language. It may indeed be that Panurge, and the reader, have learnt something by this time. But the lesson can only be made evident by the mediation of language, whether that of dithyrambic poetry or of critical commentary. Panurge, true to his initial characterization (and here it does not matter whether or not he is the Panurge of some surrogate author),[60] remains within

---

[59] I owe this gloss to Professor Demerson's edition of the text, pp. 908–9, note 10.

[60] I am willing to concede that the foregoing analysis, by integrating the end of the *CL* with the themes and episodes of earlier books, reveals—no less than the hypotheses of Masters or Weinberg—a desire for total interpretation. It is, indeed, much easier to 'totalize' texts than to conceive of them as inherently discontinuous, particularly where there is continuity of narrative structure. On the other hand, I have not ascribed this unity to the intention of an author who set out to write a neoplatonist allegory; I have tried to stress the ways in which

the limits of language and thus of the deferment problem, carrying both reader and writer irresistibly with him.

In the opening stages of the dialogue of Cicero's *De oratore*, Crassus sketches out the means of acquiring eloquence. His treatment is so compressed that his interlocutors feel the need for further elaboration. As Cotta says:

so great was the speed of his words, and so swiftly winged his discourse that, while realizing its rushing energy, I could hardly follow the traces of its advance; and just as though I had entered some richly stored mansion (*aliquam locupletem ac refertam domum*), wherein the draperies were not unrolled (*non explicata veste*), nor the plate set forth, nor the pictures and statuary displayed to view, but all these many and splendid things were piled together and hidden away: even so just now, during this discourse of Crassus, I discerned the wealth and magnificence of his mind (*divitias atque ornamenta eius ingenii*) as through some wrappings and coverings (*per quaedam involucra et integumenta*), but though I was longing to scrutinize them, I had hardly the chance of a peep. And so I cannot say either that I know nothing at all of the extent of his possessions, or that I know and have seen them clearly.[61]

The dialogue takes place in the garden of Crassus's country house at Tusculum, explicitly echoing the setting of the *Phaedrus* (*De or.* I. vii. 24–9). Thus Cotta's speech evokes a figure germane to the fictional décor; Crassus's concise eloquence is mirrored in a place of abundance. Or rather, of potential abundance, since the speakers find themselves suspended between an initial awakening

the text parodies a fictional and philosophical *telos* while enacting it (so that the integration is seen as negative and ironical, rather than positive and 'serious'); and, above all, by deflecting the problem of the gloss into my own analysis, I have pointed to the *post hoc* nature of all interpretative projects (the meaning they discover is always added at the end—or in a footnote—rather than located at the beginning of the text or beneath its surface).

[61] I. xxxv. 161. Among the various metaphors of this passage, one might note the notion of a 'winged' discourse (the Latin has the verb 'evolavit'), which recalls the Homeric *topos* of 'winged words', and perhaps the Aristotelian passage which links the 'animated' character of Homer's language with the concept of *energeia* (echoed in the Latin 'vim') (see above, p. 28, note 39). The kinetic character of eloquent discourse is thus presented here as both provoking the desire for sense and preventing its realization, which requires a second process, a reiteration.

of appetite and the full exposition of their topic. Scaevola takes up the image:

Why not do then ... as you would do, if you had come to some mansion or country house that was full of objects of art (*ornamentorum*)? If these were laid aside, as you describe, and you had a strong desire to behold them, you would not hesitate to ask the master of the house to order them to be brought out (*proferri*), especially if you were his familiar friend. So too now will you beg Crassus to bring out into the daylight the abundance of his treasures (*copiam ornamentorum suorum*), of which, piled together in one place, we in passing have caught a glimpse, as through a lattice (*quasi per transennam praetereuntes strictim aspeximus*), and also to set up every piece in its proper position? (I. xxxv. 162)

A theory of eloquence, then, is implied in the folds of an eloquent speaker's discourse; its unfolding, the resolution of the 'lattice' figure, brings into operation the movement from *copia* as *brevitas* (compression, ellipsis) to *copia* as expansion or explication.

There is nothing problematic here: Crassus will merely have to supplement his previous remarks, repeat them in such a way that the first 'glimpse' becomes plain evidence. When Erasmus echoes this passage at the beginning of Book II of the *De copia*, he remains broadly within the same context, except that now the lattice becomes a quasi-theoretical figure, associated with the *prima ratio locupletandi*:

Having said as briefly as possible what came to mind on *copia* of words, it remains for us to touch on (*perstringamus*) *copia* of 'things' with similar concision. Let us begin this part of the work with topics as closely related as possible to those treated above. Thus the first method of enriching one's thought (*sententiae*) is to be observed where something which could be said summarily and in general is more extensively unfolded (*latius explicetur*) and separated into parts. This is just as if someone first shows his wares through a lattice or a rolled-up cover (*per transennam aut peristromata convoluta*), and then unrolls (*evolvat*), opens up, and exposes the same things wholly to the gaze. (Fr. I, p. 63; LB 75)

By means of a characteristically Erasmian manœuvre, the figure, and the first method itself, are brought into contact with the method and structure of the *De copia*: the treatise is a compressed account, which the reader may unfold for himself; and the relationship between compression and extension is seen to be common to both parts of the work, since this book begins with topics germane to the first book. One might add that the first example that Erasmus provides is 'He lost everything through loose living' ('rem universam luxu perdidit'), a moral paradigm which, when expanded, becomes a narrative of prodigality; and that the second example, 'He completed his general education' ('cyclopaediam absolvit') evokes the universe of knowledge compressed microcosmically in the 'circle' of the disciplines. Such examples do not simply illustrate a device: they bring into play, through the lattices of a concise theoretical formulation, the dynamics of plenitude or prodigality in domains beyond the rhetorical.[62]

In the *Convivium religiosum*, as indicated earlier, the 'lattice' is re-sited in the context of hermeneutics. The décor of the country house and its gardens is re-evoked in order to reflect the problematic nature of figures and what they hide; abundance is a consequence of the epiphany of *sensus*, but only where the lattice is never wholly removed, explicitation never fully accomplished. The juxtaposition of these texts (and indeed the ways in which they operate *as* texts, with their figurative convolutions) will indicate the extent to which the laws governing *copia* as deployment of discourse are deeply linked to the problems of the pursuit of sense. The itinerary of the *transenna* figure encapsulates the movement from Erasmus's performative theory of writing in the *De copia* through the *Adages*—which manifest central aspects of that theory in terms of half-revealed figures or enigmas—to the interpretation theory of the 1520s. The rhetorical model which makes *brevitas* and *copia* mutually dependent is directly comparable, even interchangeable, with the hermeneutic model which links obscure places to clear places, allegories and enigmas to paraphrastic explication. At the same time, this equivalence undermines the fundamental presupposition governing the desire for full

---

62 The third example is 'A man endowed with all the gifts of nature and of fortune' ('Omnibus naturae fortunaeque dotibus praeditus'), another microcosmic figure of a totality waiting to be unfolded.

possession of meaning: namely, that linguistic (or other) signs are a 'surface' hiding a recoverable 'content', that *res* are really there beyond the lattice of *verba*. The *involucra* and *integumenta* of Crassus's mind are hardly enigmatic figures of a real presence; they will be dissipated by another, more extensive discourse. Significance, pregnancy of meaning (as they occur, for example, in Erasmus's adages and enigmas) may be defined reductively, not as a bonding of *verba* and *res*, nor as a relationship between an outside and an inside, but as the power of a given instance of discourse to generate further discourse. The reassuring antithesis of form and content is a false one, since both are articulated in the same medium; the implicit and the explicit are two modes of discourse, the second of which may turn out to be disquietingly similar to the first since 'something' will always remain caught in the folds. In consequence, interpretation (explication or explicitation) is a regressive movement; one gloss follows another, one figure invites another, according to a law of supplementation which undoes any possibility of full presence. Once again, the exiled *sensus* is seen to shift with the surface, pointing endlessly towards some absent *proprietas*, and thus inviting the game of language to continue.

4

Improvisation and Inspiration

ERASMUS's allusion to Proteus as a figure for copious discourse leads directly to the theme of extempore fluency, whether in speech or in writing.[1] Such passages make evident once again the extent to which *copia* is a term that eludes the constraints of precept, and is indeed hardly reducible to theoretical formulation. The margin by which utterance exceeds the planned articulation of a *sententia* is, by its very nature, unquantifiable; 'improvisation' is literally a leap into the unforeseen. Nevertheless, certain areas of rhetorical theory are concerned with the location and preparation of this moment in which discourse reaches self-mastery. Studies of sixteenth-century poetics have been inclined to emphasize the theory of inspiration, partly because it is so prominent in France, partly because its neoplatonist provenance allows it to be reconstructed without much difficulty as a *topos*.[2] This chapter will attempt to shift the perspective somewhat by first drawing attention to discussions of improvised or—to evoke its fundamentally temporal character—extempore discourse itself; by indicating the ways in which the notions of improvisation and inspiration mirror one another (thus denouncing another duplicity); and by suggesting that the whole question of the use of language, reading, speaking, and writing, turns on this evasive centre. Some of the most deeply rooted conceptual structures of Western thought are inevitably brought into play here; as in preceding chapters, the object will be not to restate them in all their complexity, but

---

[1] See above, p. 23. The passage continues as follows: 'This exercise will also contribute greatly to the capacity (*facultatem*) for speaking or writing extempore, and will ensure that we do not either become confused and hesitate, or fall into embarrassing silences.'

[2] See Lefranc, *Grands Écrivains*, pp. 63–137; Castor, *Pléiade Poetics*, chapters 3–4; Levi, 'The neoplatonist calculus'.

to point towards them through the lattice of specific textual examples.

The theory of improvisation is transmitted from classical to Renaissance rhetoric as a *locus* in Quintilian's tenth book; Cicero occasionally speaks of extempore composition,[3] but does not develop the topic theoretically. It falls broadly within the domain of *hexis*, rendered by Quintilian as 'firma facilitas' (X. i. 1), although its stricter Latin equivalent might be *habitus*. Arising from a root meaning 'to have', it indicates a capacity which has been appropriated, is fully possessed; thus the common renderings 'disposition' or 'habit' somewhat limit its semantic field, which is enriched and made more active by a sense of 'mastery'. This concept is the topic of *Institutiones* X, and is thus inseparably linked with *copia*: the amassing of a treasure (reading, imitation, lexical accumulation, and the modes of figurative transformation) is considered throughout in the perspective of its eventual expenditure, that is to say, of mastery, the exercise of rhetorical power.[4] The notion of 'having ready for production', 'having at one's fingertips' (*in promptu habere*) is present from the outset in the negative image of the miser hoarding his treasure,[5] but it is at the end of X. vi that the theme of improvisation begins to impose itself explicitly, appearing as the climax of the tenth book as a whole in X. vii.

Its emergence characteristically disrupts and restricts a discussion of *cogitatio* or 'premeditation'; the indispensable ability of the orator to plan his discourse in advance must not be allowed to

---

[3] *De orat.* I. xxxiii. 149–53; also ibid. III. l. 194, and *Pro Archia poeta* viii. 18. In the two latter cases, the reference is primarily to improvisation in verse, while in the *Pro Archia*, improvisation is further seen as being akin to inspiration.

[4] Cf. XII. x. 78: 'our orator, brilliant, sublime and opulent (*locuples*) of speech, is lord and master of all the resources of eloquence, whose affluence surrounds him (*circumfluentibus undique eloquentiae copiis imperat*).'

[5] X. i. 2; the phrase used here is 'in procinctu', but 'in promptu' occurs in X. i. 6 together with the visual metaphor 'in conspectu': indeed, Quintilian stresses the metaphorical register by inserting an 'ut ita dicam'. Erasmus uses 'in promptu' in the 'Proteus' passage referred to above. The figures of expenditure relate improvisation to the ambivalent theme of prodigality or 'improvidence' alluded to above, I. 3; they will recur below in II. 2 and 3.

obstruct the unlimited possibilities of the moment; it must not eliminate chance:

If, however, some brilliant improvisation (*extemporalis color*) should occur to us (*effulserit*) while speaking, we must not cling superstitiously to our premeditated scheme (*cogitatis*). For premeditation is not so accurate as to leave no room for happy inspiration (*ut non sit dandus et fortunae locus*) . . . For, although it is essential to bring with us into court a supply of eloquence which has been prepared in advance. (*paratam dicendi copiam*) and on which we can confidently rely, there is no greater folly than the rejection of the gifts of the moment (*temporis munera*). (X. vi. 5–6)

Although according to this account extemporization is a special instance of performance, occurring 'inter dicendum', it is clearly also the paradigm of performance, the moment when discourse asserts its freedom to exercise intrinsic powers. Not only does this moment appear in Quintilian's theory as the goal or fruition of all conscious preparation (X. vii. i); it also presupposes (as does the distinction between true and false imitation) the authenticity of a hidden nature.[6] All this theory depends, indeed, on the art–nature antithesis as an opposition between reflection and intuition, or between the rational and the irrational; impromptu speech is a transgression presided over by *fortuna*. Likewise, Erasmus's Folly, from the beginning of her demonstrative exercise, will repeatedly reject rhetorical planning in favour of extempore speech; immediacy, in her view, is a sign of nature and consequently a guarantee of authenticity.[7] A related though contextually different example occurs in the *Ciceronianus*: Bulephorus quotes the passage from Lucian's *True History* where Homer, asked by the narrator to solve the problem (debated by innumerable scholars) of why he chose *menin* as the first word of the *Iliad*, replies 'it just happened to occur to me at that moment (*tum forte venit in mentem*)' (Am. I–2, p. 627). This inaugural accident blocks any attempt at formal

---

[6] X. ii. 11–12; cf. also II. xx. 6.

[7] 'From me you're going to hear a speech which is extempore and quite unprepared, but all the more genuine for that' (Fr. IV, p. 354; LB 407). Cf. ibid., pp. 361, 374 (LB 423, 459–60).

imitation or analysis; the master-epic originates in a strictly non-measurable event.

Hence the aleatory character of improvisation marks a detour in the predictable paths of both theory and practice. From this point of view, the extempore moment is always, by definition, 'ahead'; displacing the moment of *cogitatio*, it constitutes an elusive present as the place, or time, of licence. At a central point in his discussion, Quintilian sketches out some of the temporal convolutions which arise from any attempt to locate this event:

> For although we need to possess a certain natural nimbleness of mind (*naturali quadam mobilitate animi*) to enable us, while we are saying what the instant demands (*dum proxima dicimus*), to build up what is to follow (*struere ulteriora*) and to secure that there will always be some thought formed and conceived in advance (*provisa et formata cogitatio*) ready to serve our voice (*vocem*), none the less, it is scarcely possible either for natural gifts or for methodic art (*aut natura aut ratio*) to enable the mind to grapple simultaneously with such manifold duties . . . For our mental activities must range far ahead (*Longe enim praecedat oportet intentio*) and pursue the ideas which are still in front (*prae se res agat*), and in proportion as the speaker pays out what he has in hand, he must make advances to himself from his reserve funds (*quantumque dicendo consumitur, tantum ex ultimo prorogetur*), in order that, until we reach our conclusion, our mind's eye may urge its gaze forward, keeping time with our advance; otherwise we shall halt and stumble, and pour forth short and broken phrases, like persons who can only gasp out what they have to say. (X. vii. 8–10)

What appeared earlier as plenitude, the fruition of discourse in a privileged present, now reveals itself as duality or even as emptiness; the instant of speech ('dum proxima dicimus') is separated from the presence of mind. It is *cogitatio* which moves ahead, supplying 'ulteriora', 'provisa', and 'formata' to an unthinking voice; neither *natura* nor *ratio* can wholly master this multiplicity of the speech-act and restore it to unity. A movement of *intentio* points ahead of *verba* towards the fleeing shadow of *res*, while saying is represented as the improvident dissipation of some future (or past?) store. The place of utterance (the *locus* given to *fortuna*) is a kind of leak, a principle of *écoulement*.

The automatism which is implicit in this account emerges in Quintilian's subsequent reference to 'a certain mechanical knack (*usus quidem irrationalis*)'

which the Greeks call *alogos tribe,* which enables the hand to go on scribbling, while the eye takes in whole lines at once as it reads, observes the intonations and the stops, and sees what is coming before the reader has articulated to himself what precedes (*ante sequentia vident quam priora dixerunt*).   (X. vii. 11)

The Greek word which is rendered as 'usus' has a range of meanings which include 'wearing down' (rather as in the French verb *user*) and 'spending': it is 'habit' seen as a kind of erosion, the obverse face of *hexis* (hence no doubt the translator's choice of the slightly pejorative 'knack').[8] The facility which is here exercised by virtue of the absence of *logos* is clearly an empty one. It is no doubt crucial that this 'knack' is defined in terms of writing rather than speaking: the movement of the hand is voiceless and thus, in a sense, 'wordless', *logos* assuming its other sense. This invasion of *viva voce* improvisation by writing will be considered again shortly; for the present, one may note that the perilous freedom of the alienated voice provokes first a caution from Quintilian, who attempts to ground the non-rational in reason and distinguish between pernicious 'random talk' and truly copious discourse;[9]

[8] Cf. X. vii. 8: 'For facility is mainly the result of habit (*consuetudo*) and exercise'; and X. vii. 18: 'we must develop improvisation (*facilitatem . . . extemporalem*) by gradual stages from small beginnings, until we have reached that perfection (*summam*) which can only be produced and maintained by practice (*usu*).' But is the facility thus achieved a supreme skill or a knack, a facile habit? One might add here that *tribe* has the further sense of 'delay' or 'evasion', as if the production of language were a continuous deferment of presence.

[9] 'But this knack (*usus*) will only be of real service if it be preceded by the art of which we have spoken [in vii. 5–7], so that what is irrational in itself will nevertheless be founded on reason (*ut ipsum illud, quod in se rationem non habet, in ratione versetur*). For unless a man speaks in an orderly, ornate, and fluent manner (*disposite, ornate, copiose*), I refuse to dignify his utterance with the name of speech, but consider it the merest rant. Nor again shall I ever be induced to admire a continuous flow of random talk (*fortuiti sermonis contextum*), such as I note streams in torrents even from the lips of women when they quarrel . . .' (X. vii. 12–13). Cf. X. iii. 2: 'For without the consciousness of such preliminary study our powers of speaking extempore will give us nothing but an empty flow of words, springing only from the lips (*inanem modo loquacitatem dabit et verba in labris nascentia*).'

but this is followed by a further concessive reversal, giving licence once again to an extemporization released from the constraints of preparation.[10] The ghosts of past and future *cogitatio*, which were supposed to fill the empty word-machine, must be kept in abeyance if the machine is to work properly. Language, in such a view, must always in some sense evade the speaker, be alienated from him, as it pursues and displaces its own moment of presence. The unlocking of the miser's hoard, the release of *copia*, is enacted ideally in a non-place whence the stream of language flows away unchecked.

The spatial analogies by means of which temporal aspects of discourse have been represented in the above analysis, as well as in Quintilian's, exhibit their character at certain moments by taking on a sensible colouring. The movement towards presence ('praesentem fortunam' in X. vii. 32) is also a movement into the field of vision. Quintilian insists that words must be not only known but held, as it were, in full view ('in conspectu', X. i. 6). The power (*vis, facultas*) of improvisation depends on keeping the images of things (*rerum imagines, phantasiai*) clearly before our eyes (*in oculis*) (X. vii. 15). Thus it is not surprising that the chance extempore event shines out as 'colour' in the midst of discourse (see above, quotation on p. 127): *copia* erupts like a magic firework display, or a theatrical *mise en scène*. At such moments, the *energeia* of speech becomes visible as a mode of *enargeia*. For if *evidentia-enargeia* is not an explicit topic of this part of the *Institutiones*, it may nevertheless be invoked here as the figure of immediate presentation, bringing to life the coloured images of things in the instant of discourse. *Enargeia* and improvisation converge in Quintilian's rhetoric of presence.

It is no accident that the tenth book ends by pointing towards the treatment of memory in Book XI. The movement by which

[10] 'although, if a speaker is swept away by warmth of feeling and genuine inspiration (*si calor ac spiritus tulit*), it frequently happens that he attains a success from improvisation which would have been beyond the reach of the most careful preparation (*cura*)' (vii. 13). This reversal leads directly to the discussion of inspiration quoted below, pp. 141–2, and thence to the central passage on *phantasiai*, *pectus*, and *vis mentis* (vii. 15). Thus the evidence of spontaneous discourse gains priority, in Quintilian's theory, over rational judgement.

cogitatio appears to 'go ahead' of speech turns out, as the earlier discussion implied, to be dependent on the power of memory as a transmitting agent between the thought-forming process (*inventio*) and enunciation (*elocutio*, as the sensible surface of speech) (XI. ii. 3). Thus improvisation, which might have seemed the antithesis of memory, is in fact dependent on its hidden activity ('extemporalis oratio non alio mihi videtur mentis vigore constare'). Memory perpetually constitutes and reconstitutes the store ('copias') or treasure-house ('thesaurus') which speech dissipates; it presents ('praesentat') the abundance of materials which the orator must always have 'in promptu' (XI. ii. 1). Its unfathomable and unpredictable powers of representation or repetition are invoked by Quintilian in a strictly rhetorical movement, which culminates in the claim that the flowering of oratory, its present lustre, is due to the quasi-supernatural power of memory, which in turn is made manifest by the *vis orandi*:

Again, is it not an extraordinary inconsistency that we forget recent and remember distant events, that we cannot recall what happened yesterday and yet retain a vivid impression of the acts of our childhood? And what, again, shall we say of the fact that the things we search for frequently refuse to present themselves and then occur to us by chance, or that memory does not always remain with us, but will even sometimes return to us after it has been lost? But we should never have realised the fullness of its power nor its supernatural capacities, but for the fact that it is memory which has brought oratory to its present position of glory (*Nesciretur tamen, quanta vis esset eius, quanta divinitas illa, nisi in hoc lumen vim orandi extulisset*).   (XI. ii. 6–7)

Oratory and memory thus appear as interdependent, as the twin light and dark—external and internal—faces of a single power. Speech is the visible surface; it is, as it were, the stage on which the characters and properties of memory are brought to life. In consequence, Quintilian's ensuing treatment of the art of memory clarifies and confirms the convergence of improvisation and *evidentia* suggested above.[11] This art depends at once on vivid visualization and on symbolic transference: 'things' are

[11] See Yates, *The Art of Memory*, on the transmission of this 'art' from classical to modern times.

represented and recalled by their verbal 'images'. Although Quintilian has reservations with regard to the value of this system, he retains its central components of visualization and symbolism in his own advice on how to learn a speech by heart (XI. ii. 17–31). It is at this point also that the complicity of memory with extempore *oratio* is taken to its logical conclusion: a perfectly memorized speech may be delivered as if it were improvised (XI. ii. 39, 45–6), no doubt because memorization, like extemporization, makes utterance an *alogos tribe*, an alienation from full presence. The situation of the orator is similar to that of the actor, even if he does not always memorize his speeches in the strict sense. In Quintilian's theory, the erosion of the difference between natural and artificial improvisation is but one consequence of the overwhelming movement of rhetoric towards the surface, and more specifically towards an audience. Thus he cites as an example of the 'mechanical knack' the way in which jugglers and conjurers conceal from the spectator the mechanics of their art; he speaks of the presence of an audience as a powerful stimulus to improvisation, since the orator will wish to display his talents and gain the reward ('praemium') they deserve (X. vii. 16–17); and the account of memory is followed by a treatment of *pronuntiatio*, that is to say, delivery and gestures, *par excellence* the sensible surface of oratory.

Quintilian is here, of course, adopting the division of rhetoric into five parts according to a scheme in which the quasi-theatrical character of Latin oratory is presupposed. In one sense, therefore, his particular configuration of theories, examples, and metaphors is merely the rewriting of a *topos*. Yet this is precisely, perhaps, the point. The itinerary of the tenth book, facilitated by the metaphor-concept of *copia*, leads directly (or *automatically*, since Quintilian's writing follows by 'habit' what one might think of as a printed circuit) to the centre of the problem mimed by rhetorical theory itself: namely, to the duplicity of mimesis, conceived of on the one hand as full and immediate re-presentation, and on the other as an empty (automatic) copy.

If, then, the deployment of *copia* depends on the voice and its instantaneous bid for presence, it depends also—by an inverse movement—on the silent, hidden circuits of *cogitatio*, of memory, or of writing. For we find, in consequence of another quasi-paradoxical convergence, that extemporization is in Quintilian's text grounded no less in writing than in memory. Although it appears at first that the *extemporalis fortuna* is separated from the *scribendi labor* by the mediation of *cogitatio* (X. vi. 1), the firm priority of writing is nevertheless established by this very sequence: the whole of the earlier part of the book, with its topics of *elocutio* and imitation, is predominantly concerned with the written, so that utterance—and particularly extempore utterance —will emerge as the 'fruit' of writing (and reading). This priority is maintained throughout. Whether in the form of a preliminary rehearsal of style, or of the memorization of a written speech, written discourse pervades all the approaches to the moment of spoken performance:

We must acquire a store of the best words and phrases (*copiam sermonis optimi*) on lines that I have already laid down, while our style must be formed by continuous and conscientious practice in writing, so that even our improvisations may reproduce the tone of our writing (*ut scriptorum colorem etiam quae subito effusa sint reddant*) . . . (X. vii. 7)

Or again (and it is here that the dependence of voice on pen is most evident):

As regards writing, this is certainly never more necessary than when we have frequently to speak extempore. For it maintains the solidity of our speech and gives depth to superficial facility. We may compare the practice of husbandmen who cut away the uppermost roots of their vines, which run close to the surface of the soil, that the taproots may strike deeper and gain in strength. (X. vii. 28)

In this account, writing provides a hidden (even a natural) 'depth' and prevents the superficial proliferation of speech. On the other hand, Quintilian's paradigm of improvisation—the *alogos tribe*—is drawn precisely from the domain of writing, which is thus seen to escape the constraints of 'reason' no less than does spontaneous speech. However it is approached, Quintilian's theory presents the orator's speech-act as being an imitation of writing: it masquerades as living utterance, as a natural fruition of the seeds of discourse planted in all men, but the matrix from which it emerges is an anti-nature, a well-rehearsed script.

It is true that Quintilian, as indicated in an earlier chapter (p. 37 above), invokes *pectus, adfectus, spiritus, calor, vis mentis* and so forth as the immediate grounding of improvisation (as opposed to its mediate groundings, writing and memory). These are the energies which animate the *imagines rerum* on the surface of discourse with such power that the listener appears to be struck ('set on fire') by the living things themselves conceived anew, rather than by their images.[12] But the surrounding analysis severs them from their implied root in the affective essence of the speaker; they are, once again, the attributes of the actor rather than of the natural man whose speech mirrors his affections. If *pectus*, which seemed inalienable from the hidden self, is intrinsic to effective improvisation, and if improvisation is in its purest form an accidental shift into a mode of automatism, then the language-self which is generated by the orator's performance can claim no authentic origin.

Although *Institutiones* X was certainly well known in the sixteenth century, it was not systematically imitated by humanist theorists (perhaps precisely because it *was* well known). Thus many of the problems discussed above do not emerge explicitly in their works. It is important, however, to consider the topic as a whole, not least because of its pertinence to imitation theory and to the notion of *copia* itself: Erasmus's 'variation exercise' is no less than a piece of virtuoso (written) extemporization. In the context of the present chapter, one needs to be aware of what sixteenth-century accounts select and suppress; moreover, the analysis given above lays bare

---

[12] See X. i. 16: 'The speaker stimulates us by the animation of his delivery (*spiritu ipso*), and kindles (*incendit*) the imagination, not by presenting us with an elaborate picture, but by bringing us into actual touch with the things themselves (*nec imagine et ambitu rerum sed rebus*). Then all is life and movement (*vivunt omnia enim et moventur*), and we receive the new-born offspring of his imagination (*nova illa velut nascentia*) with enthusiastic approval.' Cf. X. ii. 11–12, on imitation and authenticity; and compare both passages with the development of similar themes and images in Erasmus's *Ciceronianus*.

many problems which humanist discussions will seek, in their different ways and often by implication, to circumvent.

Thus when in 1534 Nicolaus Beraldus (Bérault) produces a treatise on extemporization, he gives it a title which echoes Quintilian, but presents it as a dialogue, a form which itself imitates extempore speech by providing a script for imaginary actors: *Nicolai Beraldi Aurelii Dialogus. Quo rationes quaedam explicantur, quibus dicendi ex tempore facultas parari potest.*[13] Many verbal traces of *Institutiones* X are evident in this dialogue: improvisation is classed as a type of *hexis*; it is the principal fruit of study; *pectus* and *vis mentis* are the immediate source of eloquence; extempore speech floods discourse with colour; the empty quarrelling of women is to be avoided; *cogitatio* mediates between the labour of writing and the *extemporalis fortuna*; and so on. Furthermore, much of the exposition summarizes Quintilian's recommendation of wide reading, imitation, paraphrase, stylistic practice, and oral practice. But by an odd strategy of presentation, Beraldus never develops in full the topic of extemporization itself, which is often alluded to as the end-product but always deferred or set aside in favour of the means of approach. There is nothing, for example, on the intricate temporal relationship of *cogitatio*, memory, and utterance; nothing on the *alogos tribe*; and very little on the psychology of maintaining the flow of speech. Indeed, the pedagogue-figure Leonicus at one point simply advises his pupil Spudaeus to follow the guidance of Cicero and Quintilian; Spudaeus says that he foresaw that reply, and has already read both in detail.[14]

The reference to Quintilian is not, however, sufficient explanation of the absence of the proposed topic. Why does the discussion give space to many other themes which are no less amply developed in classical theory? Why invent a dialogue on extemporization

[13] On Beraldus, a humanist from Orléans, see Allen 925, introduction. Erasmus dedicated the *De conscribendis epistolis* to him.

[14] fol. A8 v°. The inclusion of Cicero here is indicative of Beraldus's approach. Leonicus clearly sees extemporization as dependent on the whole apparatus of rhetorical theory and on the detailed study of practical examples, in particular those provided by Cicero's orations; Spudaeus has carried out much of this programme (see fol. B1 r° and especially B2 r°).

if it has been adequately treated elsewhere? These are, of course, ghost questions to which there is no demonstrable answer. But they none the less point towards central features of the work. For example, the supreme difficulty of acquiring this habit is often stressed. The extempore speaker is, it appears, a rare phenomenon at which one can only marvel; indeed, as will shortly be indicated, the supernatural character of the gift is endorsed without reservation. The *ex tempore* moment is treated not directly but as an almost inaccessible past event or future possibility; the teacher Leonicus, who says that he has spent too many years among the 'barbarians' to be able to aspire to such heights, is contrasted likewise with his pupil born in a more favourable age.[15] A familiar structure is apparent here. The Latin language, still more the Greek, is in exile: the society of 'pseudo-theologians' with their impure Latin, or of vernacular speakers, makes the fruition of copious Latin speech in the present virtually impossible (fol. C5 v°). Spudaeus refers to the historical shift which has made forensic performance irrelevant,[16] and later takes up with Leonicus the question why Latin and Greek (always excepting Hebrew as the mystic language of God) have maintained their power after the fall of Greece and Rome (fols. C2–3). The rigour of their structure and the abundance of their lexicon are cited as the primary reason. The vernacular is spurned and excluded for its corresponding indiscipline and *inopia*; even assuming that anything worthwhile can be written in a modern language, few will read it. Yet in spite of a reference to the recent progress of Latin and Greek studies in Paris, authentic mastery of utterance in the classical languages is out of reach of Leonicus and not yet acquired by Spudaeus. Thus the special difficulty of extemporization in a non-vernacular tongue is placed in a temporal perspective by means of a 'biographical' situation which enacts a historical one.[17]

---

[15] fols. A8 v°, B7 v°–8 r°, C4 r°–v°.

[16] fol. B3 v°: 'For since the ancient forensic art of speaking extempore is little needed in our own day, I don't greatly covet it.'

[17] The most celebrated contemporary example of this awareness of cultural change in the course of the fictional speaker's lifetime is provided by Gargantua's letter to Pantagruel in *Pantagruel* 8 (published only a year or two before Beraldus's dialogue).

The deletion (or at least non-reproduction) of those parts of Quintilian's account which deal with the suspense of reason or of *cogitatio*, and with the fortuitous or aleatory character of extempore speech, indicates a caution also apparent in the frequent emphasis on restraint, sobriety, and the cultivation of *res* rather than *verba*. The tone of Leonicus's discourse is distinctly moral. Dialectic and, eventually, *philosophia* as a whole are evoked as grounding and as constraints for *viva voce* speech (fol. C1). Such a suppression of 'licence' might well betoken a certain anxiety of the kind observable in other humanists (Agricola, for example) rather than a lack of interest or comprehension. At all events, it is compensated for in some measure—although in a very different register—by the redirection of Quintilian's advice on writing practice towards the more relaxed genres, in which fluency is easier to acquire: fables, letters, comedies, and above all dialogues (fols. B4–5). Leonicus is no enemy of *voluptas*, although at the end of the dialogue he founds it characteristically on frugality.[18] He is, after all, himself a character in a dialogue; his rambling and unpretentious conversation with Spudaeus takes place on a journey, in a pleasant landscape, and with a happy *inopia* of books.[19] When he advises, as another way of practising fluent speech, the introduction of correct Latin into ordinary, domestic situations (fols. B7 v°, 8 v°), he is mirroring the mode of the dialogue itself. The theatrical eloquence of the Roman orator is eclipsed by a model of informal and relatively unambitious colloquy: only thus, perhaps, can Latin be naturalized in a modern context. The student writes colloquies to practise impromptu speech, and converts his everyday conversation into a colloquy.[20] Extempore

---

[18] fols. C5 v°–6 r°. Cf. Quintilian, *Inst. orat.* X. iii. 26; this *topos* is displaced by Beraldus to a position of greater emphasis.

[19] fols. A6, B1 r°, C6 r°. The journey is a *peregrinatio* through French Navarre; the theme of the journey is echoed in the discussion, as when art is said to provide a *via* to which one can safely return after the wanderings of improvisation (*aberrare*) (fol. B1 v°). The passage, early in the dialogue, in which Spudaeus invites Leonicus to sit under a tree to escape the heat of summer, while Leonicus prefers to go indoors to avoid distraction, dramatizes a theme from Quintilian (X. iii. 22–5); but the combination of the dialogue setting, the journey motif, and the theme of extempore colloquy, inevitably recalls Erasmian parallels.

[20] Compare fol. B5 r° (on dialogue as a writing exercise) with B8 v° ('So make

speech is domesticated as colloquial speech: or rather, colloquial writing, since writing provides the paradigm. The voices of Leonicus and Spudaeus are absent, their mime of improvisation being fixed inaudibly on the written or printed page.

Besides, despite the many local and quasi-personal references of the text, the fictional nature of this conversation is made doubly clear from the outset by its explicit engagement—on the side of Erasmus—in the debate on Ciceronianism. The characters rehearse, puppet-like, many of the motifs from this polemic before the question of extemporization is raised at all. When it is raised, however, a strategy is revealed. Ciceronians, it seems, are unable to speak extempore; their purism makes them hesitate and stammer. Deflecting a sentence from Quintilian, Leonicus attempts to show that the desire for perfect eloquence suppresses the source of that eloquence:

If we suppress feeling (*Pectore . . . represso*), by means of which we become eloquent, and if we also immobilize our mental powers (*fraenata . . . vi mentis*) . . . , the tongue will be brought to a standstill . . . (fol. A5 vº)

In such circumstances, the *fructus studiorum* can never be reaped. By making this issue central to the polemic, Beraldus highlights an aspect of Erasmus's *Ciceronianus* which might otherwise have seemed of minor importance; in this sense, the very decision to compose a dialogue with such a title at such a time, notwithstanding its lack of theoretical range, is rich in implications.

Extemporization is explicitly discussed in the *Ciceronianus* only at an early stage when Nosoponus, having described his *scribendi ratio*, is asked by Bulephorus how he prepares himself for speech ('ad dicendum') (Am. I–2, p. 615). He replies that he avoids speaking Latin wherever possible, using the vernacular for trivial everyday matters ('ad garriendum de quibuslibet nugis'). When forced to speak Latin, he says as little as possible, and uses set formulas of greeting, thanks, congratulation, and so on, excerpted beforehand from Cicero and learnt by heart for extempore use

sure, my Spudaeus, that when you are dining, walking, riding with your companions, your friends and your equals, you talk about everything, as far as possible, in good Latin').

('quo possim uti velut ex tempore'). After longer speeches, he 'washes away the infection of his lips' by extensive reading: 'protinus multa lectione diluo quod contractum est labis'. Normally, he avoids public situations in which he might be forced to speak extempore, citing the example of Demosthenes, who would never make a speech without preparation; he learns his formal speeches by heart, so that he can recite as if from a written script ('de scripto').

Thus the issue of extempore speech is decisive in determining the opposition between a written (Ciceronian) and a spoken (Erasmian) model of discourse; it will be implied again later when Bulephorus (in a passage which Beraldus echoes) refers to the anxieties and hesitations of the Ciceronian when speaking *viva voce* (p. 655). That it is central to the movement of Erasmus's dialogue is moreover evident from the fact that the conversation paraphrased above leads directly to the turning-point of the discussion, where Bulephorus, disturbed by the gravity of Nosoponus's 'disease', begins his attempt at therapy. The project of Ciceronian imitation is enclosed within the space of the written; its commitment to the past, to isolation and absence, excludes it from life, presence, the accident of the moment. Thus the very appearance of Nosoponus in this dialogue, as he himself remarks, is an anomaly:

Nor does it escape me what an offence I commit, how much damage I am doing to my labours, by participating in this very dialogue (*colloquio*) with you. It will take at least a month of reading to repair it. (p. 615)

Ciceronians cannot participate in colloquies; the sterilized univocity of their model is disrupted by the unpredictability of dialogue. Nosoponus is the face of silence, appearing in a masque of voices so that the power of colloquy may be restored to him.

In the through-the-looking-glass world of Dolet's counter-dialogue, the topic of *viva voce* utterance recurs. Nosoponus's remarks on avoiding the speaking of Latin except after long pre-meditation or by means of Ciceronian formulas are summarized by 'More', who asks Villanovus if he can approve of such superstition or madness (*De imitatione*, p. 92). Villanovus accuses

Erasmus of crude caricature; such absurdities could never be committed by anyone who had fully studied the rich resources of Cicero. Having resited the notion of Ciceronian *copia* on a less purist basis than the Erasmian caricature, Villanovus admits the value of extempore speech, but only as a rare exception:

I admire as vigorously as anyone a prompt and ready capacity for speaking, but I have known very few who were endowed with it. Nor must you think that, by any happy gift of nature, or assiduous study, or power of mind and memory, or any practice and habit, we can succeed in speaking extempore as skilfully and elegantly as we can write in peace and leisure after much reflection (*excogitationem*). What we put down on paper is fuller and richer (*pleniora . . . et uberiora*) than what we discuss among ourselves; reflection nourishes and increases style (*stilum cogitatio alit et auget*) . . . Therefore those who love a perpetual uniformity of style and an uninterrupted flow of discourse, do not willingly, nor unless absolutely necessary, speak the Latin language; and they avoid with the greatest care being suspected of ostentation, as rightly happens to those who, lest they should be thought to speak an insufficiently colloquial and domestic Latin, fall into ugly dog-Latin, address in Latin servants and women ignorant of the language, and in short chatter about everything in Latin. (pp. 93–4)

A similar point is made shortly afterwards (p. 95), when Villanovus claims that Erasmus has eroded the difference between the gravity of written eloquence and 'familiare colloquium'. Dolet's Ciceronian thus accords improvisation a special and necessarily restricted place *within* the terrain of written style, since writing is always the criterion by which speaking is judged. The mastery of eloquence on paper represses the use of the Latin tongue as a perilous freedom leading to erosion and devaluation. Writing is a mode of conservation, whereas the improvident tongue is always tempted by prodigality and dissipation.

In practical terms, Dolet's Ciceronianism might be said to anticipate the later development of classical studies: Latin is preserved as a privileged model of writing in vernacular cultures, while its oral use rapidly declines; Erasmus's bid for the re-dissemination of Latin as a colloquial language has no future. So much is clear if one considers the topic of improvisation as being debated specifically in terms of Latin competence. On the other hand, the 'colloquial' mode is of the greatest significance for vernacular writing in sixteenth-century France. The fictions of Rabelais and Marguerite de Navarre, the quasi-dialogic movement of Montaigne's *Essais*, all attempt to escape the space of the written text, to disrupt it or open it up, while yet retaining fragments of writing consecrated by tradition as an integral part of their movement. As with the trilingual inscriptions of the *Convivium religiosum* (or Rabelais's many devices for blocking the vocalization of his script), such fragments enter into a dialogue with the oral mode, almost as if some kind of perverse Nosoponus had infiltrated enemy terrain; the desire of the text being always to neutralize and naturalize such foreign bodies. In this perspective, the Erasmus–Dolet pantomime—with the interlude performed by Beraldus—has an exemplary value in that it raises the question of improvisation as a pivot of the problematic relationship between speech and writing. As in the theory of imitation, it is the exchange and even equivalence between Dolet and Erasmus (Nosoponus and Bulephorus, Villanovus and More) which is striking rather than their polemical difference. If Erasmus traps and mobilizes the face of writing in his oral model, Dolet in turn traps and immobilizes the face of garrulous oral speech in his written model (Erasmus's text can be reproduced verbatim in Dolet's because it is *written*). Both texts are dialogues, the two together constituting a third: dialogue and anti-dialogue. Both are also written, conserved and immobilized like insects in amber. Thus both win, and both lose: the written dialogue is a self-destructive as well as a self-preserving form. The primary factors of difference—Erasmus's insistence on eclectic imitation and on the value of improvisation—are supplied by fragments of *Institutiones* X, which may thus be perceived, still repeating its theory of presence, in the interstices of the Ciceronian deconstruction.

Quintilian speaks of a divine presence in extempore speech only to replace the supernatural explanation with a rational one:

if a speaker is swept away by warmth of feeling and genuine inspiration (*calor et spiritus*), it frequently happens that he attains a success from improvisation which would have been beyond the reach of the most careful preparation. When this occurred, the old orators, as Cicero says, used to say that some god had inspired the speaker (*Deum tunc adfuisse, cum id evenisset, veteres oratores, ut Cicero dicit, aiebant*). But the reason is obvious (*Sed ratio manifesta est*). For clearly conceived affections and freshly imagined materials (*bene concepti adfectus et recentes rerum imagines*) sweep on with unbroken force ...[21]

The power of 'calor', 'spiritus', 'adfectus', and 'imagines' is further elaborated in the following paragraph, where 'pectus' and 'vis mentis' are located as the centre of the psychology of extemporization, and thus of eloquence in general. When Beraldus touches on the possibility of a supernatural agent, he reverts (without acknowledgement) to the key sentence in Quintilian ('Deum tunc ... aiebant'). But he omits Quintilian's rationalization and proceeds instead to endorse the supernatural interpretation given by the 'old orators':

They rightly considered that it was a divine gift, only bestowed by supreme heavenly favour, to be able to extemporize wisely and felicitously on important matters before a large audience of neither foolish nor ignorant people.   (fol. A7 v°)

The juxtaposition of these two passages reveals the extent to which the topic of inspiration may converge with that of improvisation, providing an alternative explanation of the same unforeseen surge of productivity. That the superstructure of divine presence should have been added (or re-added) by Beraldus is perhaps due to the prestige in the earlier sixteenth century of neoplatonist thought as filtered through such texts as the *Praise of Folly*. Whereas Boccaccio, in *De Genealogia* XIV. 8, had made a careful distinction between the divine inspiration of the Biblical prophets and the *vis mentis* of the pagans—a distinction which becomes necessary precisely because of the ambiguity of the phenomenon— many sixteenth-century theorists speculate on the identity of the two.

A rather different kind of example of the linking of nature and

[21] *Inst. orat.* X. vii. 13–14. In quoting Cicero, Quintilian is presumably referring to the comment on inspiration in the *Pro Archia poeta* (see above, note 3).

supernature is provided by Talon's description of the mental origin of thought and language:

God has engendered (*ingeneravit*) in us rapid movements of the mind (*celeres ingeniorum motus*) which are rich and abundant (*uberes et copiosi*) in unfolding and embellishing (*explicandam et ornandam*) all mental reflection (*cogitationem mentis*) and rational judgement (*prudentiamque rationis*). When they have been strengthened by the knowledge of method (*doctrinae cognitio*) and by diligent premeditation, the noble and exceptional gift of eloquence becomes manifest. (*Institutiones oratoriae*, p. 6)

The context here is that of a traditional distinction between *natura*, *doctrina*, and *exercitatio*. The essential basis for fluency of discourse is seen as *natura*, identified explicitly with God's creative action in producing copious movements in the mind which 'unfold' both its cognitive and its expressive powers. The terminology appears to be derived from Cicero's *De oratore* I. xxv. 113, which refers to the rapid movements of the mind ('animi . . . celeres . . . motus') arising from *natura*, and describes them as 'uberes'. Talon adds the word 'copiosi', perhaps simply as a reflex action ('uber et copiosus' being a commonplace doublet in rhetorical contexts); more importantly, he attributes the *motus* to a specifically divine source, showing, like Beraldus, the desire to locate his psychology of fluent speech in a supernatural origin. Within neoplatonist theory proper, a similar desire governs the attempt to align classical notions of inspiration (*enthousiasme*, Ovid's 'est deus in nobis') with the Christian theology of grace.[22]

The theory of the 'divine furies' and its dissemination in Renaissance Europe is too well known to require detailed exposition here. What is important is that it performs a function comparable with that of improvisation theory in subjecting writing to what is essentially an oral model, with all the problems that such a project entails. Thus, for example, the platonist myth of the invention of writing as the betrayal of a divine origin is echoed (however restrictively and pragmatically) by Quintilian in his discussion of

---

[22] The most striking instance is no doubt Richard Le Blanc's preface to his translation of the *Io*, reprinted in full in Lefranc, *Grands Écrivains*, pp. 125–6, note. Cf. above, p. 109, note 44.

memory (XI. ii. 9), and later, with a wider resonance, in the *Praise of Folly*:

[The sciences] are quite useless as regards happiness, they are in fact an obstacle to the very thing for which they were specially invented, as that sensible king in Plato neatly proves in discussing the invention of letters . . . But the innocent folk of the Golden Age had no sciences to provide for them and lived under the guidance of nothing but natural instinct. What need had they of grammar when all spoke the same language, and the sole purpose of speech was to make communication possible?   (Fr. IV, pp. 364–5; LB 433–4) (trans. Radice)

The Golden Age as presented here is an age before writing, when all discourse, not yet being radically dislocated from 'things', naturally achieved immediacy of presence. The neo-platonist notion of a *prisca theologia* likewise gives priority to oral utterance by supposing an unwritten transmission of supreme wisdom from the earliest poets and prophets via Christ and the Apostles to the Christian era: the ultimate triumph of the oral mode is a kind of silence.[23]

When Aristotle, in a *locus* quoted by Rabelais at an important moment of the *Quart Livre*, describes the discourse of Homer as 'animated',[24] he is in effect using an oral metaphor to characterize

[23] Cf. Wind, *Pagan Mysteries*, pp. 18–20; to infer such a transmission is, in more than one sense, to argue *ex silentio*. One might add here that the antithesis between oral and written is analogous to that between spirit and letter, 'spirit' being connected with breath, 'letter' with writing.

[24] Rabelais, *QL* 55, p. 730: 'Me souvient aussi que Aristoteles maintient les parolles de Homère estre voltigeantes, volantes, moventes et par conséquent animées.' The Aristotelian passage in question is almost certainly the one quoted above (p. 28, note 39), which contains both the notion of things made animate (*empsucha*) by Homer's metaphorical language, and of things in movement (*kinoumena*). However, it is not unlikely that Rabelais was reminded of the Aristotelian *locus* by another in Plutarch's *De Pythiae oraculis* 8 (398 A): 'Aristotle used to say that Homer is the only poet who wrote words possessing movement (*kinoumena . . . onomata*) because of their vigour (*energeian*).' Frequent allusion is made in the later part of the *QL* (and specifically in the context of the 'frozen words') to Plutarch's essays, not least to those on the oracles. Neither Plutarch nor Aristotle has the notion of 'flight' ('voltigeantes, volantes'), which recalls the Homeric *topos* of 'winged words': Rabelais's rewriting of his quotations is richly creative, as Guiton suggests in his article 'Le mythe des Paroles gelées'. There seems to be no reason to reject the reference to the *Rhetoric* in favour of an Aristotelian

a paradigm of writing. For breath, being synonymous with *anima*, is inseparable from spoken language as a movement proceeding from inside a living being (an incorporated mind or *animus*) to manifest itself outside in sensible form. Echoed also in Homer's own phrase 'winged words', the notion of a language animated or inflated by some authentic wind is one of the most persistent *topoi* of Western language theory; the erasure of its purely metaphorical character gives it the prestige of a constitutive concept, a limit which cannot be bypassed. Thus, for example, Quintilian's 'rationalization' of extempore speech (above, p. 142) is embedded in a vocabulary presided over by *spiritus*, so that the strange behaviour of the speaker is credited to the operation of some unseen super-breath. The denial of godhead is outwitted by a disguised presupposition of metaphysical essence.

Erasmian language theory elaborates this *topos* with a sophistication which comes near at times (as indicated in I. 2 above) to displacing its limits, or at least recognizing them. His concept of *pectus*—the internal place where breath or spirit is generated—is developed by means of a recurrent set of metaphors of corporality (lips, tongue, skin; intestines, veins); the objective being to construct the image of a mirror-discourse, a reproduction or representation so carried and animated by the authentic *spiritus* of the speaker that, like Galatea, it lives and breathes.[25] This model is applied to *viva voce* situations proper, to their surrogate in dialogue, and to the writing of great men (like Cicero); in consequence, the circulation of breath animates, ideally, the whole system of language production and language consumption. Everything depends on that invisible emission, on the blowing of

fragment which Marichal (ed. *QL*, p. 227), followed by Demerson, misleadingly numbers '151a'. The fragment in question appears on *page* 151a of the 'Didot' edition of 1869, where it is numbered 49 (214). The same fragment appears as no. 129 in the Bekker edition (p. 1500a). It consists of two Homeric scholia which add nothing to the *loci* mentioned above and which Rabelais is not likely to have known. I am grateful to Donald Russell for help in identifying the scholia.

[25] See, for example, the passages from the *Ciceronianus* discussed above, pp. 41–6. For parallels in Rabelais and Montaigne, see Jeanneret, 'Rabelais et Montaigne: l'écriture comme parole'.

a wind whose unpredictability may be stabilized by the reciprocal 'inspiration' of a properly attuned reader.[26]

In dialogues such as the *Convivium religiosum* or the *Ciceronianus*, the colloquial relationship of writer and reader is enacted and almost, as it were, pre-empted by the *sermocinatio* of the characters in the dialogue. Rabelais and Montaigne likewise dramatize their would-be oral communication with the reader, caricaturing him, tricking him, simultaneously inviting and excluding him. Their works, like certain of Erasmus's, are strictly unreadable according to the model they explicitly propose in their prefatory statements and elsewhere. The express desire for total immediacy of contact between the minds or wills of writer and reader (seeming to imply a total evaporation of the written text, as of the transitory sounds of speech) is deeply connected in such instances with textual plurality, no doubt precisely because that desire is written into a 'script' which controverts its means of oral performance by imposing the absence of either writer or reader (or even of both).

The rhetoric of presence—the rhetoric which represents its own movement towards presence—is intermittently visible in *Institutiones* X in the image-motif of a ship at sea. It occurs, for example, in a passage where Quintilian is discussing the acquisition of facility in writing, and the necessity of finding a balance between hasty, chaotic composition and laborious self-correction:

At times, however, we may spread our sails before the favouring breeze (*si feret flatus, danda sunt vela*), but we must beware that this indulgence does not lead us into error. (X. iii. 7)

It reappears early in X. vii in conjunction with the topic of extempore speech: this double instance (vii. 1 and 3) evokes the pressures of forensic oratory in terms of strong winds or storm. Such uses anticipate a particularly striking one in X. vii. 23. Quintilian allows an initial slowness of speech in an unforeseen situation:

This precaution may be employed while we are clearing harbour, if the wind drive us forward before all our tackle is ready. Afterwards,

[26] Evangelical theories of biblical reading insist that the reader must be inspired in order properly to understand the divinely inspired message of Scripture. For a secular equivalent, see Aneau, preface to the *Metamorphose*, fol. b4 r⁰.

as we proceed upon our course, we shall trim our sails, arrange our ropes, and pray that the breeze may fill our sails (*impleri sinus optabimus*). Such a procedure is preferable to yielding ourselves to an empty torrent of words (*inani verborum torrenti*), that the storm may sweep us where it will.

These metaphors could be considered in relation to others in the text of the *Institutiones* (walking, running, looking ahead, acquiring athletic or military skill, controlling an orderly household, etc.). But as an archetypal image-trace, converging here with a theory of the speaking voice, the blowing of the wind and the filling of the sails is a privileged sign of plenitude. The viewless winds are made evident in the sensible curve of a fabric and in the beginning of a movement: the ships put to sea, the voyage unfolds; the wanderings of epic heroes (or of explorers) towards unknown places are inscribed in accordance with the vicissitudes of the wind—whether it blows favourably, not at all, or to excess. Between Homer and Rabelais, Quintilian's pedagogical *topos* carries its effaced cargo of associations of wind with voice.

Wind is indeed, in certain respects, the most pervasive of all the figures of abundant discourse. Next to the etymologies of breath as *anima* (Greek *anemos*), or of inspiration-spirit-*spirare*, *flatus-afflatus* takes its place, suggesting a possibility of inflation and eventual deflation. For if the wind or spirit, as the bestower of grace, bloweth where it listeth ('L'esperit inspire là où il luy plaît', as Lefèvre d'Étaples renders it),[27] the randomness of its wanderings and its necessary invisibility constantly risk denunciation as absence or inanity. The *spiritus* which animates extemporization can easily be reduced—as it is in at least one passage of the *Institutiones*—to the automatic printing-out of well-programmed circuits. The same reversibility underlies Montaigne's revision of a passage in the 1588 text of *De la vanité* where he speaks of the movement of his own writing. The later version interweaves a series of allusions to Plato's dialogues (among them the *Phaedrus*, which he cites as an example of non-logical structure), to Plutarch, and to the divine fury:

(c) [Plato's dialogues] ne creignent point ces muances, et ont une

[27] Rice, *Prefatory Epistles*, no. 138, p. 465; cf. John 3: 8.

merveilleuse grace à se laisser ainsi rouler au vent, ou à le sembler.
(b) Les noms de mes chapitres n'en embrassent pas tousjours la
matiere; souvent ils la denotent seulement par quelque marque . . .
(c) O Dieu, que ces gaillardes escapades [Plutarch's], que cette variation a de beauté, et plus lors que plus elle retire au nonchalant et fortuite . . . (b) Je vais au change, indiscrettement et tumultuairement.
(c) Mon stile et mon esprit vont vagabondant de mesme . . . (b) . . .
la meilleure prose ancienne (c) (et je la seme ceans indifferemment
pour vers) (b) reluit par tout de la vigueur et hardiesse poetique, et
represente l'air de sa fureur . . . (c) Le poëte, dict Platon, assis sur le
trepied des Muses, verse de furie tout ce qui luy vient en la bouche,
comme la gargouille d'une fontaine, sans le ruminer et poiser, et luy
eschappe des choses de diverse couleur, de contraire substance et
d'un cours rompu. Luy mesmes est tout poëtique, et la vieille theologie
poësie, disent les sçavants, et la premiere philosophie. C'est l'originel
langage des Dieux.[28]

The accidents and wanderings of writing are endorsed here as
intrinsically productive; the divine fury—the whole metaphysical
superstructure with its nostalgia for origins—is invoked nominally, not as a theory to be believed, but as a kind of rhetorical
figure, an elaborate *sententia*: 'dict Platon', 'disent les sçavants'.
The phrase 'se laisser . . . rouler au vent' determines the reading
from the outset; the vocabulary of chance ('escapades', 'nonchalant', 'fortuite', 'vagabondant') unmasks the divine wind of
fureur and makes *esprit* coterminous with the movement of the
pen, 'stile' being the means of inscription as well as the arabesques
it traces. Similarly, the source or fountainhead of inspiration is
transmuted into a random outpouring. And, most strikingly,
classical writing is said to mime its inspiration, 'represent the air
of its fury': Montaigne is specifically not claiming that it is
divinely inspired, but that it confidently adopts the mask of
inspiration. This reduction is characteristic of Montaigne, and
could be historically located as the symptom of a reaction against
neoplatonist optimism. But its possibility is foreseen long before,

---

[28] III. ix, pp. 994–5. In addition to the thematic elements indicated below, note
the recurrent motif of transformation and variation: 'ces muances', 'cette variation', 'Je vais au change', 'des choses de diverse couleur'. Change and chance are
the twin qualities of the Protean text.

is indeed present in the congenital duplicity of inspiration, whether as a 'decorative' figure (Quintilian's sailing boat) or as an eroded metaphor masquerading as a concept. *Afflatus* may always surface as inflation, *anima* revert to flatulence (Greek *anemia*).

Around the *topos* coalesce the many figures of incorporation. Breath is shaped, as it emerges from the unseen interior, by tongue, lips, and mouth: the physiology of speech becomes the metaphor of coming-into-presence; by extension, the whole body offers itself as the model *par excellence* of a discourse articulated in the mode of life. Oral emission is linked, by means of what is at once a figure and a physiological theory, with genital and anal emission; to the functions of discourse as a body—dissemination, propagation, reproduction of father in son—correspond its malfunctions and diseases. The virtues of the seminal flow may be lost by prodigality, or impotence; loquacity, the flux of words, is germane to the flux of the bowels.[29] Or again, the reading and imitation processes are interwoven with their organic counterparts, ingestion and expulsion. This model, like that of the breath, is endemic in Western theories of language; but it manifests itself with particular vigour in the treatises, dialogues, and literature of the sixteenth century. Erasmus's *Lingua*, for example, elaborates profusely the platonist notion (as transmitted in particular by Plutarch) of the diseases of the *logos*;[30] the same theme recurs, though with lesser concretion, in Bulephorus's diagnostic and therapeutic colloquy with the onomastically sick Nosoponus. The outgrowths of 'incorporation' in Rabelais, Ronsard, and Montaigne will form a recurrent topic of Part II of the present study; its two predominant thematic modes—the sexual and the alimentary—will there provide a constant yet flexible frame of reference for the exploration in their texts of the generative powers, the deviations, and the intermittences of writing. The

[29] Cf. the association between defecation and interpretation in *Pant.* 5, p. 234 and *Garg.* 23, p. 106, or between the chattering and the incontinence of Panurge in the *QL*; also below, p. 165.

[30] Erasmus translated into Latin the *De tuenda sanitate praecepta* and the *Animine an corporis affectiones sint peiores* of Plutarch, but it is the *De garrulitate*, with its metaphors of sickness affecting the tongue and the hearing, which is most relevant here. See also below, pp. 165–6.

inflation of the body, its mental faculties and its 'animal spirits', whether by words, wine, or sexual desire, might indeed be said to be their most central figure and their prescribed means of self-perpetuation.

Many tricks can be played with this model of the body; all of them have to do with the fabrication of a grounding or a set of oppositions (health–disease, inner–outer) by means of which discourse can claim authenticity. The contrast, frequent in Erasmus and Montaigne, between a language-act inscribed, as it were, on the surface of the body (lips, skin) and one proceeding from intestinal depths is a characteristic example in that it evades the problem of locating a disembodied (but privileged) mental operation 'beneath' a suspect linguistic surface. A figure of consubstantiality allows the text to indulge its own concretions and to controvert any attempt to derive from it an abstract conceptualized structure. Presenting itself as a body, the text claims the living body's sovereign right to resist being dissected or turned inside out in the search for its principle of life. The subterfuge is a powerful one. But the example given above reveals its mechanism. Discourse *personifies* itself as a nature, fabricates itself quasi-organic credentials which permit it to entrench itself and its own devious operations. The body mimed by language is not Pygmalion's Galatea, but a replica; the subcutaneous articulation of its tropes, its syntactical control-mechanisms, function in a way wholly alien to organic life. Rabelais's fictions depend on this prodigious illusion; but they also unmask it by bringing on to the stage anti-natures like that of Quaresmeprenant, whose anatomies block the circuits of *enargeia* and dissolve the body into an 'unreadable' sequence of verbal figures (see below, pp. 208–9). Even in less striking instances, where the trick is skilfully concealed, the duplicity of such a device leaves its traces at all the levels of textual process. If writing mimes the body in order that its detours, congenital irregularities, improprieties, figures, and semantic indeterminacies will appear as the inscription of an *anima* (*natura, ingenium, vis mentis, afflatus*), it necessarily follows that the textual body will display with unrestrained evidence the topologies and tropologies of writing.

The discourse of such an incorporated text might be characterized as a kind of perpetual prosopopeia: a figure of speech presenting a speaking figure. In this sense, it is connected by extension with *evidentia*; not only because rhetoric locates prosopopeia next to *evidentia*, but also because animation, illustration, and concretion, chiefly in the visual field, are the primary functions of such a discourse. Acting *in loco dicentis*, the text proffers itself as being affectively engaged in its materials, as representing 'l'air de sa fureur'; above all, it is an eyewitness, communicating first-hand with the world on one side and the reader on the other. The self-effacing theory of *exercitatio* or *experientia* demands that *res* shall crystallize in words as if they were the property of the enunciator; the guests of the *Convivium religiosum*, the actors in the Rabelaisian comedy, the *je* of the *Essais* thus impose their deictic situation. 'I am here', 'look at this', 'listen to what I say' belong to the grammar of *evidentia*, and Montaigne's claim that he is describing personal experience (together, for example, with key aspects of the Ignatian system of meditation) may plausibly be analysed as the complex articulation of a rhetorical category.

In the domain of poetics, the deployment of inspiration may be examined most characteristically in terms of a particular relationship between *afflatus* and *enargeia* (the figure appearing here as a metonymy for *elocutio* as a whole). Whereas the evangelism of Lefèvre d'Étaples or of Marguerite de Navarre had envisaged a maximum reduction of aesthetic resistance to the supernatural energy of grace—a position which constantly attempts to approximate to the self-evidence of a contemplative silence[31]— mid-century poetics give full play to *elocutio* as the visible sign of 'inspiration'. In doing so, they draw on a theoretical *topos* which

---

[31] I am thinking here in particular of the more mystical reaches of Lefèvre's thought and of Marguerite's later poetry; but suspicion of aesthetic elaboration is characteristic of the whole range of their work. Cf., for example, the Prologue of the *Heptaméron* (p. 9), where 'ceulx qui avoient estudié et estoient gens de lettres' are said to have been excluded from the circle of court story-tellers: 'car monseigneur le Daulphin ne voulloit que leur art y fut meslé, et aussy de paour que la beaulté de la rethoricque feit tort en quelque partye à la verité de l'histoire.' See also the aesthetic of Marot's psalm-paraphrases as discussed by Jeanneret, *Poésie et tradition biblique* I. 3.

could be illustrated by quoting not only Ronsard but also much earlier theorists: Boccaccio, for example, who defines poetry as a divine gift, stresses its 'unforeseen' quality, and specifies its function as the weaving of a fabulous veil or garment:

Poetry . . . is the fervour of exquisitely 'inventing', and of speaking or writing what has been invented (*Poesis . . . est fervor quidam exquisite inveniendi atque dicendi, seu scribendi, quod inveneris*). It proceeds from the bosom of God, and few, I find, are the souls in whom this gift is born; indeed so wonderful a gift it is that true poets have always been the rarest of men. This fervour of poetry is sublime in its effects: it impels the soul to a longing for utterance; it brings forth strange and unheard-of creations of the mind; it arranges these meditations in a fixed order, adorns the whole composition with unusual inter-weaving of words and thoughts; and thus it veils truth in a fair and fitting garment of fiction.   (*De genealogia* XIV. 7)

The kernel of this theory—which is briefly echoed in a well-known passage of Ronsard's *Hymne de l'Autonne* (lines 79–82)—is precisely similar in structure to that of the improvisation-*evidentia* model analysed above on the basis of *Institutiones* X and XI. A hidden energy becomes evident, is indeed only evident, in the articulation of a vivid, highly coloured surface.[32] To imitate nature by means of a profusion of ornament is to repeat the movement which is said to animate nature; the distinction be-tween poetry and rhetoric being here constituted precisely by the inference of an original, authentic *anima*.[33] Sixteenth-century accounts elaborate this theory by constructing a psychology of the imagination which is virtually a metaphysics, since it always

[32] Cf. the sentence immediately following the quotation from Boccaccio given above: 'Further, if in any case the invention so requires, it can arm kings, marshal them for war, launch whole fleets from their docks, nay, counterfeit sky, land, sea, adorn young maidens with flowery garlands, portray human character in its various phases . . .' (I use the translation of Osgood in *Boccaccio on Poetry*).

[33] This seems to be the implication of the concluding passage of *De genealogia* XIV. 7: 'among the disguises of fiction rhetoric has no part, for whatever is composed as under a veil, and thus exquisitely wrought, is poetry and poetry alone.' If allegory is peculiar to poetry, and if, as shown earlier, inspiration mani-fests itself in the invention of allegories, it follows that rhetoric is here regarded purely as an art, unaided by supernatural gifts. A similar distinction is implied by the opening chapter of Sebillet's *Art poétique*; cf. Castor, *Pléiade Poetics*, chapter 3.

seeks an identity between the operation of a superior imaginative faculty and the divinely grounded energy of inspiration. This terrain and its duplicity have been well explored;[34] some of its textual implications will be considered below (II. 3). For the moment, two Ronsardian examples will indicate the ways in which the rhetoric of presence may be modulated into a poetic of presence.

The first is taken from a familiar, instantly recognizable, instance of imitation. Horace's *Exegi monumentum*, evoking its writer's death by representing itself as a tomb, reappears in Ronsard's 1550 ode *A sa Muse*. The Ronsardian version effaces the name of Horace from the monument, inscribing a new name ('Ronsard') and a new deictic voice ('Je', 'mon renom', 'mes vers'). The movement from death to life is enacted by the substitution of images of fertility for the monumental metal and stone; the death of the poet will be redeemed by the organic after-life of his text, incarnate in the fields of Vendôme:

> Quand ce viendra que mon dernier trespas
> M'asouspira d'un somme dur, à l'heure
> Sous le tumbeau tout Ronsard n'ira pas
> Restant de lui la part qui est meilleure.
> Tousjours tousjours, sans que jamais je meure
> Je volerai tout vif par l'univers,
> Eternizant les champs où je demeure
> De mon renom engressés et couvers:
> Pour avoir joint les deus harpeurs divers
> Au dous babil de ma lire d'ivoire,
> Se connoissans Vandomois par mes vers.
>
> (*L* II, pp. 152–3)

Thus the poem both embodies implicitly the doctrine of imitation and claims explicitly to have brought to fruition in an authentic sound ('Au dous babil de ma lire') that grafting and naturalization of alien elements which imitation requires. In the *Deffence et illustration*, the ambition to 'voler au ciel' by means of words is always projected into a difficult future; in the *Regrets*, it is already past, renounced by the self-deflating voice of a poet reduced to

---

[34] See Castor, op. cit., chapters 2–4, 13–17.

'mere' writing. By contrast, the future of Ronsard's text is one of facility and mastery: the privilege of flight, that uninhibited animation bestowed by *afflatus*, is germane to the privilege of the voice in its bid for presence. But, once again, the perspective is reversible: next to the tombstone of Horace, the Ronsardian variant may equally appear as a mortuary inscription, or at most as the figure of a chronically deferred presence.

The topic of inspiration as such frequently appears in Ronsard's poems in contexts where the powers of *elocutio* are flamboyantly displayed. The *Chant pastoral* of 1559 provides a central example of this phenomenon, and of a certain shift from *afflatus* to *evidentia* which displaces the breathing spirit, or absorbs it into the suspended animation of figures:

> Apres qu'ilz [sc. the 'shepherds' Du Bellay and Ronsard]
>   eurent fait aux deux coings de la porte
> Le devoir à Pallas qui la Gorgonne porte,
> Et à Baccus aussi, qui dans ses doigs marbrins
> Laisse pendre un rameau tout chargé de raisins:
> Ilz se lavent trois fois de l'eau de la fonteine,
> Se serrent par trois fois de trois plis de vervene,
> Trois fois entournent l'Antre, et d'une basse voix
> Appellent de Meudon les Nymphes par trois fois,
> Les Faunes, les Sylvains, et tous les Dieux sauvages
> Des prochaines forests, des mons, et des bocages,
> Puis prenant hardiesse, ilz entrerent dedans
> Le sainct horreur de l'Antre, et comme tous ardans
> De trop de Deité, sentirent leur pensée
> De nouvelle fureur saintement insensée.
>   Ilz furent esbahis de voir le partiment,
> En un lieu si desert, d'un si beau bastiment:
> Le plan, le frontispice, et les pilliers rustiques,
> Qui effacent l'honneur des colonnes antiques,
> De voir que la nature avoit portrait les murs
> De crotesque si belle en des rochers si durs,
> De voir les cabinets, les chambres, et les salles,
> Les terrasses, festons, guillochis et ovales,
> Et l'esmail bigarré, qui resemble aux couleurs
> Des préz, quand la saison les diapre de fleurs,

Ou comme l'arc-en-ciel qui peint à sa venue
De cent mille couleurs le dessus de la nue.
(*L* IX, pp. 77–8)

In pastoral guise, two poets perform a mime of inspiration. Invoking the harmonious fusion of mental and physical powers allegorized by Pallas and Bacchus, they carry out—in a present tense—the rites of an alien religion. This is neither a theory of *fureur*, nor an example of its operation: it is given as the visible entry into a place of inspiration, as a *rite de passage*. The colours of this place—the 'grotte de Meudon' built by the Cardinal of Lorraine[35]—are wholly unforeseen; the liminary performance has led to a point where the treasure-house is unlocked and reveals its exuberant contents. Indeed, it is the contents, in this fiction, which induce the *fureur*; so that as the text mimes the fabulous décor, it also mimes the epiphany of inspiration. The movement of presentation is thus particularly clearly articulated here, the more so as 'nature' is written into the arabesques of this virtuoso display of art. The proliferating figures of *evidentia*, which begin in *enumeratio* and end in elaborate tropes, are the sign of a *fureur* which is now hidden, since it can only articulate itself on the surface as a prelude, not as pure performance. The present tenses of that prelude shift back into the past at the moment of entry into the *grotte*; from the interior of its imaginary space, nothing is visible but the verbal traceries.[36]

The desire for immediacy which is apparent in all of the theoretical models considered in this and earlier chapters is most clearly revealed in the attempts of sixteenth-century texts to 'oralize' themselves, or at least to propose themselves as animated utterance, which amounts to the same thing. The model itself, as theory, is no doubt deeply implicated in the problems of a writing which purports to be phonetic: in the theoretical writing of

[35] The eloquence of the Cardinal is one of the key themes of the earlier part of the *Chant pastoral*, where it is associated with figures of natural abundance and fertility.

[36] It appears, too, that the 'voices' of the poets as they invoke supernatural aid (quotation, lines 7–8), are displaced by the exclusively visual masque of the *grotte* ('Ilz furent esbahis de *voir* . . .').

Jacques Peletier Du Mans, imitation and inspiration coincide with (are indeed written in) a reformed orthography which claims to be purely phonetic, a transparent copy of the voice. The release of *copia* (itself initially a figure of would-be oral utterance) thus depends on what might be imagined as an exact superimposition of the oral on the written frame, a principle of equivalence or interchangeability. Since the correspondence is always inexact if not fallacious, such an attempt to re-route writing along the axis of the voice—repeating, albeit with far-reaching differences of materials and context, a gesture written into Western thought—will necessarily create a series of shock-waves and displacements in the fabric of writing. These are often marked by the appearance of reflexive topics, just as, in hermeneutics, the desire to avoid expressing a gloss produces thematic representations of unglossed reading; or as the effacement of models in the course of imitation may be accompanied by an explicit indication of their elimination: Ronsard's *A sa Muse* is in this respect comparable with many passages in Montaigne. But in every instance, the reflection is articulated as part of the performance. The text, as a self-designating figure of prosopopeia, absorbs and exploits its own disruption. It is in this sense that the prestige of the voice—'prestige' being etymologically related to illusion or sleight-of-hand (*praestigiae*)—nourishes the textual experiments of sixteenth-century French writers and their humanist forerunners.

5

Lingua

THE theories of discourse outlined so far are all, in essence, attempts to construct satisfactory models of writing and reading in the face of an awareness of the inherent duplicities of language. In the 1520s and 1530s, language problems to which every major phase of Western culture had responded with its own philosophical and literary devices were restated with particular force. Immense pressures were being exerted on the epistemological status of language by the intensive reappraisal of Scripture and of classical culture, that is to say, the whole corpus of consecrated writing; the fissures which began to appear in long-established theological and ethical structures provoked an urgent desire, in all camps, to seal the leaks and prevent the fragmentation of the *logos*. The figures of Babel—whether the Old Testament *topos* itself, Proteus, Mercury, or the dismemberment of Orpheus— proliferate at this time. Des Périers's dialogues contain powerful emblematic representations, at once penetrating and unresolved, of the imperfections of discourse; the problems raised by Erasmus and other humanists thus re-emerge, in all their sophistication, in vernacular texts. Theoretical and semi-theoretical writing of this period repeatedly expresses its inability to produce a coherent account of the relationship of language to 'world', 'thought', 'truth'.

The crisis is most strikingly exemplified by a preoccupation with the ancient question of specious argument. Aristotle's attempt to separate a rigorously apodeictic language from the eristic and sophistic modes had been echoed in the scholastic preference for logic over rhetoric. But logic, as the humanists observed, preserves rigour only by isolating itself from the conditions in which language is commonly used, from performance.

Hence the desire of Agricola and others to construct a performative logic (dialectic) which would guarantee the validity of each utterance as it is produced. The slippage in such systems is easily perceived, as in the instance of Agricola's gravitation towards the pleasure of writing. In more open forms of discourse—dialogue as a genre being the most central—the reversibility of propositions, their lack of anchorage in any criterion which is not simply additional language, breaks out almost uncontrollably. In the *Convivium religiosum*, for example, the apparent harmony of the discussion only half conceals an anxiety carried by the repeated preoccupation with *species*. 'Appearances often deceive' ('non raro fallit species'), says Eusebius, with reference to the marble which proves to be an imitation; and the whole décor is full of appearances which point to the mobility of the interlocutors' utterances as *species*, even if not, in this instance, as specious.

This disquiet is conceptualized with considerable elaboration in the *Ciceronianus*. Bulephorus-Erasmus makes two kinds of distinction between true and false *oratio*. The first depends simply on the criterion of affectivity or intuitive response: imitation grounded in the *pectus* of the speaker or writer is marked by its ability to persuade and move, inauthentic *oratio* (like inauthentic allegories) being 'cold' and 'lifeless'. But the second draws the boundary line *within* the realm of affective discourse. Mendacious rhetoric penetrates and does violence to the mind; the power of moving the affections is a kind of magic or poison:

For your rhetoricians permit the orator to lie on occasion, to magnify humble matters (*res*) with words, and to depreciate important ones, which is truly a kind of magic (*praestigii*), penetrating insidiously into the mind of the listener. Furthermore such rhetoric does violence to minds by moving the affections, which is a kind of poison (*veneficii*). (Am. I–2, p. 636)

Here intuition alone cannot be a criterion, since the distinction presupposes that there may be good and evil (true and false) intuitions: everything lies in the correspondence of the discourse to truth, rather than in its immediate impact. But how is this veracity to be determined? At this point in the dialogue, Nosoponus simply replies that such magic only tricks the listener who is worthy of being tricked ('. . . ubi dignus est auditor qui fallatur'); but this scorn for the gullible is of no help to the *auditor* who wants to know how to avoid gullibility. The problem is posed again in an important passage where Bulephorus, having quoted parallel phrases and formulas from the classics and the Bible, asks what it is that makes classical language seem more beautiful and persuasive than biblical language. Hypologus replies by invoking intuitive response:

To tell the truth, only that which is most valid among men: either the conviction which immediately occupies the mind, or the impression that strikes fully home (*penitus hausta imaginatio*). This we accept, this totally invades our minds: that one set of words is polished and elegant, the other ugly and barbaric.   (Am I–2, p. 645)

Thus there is no question of a rationally demonstrable superiority intrinsic to one particular form of language; Hypologus can only point to the fact of intuition, of the total and immediate 'occupation' of the mind by one mode of discourse rather than the other. Bulephorus tells him that he has got to the heart of the matter ('Rem acu tetigisti'). But then what is it that persuades? The subject in itself ('Res ipsa')? Hypologus doesn't think so (and thus implies, significantly, that *res* as well as *verba* may themselves be neutral or ambivalent). Finally, Bulephorus answers his own question in a celebrated outburst:

It is paganism, believe me, Nosoponus, it is paganism, which persuades our ears and our minds of these things . . . Let us throw out, extirpate, expel from our minds this paganism, and bring a truly Christian heart (*pectus*) to our reading.   (loc. cit.)

The crucial factor is the moral and psychological predisposition of the reader. Thus the grounding for authenticity which is offered in the last analysis is, once again, *pectus*, but only where *pectus* is itself grounded supernaturally (or at least evangelically) in Christ. The aesthetic illusion fostered by Ciceronian discourse is not simply a lie, it is a sign of the alienation of both speaker and listener from their true (Christocentric) nature.

The later part of the dialogue elaborates on this guarantee by means of a play on the word *logos*. Bulephorus admits that he had once been afflicted by the same rhetorical sickness as Nosoponus; but he found a doctor who could heal man's inward nature ('hominis intima sanet'). Having strategically deferred a gloss on this metaphor, Bulephorus finally produces one, but only in the form of another 'enigma': you shall know both the name and the healer, he says; the *logos* has cured me by the *logos* ('et nomen et pharmacum scies, ὁ λόγος τῷ λόγῳ mihi medicatus est') (Am. I–2, p. 656). The ambivalence of *logos* here turns no doubt on the two primary antique senses: 'word', 'language'; and 'natural' or 'right reason' (*oratio* and *ratio*).[1] But, by the end of the dialogue, a Christological sense has been added. All utterance is empty and 'sick' unless it arises from an alignment of *ratio* and *oratio* which is grounded in Christ as Logos. The single Greek word thus provides an apparent identification, in a unique origin, of Erasmus's authenticity principles at both the natural and the supernatural level.

There may seem to be a certain irony in the fact that Erasmus's final cure for the duplicity of discourse is sited in a play on words, in a pun which manifests both the etymological preconditioning of language (the senses of *logos* being determined by the history of the contexts in which it appears) and its susceptibility to chance (a pun being above all a productive accident). Moreover, if discourse is anchored by a word which means 'word', it turns on its own centre, is self-regulating, and thus incurably specious, whatever the metaphysical prestige of that particular word.[2]

---

[1] At the beginning of the *De garrulitate*, Plutarch specifies the *logos* as the cure (*pharmakon*) for talkativeness; in the context, a play on the double meaning of the word seems implied. Later in the essay (16. 510D), it appears in the form *to logo*, again as the means of curing spiritual ailments. Mesnard argues in favour of restricting Erasmus's use of *logos* to language or discourse alone (Am. I–2, notes on pp. 656 and 710); although this reading accentuates the paradox of a cure which is identical with the disease, it reduces the semantic reverberations of Erasmus's doubling of the word. Note that, in Hypologus's ensuing quotation from Aeschylus (*Prometheus* 378: 'words are the doctors of the sick soul'), the plural *logoi* is changed to singular *logos*, a modification which restores the philosophical implications of the term. Mesnard is no doubt unwilling—understandably so—to attribute to Erasmus the praise of some Voltairean form of reason. Cf. also above, p. 86, note 15, on the translation of *logos* as *sermo*.

[2] The point made here is related to some of the topics of Burke's *The Rhetoric of Religion*.

However, the acrobatics which result from an attempt to escape the inescapable space of language are perhaps less intrinsically interesting here than the fact that the text of the dialogue had succeeded in posing the problem in a form which made it virtually insoluble. The relapse into a conventional metaphysics only occurs after a prolonged exploration of the perilous autonomy of linguistic acts.

In the dialogues of the *Heptaméron*, Marguerite de Navarre provides recurrent enactments of specious argument. In particular, when Saffredent pieces together Pauline and neoplatonist *topoi* to endorse a doctrine of erotic licence, he is mimicking very precisely Parlamente's celebrated exposition in the discussion following the nineteenth *nouvelle*; the verbal formulas and quotations are at certain points identical. Who is to prove that Saffredent's discourse is only a false copy? Oisille's response is reminiscent of Bulephorus's strictures on the poisonous mendacity of the Ciceronians:

gardez-vous de faire comme l'arignée qui convertit toute bonne viande en venyn. Et si vous advisez qu'il est dangereulx d'alleguer l'Escripture sans propos ne necessité! (*Heptaméron*, p. 265)

But it resolves nothing; the subversion personified by Saffredent continues to assert itself, drawing on an evangelical vocabulary of inner conviction, of a faith confirmed by charity:

Vous voulez doncques dire que, quant, en parlant à vous aultres incredules, nous appellons Dieu à nostre ayde, nous prenons son nom en vain; mais, s'il y a peché, vous seules en debvez porter la peyne, car voz incredulitez nous contraingnent à chercher tous les sermens dont nous pouvons adviser. Et encores, ne povons-nous allumer le feu de charité en voz cueurs de glace. (loc. cit.)

Longarine attempts to turn Saffredent's argument against him; but by locating the criterion of truth so firmly in the power to convince ('si la verité estoit en vostre parolle, elle est si forte, qu'elle vous feroit croyre'), she remains within the problem of duplicity, as her own final reservation betrays: 'Mais il y a dangier que les filles d'Eve croyent trop tost ce serpent.' The paradigm of the Fall makes all forms of persuasive discourse suspect in advance.

Whose 'parolle', after the serpent's, can be so full of truth that it attracts both automatic and authentic belief?

The issue recurs in the discussion after the forty-fourth *nouvelle* in the context of whether preachers are to be believed or not; the scandalous equivalence between the credibility of the Gospels and that of Caesar's *Commentaries*, although rejected by Parlamente, cannot be controverted by her insistence that the word of God is the true touchstone ('la vraye touche') by which the truth or falsity of language may be tested.[3] Saffredent had already proved the contrary by his specious citations of Scripture. Oisille's development of the evangelical criterion, by referring to 'human fictions and inventions' as clearly separable from evangelical truth, manifests the desire of the text (Marguerite's) to resolve itself, to find an anchor outside itself; but the *Heptaméron*, as a fiction or invention founded on an essentially dialogic movement, cannot thus escape from its own space. In so far as it presents itself as an alternative mode of preaching, redeploying scriptural *topoi* in the context of erotic fictions (which, like Rabelais's gigantic fictions, are strangely claimed as being 'authentic' in their turn), it seems designed for a world from which the reader 'qui a l'esprit remply de verité' is noticeably absent. It is a world where, to rephrase Nosoponus, all listeners deserve to be tricked.

The device of the double gloss which is endemic in Rabelais's work performs a similar function. The difficulty of deciding between two incompatible interpretations of a given text always raises, whether explicitly or implicitly, the question of what constitutes a valid criterion. Thus, at the end of *Gargantua*, the giant's evangelical interpretation of the *Énigme en prophétie* is marked by an affective movement: he sighs deeply, so that his tragic vision of the persecution of the faithful takes on an authentic inwardness which is lacking in Frère Jan's reductive reading. Yet Frère Jan is also correct, in that he supplies the key to the riddle poem as originally composed by Mellin de Saint-Gelais.[4] He also

---

[3] pp. 303–4. Du Bellay's *pierre de touche* for authentic poetry—its power to transform the reader affectively (see above, p. 63, note 37)—shows that, in a profane context where no metaphysical guarantee is called upon, full licence may be given to the 'prestige' of discourse.

[4] See Screech, ed. *Gargantua*, pp. 306–14, notes.

prevents Gargantua from destroying the comic fiction: to accept Gargantua's reading and discard the apparatus of comedy would be to controvert the fundamental premise of the book ('rire est le propre de l'homme'). The possibility of a criterion must be suggested but not imposed, since it carries the threat of an intolerable finality.

In the *Tiers Livre*, the problem of specious argument is endemic. Heralded by the praise of debt, it erupts in Panurge's attempts to attribute a favourable sense to the enigmatic answers he receives. Pantagruel's firm rejection of Panurge's mendacity and defective cognition, like the evangelical confidence of Bulephorus or Oisille, carries a pragmatic reassurance, temporarily arresting the movement of disruption initiated by his companion.[5] But the difficulty—like the Hydra, or Proteus—incessantly reasserts itself in a new form, forcing Pantagruel to have recourse, not to self-evidence, but to authority. Thus, to impose his reading of Panurge's dream, he cites cabalistic exegesis of Scripture:

Vrayement je me recorde que les Caballistes et Massorethz interprètes des sacres letres, exposans en quoy l'on pourroit par discrétion congnoistre la vérité des apparitions angélicques (car souvent l'Ange de Sathan se transfigure en Ange de lumière), disent la différence de ces deux estre en ce que l'Ange béning et consolateur, apparoissant à l'homme, l'espovante au commencement, le console en la fin, le rend content et satisfaict; l'ange maling et séducteur au commencement resjouist l'homme, en fin le laisse perturbé, fasché et perplex. (*TL* 14, p. 423)

Later, in the discussion of Bridoye's judgement, Epistemon quotes the same Pauline reference to Satan disguising himself as an angel of light (*TL* 44, p. 529); the question of 'discernment' had also been raised by Erasmus in the letter-preface to his paraphrase of St. Matthew.[6] It is true that the affective state of the dreamer after

---

[5] See *TL* 5, where Pantagruel reverses Panurge's theme by quoting St. Paul and referring to the immediate, intuitive rejection by society of the avowed debtor.

[6] See Levi, 'Erasmus, the early Jesuits and the classics'. Erasmus is of course not concerned with dream interpretation, and makes no mention of the cabalistic rule for distinguishing angelic illumination from its satanic counterpart. The

his dream might be classed as a 'natural sign' (not unlike Gargantua's sigh), stabilizing the arbitrariness of linguistic signs. But its function still needs to be recalled and recognized by the authoritative Utopian wisdom of Pantagruel; the fallen Panurge refuses to hear.[7] In such episodes, Rabelais uncovers a danger which cannot thereafter be fully eliminated. The interval between the word and the rectifying gloss means that the question of *species* remains undecidable. The *ange de lumière* is indissolubly wedded to his twin; the figure of significant utterance might always be a satanic transfiguration.

It is around this ambivalent centre of discourse that the dual series of possibilities—*copia* and *garrulitas*, fruitful imitation and empty repetition, the authentic sense and the spurious gloss, Homer's winged words and Mercury's grains of sand—organize themselves, revealing not so much the reversibility as the identity of their apparent polarities. The absence of any extra-linguistic criterion ruins the possibility of a reassuring dialectic and imprisons the speaker or writer in the labyrinthine detours of language, in its surface or *species*. That the recognition of this problem is itself productive is evident from the very fact that in Erasmus, Marguerite de Navarre, Rabelais, it provokes strategies which seek to escape from the impasse by mirroring it in every conceivable way: the rhetoric of Erasmus's Folly denounces the folly of rhetoric, while the dialogue narratives of Rabelais and Marguerite insistently revert to their own fictional status.

Towards the beginning of his essay *Lingua* (the title plays, appropriately, on the *double* sense of the word 'tongue'), Erasmus alludes to Pandora's box as a paradigm for the inseparability of good from evil:

For we see that things have been so arranged by nature that from the very things which have the greatest utility arises also the most extreme damage . . . Hence the universal value of the proverb 'where there is

topos reappears in his *Lingua* (Am. IV–1, p. 299), where Satan's lies are seen as the cause of the Fall.

[7] *TL* 15, p. 424: 'Je vous voy très bien, mais je ne vous oy poinct. Et ne sçay que dictez. Le ventre affamé n'a poinct d'aureilles.' Panurge here ironically inverts the Socratic 'Speak, that I may see you' (see above, p. 48, note 16).

honey, there also is poison; the source of nourishment is also the source of cancer' (*ubi mel, ibi fel, ubi uber, ibi tuber*). (Am. IV–1, pp. 239–40)

Thanks to yet another accident of language, Erasmus inverts a breast-like plenitude to reveal a cancerous growth: this is the darker side of the logocentrism of an *oratio* confidently grounded in *ratio*. *Uber* (which is semantically close to *copia*) is inseparable from *tuber*. According to this same text, the tongue (or language) is not only the mediator between mind and body, placed close to heart, senses, and brain; it is also the neutral place, the shapeless, Protean plasma from which the innumerable virtualities of speech arise:

it is instructive to see how such a tiny and shapeless portion of the body, like a crude mass of flesh, has been created in such a way as to be adapted to such a wide range of uses. (p. 243)

Erasmus is referring here not only to virtuosity of speech (he cites Mithridates as master of twenty-two languages),[8] but also to that of singing, and to the function of the tongue in breathing, eating, tasting (see also above, p. 104, note 41). Elaborating Plutarch's *De garrulitate*, he describes in minute detail the physiology of the tongue and its relationship to other parts of the mouth and throat (pp. 243–5); the passage is full of metaphors such as 'the rampart of the teeth' (borrowed from Plutarch). Rabelais's imaginative explorations of the mouth (notably in *Pant.* 32 and *Garg.* 38), while certainly not directly based on the *Lingua*, suggest a similar preoccupation with the organs of eating, drinking, and talking; or, to cite another example from vernacular literature, Des Périers's fourth dialogue (concerning the dogs who have been endowed with speech by eating their master's tongue) exploits the figure of the tongue in order to make comments on the use of language. In the *Lingua*, Erasmus marshals familiar ethical and metaphysical notions (right reason, moderation, the

[8] p. 244. Cf. Quintilian, *Inst. orat.* XI. ii. 50. This *topos* recurs frequently in Erasmus. Panurge's exhibition of language skills in *Pant.* 9 connects him, from his fictional origins, with the versatility of *lingua*.

evangelical *logos*) to counter the tongue's dangerous versatility;[9] but the corporal power of the image—associated as it is not only with alimentary functions, but also, only slightly less directly, with sexual ones[10]—makes it, like Proteus himself, infinitely capable of eluding such constraint. *Lingua*, the tongue personified, is already a kind of Panurge, and in Panurge, its duplicity will be given full play.

Since a principal object of the analysis up to this point has been to show the performative character of Erasmian texts, their tendency to enact problems which go beyond the codifying grasp of theory, the *Praise of Folly* may be cited once more as a conclusion to this discussion of primarily theoretical texts and a means of transition to the more evidently performative ones of Rabelais, Ronsard, and Montaigne. The voice of Folly claims immediacy and sincerity; it is the 'wise' man, she says, who has two tongues (Fr. IV, p. 366; LB 438). Recalling a prelapsarian Golden Age in which all men shared a single tongue and had no need of rhetoric or dialectic, her copious speech invokes the priority of the oral mode, of extempore discourse, of *oratio* as *speculum animi*. Yet she herself is evidently a voice from a fallen world. She uses, however playfully, the devices she condemns; she refers at the end of her discourse to her own transgressions and to her garrulousness; and her reversals and disjunctions make her as hard to pin down as *lingua* itself. Folly is, of course, like the drunkenness and love in which she manifests herself, another instance of 'ubi uber, ibi tuber'. Besides, she speaks as a *larva* or mask, hiding the 'real' voice of Erasmus as author. Like Socrates

---

[9] Like the *Praise of Folly* and the *Ciceronianus*, the *Lingua* culminates in a Christocentric argument designed to resolve all the foregoing ambiguities. The *Ecclesiastes* may be seen as the logical extension of such arguments in that it attempts to prescribe a hygienically evangelical rhetoric. I am grateful to George Kerferd for drawing my attention to this aspect of Erasmus's later works; cf. also Schalk's introduction to the *Lingua* (Am. IV-1, pp. 226–8).

[10] The link is made explicitly in Erasmus's preface, where he compares linguistic disorder to venereal disease (Am. IV-1, p. 235). Plutarch uses alimentary metaphors such as the following: 'while others retain what is said, in talkative persons it goes right through in a flux (*diarreousin*)' (*De garrulitate* 1. 502D); and the sexual simile: 'just as . . . the seed of persons too prone to lusts of the flesh is barren, so is the speech of babblers ineffectual and fruitless' (ibid., 2. 503B–C).

in the *Phaedrus*, Erasmus locates the generation of this frivolous discourse in the country; he also cites the passage in the same dialogue where Socrates hides his face in order to speak of love.[11] Only in a very special sense, then, could the speech of Folly be said to be a *speculum animi*: there is only a mirror, constituting a 'mind' as text in all its plurality.

For the duplicity which causes antitheses such as that between wise and foolish—or *res* and *verba*—to slide and crumble can only be performed in a plural discourse, one that keeps in play all the thematic (and linguistic) disjunctions which a monologic text purports to eliminate. Any text which seeks to reveal the fissures in conventional conceptual frameworks without proposing a new reassuring model becomes committed to plurality. Placed under the sign of *lingua*, of Proteus, Pandora, the Danaides, or the cornucopia, writing begins to enact and to thematize, in the major vernacular works of the French Renaissance, its own unending versatility.

[11] See the 1515 letter to Martin Dorp (Allen 337, p. 95): 'When I wanted to play the fool, I assumed the character of Folly (*Stulticiae personam obtexui*), and just as in Plato Socrates masks his face in order to sing the praises of love, I too have played my comedy in character (*ipse fabulam hanc personatus egi*).' For the allusion, in the *Folly* itself, to the myth of Thoth (the invention of writing and the 'fall' of language), see above, p. 144.

II

assiduae repetunt, quas perdant, Belides undas
(Ovid, *Metamorphoses* IV. 463)

1

Cornucopia

IN a celebrated passage of the Prologue to the *Tiers Livre*, Rabelais speaks of the inexhaustibility of his book, here figured as a barrel which he will constantly refill:

Et paour ne ayez que le vin faille, comme feist ès nopces de Cana en Galilée. Autant que vous en tireray par la dille, autant en entonneray par le bondon. Ainsi demeurera le tonneau inexpuisible. Il a source vive et veine perpétuelle. Tel estoit le brevaige contenu dedans la couppe de Tantalus représenté par figure entre les saiges Brachmanes; telle estoit en Ibérie la montaigne de sel tant célébrée par Caton, tel estoit le rameau d'or sacré à la déesse soubsterraine, tant célébré par Virgile. C'est un vray Cornucopie de joyeuseté et raillerie. Si quelque foys vous semble estre expuysé jusques à la lie, non pour tant sera-il à sec. Bon espoir y gist au fond, comme en la bouteille de Pandora, non désespoir, comme on bussart des Danaïdes.   (pp. 370–1)

The affirmative tone, culminating in the figure of cornucopia, the magic vessel which supplies goods on demand, seems to be without reservations. Indeed, the passage enacts what it affirms by producing a rich sequence of analogous figures, echoing the *celebration* of plenitude in fragments of ancient text, both classical and evangelical. But what appears rhetorically as a productive movement turns out to constitute, in thematic terms, a falling away from the ideal. The unifying pattern of anaphora masks a figurative discontinuity, just as the syntactic devices enlisted to affirm the theme of inexhaustibility admit counter-examples into the text ('Et paour ne ayez que le vin faille, comme feist . . .'; 'Si quelque foys vous semble estre expuysé jusques à la lie, non pour tant . . .'). Indeed, although the infernal labour of the Danaides is given as a counter-example, it is nevertheless anticipated by the cup of Tantalus, ever full but ever inaccessible, which is assigned to the 'positive sequence. Similarly, Pandora's box, supposedly the antithesis of the Danaides' vessel, is an emblem of trickery and duplicity, and of the release of evil: it denotes a fall, Pandora being analogous to Eve. What appeared at first as an ideal, pre-lapsarian movement of plenitude is revealed as a post-lapsarian attempt to overcome temporality or *écoulement*: the reference to 'bon espoir', which is envisaged as remaining when the barrel is empty, only serves to emphasize the rupture between an apparent fullness located in the past and the possibility of future plenitude. Any such rupture necessarily puts in doubt the whole cornucopian movement.

A late text by Ronsard, the *Discours ou dialogue entre les Muses deslogées, et Ronsard*, provides another instance of an author confronting the dubiously cornucopian properties of his writing. The poet himself, as persona, appears in a décor of solitude and exile. He meets a band of hungry, dirty, and tattered women, who turn out to be the Muses; thereupon, he elaborates on what is already a fractured myth by accusing them of having tricked him:

> Je pensois qu'Amalthée eust mis entre vos mains
> L'abondance et le bien, l'autre ame des humains;
> Maintenant je cognois, vous voyant affamées,
> Qu'en esprit vous paissez seulement de fumées,
> Et d'un titre venteux, antiquaire et moysi,
> Que pour un bien solide en vain avez choisi . . .
>   Que vous sert Jupiter dont vous estes les filles?
> Que servent vos chansons, vos temples et vos villes?
> Ce n'est qu'une parade, un honneur contrefaict,
> Riche de fantaisie, et non pas en effet.
>   (*L* XVIII, pp. 92–3)

As in the Rabelais passage, the act of writing is here seen, ideally, as arising from an inexhaustible source figured by the cornucopia. This source or origin was supposed to guarantee the plenitude of the text: Rabelais had alluded, in the same Prologue, to the neo-platonist doctrine of divine inspiration, although with enough irony to suggest an ambivalence; while for Ronsard, the Muses had throughout his *œuvre* appeared as mediators of a supernatural energy. But if Rabelais's 'bon espoir' shows signs of contamination, this retrospective Ronsardian text is unequivocal in its negative tone. The cornucopia is full only of smoke and wind: a mythological figure to which contemporary glosses assign almost universally favourable connotations is strikingly conjoined with those emblems of vanity, emptiness, and ephemerality which fill the moral and pious literature of the late sixteenth century.[1] The lapsed Muses have lost contact with their origin, so that the whole structure which was to vindicate the poet's productivity falls to the ground.

These two texts, separated historically by nearly forty years, may be read as signs both of a recurrent ideal of French Renaissance writing, and of a recurrent anxiety.

The notion of the text as a cornucopia was not a new one in the mid sixteenth century. Aulus Gellius twice refers to *copiae cornu* as an appropriate title for a miscellany,[2] and the caption was quickly picked up by humanists. Melanchthon calls the works of Pliny a cornucopia of *paideia*;[3] Erasmus, in the 1515 letter to Martin Dorp, speaks in characteristically scathing tones of theologians who borrow materials from the *Catholicon*, the *Mammetrectus*, 'and other dictionaries of the same sort which will serve them as a *Horn of Plenty*'.[4] Next to these compilations which, however enormous, must nevertheless be considered as 'finite' horns of abundance, may be set the great edition in Greek, with commentaries by Eustathius, of Homer's epics under the title *Copiae cornu sive Oceanus enarrationum homericarum* (Basle, 1558). The preface of this edition, dedicated to the President and Fellows

[1] On the range of positive values associated with the cornucopia in Renaissance iconography, see de Tervarent, *Attributs et symboles*, vol. I, cols. 116–22. A characteristic selection of 'illusion' metaphors is provided by Rousset, *Anthologie de la poésie baroque*, vol. II, section IV. 3; cf. also my *Devotional Poetry in France*, pp. 147–56.

[2] *Noctes Atticae*, Praef. 6; I. viii. 1.

[3] In *De corrigendis adolescentiae studiis* (*Corpus Reformatorum* XI, p. 22).

[4] Allen 337, p. 99. A further example is provided by the *Cornucopiae, sive linguae latinae commentarii* of N. Perottus, a commentary on the first book of Martial's epigrams; many editions of this work appeared between 1489 and 1527.

of Magdalen College, Oxford, by one Laurence Humphrey,[5] celebrates Homer in traditional manner as a master of *copia* and *brevitas*, as a source of tropes, figures, and adages, and as a fount of wisdom, using images from the *Odyssey* itself to render imaginatively the qualities of the whole work:

Here is the nectar of the gods, here is the most beautiful house of Alcinous constructed by the art of Vulcan, here are the gardens of Alcinous in which pears and apples abound, and the goddesses flourish whose fruit never perishes, nor is absent in winter or summer. Here is the moly with its milky flower and black root, here is nepenthe, remedy of evils and purger of vices.   (p. 2)

Not only Homer, but also Hesiod, Virgil, Ovid, and other major classical authors were explicitly presented by their humanist editors as encyclopedic treasure-houses (*copiae*) of knowledge and of rhetorical or poetic ornament, each containing a quintessence of the whole range of classical literary insights and styles. Melanchthon gives Homer and Hesiod priority among those authors 'who both foster knowledge of things (*rerum scientiam*) and contribute greatly to the acquisition of eloquent discourse (*sermonis copiam*).'[6] Similarly, Salel's French translation of Homer, echoing the classical commonplace transmitted by Politian among others, emphasizes his universality, while Habert and Aneau claim the same advantage for Ovid in the prefaces to their translations of the *Metamorphoses*.[7]

Thus a long-standing reverence for Virgil as a source of *loci*, or for the *Metamorphoses* as a *Bible des poètes*, is reconstituted in

---

[5] Humphrey was a Marian exile, later to be President of Magdalen. See Garrett, *The Marian Exiles*, pp. 193–4.

[6] *Praefatio in Hesiodum*, in *Liber selectarum declamationum*, p. 613. Cf. also the *Praefatio in Homerum* in the same collection, pp. 385–406. The principal classical source for the view of Homer as universal author is the pseudo-Plutarchan *De vita et poesi Homeri*.

[7] Salel, *Les Iliades d'Homere*, 'Epistre de Dame Poesie, au treschrestien roy de France François, premier de ce nom'; Habert, *XV livres de la Metamorphose*, 'Epistre au Roy' (i.e. Henri II); Aneau, *Trois premiers livres de la Metamorphose*, preface, fol. b5 r⁰ (quoted below). Cf. Politian's *Praefatio in Homerum*, in *Opera* (1519), vol. II, fols. lvi r⁰–lxii r⁰. The *topos* of Homer as an 'ocean', derived from a figure in his own works, originates in Quintilian, *Inst. orat.* X. i. 46: *Oceanus* is the paradigm of a universal source.

terms of a much enlarged frame of reference and a new stress on significant abundance. There emerges from these various editions and translations an image of an ideally rich work of literature, a living and inexhaustible paradigm of the humanist encyclopedia, here conceived not as a prescribed set of disciplines to be acquired systematically but rather as a kind of privileged myth: such texts hold suspended an infinite potentiality, transcending the dichotomy of philosophy and eloquence. The size or length of a work is not of cardinal importance here; one episode of the *Iliad*, the making of Achilles' shield, embodies the notion of a complete microcosm expressed mythically in a decorated surface; in the *Metamorphoses*, what counts is not only the bulk of myths it contains (as a kind of dictionary), but also the principle of change itself, which operates at a level more profound than that of narrative content:

Or est il vray que entre toutes les Poësies Latines n'en y a point de si ample, ne de tant riche, si diverse, et tant universelle que la Metamorphose d'Ovide qui contient en quinze livres composez en beaux vers Heroiques toutes les fabulations, (ou à peu pres) des Poëtes, et scripteurs anciens tellement liées l'une à l'autre, et si bien enchainées par continuelle poursuyte, et par artificielles transitions: que l'une semble naistre, et dependre de l'autre successivement, et non abruptement: combien qu'elles soient merveilleusement dissemblables de diverses personnes, matieres, temps, et lieux. Par toutes lesquelles fables il ne veult autre chose faire entendre sinon qu'en la nature des choses les formes se muent continuellement, la matiere non perissante: comme luy mesme le demonstre au quinsiesme et dernier livre soubz la personne et en l'opinion de Pythagoras.[8]

Much as Humphrey uses episodes from the Homeric epics themselves to designate reflexively the intrinsic values of the model text, so Aneau in this passage attempts to grasp the productive principle from which Ovid's poem arises. Its structure, based on continuous *enchaînement* of diverse materials, reflects the theme of metamorphosis itself, figured in the narrative transformations of gods and mortals, and endorsed by a physical paradigm of the relationship between form and matter. In its variety, its

---

[8] Aneau, op. cit., preface, fol. b5 r°–v°.

productivity, its capacity for endless transformation, the *Meta-morphoses* is very precisely a Protean text.

The inexhaustibility of such works is necessarily dependent on the conservation of their potentiality for the production of meaning, and thus on the downgrading of the allegorizing gloss. Once the *Metamorphoses*, for example, has been converted into a set of allegorical notations, its significance becomes finite; the text is quite literally circumscribed. In many of the editions referred to above, glosses of an allegorical kind are provided in addition to linguistic and historical or archaeological clarifications; but they are given a subordinate role. Instead of replacing the text, they point back towards it, allowing the reader to make contact with the cornucopian source as designated by the prefatory metaphors. The literary work as *locus amoenus*, as a place of plenty, always exceeds the rewriting of any part of its content. This is very clearly indicated by the prefaces of the *Grand Olympe* (see above, pp. 96–8): allegory is superfluous to the self-allegorizing text. It is also suggested by Melanchthon's cautious limitation of his glosses on Hesiod;[9] Aneau, in his *Metamorphoses* preface, specifically recalls Melanchthon's rule;[10] and the neoplatonist allegories of Pontus de Tyard's *Solitaire premier* are subject to an analogous restriction.[11]

The notion of the classical text as a cornucopia, as a universal

---

[9] Cf. *In Hesiodi libros de opere et die* (1543), fol. 13 r°: 'one should not always seek for a reason in fables (*non est semper in fabulis ratio quaerenda*); it is enough to have grasped in some measure what they signify.'

[10] Op. cit., fols. c5 v°–c6 r°: 'Toutefois soit observé ce que a tresbien annoté le Chevalier de Terre noire [Melanchthon] sur Hesiode: c'est que tousjours ne fault exactement chercher es fables Poëtiques raison, suycte, et Lyaison convenante et consequente, en une chescune menue partie d'icelles, mais sufict aucunement avoir trouvé, et monstré ce que en somme les Poëtes ont voulu en toute la fable signifier . . .'.

[11] See *Solitaire premier*, pp. 52–3: 'Combien . . . que je ne sois de l'opinion de ceux, qui estiment que des fables une grande partie est plus vestue de delectation, que remplie de secrets ou naturels, ou moraux, je ne pense toutesfois estre chose fort necessaire de s'effiler le cerveau à tant serve curiosité, aussi que si desjà je vous en ay fait ouir quelques allegories, je ne pourrois pourtant vous promettre de continuer en toutes les autres fables.' This concessive view of allegory may be compared with Erasmus's (see above, p. 87).

source, is always justifiable by the strategies of syncretist thought, even where Scripture is accorded the firmest priority. Melanchthon's enthusiasm for Homer, for example, is made possible by an optimistic application of the *duplex regimen*, and by a rigorous distinction between material and spiritual goods:

Homer does not swell our purse with gold and silver, nor our stomach with gluttony, nor does he adorn our fingers with jewelled rings. But he surely fills, adorns, and endows the mind, which is more excellent, which is the immortal part of us, with enormous, and far more noble, and eternal riches.[12]

This encomium of Homeric plenitude may be compared (and contrasted) with Budé's strictly evangelical interpretation of the cornucopia image in the *De contemptu rerum fortuitarum* (1520) and the *De transitu hellenismi* (1535). In the earlier text, he concedes that pagan moral thought may be fruitful, but denies to it the power of overcoming all worldly afflictions:

Not even moral philosophy has such a rich store (*tam uberem penum*) from which it can produce cures and medicines for soothing and healing the sickness of the soul. It teaches, indeed, many worthwhile, pleasant, and fruitful things, but they are often unequal to suffering ... (*Omnia opera*, I, p. 128)

Once *doctrina*, *ratio*, and *natura* have been defeated by adversity, 'the only hope of salvation is to approach the sacred oracles and hierographic texts, and to turn to faith and divine riches.' This strongly evangelical emphasis determines the sense of the subsequent reference to the 'cornu Amaltheae' itself, glossed as the *aequitas animi* (tranquillity of mind) which arises from faith. In the *De transitu*, the contemplation of Christ crucified similarly provides the essential foundation for true tranquillity of mind, and is translated again into an image of cornucopia:

philosophy considers this as a divine cornucopia, whence it supplies

---

[12] *Praefatio in Homerum*, in *Liber selectarum declamationum*, p. 405. On the *duplex regimen* as applied to Hesiod, see *Praefatio in Hesiodum*, ibid., p. 617: the study of Hesiod is of no use for 'transforming the mind' and imbuing religion, which is effected by the heavenly spirit operating through Scripture; but the knowledge of Greek is necessary for the understanding of Scripture, and secular disciplines are of value in training literary judgement ('ut de sermone rectius iudicemus') and the ability to expound religious dogma.

not only nourishment for contemplation, but also pleasures for lofty and profound meditation; whence it draws out faith, hope, and charity, those supreme riches of the diligent soul; whence it furnishes a calm mind amid the harshest circumstances, and contempt for life amid good fortune.[13]

Although in such passages Budé is not speaking explicitly of the productivity of Scripture, the contemplative movement figured by the cornucopia clearly arises from the reading of the sacred text.[14] Perhaps, more precisely, it represents an ideally internalized end-product of the reading process, the point at which the potentiality of Scripture is gathered together and redeployed in a spiritual ascent beyond language. A variant of this ideal appears in the neoplatonist vocabulary of Pantagruel's advice to Panurge on prophetic dreaming in *Tiers Livre* 13:

Car, comme jadis le grand vaticinateur Proteus estant desguisé et transformé en feu, en eau, en tigre, en dracon et aultres masques estranges, ne praedisoit les choses advenir, pour les praedire force estoit qu'il feust restitué en sa propre et naïfve forme: aussi ne peult l'homme recepvoir divinité et art de vaticiner, sinon lorsque la partie qui en luy plus est divine (c'est *Noῦs* et *Mens*) soit coye, tranquille, paisible, non occupée ne distraicte par passions et affections foraines. (p. 415)

Here, Proteus plays the role of cornucopia: beyond (or prior to) the infinity of external, material transformations, is a place of silence and tranquillity, the still point of the turning world. Except that in this instance, tranquillity is a mode of preparation for prophetic discourse; it has not superseded language.

Erasmus is less concerned than Budé with a contemplative ideal. When he speaks of Christ as Proteus, he is referring to the polyvalence of the words attributed to Christ in the Gospels, not to some transcendent state of mind. Scripture is in this sense a cornucopian text, a paradigm analogous (though doubtless also superior) to the Homeric poem. The point is well demonstrated by Erasmus's use of the phrase *orbs doctrinae Christianae* to designate

[13] *Omnia opera*, I, p. 166. The image recurs towards the end of the *De transitu* (p. 231).

[14] Cf. *De transitu*, p. 157, where Scripture is described as copious and inexhaustible; see also above, p. 110, note 46.

the scriptural corpus, or more specifically the New Testament. *Orbs doctrinae*, 'the circle of learning', is an exact Latin transposition of the Greek *encyclios paideia*:[15] the Bible is a global text, an ideal encyclopedia.

It is important that such presentations of the paradigm text, whether classical or Christian, bring together the notion of infinite fruitfulness and that of closure: the imagery of circle, *locus amoenus*, or prelapsarian garden, connotes the self-sufficiency of the text and announces the exclusion of any supplementary discourse. *Copia* and *brevitas* are here in perfect equilibrium; the textual surface, like that of Achilles' shield, or the winged words of Homer, remains in suspended animation. Similarly, in a temporal perspective, the consecrated book presents itself as immortal, as released from the conditions of time. The linear extensibility of writing, which is a consequence of its commitment to the temporal order, is here redeemed by the figure of the closed circle, representing eternity. The entropy of the Bible and of Homer is zero. Each achieves a *telos*, whether apocalyptic or narrative, which conserves the energies deployed in its textual transformations.

But the very act of conceiving of such a Utopian fiction necessarily places the 'modern' writer outside the circle, in the postlapsarian space and time of his own composition. His project necessarily begins with a transgression: his desire to write challenges the ideal, presupposes the necessity of its replacement; his materials will be fragments of its dismembered corpse. This predicament is particularly apparent in Du Bellay's *Deffence et illustration*, with its imagery of ruined buildings, or of Aesculapius piecing together and resuscitating a dismembered body.[16] In Rabelais's *Gargantua*, the genealogies and a corrupt text culminating in a pseudo-apocalypse are found in an excavated tomb; likewise, the book ends with another apocalyptic riddle discovered

[15] On the notion of encyclopedia in the sixteenth century, see the contributions of Levi and Simone to *French Renaissance Studies 1540–70*. For a visual equivalent, see Tory's design for the letter O reproduced as the frontispiece of the present study.

[16] *Deffence*, I. xi, p. 79. See above, pp. 68–9; also pp. 116–17, on Rabelais's reference to the dismemberment of Orpheus.

in the foundations of the Abbey of Thélème.[17] Thus we return, from another angle, to the problems of imitation. The major literary works of the sixteenth century in France are all marked by an acute and persistent consciousness that they are produced in the shadow of a 'father-text', which must be in some sense destroyed if life is to continue. One of the problems, of course, is that the manifestations of the father are multiple: no doubt, the Bible has a unique status, and the Ciceronians may yearn for the purity of a single model, but in practice, and particularly for an Erasmian generation, the space of utopian writing broadens out to include, potentially, the whole corpus of classical and biblical works (or even modern ones like the *canzonieri* of the Italian poets). Hence the notebook method popularized by the *De copia*; hence also the compilations and dictionaries which attempt to preserve a durable 'matter' while destroying the particular 'form' of the source-texts. In the titles and prefaces of such collections, the *locus amoenus* imagery recurs: mention has already been made of the use of 'Cornucopia' as a title for miscellanies; likewise, the preface of the 1556 *Dictionarium poeticum* speaks of weaving a garland of flowers derived from the fertile gardens of Hesiod, Homer, Quintus Calabrius, Ovid, Diodorus, Hyginus, Cornutus, and Palephatus. The erased etymology of 'anthology' and 'flori-lege', deriving from the same metaphor, reveals the extent to which the ideal has absented itself from these fallen gardens.

When Du Bellay encourages the transplantation of the classical cornucopia, he is speaking *idealiter*, in the moment before any virtuality has to be realized:

Donques, s'il est ainsi que de nostre tens les astres, comme d'un accord, ont par une heureuse influence conspiré en l'honneur et accroissement de notre Langue, qui sera celuy des scavans qui n'y voudra mettre la main, y rependant de tous cotez les fleurs et fruictz de ces riches cornes d'abundance Greque et Latine? (*Deffence* II. xii, p. 182)

But within a modern text, the ghostly presence of its destroyed

---

[17] Through a textual irony which is no doubt accidental, Rabelais's phrase 'aux fondemens de l'abbaye' (*Garg.* 57, p. 203) might refer to the time when the foundations were laid, or to some later time when the ruins of the Abbey were being excavated.

antecedents is more problematic, as Rabelais illustrates with especial clarity. In the first place, his work both continues and denies a romance tradition. The prologue to the allegorized edition of the *Roman de la Rose*, attributed to Clément Marot and dated 1526, not only speaks of its 'mouelle neupmaticque', accessible with the aid of inspiration (see above, p. 95, note 30), but also presents the work as an encyclopedia.[18] Whether or not Rabelais's Prologue to *Gargantua* specifically echoes this text, his comic redeployment of traditional fictions hangs in the balance between the supposed plenitude of such paradigms and the emptiness of simple entertainment. At the same time, the proximity of the Bible, now becoming available as a vernacular text, creates its own turbulence within the fictional medium. When the narrator of the Prologue to *Pantagruel* claims that more copies of the *Chronicque Gargantuine* were sold in two months than of the Bible in nine years, his irony turns back on his own text, on its productive but also perilous chances of dissemination. Throughout Rabelais's work, indeed, the rewriting of classical and biblical *topoi* creates tensions which cannot be resolved. Such textual fragments appear as moments of possible insight, verbal echoes of an ideal source; but they do not, *per se*, represent the 'substantificque mouelle': to excerpt them from the textual continuum is to destroy the movement which gives them, as well the fiction, its possibility of fruition. It is as if, having recognized its commitment to a postlapsarian world in which people prefer romances and giant-stories to the Bible, Rabelais's text aimed at a maximal confrontation between paradigmatic fragments and a wilfully deviant discourse. The acceptance of such a fallen plurality, transposing and betraying the harmonious plurality of ideal models, is the only strategy open to a writer conscious that he is undertaking an impossible project.

The redeployment or re-grounding of *topoi* is, of course, a

---

[18] Fol. iii r⁰: 'Les philosophes naturelz et moraulx y pevent apprendre / les theologiens / les astrologues / les geometriens / les archimistres [*sic*] / faiseurs de mirouers / paintres et autres gens naiz soubz la constellation et influence des bons astres ayans leur aspect sur les ingenieux et autres qui desirent scavoir toutes manieres dars et sciences.'

major preoccupation of French Renaissance writing in general.[19] Rabelais, Ronsard, and Montaigne are all caught, in their different ways, in the same problem: the resistance of alien fragments within a new formal context tends to disrupt the movement of the text towards a stable meaning, and thus draws attention to the mode of operation rather than to the product of the writing system. As a corollary, this same phenomenon blocks the possibility of full thematic closure. The major French Renaissance texts are characteristically reflexive, dialogic, and open-ended. Written in the shadow of an impossible ideal, they proliferate in order to question themselves and to lay bare their own mechanisms. Thus they inevitably represent *copia*, or the cornucopia, as a centrifugal movement, a constantly renewed erasure of their origins.

[19] Cf. Screech, 'Commonplaces of law, proverbial wisdom and philosophy'.

2

Rabelais

RABELAIS's image of the book as a cornucopia is anticipated by a particularly striking instance of the same figure: in *Gargantua* 8, the magnificent *braguette* worn by the child Gargantua is assimilated to the horn of plenty. The myth is here, it would seem, attached firmly to the theme of sexual performance rather than to that of writing. Yet one may perceive, by tracing its figurative development, a fundamental movement inscribed in Rabelais's text at many different levels—rhetorical, grammatical, and lexical, as well as thematic; it may thus be taken as a point of departure for a textual exploration which will point back insistently to the two-faced myths of plenitude in the Prologue to the *Tiers Livre*. Like other Utopian myths, the cornucopia always presages a fall: its dynamic productivity will sooner or later begin to appear, in the post-lapsarian world, as an emptying out, or as mere flux or repetition.

In this particular passage, the pleasure of describing Gargantua's codpiece sets in train a series of phallic figures. It begins with the image of a flying buttress ('et fut la forme d'icelle comme d'un arc-boutant') and, passing through the details of its shape and embroidery and of the precious stones with which the material is encrusted, culminates in the cornucopia:

Mais, voyans la belle brodure de canetille et les plaisans entrelatz d'orfèverie, garniz de fins diamens, fins rubiz, fines turquoyses, fines esmeraugdes et unions persicques, vous l'eussiez comparée à une belle corne d'abondance, telle que voyez ès antiquailles, et telle que donna Rhea ès deux nymphes Adrastea et Ida, nourices de Jupiter: tousjours gualante, succulente, resudante, tousjours verdoyante, tousjours fleurissante, tousjours fructifiante, plene d'humeurs, plene de fleurs, plene de fruicts, plene de toutes délices. Je advoue Dieu s'il ne la faisoit bon veoir! Mais je vous en exposeray bien dadvantaige au livre que·j'ay faict *De la dignité des braguettes.*   (pp. 60–1)

The thematic function of this cornucopian codpiece is, apparently, to designate the sexual potency and fertility of what it contains. The recurrence of 'tousjours' and of 'plene' establishes perpetual fullness as the thematic axis of the figure; and the notations of dampness, fructification, and the seasonal cycle unambiguously evoke the world of nature. Yet this glimpse of natural plenty is perceived through the lattice of art: not only is the codpiece an artificial object; the cornucopia itself appears as an antique cameo, as the *representation* of a myth. Furthermore, the precious stones recall the textual domain of lapidaries (Rabelais cites, erroneously, the pseudo-Orpheus and Pliny), and the reference to a further commentary (future or past?) composed by the 'author' himself closes the parenthesis firmly within the realm of writing.

In this passage, as so often in Rabelais, the cornucopian movement depends primarily on lexical productivity, that is to say, on the list of epithets: the horn generates an exuberant display of adjectival terms, seeming to initiate an open-ended movement, via the multiplicity of phenomena, towards plenitude. The list proceeds by synonymy and by associative devices of a phonological kind (alliteration and assonance). Both these devices are forms of partially concealed repetition, and here repetition asserts itself in a particularly prominent way: not only in the insistence on 'tousjours' / 'plene', but also in the doubling of 'fleurissante' / 'fructifiante' in 'plene de fleurs', 'plene de fruicts'. This cornucopia, to rephrase a little, produces flowers and fruits; and flowers and fruits; and flowers and fruits; *ad infinitum.*

At the rhetorical level, the horn of Amaltheia appears as an emblem, comparable with the Androgyne figure which occurs later in the chapter. It confers a mythical status on the *braguette*: hence the references to 'antiquailles' and to explanatory commentaries. However, it is, initially at least, only a simile ('vous l'eussiez comparée . . .'). No cornucopia is embroidered on the codpiece in the way that the Androgyne emblem is attached to the hat. As a simile, its function is to enrich an instance of *descriptio*:

the chapter as a whole is a verbal surface purporting to represent
a series of physical surfaces (the child's clothing) which themselves
stand for, or replace, the giant-child himself. Thus the cornucopia,
as consigned to the written text, shifts between the function of an
ornamental simile (a singularity within the writing process) and
that of a sign pointing beyond the text towards an intended or
virtual fullness. In this sense, it displaces the *braguette* itself, imitating or mirroring its function of designating plenitude. Now this
ambivalence or displacement is fostered in particular by an ambivalence of genders ('braguette' and 'corne d'abondance' being
both feminine) which is prolonged throughout the list of epithets
and the ensuing sentences. A rationalization might attribute the
adjectives to the cornucopia (their immediate antecedent), and
the pronouns of the following sentences to the *braguette*. But
no rationalization can eliminate the textual ambivalence of the
grammar. It is particularly noticeable, of course, because the
codpiece and its contents are specifically male in character.
Gargantua's virility is already in some measure androgynous.
The grammatical accident of gender is reinforced, for example,
by the reference to the 'nourices de Jupiter', which evokes the
mammalian rather than the phallic properties of the horn; one
might see here encapsulated, in a *mise en abyme*, the relationship
between Gargantua and his nurses (chapters 7 and 11), which is
first mammalian and then phallic (introducing in the latter instance
a castration motif).[1] In the *Quart Livre*, too, the female Andouilles

[1] The myth of the suckling of Jupiter by Amaltheia (variously a nymph or
a she-goat) associates the classical cornucopia primarily with the female breast.
However, other versions of the myth have male and phallic connotations. According to Diodorus Siculus (IV. 35. 3–4), the horn wrested by Heracles from the
river-god Acheloüs (who had taken the form of a bull) symbolizes the stream and
the fruit-trees in its valleys, a physical allegory of nature rendered fertile by
cultivation; and Diodorus adds an etymology of 'Amaltheia', linking it with the
vigour of Heracles (*amalakistia*: 'hardness', literally 'inability to be softened').
Another late classical gloss is provided by Cornutus (Rabelais's 'Phornute',
Garg. Prol., p. 40): Amaltheia's horn is carried by the Good Daimon either because he ripens everything, or because he destroys (*amaldunei*) and ravages everything, or because of the exhortation to labour that comes from it (? him),
'because good things accrue to those who are not softened' (ed. Lang, pp. 51–2)
(I am grateful to Donald Russell for indicating these glosses to me). The 'good
daimon', who ravages as well as ripens, recalls the ambivalence of Dionysus,

will take on a phallic character emblematized in the name of their queen Niphleseth, which, as the *Briefve déclaration* tells us, means 'membre viril'.² These secondary thematic perspectives opened up by the grammar might be said to compensate for the suppression of the mother figure in both of the first two books; or to figure a double plenitude, an ideally hermaphroditic fusion; or to introduce the possibility of inversion into what appears as an aggressively male fiction. It is important, within the play of the plural text, to allow such motifs to retain their virtuality. What is quite explicit, however, is the subsequent movement of the passage from a positive to a negative register:

D'un cas vous advertis que, si elle estoit bien longue et bien ample, si estoit-elle bien guarnie au dedans et bien avitaillée, en rien ne ressemblant les hypocriticques braguettes d'un tas de muguetz, qui ne sont plenes que de vent, au grand intérest du sexe féminin.   (p. 61)

This sentence clarifies the character of the codpiece both as a beautiful object and as an emblem by evoking its antithesis, which is associated ethically with hypocrisy and figuratively with a windy emptiness (a conjunction to be found elsewhere in Rabelais). Ornamental codpieces, like rhetoric, may turn out to be mere surface. But here—if we are to believe the fiction—a natural fullness guarantees the artificial object, just as the decorative description is furnished with emblematic significance. If we are to believe the fiction. But in this most consciously fictional of all works, belief is necessarily suspended. And the suspension here draws our attention to the reflexive operation of the passage. The

who is himself often depicted with horns (or indeed the cornucopia). The phallic implications of such figures, and their connection with fertility, link them also with the more overtly phallic deity Priapus (cf. the *Songe de Poliphile*, fols. 66 vᵒ–69 rᵒ, triumph of Vertumnus and Pomona).

² p. 778. It is in the 'Andouilles' episode that the cratylist theory of names is cited (QL 37, p. 684). The narrator inverts the relationship between nature and language by creating a 'nature' to fit the name: cratylism thus becomes a device of fiction. But the device also shows how the writer may give new value to neutral conventions of language—including, perhaps, the antithesis of genders. The theme of the *braguette* and other related topics of the present chapter formed the basis of a paper which I gave at a conference at the University of Kentucky, Lexington, in April 1976. I note that the same theme has subsequently been developed in J. Sacré's 'Métamorphoses d'une braguette'.

textual surface is a rhetorical *braguette* enacting, through the cornucopian analogy, a plenitude; but at the same time it also undercuts this plenitude by introducing its own thematic inversion.

One might restate this point by saying that, while the text as cornucopia delights in its own productivity, its generative movement depends on its fictionality, on its lack of origin or grounding, as manifested by the gratuitousness of simile, or by the series of replacements 'Gargantua–clothing', '*braguette*–cornucopia', 'genitals–*braguette*', 'inner plenitude–textual surface'. Its very celebration of fertility, plenitude, presence, reveals an inverse movement towards emptiness or absence. And this movement was already prefigured in the repetitions of the mythical figure itself, in its supposedly positive presentation. The thematic notation of emptiness only confirms what was always there in a disguised form.

When *Gargantua* 8 was first written and disseminated, the fertility of the contents of Gargantua's codpiece had already been demonstrated at both the narrative and the textual level: *Pantagruel* was published before *Gargantua*; Pantagruel the son was generated before his father. It should be noted at once that, in replacing the anonymous *Chronique Gargantuine* with his own pseudonymous 'father-text', Rabelais–Nasier makes doubly prominent the fictional character of his writing; and that the 'second' book is thematically and structurally a repetition of the first, whether one follows the order of the fiction (*Gargantua–Pantagruel*) or the order of publication (*Pantagruel–Gargantua*). The demonstration of potency thus depends, once again, on a kind of synonymy or replacement. The desire to rewrite seems to throw doubt on the adequacy of the initial performance.

The early chapters of each book are dominated by the theme of generation. In both instances, the exuberance and productivity of the generative act are essential to the epiphany of the giant-world (that is to say, of the whole of Rabelais's fiction);[3] in both

---

[3] In the opening chapter on Pantagruel's genealogy, the race of giants is said to originate in the excessive eating of a particularly fertile crop of medlars, which

instances, this exuberance is immediately threatened thematically by the death of Badebec in child-bed and by the imagery of dissolution, decay, and defecation which announces the birth of Gargantua. Hence the importance of Gargantua's letter to Pantagruel (*Pantagruel* 8), with its encomium of the perpetuation of the species: 'propagation séminale' repairs in some measure the damage done by original sin.[4] After his death, Gargantua will continue to converse with his friends, to be present to the world, in the shape of his son:

> quand ... mon âme laissera ceste habitation humaine, je ne me réputeray totallement mourir, ains passer d'un lieu en aultre, attendu que en toy et par toy je demeure en mon image visible en ce monde, vivant, voyant et conversant entre gens de honneur et mes amys comme je souloys. (p. 245)

Moreover, this replacement of the individual permits a movement towards ethical fulfilment ('ainsi te y ay-je secouru comme si je n'eusse aultre thésor en ce monde que de te veoir une foys en ma vie absolu et parfaict ...');[5] it is closely linked to the theme of education, and is reproduced on a broader scale in the notion of a new historical era, replacing the 'Gothic darkness'. The generative cornucopia, while admitting of the operation of a negative principle (corruption and death), thus appears here primarily as a principle of positive, *telos*-directed repetition. According to this reading, the eighth chapters of each of the first two books complement one another in their thematization of the generative movement at a sexual level, uncovering the erosion and death which this movement necessarily carries with it, and reflecting the productivity of the text as it begins to be written. At the

---

produce 'une enfleure très horrible' in various parts of the body (including, of course, the genitals: but the race of those thus afflicted has regrettably vanished) (pp. 218–19). The swelling is presented both as a deformity and as a superior endowment; *uber* is inseparably linked to *tuber* from the outset of the fiction. Cf. Glauser, *Rabelais créateur*, pp. 64–70. The themes of the 'grotesque body' are central also to Bakhtin's imaginative study, *Rabelais and his World*.

4 See Gilson, *Les Idées et les lettres*, pp. 230–6, on the theological background to this theme. Cf. also Telle, 'A propos de la lettre de Gargantua à son fils'.

5 See Screech, *The Rabelaisian Marriage*, pp. 14–22. Rabelais is also drawing in this passage on Erasmus's educational treatise *De pueris ... instituendis*.

same time, the duplicity of writing, its tendency to enact the cornucopian movement as an emptying out rather than a filling up, is adumbrated, but at least partially disguised.

In the *Tiers Livre*, as its Prologue already suggests, things will be different. It is true that the sexual mythologies of this book begin, on the first page of the first chapter, with an allusion to the extraordinary fecundity of the Utopians: just as the ethical perfection Gargantua hopes for in his son (or that of the Thelemites) presupposed a set of conditions minimizing the effects of the Fall, so too the proliferation of the Utopians may be read as a sign of their affinity with a largely rehabilitated nature. But, thanks to Panurge, the consequences of original sin soon reestablish themselves. From the praise of debt onwards, he is a professional subverter of productive systems. He is a master of dissipation; and, of course, of rhetoric.

This dissipation is thematized sexually in two ways. First, through Panurge's defence of his desire to maximize his sexual activities by reference to the temporal cycle which will come to an end with the world itself: Frère Jan tells him to marry so that he will not be found 'les couilles pleines' at the Last Judgement (*TL* 26, p. 468), and Panurge himself takes up the argument that sexual regeneration is the mode of permanence or immortality appropriate to fallen nature.[6] His decision to allow criminals to empty their 'vases spermaticques' before execution is based on an affirmation of the cycle of replacement:

Chose si précieuse ne doibt estre follement perdue! Par adventure engendrera-il un homme. Ainsi mourra-il sans regret, laissant homme pour homme.   (p. 468)

But here, the replacement is flagrantly undifferentiated, there being no progress towards perfection as had been envisaged in Gargantua's letter. The generative movement reverts to mere repetition ('laissant homme pour homme'), to an *emptying* of the 'vases'.

In the second place, the threat of impotence emerges as a key theme, once again in the discussion with Frère Jan. It appears

---

[6] Cf. *TL* 4, pp. 387 and 389; *TL* 8, pp. 397 and 399.

first in the monk's warning that impotence may occur if inter-
course is not practised regularly (*TL* 27, p. 469). Panurge takes
this as a slight on his 'paternité, comme ayant peu favorable le
roydde dieu des jardins', and proceeds to boast at length of his
Priapic potency. His *braguette*, outdoing that of Hercules and other
champions, is '*prime del monde*';[7] women may be insatiable, but
his 'ferrement infatiguable' will answer their needs. He thus
appears to discount in advance Rondibilis's pessimism about the
possibility of providing the continual satisfaction which alone will
tame the female animal (*TL* 32, p. 492). In this episode, he also
sets aside Frère Jan's mocking reference to his grey hair and beard
as signs of an imminent loss of potency. His ostensible reason for
anxiety about his future wife's fidelity is simply that he might
be forced to leave her from time to time in order to follow
Pantagruel (*TL* 28, pp. 471–2). Yet the threat of impotence
asserts itself obliquely but unanswerably in the antithetical lists of
epithets for *couillon* which provide a counterpart for these chapters, transposing as it were to a purely rhetorical level Frère Jan's
metaphor 'marie-toy, et carrillonne à doubles carrillons de
couillons' (p. 468). Thematically, the cornucopian vigour of the
first list, which recalls Gargantua's *braguette* and is associated with
Frère Jan by Panurge's apostrophe, is reversed in the insistence on
debility in the list which Frère Jan directs at Panurge. By inserting
himself recklessly into the cycle of generation, Panurge must
inevitably accept loss as well as gain: the ravages of time on the
individual. His reference to his 'ferrement *infatiguable*' (like the
'tonneau inexpuisible' of the Prologue) is a flagrant absurdity in
an order governed by time, and thus by decay as well as generation. Priapus, the 'roydde dieu des jardins', asserts himself in
favour of the race rather than of individuals: to endorse (as
Panurge does) Galen's theory of the priority of the testicles,[8]
and thus of the race over the individual, necessarily implies a

[7] p. 470. The metonymic substitution of the *braguette* for what it contains in
itself suggests a parallel with those whose *braguette* 'n'est pleine que de vent':
as usual, Panurge substitutes rhetoric for achievement. The fact that he is supposed
to have abandoned his *braguette* compounds the irony.

[8] See Screech, ed. *TL*, p. 73 (note on line 81), p. 191 (note on line 106), and
pp. 218–19 (note on line 60); *Rabelaisian Marriage*, pp. 96–8.

surrender of the self to time. In sex as in economy, Panurge espouses a doctrine of self-dissipation. He envisages an endless expenditure, as if he had at his disposal a mythical cornucopia supplying goods and energies on command. But, like the author, all he has is language, rhetoric, loquacity. The lists of epithets, with their antithetical arrangement, may recall Erasmus's *copia* and his classification systems; but they also recall the epideictic categories of Fliscus (see above, p. 10). Thus the thematic inversion of potency points back towards the uncertainties of language: what at first appears as articulate energy may revert to gratuitous expenditure, presaging exhaustion.

This recurrent structure—which is personified in a certain sense by the interplay between Frère Jan and Panurge—is already apparent in chapters 7 and 8 of the *Tiers Livre*, which form a counterpart to *Gargantua* 8. Here Panurge manifests his desire for marriage by appearing in an emblematic costume whose drabness and absurdity are a farcical inversion of Gargantua's clothing. In particular, he wears no *braguette* (chapter 7 is entitled 'Comment Panurge . . . désista porter sa magnifique braguette'), an omission which he defends in chapter 8 in a new variation on the theme of codpieces. His argument excludes man from a natural order in which seeds are always protected by some form of shell, husk, or pod: man is unprotected, and so has had to devise the codpiece, the fig-leaf being the first example (pp. 397–8). Panurge's omission thus appears as a kind of reversion to nature, but to a nature in which man is defective, denatured: he is a kind of walking parody of the Edenic state. The absurdity of this gesture of exposure is clearly denounced by the reactions of Pantagruel and his companions: hence the text would seem to imply that, in the post-lapsarian state, the mediation or protection of the *braguette* is necessary. This is already indicated by the reference to Panurge's own codpiece, before he threw it away, as an 'anchor in times of adversity':

En tel estat se praesenta davant Pantagruel, lequel trouva le desguisement estrange, mesmement ne voyant plus sa belle et magnificque braguette, en laquelle il souloit comme en l'ancre sacré constituer son dernier refuge contre tous naufraiges d'adversité.   (*TL* 7, p. 394)

Thus Panurge's lack of protection is a deviation no less pernicious than the emptiness of the hypocritical codpieces of *Gargantua* 8. As the ensuing chapters will suggest, the thing itself, unmediated, becomes a principle of empty repetition, associated with self-expenditure, sterility, and non-performance.

One further gloss may be added at this point. If Gargantua's sexual organs were both disguised and designated by a *figure* (simile, metaphor, emblem) full of significance, Panurge's are all too *literal*. The relationship between shell and seed recalls that between sign and thing signified, between allegory and truth, as elaborated in the traditional imagery of exegetical theory (see above, p. 92). In this sense, Panurge's self-justifying rhetoric in these very chapters (as well as many others) concurs with his devious reading of the signs provided by those he consults in the course of his quest: he is attached to the flesh rather than the spirit. Thus there is a marked reflexivity in these passages, as if, when the Rabelaisian text touched on the *braguette* theme, it invoked its own relationship as surface with what it purports to signify. At all events, the two variants of the theme (*Gargantua* 8 and *Tiers Livre* 7–8), when juxtaposed, clarify the duplicity of the cornucopian movement. On the one hand, the Gargantuan codpiece asserts itself as a powerful mediation, but invites the reader to consider its potential emptiness; on the other, Panurge rejects mediation as an obstacle to desire, but falls into the obverse problems of repetition and impotence. Between the two apparent poles (which are also identical: the *Gestalt* duck–rabbit rather than the two-faced Janus), the possibility of a firm distinction between outside and inside, surface and content is eroded. *Copia* and *loquacitas* are, once again, perilously intertwined. The author's 'tonneau fictil' is all that remains to him after the 'naufrage faict par le passé on far de Mal'encontre';[9] but his protagonist will throw away the 'magnifique braguette' which was 'son dernier refuge contre tous naufraiges d'adversité'.

[9] *TL* Prol., pp. 365, 367. The phrase 'tonneau fictil' is used specifically of Diogenes' barrel; 'fictil' means 'made of clay', and thus has nothing to do with 'fiction'. But since Rabelais appropriates the Diogenic barrel as a metaphor for his fiction, a play on words is perhaps legitimate here.

When Panurge dreams that he has grown horns, his companions read the sign according to its conventional sense; but in an ironic inversion of a familiar theme, Panurge himself 'misreads' the horn as an emblem of abundance and potency (*TL* 14, p. 421).

Panurge, then, disrupts the myth of cornucopia. Yet by doing so, he reconstitutes it, for he enacts the absurdities of language which enable the text to continue. The only difference—though a fundamental one—between the earlier books and the *Tiers Livre* within this perspective is that the scandal of language as personified by Panurge has now moved to the front of the stage: the sense of gratuitousness which announced itself at the beginning of the enterprise as an exhilarating freedom from constraint is rephrased, from the prologue of the *Tiers Livre* onwards, in more rigorous and corrosive terms. Panurge, the impresario of Babel, is in full flight from prelapsarian nature and from an original truth: the Dive Bouteille is not ahead of him, but behind him. His language is not the mirror of his soul; rather, he lives within the confines of deviant language, so that his soul is a product of his linguistic performance.

The predominant structural principle of the *Tiers Livre* is that of repetition, and is imposed by the series of consultations laid on for Panurge.[10] A question and its answer are repeated, forming a dialogue which systematizes one of the central problems of Rabelais's whole text: namely, the relationship between fragments of 'serious' language, usually excerpted or paraphrased from consecrated texts, and the comic narrative in which they are redeployed. This dialogue clearly cannot be resolved simply by deleting one term. On the one hand, all the evidence suggests that it would be wrong to argue that Rabelais is deliberately subverting evangelical and humanist ideals; on the other, the text makes it clear that, for fallen man and for fallen language, such conceptualizations have little persuasive force. Seen from Panurge's angle, they appear as repetitions of an uncomprehended lesson, as mere formulae. The desire of the text is to arrive at a grounding of such formulae in an authentic discourse, in a

[10] Cf. Gray, *Rabelais et l'écriture*, pp. 118–19, 124, 126; also above, pp. 115 ff.

discourse itself grounded in experience; but the repetitions and the non-resolutions suggest that such authenticity is only constituted by and in the dialogue itself, not by a univocal language of ethically harmonious truth.

Plutarch and Erasmus had already foreseen the difficulties of curing a flux of words by means of verbal medicine (the *logos*): since the sickness and the medicine are of the same substance, their polarities are liable to become inverted. This is what frequently happens in the third book. Thus when, after a laborious exposition of four methods of restraining concupiscence, Rondibilis comes to the fifth and last, his brevity already has the force of a deflating self-evidence:

[Hippocrates] maintient grande portion de la géniture sourdre du cerveau et de l'espine du dours.
'Quintement, par l'acte vénérien.'
—Je vous attendois là (dist Panurge) et le prens pour moy. Use des praecédens qui vouldra. (*TL* 31, p. 486)

The medicine is here precisely identifiable with the disease: we have returned, necessarily, to the world of concupiscence and dissemination from the ideals of seminal conservation proposed by the learned doctor. Rondibilis is himself married, and will happily accept Panurge's fee for his advice. Ethico-medical *topoi* seem fragile weapons indeed in the battle against desire; but the inversions and dissolutions of the third and fourth books have no sense unless the possibility of some kind of textual therapy is envisaged. Here, as throughout the consultation scenes, a negation engenders—however tenuously or provisionally—the possibility of affirmation. And vice versa: the duplicity of the world, and of language, is inescapable.

The Prologue of the *Quart Livre* provides an outstanding paradigm for the problem of the grounding of *topoi*. It is at first sight the least disconcerting of all Rabelais's prologues. Its central component is an Aesopic fable, and everyone knows that fables—unlike the 'enigmas' of the *Tiers Livre* Prologue—are easy to read. Their message is usually made explicit in the form of a maxim, and in this instance it is stated before, during, and after the story, so that the simplicity of the reading exercise is constantly emphasized:

J'ay cestuy espoir en Dieu qu'il oyra nos prières, veue la ferme foy en laquelle nous les faisons, et accomplira cestuy nostre soubhayt, attendu qu'il est médiocre. (p. 570)

Et, pour ce que tu as opté et soubhaité médiocrité en matière de coingnée, par le vueil de Juppiter je te donne ces deux aultres. (p. 578)

. . . voylà qu'advient à ceulx qui en simplicité soubhaitent et optent choses médiocres. (p. 580)

Soubhaitez donc médiocrité: elle vous adviendra, et encores mieulx deuement, ce pendent labourans et travaillans. (p. 581)

These repeated formulations expand the *topos* of *aurea mediocritas* in an evangelical direction. Moderation of desire, frugality, simplicity of choice, submission to the will of God, and an ethic of humble labour, are the conditions in which prayer (as the expression of a questioning or desire) may be fruitful. Such themes surface incessantly in the third and fourth books; in this same prologue, they attract other related motifs: the definition of *Pantagruélisme*, the desire for spiritual and corporal health, and the evangelical *topos* 'Physician, heal thyself', which corresponds to the Delphic injunction of self-knowledge.

Yet the simplicity of fables and of their message may be deceptive. In the first place, Aesop's version of the story of the woodcutter who loses his axe, and Erasmus's retelling of it in the *Adages*, draw different conclusions.[11] Thus a gap begins to appear between the fable and its moralization, a sign of arbitrariness. Rabelais exploits this gap by means of a virtuoso elaboration of 'borrowed' materials. He prefaces the fable proper with two biblical *exempla*, the second of which already contains the motifs of the woodcutter, the *cognée*, and the river and thus anticipates the

---

[11] Aesop: 'just as the divinity favours the honest, so is he hostile to the dishonest'; Erasmus: 'one should not covet the good fortune of others' (*Adages* IV. 3. 57: 'Fluvius non semper fert secures'). On this Prologue, see the commentaries of Glauser (*Rabelais créateur*, pp. 38–40), Rigolot (*Les Langages de Rabelais*, pp. 104–6), and Gray (*Rabelais et l'écriture*, pp. 28–30).

Aesopic narrative proper.[12] The parallelism of these exemplary
stories may seem to stabilize the sense by providing a series of
correlates; but it is also true that the variation strategy, unlike
the primary narrative unit designed to release a single message,
begins to inject a characteristically Rabelaisian plurality into the
text and thus opens up a range of possible readings which cannot
wholly be anchored by the restatement of the moral, however
insistent.

This effect is, however, primarily a consequence of the copious
extension of the fable itself, and of the deflections to which it is
subjected. If one leaves aside for the moment the insertion of a
Lucianic scene in which Zeus, Priapus, and other gods act out the
comic paradoxes of destiny, it appears that the central area of
expansion is constituted by an interplay between verbal and
thematic motifs. The opening of the story places the word
cognée in the focus of attention: it occurs ten times (five in the
initial reference to its loss, five in Couillatris's prayer). The
cognée is also established as Couillatris's only source of material
wealth; its absence would lead to hunger and eventually death:

de sa coingnée dépendoit son bien et sa vie, par sa coingnée vivoit
en honneur et réputation entre tous riches buscheteurs, sans coingnée
mouroit de faim. La mort, six jours après le rencontrant sans coingnée,
avecques son dail l'eust fausché et cerclé de ce monde.   (p. 571)

In the corresponding section at the end of the fable, where the
habit of losing *cognées* spreads to the whole neighbourhood, the
same word occurs fifteen times (pp. 579–80); on nine occasions it
is associated with *perdre* or a variant thereof. Thus the two parts of
the story echo one another, but with a major shift to the theme of
loss, or 'défault de coingnées'. Here lexical and semantic repetition
is associated with the theme of emptiness; it denotes a gratuitously
repeated gesture of self-destruction, a dead copy of Couillatris's
original and fortuitous gesture:

Adoncques tous perdirent leurs coingnées. Au diable l'un à qui de-
moura coingnée! Il n'estoit filz de bonne mère qui ne perdist sa coingnée.

[12] pp. 570–1. Rabelais adjusts the story of the prophet's son to fit the proverb
'jeter le manche après la cognée', while in the Couillatris story he omits the
Aesopic motif of the river.

Plus n'estoit abbatu, plus n'estoit fendu boys on pays, en ce défault de coingnées. (p. 579)

The effects of losing the *cognée*, as foreshadowed in the opening section, are now realized: productive labour ceases, and death follows with Mercury's symbolic decapitation of the seekers after easy money. Phrases denoting wealth—'richesses tant grandes et inopinées', 'grand thesaur', 'montjoye d'or et d'argent'—are here presented in a negative context. True abundance remains absent: we are left with the empty echoes of unfulfilled desire ('L'air tout autour retentissoit aux cris et hurlemens de ces perdeurs de coingnées'), and with the baldly stated equivalence of lost *cognées* and chopped heads.[13] By contrast, the riches acquired by Couillatris are enumerated copiously. A dynamic proliferation (semantic, lexical, phonological) appears to assert itself in contradistinction to static repetition:

En Chinon il change sa coingnée d'argent en beaulx testons et aultre monnoye blanche; sa coingnée d'or en beaulx salutz, beaulx moutons à la grande laine, belles riddes, beaulx royaulx, beaulx escutz au Soleil. Il en achapte force mestairies, force granges, force censes, force mas, force bordes et bordieux, force cassines, prez, vignes, boys, terres labourables, pastis, estangs, moulins, jardins, saulsayes; beufz, vaches, brebis, moutons, chèvres, truyes, pourceaulx, asnes, chevaulx, poulles, cocqs, chappons, poulletz, oyes, jars, canes, canars, et du menu. (p. 579)

Thus the story as a whole has a ternary structure or rhythm in which the verbal figuration of loss, sterility, and death is distributed on either side of a figure of true abundance and its discovery (or recovery).

At one level, these themes may be read as transposing the original ethical *topos* into a socio-economic context. The ethic of labour is explicitly announced by one of the later enunciations of the *topos* itself ('. . . ce pendent labourans et travaillans'). Labour sustains both individual life and the fabric of society; excessive desire for gain destroys them. Couillatris exchanges his gold and

[13] In the further *exempla* which follow the Couillatris story (pp. 580–1), the desire for fabulous wealth, represented in images of impossible multiplication, is again bluntly rewarded with empty purses and disease.

silver *cognées* for money only in order to buy land and stock
which will provide him with an enduring means of production.
He thus moves back through the conventional, arbitrary medium
of exchange to natural goods. Conversely, the landowners and
minor nobility who sold their meadows and mills did so 'pour
soy gourgiaser à la monstre', that is to say, in order to indulge in
pure display (they no doubt wore ostentatious codpieces); they
now take the further step of exchanging their swords for *cognées*
'affin de les perdre'. Thus they abandon the authentic means of
production in order to speculate in the chimerical currency of
cognées, an investment which has spectacularly negative returns.
One is reminded of Panurge's policy of loan-financed consumption in Salmiguondin: the metaphor 'manger son blé en herbe',
epitomizing the theme of negated fertility, is paralleled in the
Couillatris fable by the cessation of wood-cutting ('Plus n'estoit
abbatu, plus n'estoit fendu boys on pays . . .'). In both instances,
the natural cycle of agricultural labour as a source of wealth is
interrupted.

The model of economic exchange inverted by Panurge and the
'perdeurs de coignées' is parallel and interchangeable with another
key *topos* deployed by Panurge in his speech on debt, namely, the
notion of charity as *copula mundi*.[14] Charity institutes a dual exchange, fostering ethical productivity amongst men (as at
Thélème, with its imagery of wealth and its cornucopian fountain of the Graces) and salvific co-operation between men and
God (as in the storm scene of the *Quart Livre*).[15] Its negative
counterpart is represented in the Prologue of the fourth book
by the 'petitz Romipètes, vendens le leur, empruntans l'aultruy
pour achapter mandatz à tas d'un pape nouvellement créé'
(p. 580), a reference which may no doubt be associated with the
Papimanes episode: in each instance, evangelical law has been
translated into a purely nominal currency (Papal mandates,

---

[14] Rabelais is here playing on an alignment of stoic, neoplatonist, and Pauline
motifs: see Mayer, 'Rabelais's satirical eulogy'; Kaiser, *Praisers of Folly*, pp. 132–
3; Marichal, 'Rabelais devant le néoplatonisme'; and Screech, ed. *TL*, chs. 3–4,
notes. The iconography of these themes is discussed in the context of Italian
Renaissance art by Wind, *Pagan Mysteries*, chs. II–VII.

[15] See Screech, *L'Évangélisme de Rabelais*, ch. 3.

Decretals).[16] Thus, as a figure of charity, gold denotes authentic—inward and salvific—abundance:

> Or donné par don
> Ordonne pardon.   (*Garg.* 54, p. 198)

But taken in its literal sense, the same phrase recalls the purchase of indulgences (paper pardons). Two identical systems of exchange are thus immanent in a single verbal formula: the shift between positive and negative depends on a change of aspect, or of rhetorical function, between literal and figurative. In the last instance quoted, the duality is mimicked by the reduplication of the sound-pattern: the same reappears as another. In a fiction, or a poem, it is evident that such oscillations can only be stabilized if the fiction eliminates itself (as in a fable) by generating a maxim which then replaces it; or vice versa. When the moral has been crystallized, the story is no longer present, just as, conversely, a metaphor (or fiction) imposes absence on what it signifies. Rational and figurative discourse, *topoi* and narrative, circle endlessly around the same centre, unable to resolve their duality. The mutual attraction and hostility between Pantagruel and Panurge (whose names are semantically and orthographically similar) represent the dilemma in quasi-allegorical manner.

There are clear parallels between the presentation of the Couillatris story and the *braguette* motif of the earlier books. A movement towards plenitude and presence is established, but is constantly threatened by the possibility of inversion or subversion, whether thematically or rhetorically; once again, the distinction between lists or repetitions carrying a thematically positive sign and those with a negative sign may seem, within a linguistic perspective, to be a mirage rather than the affirmation of a value-system. And this indeterminacy is exacerbated by the figure of Priapus, who presides over the radical irony of the Aesopic fable in Rabelais's deviant version.

The original story has no overtly sexual implications; or at least it has none until it is retold in French and the axe is rendered

---

[16] On this aspect of the satire of the Papimanes, see Jeanneret, 'Les paroles dégelées', pp. 15–17.

as *cognée*. The insistence on the word as the narrative begins heralds a pun which Priapus, in his Lucianic heaven, will make explicit; for when Mercury reports to Zeus the prayer of Couillatris, Priapus raises a problem:

Roy Juppiter, on temps que, par vostre ordonnance et particulier bénéfice, j'estois guardian des jardins en terre, je notay que ceste diction, *coingnée*, est équivocque à plusieurs choses. Elle signifie un certain instrument par le service duquel est fendu et couppé boys. Signifie aussi (au moins jadis signifioit) la femelle bien à poinct et souvent gimbretiletolletée, et veidz que tout bon compaignon appelloit sa guarse fille de joye: ma coingnée.[17]

From the strictly narrative point of view, the equivocation is gratuitous. There appears to be no continuity between Priapus' semantic doubling and Zeus' decision to send Mercury to earth with the three *cognées*. Couillatris will not, apparently, be invited to choose between different meanings of a word but between different material objects. And yet, precisely perhaps because of this comic arbitrariness, Priapus introduces a disruption into the reading of the fable: a sexual register announced, not only by the pre-existing pun, but also by the act of naming the woodcutter 'Couillatris', has now inserted itself into the thematic nexus of the tale. Hence the scene in which Couillatris joyfully recognizes his mark 'au bout du manche' appears, by a shift of aspect, as a figure of sexual conjunction; the fertile domains acquired by Couillatris recall the productive gardens of which Priapus is the guardian; and the sterility of the 'perdeurs de coignées' is rewarded by a kind of castration.

A reading within this thematic context immediately suggests further parallels. Like the Androgyne emblem, the fable of Couillatris figures the recovery of a lost unity as the fulfilment of authentic desire; it also concurs with Rabelais's distrust of monasticism (in which sexual deprivation is supposed to be a passport to spiritual abundance); or with Frère Jan's argument in the *Tiers Livre* that to 'labour' incessantly is to conserve potency;[18]

---

[17] p. 576. The same pun occurs in the Ennasin episode, QL 9, p. 606.

[18] *TL* 27, p. 469. The metaphor of 'labouraige sempiternel' used by Frère Jan makes explicit the equivalence between the sexual theme and the theme of productive labour.

or again with the warning ignored by Panurge that excessive desire for sexual gain (obsession with testicles and *cognées*) leads to self-expenditure. No doubt these topical fragments could be reconciled in a coherent rationalization. What matters more, perhaps, is the fact that, whichever way the thematic kaleidoscope shifts, the contamination of a principle of abundance by a principle of *écoulement* or entropy remains central.

Finally, the Prologue seems to suggest, at all its levels, that some kind of equilibrium between mind and matter, or between ethics and desire, is necessary to the achievement of plenitude. But if this is so, the balance cannot be understood as a banal recommendation of rational control. Couillatris is hardly a master of conscious ethical activity. He makes no calculations, no ethical judgements; he rejects the gold and silver *cognées* because they are alien to him; it is almost as if he despises them as counterfeit versions of the real thing. When he sees his own, an extraordinary excitement possesses him:

il reguarde au bout du manche, en icelluy recongnoit sa marque et, tressaillant tout de joye comme un renard qui rencontre poulles esguarées et soubriant du bout du nez, dict: 'Merdigues, ceste-cy estoit mienne!...' (p. 578)

This is the excitement of recognition, echoing at however great a distance the recognition scenes of Greek tragedy, in which a birth-mark or scar designates the recognized object as authentic. It is almost as if the reward conferred by Mercury, and the subsequent release of abundance in Couillatris's life, were brought about by this intuitive event rather than by the operation of a moral code. Couillatris stumbles, as it were by accident, on a fundamental principle which is prior to the *topos*, and thus 'grounds' it. In this sense, the role of Priapus is central not only as part of a narrative strategy which multiplies the thematic strata of the fiction. In the Lucianic scene, he is essential to Zeus, who is incapable of making judgements without his mediation. The Androgyne, the advice of Hippothadée and Rondibilis, the evangelical and neoplatonist injunctions which surface throughout the Rabelaisian text can no more dispense with the 'roidde dieu des jardins' than he with them. Zeus' remark to Priapus, 'habet tua mentula mentem',[19] might be read as a constructive inversion of Hippocratic theory on semen and the status of testicles; as such, it deserves to take its place amid the various 'morals' generated by the Couillatris fable. Mind is a function of desire; the problem of Panurge is constitutive of the text as a reflection of, and a reflection on, the conditions in which insight may be achieved; the *topos* as a conceptual fragment has no sense outside the hazards of an accidental fiction.

Priapus' brief re-entry into the *Quart Livre* in a gloss on the Andouilles (chapter 38) provides a postscript to the Prologue and indeed to the thematic representation of sex in the work as a whole. His presence here, as in the fable, seems to deflect, for a moment at least, the sense of the whole episode. Whereas the anatomy of Quaresmeprenant—like the second list of *couillon* epithets in the *Tiers Livre*—evokes a perspective of sterility, or of futile generation,[20] the prolific Andouilles are not only a figure of porcine consumption but also inherently phallic.[21] They incarnate the fundamental duplicity of sex:

Le serpens qui tenta Eve estoit andouillicque: ce non-obstant est de luy escript qu'il estoit fin et cauteleux sus tous aultres animans. Aussi sont andouilles.

Encores maintient-on en certaines Académies que ce tentateur estoit l'andouille nommée Ithyphalle, en laquelle feut jadis transformé le bon messer Priapus, grand tentateur des femmes par les paradis en Grec, ce sont jardins en François.[22]

According to this gloss, the gardens of Priapus become typolo-

[19] p. 573. Cf. p. 576: 'car j'ay mentule, voyre diz-je mémoire . . .'; the semantic equivalence of mind and member originates, as does so much else in Rabelais's fiction, in an accidental homophony.

[20] See *QL* 29, p. 661 ('Jamais ne se trouve aux nopces') and 30, p. 666 ('estant marié avec la Myquaresme, engendra seulement nombre de adverbes locaulx et certains jeûnes doubles'). His physical organs, as described by Xenomanes in *QL* 30-1, are markedly lacking in vitality (see also below, p. 208).

[21] 'Andouille' is one of the metaphors used by Gargantua's nurses to designate his phallus (*Garg.* 11, p. 74).

[22] *QL* 38, p. 687. Marichal (ed. *QL*, pp. 169-70, note on line 15) quotes Cornelius Agrippa's *De originali peccato* (1532) for the identification of the serpent with the 'andouille . . . Ithyphalle'.

gically (and etymologically) equivalent to the garden of Eden:
the god of horticulture, potency, and fruition, the cornucopian
god who, in other contexts, provided a remedy for the mortality
of fallen man, assumes the *persona* of the tempter himself. The
phallus both destroys and repairs, ravages and ripens (see above,
note 1); it is the origin of deviation from the paradisiac ideal, and
the means of reproducing (repeating) paradise-gardens indefatig-
ably until the Last Judgement. Like the Protean tongue, this
dubious fragment of flesh is the source of all abundance and all
waste: 'ubi uber, ibi tuber.' In this respect, 'le bon messer Priapus'
also resembles 'messer Gaster', whose opacity and materiality
are an obstacle to spiritual perception, and who nevertheless
initiates the constantly expanding movement of civilization.
Both are symbols of the duplicity of the fallen world; both must
be reckoned with in any quest for understanding or happiness,
indeed they are the necessary mediators of desire for a transcendent
telos; yet both are marked by original sin and may even be associated with the satanic source of perversion (or inversion).[23]

In this same passage, the female principle reappears in the
archetypal figure of Eve, that is to say, as the *victim* of temptation:
congenitally weak, no doubt, but not the origin of weakness,
since it is the phallic serpent who incarnates trickery and subversion. But in Rabelais's text, a further equivocation—heralded,
as we have seen, by the cornucopian *braguette*—is immanent. The
slippery phallus may change in gender as well as in its typological
figuration. In the passage quoted above, the duplicity of gender
surfaces in the phrase 'andouille nommée Ithyphalle' and is endorsed by the bisexuality of Niphleseth. The two-faced Priapic
trickster deepens his disguise and his ambivalence: a female phallus
generated the unstable duality of the world, or rather becomes the
figure of that ineradicable duality.

In so far as she is a kind of hermaphrodite, Niphleseth provides
a counterpart to the neoplatonist Androgyne. She is not simply its

[23] See the conclusion of *QL* 58 (p. 739), where the narrator himself (rather than
Pantagruel) quotes St. Paul's condemnation of 'gastrolatry'; Gaster is also the
inventor of gunpowder (*QL* 61, p. 748), which was commonly held to be a
diabolic invention (cf. *Pant.* 8, p. 246). See also the discussion of the Gaster episode
by Rigolot, *Les Langages*, especially p. 160.

dialectical opposite: rather, she is the alternative face of the same coin. One face figures a subversive movement from unity into duality, the other a redemptive movement from duality towards unity: both are aspects of a world which cannot be conceived of other than as duality. If *Gargantua* 8 is predominantly affirmative, celebrating the codpiece as a cornucopia and proposing a figure of sexual union transmogrified into 'charity', the Satanic-Priapic *andouille* is already lurking in its decorative garden; conversely, Niphleseth, who belongs to a mythical domain from which the ideal is noticeably absent, and who combines the perilous appetites of stomach and phallus, makes peace with Pantagruel: the fallibility and fallaciousness of her people are (at least provisionally) domesticated by the text.

After the systematic repetition structure of the *Tiers livre*, Rabelais's narrative abandons itself to a kind of gratuitousness. The *Quart Livre* no doubt brings into play many linking themes—ethical, historical, satirical, figurative—but the movement of the voyage from island to island imposes a high degree of narrative fragmentation. In this sense, the quest seems to take on an outward shape which acutely clarifies the problem latent in the consultation scenes of the *Tiers Livre*: the investigation of unanchored, fragmentary *topoi* is mythologized as the Pantagrueline fleet touches—always provisionally—on one alien 'place' after another. If the tautology embodied by Panurge (his *philautia*) was made evident in his dialogue with topical manifestations of *doctrina*, the fourth book breaks out of the 'circle of learning' and proposes an open-ended confrontation with *experientia*. Furthermore, the factor of displacement inherent in the voyage motif is multiplied by the dubious—sometimes virtually impenetrable—character of the narrative topologies: why Ruach, why the Physetère, why these particular episodes in this particular sequence? The quest now clearly transcends Panurge's initial question, and exhibits more and more urgently the desire to locate a place of abundance. At the same time, as has been remarked in recent commentaries,[24] it thematizes, more clearly and

[24] See Jeanneret, 'Les paroles dégelées'; Gray, *Rabelais et l'écriture*, ch. VI.

yet also more problematically than the earlier books, the character and operations of language itself. Ennasin is like an enormous outgrowth from Priapus' pun on *cognée*, illustrating a principle which is no doubt true of Rabelais's work as a whole, but is particularly apparent in the *Quart Livre*: the composition of the book is again and again dependent on the decomposition of language. At all levels of organization of the text—sounds, words, sentences, characters and their speeches, events, episodes —forward movement is a function of the deflection or interruption of normal language habits. If, as Valéry puts it, 'de grands dieux naquirent d'un calembour', it is still more evident that linguistic accidents play a major part in the generation of Rabelais's fictions.[25] The fragmentation of the macro-structure thus echoes the non-logic of the micro-structure: it repeatedly blocks the reader's attempt to constitute a story or meaning according to habitual rules of reading, while at the same time provoking his desire for unity by reverting to the thematic motifs of fasting and feasting, Lent and productive *médiocrité*. And in due course, late in the 1552 edition, the episode of the 'parolles dégelées' will provide a paradigm of the problems surrounding the epiphany of sense (see above, I. 3. ii).

In such a context, the cornucopian movement prefigured by the Gargantuan codpiece and by the inexhaustible barrel of the *Tiers Livre* Prologue is sharply accentuated, revealing all of its ambiguities. The narrative represents a constantly interrupted search for a place of abundance, uncovering on its way many places of emptiness and absence; likewise, the language of the representation owes its very proliferation and 'fruitfulness' to a principle of deviation which excludes any hope of arriving at a true *telos*, an ultimate closure of sense. The search for the 'Word' of the bottle is both perpetuated and frustrated (filled and emptied out) by the words which emerge from the barrel. 'Physician, heal thyself': so the Prologue to the *Quart Livre* insists (p. 568); but the *logos* cannot cure its own diseases, except by the (obviously fictitious) expedient of capitalizing its first letter.

The sentence 'Vray est que leurs provisions estoient aulcunement

[25] This point is illustrated, in various different ways, by both Glauser and Gray.

endommagées par la tempeste praecédente' in chapter 25 conceals a rupture, since the earlier version had ended with an abrupt formula of conclusion after 'Vray est que'. This is perhaps the clearest sign in all of Rabelais's work of the arbitrariness of the moment chosen to arrest the flow of words.[26] One might reflect on the fact that the preceding sentence refers to a central Rabelaisian theme (the generous exchange of goods which releases the cycle of abundance); or on the irony of an accident which leaves in suspense an assertion of *veracity*, even if it appears eventually as a conventional concessive phrase. At all events, it is important that the break should occur after the beginning of a new episode, so that the rupture invites a continuation: the thematic axis of the added narrative is predetermined in part by the names 'isle des Macraeons' and 'Macrobe'. The story is broken and re-opened within the domain of longevity, or rather of old age, and seems to mime in its very cessation the catastrophe which retrospectively 'explains' the preceding storm episode, namely, the death of a hero. Historically, there is little doubt that the juxtaposition of these two focal episodes allegorizes the relationship between the untimely and ominous death of Rabelais's patron Guillaume Du Bellay, champion of political and religious *médiocrité*, and the hardening of doctrinal lines at the Council of Trent.[27] Within the narrative, it is clear that a loss has occurred, a death or a funda-

---

[26] The endings of the various books are all 'inconclusive' in various ways. *Pantagruel* promises a continuation which will only be partly realized; the 'énigme en prophétie' seems unrelated to the themes of Thélème; the *Tiers Livre* ends with an anticipation of the Pantagrueline voyage. In particular, the later version of the *QL* closes with an episode which, although complete in itself, has no force as a means of integrating the narrative thread of the book as a whole: indeed, its lack of association with the major themes of the text seems to empty out the possibility of integration offered by the preceding Chaneph episode (but see Paris, *Rabelais au futur*, pp. 223–4, 236–7, where the scatological theme of the final chapter is read as emblematic of the 'désagrégation' which pervades the whole of the narrative of the *QL*).

[27] The storm is presaged, in QL 18, by an encounter with a boat-load of *religieux* on their way to the 'concile de Chesil'; it is precipitated, according to Macrobe, by the death of a hero, and Epistémon subsequently refers twice (QL 26, p. 654, and 27, p. 657) to the death of Du Bellay and to the 'prodiges' which preceded his death. On the importance of this episode, see Krailsheimer, *Rabelais and the Franciscans*, pp. 126–31.

mental rift in experience, disrupting the voyage and threatening its continuation. On the isle of the Macraeons, images of erosion abound. The island has declined from its original fertility:

icy est une des isles Sporades . . . jadis riche, fréquente, opulente, marchande, populeuse et subjecte au dominateur de Bretaigne; maintenant, par laps de temps et sus la declination du monde, paouvre et déserte comme voyez. (QL 26, p. 653)

Similarly, it is full of fragmentary remnants of a past civilization, heterogeneous in character and marked by a plurality of languages:

Et par la forest umbrageuse et déserte, [Macrobe] descouvrit plusieurs vieulx temples ruinez, plusieurs obélisces, pyramides, monumens et sépulchres antiques, avecques inscriptions et épitaphes divers, les uns en lettres Hiéroglyphicques, les aultres en languaige Ionicque, les aultres en langue Arabicque, Agarène, Sclavonicque et aultres. Desquelz Epistémon feist extraict curieusement.[28]

Rabelais's text itself, by echoing Plutarch and other antique sources, reflects this landscape of venerable but fallen *topoi*, only rediscoverable through a modern and essentially different sensibility. The motif of decline will be embodied in other episodes of the 1552 version: the Papefigues have fallen on hard times;[29] Gaster has usurped the 'Manoir de *Arété*', the earthly paradise situated on the Rock of Virtue, while his consort Penia once ('jadis') lived with Porus, Lord of Abundance, and gave birth to Amour, 'le noble enfant médiateur du Ciel et de la Terre' (QL 57, p. 735). The time is out of joint; the structure of the world has been dislocated, and the structure of Rabelais's myths mimes that dislocation.

It is true that the metaphysical nostalgia of the Macraeon episode constitutes a moment of tranquillity and contemplation after the storm. The danger is past, the ships are repaired and

---

[28] QL 25, p. 652. Cf. *Briefve déclaration*, p. 777, where the *Hypnerotomachia* is cited on the question of hieroglyphs. See also Goebel, 'Zwei Versuche'.

[29] See QL 45, p. 701: 'Au lendemain matin, rencontrasmes l'isle des Papefigues, lesquelz jadis estoient riches et libres, et les nommoit-on Guaillardetz; pour lors estoient paouvres, malheureux et subjectz aux Papimanes.'

revictualled, the journey proceeds joyfully and with a favourable wind:

Les naufz du joyeulx convoy refaictes et réparées, les victuailles refraischiz, les Macraeons plus que contens et satisfaicts de la despense que y avoit faict Pantagruel, nos gens plus joyeulx que de coustume, au jour subséquent feut voile faicte au serain et délicieux Aguyon en grande alaigresse. (QL 29, p. 661)

Equilibrium and forward movement have apparently been restored. But not for long. The voyage has hardly got under way again before Xenomanes points out the island of Tapinois in the distance and embarks on the detailed 'anatomy' of Quaresmeprenant. He does so in order to avoid a direct confrontation with the monster, not only because the 'maigre passetemps' of Quaresmeprenant threatens the 'alaigresse' of the company, but also because of 'le grand destour du chemin' which such an encounter would have caused. Yet the anatomy itself is in its own way just such a 'destour' or deflection of the voyage. It arrests the narrative, since there is no action, no event in these chapters. This particular 'Seigneur' and his domains remain absent, and are replaced by a discourse which describes them, just as in the preceding episode the discussion of heroes was a function of *their* absence. But whereas the death of heroes and even of Pan evoked, albeit in a minor key, the possibility of transcendence, the anatomy of Quaresmeprenant constitutes a negative place, an absence which remains sterile and unredeemed. His activities consist of negations, inversions, and tautologies: 'travailloit rien ne faisant, rien ne faisoit travaillant. Corybantioit dormant, dormoit corybantiant . . . Rien ne mangeoit jeusnant, jeusnoit rien ne mangeant . . .' (QL 32, p. 670). Such figures cancel one another out, producing a sense of stasis which echoes the inert *enumeratio* of his external and internal features and of his 'contenences'. Quaresmeprenant is an emptiness: the physiological disruption which is a consequence both of the catalogue device, and of the extraordinary series of incompatible similes which are used to describe him, deprives him of the coherence and dynamism of life. He is an image of the *abios bios* referred to in the Prologue (p. 570): his gigantic stature is literally abiotic in that it proliferates and extends itself according to a negative, disjunctive process which moves progressively further from any basis in experience. Once again, one is reminded of a paper currency, at one level because he is only present by virtue of *descriptio* and *enumeratio*, at another because he is said to abound in formal 'pardons, indulgences et stations'.[30] Furthermore, his likeness to Amodunt, child of Antiphysie, in the fable recounted by Pantagruel, demonstrates that he is a counterfeit, a malignant simulacrum of nature.[31] Indeed, Antiphysie, through the discourse of Pantagruel, attempts an encomium of her children which echoes Panurge's mock encomium of debt in that it constitutes at once an imitation and an inversion of a natural principle.

The tuberous malignancy of Quaresmeprenant is central to Rabelais's text in many ways. It establishes the stomach (rather than the sexual organs) as the dominant thematic axis of the later *Quart Livre*,[32] setting in train a sequence of episodes which assume a broadly antithetical pattern (Quaresmeprenant–Andouilles; Papefigues–Papimanes; Gaster–Pantagruel's feast). It may also be seen as a kind of variant of the *braguette* episodes of the earlier books: its lexical proliferation, anchored in themes of emptiness, sounds like a *reductio ad absurdum* of neutral textuality (*garrulitas*). Or again, Quaresmeprenant's monstrous features

[30] QL 29, p. 661; cf. 32, p. 669 ('S'il souffloit, c'estoient troncs pour les Indulgences'), and p. 670 ('S'il resvoit, c'estoient papiers rantiers').

[31] QL 32, p. 672: 'Ainsi, par le tesmoignage et astipulation des bestes brutes, tiroit tous les folz et insensez en sa sentence et estoit en admiration à toutes gens écervelez et desguarniz de bon jugement et sens commun. Depuis elle engendra les Matagotz, Cagotz et Papelars . . . et aultres monstres difformes et contrefaicts en despit de Nature.' On Quaresmeprenant as an 'Antiphysis esthétique', see Glauser, op. cit., pp. 249–56.

[32] As Marichal and others have shown, the themes of the QL, particularly in the later version, are determined in substantial measure by satirical aims. In 1547, the Council of Trent had reaffirmed the necessity of prescribed mortifications (cf. Marichal, ed. QL, Introduction, p. xxxiii); the expanded version of the QL appeared during or shortly before Lent in 1552; the saying 'Bien et beau s'en va Quaresme' is quoted at the beginning of the Prologue (p. 568); and the first wholly new episode in the voyage, following the visit to the Macraeons, is the account of Quaresmeprenant. Similarly, the Gallican controversy which came to a head in 1551 provides a satirical dimension for much of the new material in the 1552 edition (see Marichal, '*Quart Livre*: commentaires' (1964), pp. 100–33).

distantly recall the excrescences of Pantagruel's ancestors (*Pantagruel* 1), controverting their exuberance and exhibiting the ultimate gratuitousness of such fictional accidents.[33] The voyage, the narrative, the writing process, have here reached a nadir of which the disruptive storm, the death of heroes, and the landscapes of old age were only the prefigurations. Nature is absent, and can only be designated through her counterfeits, which in their turn are composed of absence. The text, with its interruptions, disjunctions, and non-sequiturs, enacts the grotesque deformity of Amodunt: it accepts monstrous obstruction as its mode of 'progression'.

This point may be further clarified by a brief examination of the episodes which follow. The 'Physetère' interlude restores the movement of the text with a piece of naïve narrative action: the fleet takes up fighting formation, Panurge babbles incoherently with fright, and Pantagruel performs a superlative feat of marksmanship with his gigantic harpoons. We have returned to the register of Pantagrueline domination of the world: *bios* is reasserted with unmistakable vigour and delight ('et estoit chose moult plaisante à veoir') (*QL* 34, p. 676). On the other hand, although the Physetère may graphically echo Physis,[34] the symmetry with which the harpoons are placed is clearly not that of Nature's children. It is a gratuitous piece of showmanship, a self-parodying imitation of epic. The fleet is arranged like a Greek gamma, the corpse of the monster resembles a galleon in the process of construction. Quaresmeprenant's malevolence is eluded via another corridor of fiction, where monsters are reassuringly slain by heroes.

Subsequently, the text reverts to his counterparts in excess, Mardigras and the Andouilles, by means of a new interruption:

[Pantagruel] condescendit toutesfoys descendre en l'isle Farouche pour seicher et refraischir aulcuns de ses gens mouillez et souillez par le vilain physetère à un petit port désert vers le midy, situé lèz une touche

---

[33] Cf. Glauser, op. cit., pp. 244–5.

[34] 'Physetère' literally means 'blower' (hence 'whale'); but the discussion of Physis and Antiphysie in the preceding chapter accidentally gives this monster an added dimension, as if he were a natural phenomenon, rather than a grotesque counterfeit.

de boys haulte, belle et plaisante, de laquelle sortoit un délicieux
ruisseau d'eau douce, claire et argentine. Là, dessoubs belles tentes,
feurent les cuisines dressées sans espargne de boys. Chascuns mué
de vestements à son plaisir, feut par Frère Jan la campanelle sonnée.
Au son d'icelle feurent les tables dressées et promptement servies.

Pantagruel, dipnant avecques ses gens joyeusement, sus l'apport
de la seconde table apperceut certaines petites andouilles . . . (QL
35, p. 678)

In place of the pleasure of the voyage, a *locus amoenus* in which
a dinner is served. But the arrival of the Andouilles disrupts the
meal, which will never be completed.[35] The culinary associations
of the battle with the Andouilles adumbrate, as it were, an alternative and more problematic meal: a grossly gastric form of
nourishment threatens to overwhelm the festive *topos* of the
opening. If the phantom of porcine indulgence represented by
Mardigras is held at bay with energy and even enthusiasm (on the
part of Frère Jan), the rarer delight of Pantagruel's feast will not,
in this episode, be reconstituted. A place of abundance, precari-
ously situated on the margin of the text's thematization of eating,
is rapidly invaded and replaced by a repetitious host of *andouilles*
which fill (copiously enough) the remainder of the episode. And,
strangely, Frère Jan suggests that the attack was provoked by an
error: the Andouilles mistook Pantagruel for Quaresmeprenant
(perhaps because he was dining moderately and thus appeared,
from their angle, to be fasting rather than feasting?).[36] Of course,
the mistake indicates that they, like the 'fols insensez' who believe
Antiphysie's encomium, are congenitally foolish; but the shift of
perspective which raises the possibility of a confusion between
the two giants provides a glimpse of sinister equivalences pro-
longing Quaresmeprenant's resemblance to Amodunt, and thus

[35] The motif recurs in QL 36, where Frère Jan, foreseeing trouble with the
Andouilles, says: 'Laissons ces repaissailles icy . . .' (p. 681), upon which Pantagruel
rises from table.

[36] QL 42, p. 696. Another accident occurs in 41, p. 693, where Gymnaste, in
his parley with the Andouilles, is reported to have made a slip of the tongue,
pronouncing 'Gradimars' for 'Mardigras' and thus failing to pacify the Andouilles: a chance rearrangement of sounds is given as a possible cause for a major
narrative development. For a gloss on 'Gradimars', see the Demerson edition,
note 4 (pp. 693–4).

Antiphysie's counterfeit reduplication of the children of Physis. The duplicity of the Andouilles, repeatedly emphasized by the narrative and figured in their ambivalent sexuality, thus reveals the duplicity of the text and of its gigantic fabulations.

Quaresmeprenant was followed by the Physetère; the isle Farouche is replaced by Ruach, island of wind (the name is glossed by the *Briefve Déclaration* as the Hebrew word for 'vent, ou esprit'). It had been anticipated by the Bringuenarilles episode of the 1548 version, which is explicitly recalled; but the figures of wind are now woven more intimately into the thematic fabric of the surrounding episodes. For the inhabitants of Ruach eat and drink wind; they too have appetites and banquets; and they too can be constrained to fast.[37] The narrative accords no special dignity to the island. Flatulence is, as one might expect, endemic among its people, who die farting ('Ainsi leur sort l'âme par le cul'), and their inverted festivities seem a celebration of emptiness:

> Quant ilz font quelque festin ou banquet, on dresse les tables soubs un ou deux moulins à vent. Là repaissent, aises comme à nopces, et durant leur repas disputent de la bonté, excellence, salubrité, rarité des vens, comme vous, beuveurs, par les banquetz philosophez en matière de vins. (*QL* 43, p. 697)

The accidental homophony which makes wind the obverse of wine repeats the onomastic similarity of Pantagruel to Panurge or the error of the Andouilles. It deflects the twin generative motifs of the voyage, the blowing of the wind and the convivial mood,[38] so that they become, for a moment, a strangely external object of examination, as if the text had alienated its own narrative *topoi* by stranding them on a specially designed fictional island or place (or rather, a non-place, a utopia in the strict sense of the word).

[37] *QL* 44, p. 700: Bringuenarilles's diet of windmills and bellows brings him annually at springtime to Ruach, imposing on the inhabitants 'troys ou quatre quaresmes par chascun an, sans certaines particulières rouaisons et oraisons.'

[38] These motifs often recur, together or separately, at the beginning of episodes throughout the voyage. They act both as a convention marking a shift in the narrative, and as a thematic nucleus which may be developed in the episodes themselves. The storm, which concludes the first version of the *QL*, may be read as a special instance of both functions with regard to the wind motif. See also pp. 584, 605, 609 (twice), 661, 708, 729, 751, 760.

This is also a domain where the king keeps, for its supernaturally therapeutic properties (the *maladie-santé* motif being akin to that of the 'well-tempered feast'),[39] 'une veze plene du vent propre que jadis à Ulysses donna le bon ronfleur Æolus pour guider sa nauf en temps calme':[40] the master-epic and its thematic motifs of movement and stagnation are represented in Rabelais's fiction by a magic wind-bag. The fallen text, the erratic text in which error composes the fiction, exhibits or mimes in its own mode the proper original fictional container—an epic bladder or codpiece.

In such ways, the satirical elements which polarize the thematic structure in terms of 'good' and 'evil' phenomena are dislocated by a narrative so plural that no commentary can control it. The apparent antitheses sketched out above are non-symmetrical, since their axes are manifestly different: narrative juxtaposition produces one kind of antithetical pattern, ethical evaluation another. These patterns may be reconciled if Pantagruel (or Pantagrueline festivity) is assigned a consistently positive role: he will appear then both as a principle of narrative *enchaînement*, and as a paradigm of *médiocrité* in opposition to the proliferating modes of excess. He is, as it were, the sovereign *topos*, wrestling with the Protean metamorphoses of the fiction. But this dialectical contest is subject to many uncertainties and shifts of identity. Behind the giant-hero and his opponents lurks a more radically Protean figure—that of the discourse itself—which engenders both of the protagonists and undermines their reassuring polarization. In consequence, the vicissitudes of the text appear as displacements rather than as a series of parallel pairs; and displacement is itself repeatedly enacted by disconnected episodes in which the medium of language might be said to contend

[39] Cf. *QL* I (p. 584), on the curative properties of the feast given prior to the departure of the fleet; also the therapeutic feast given by Pantagruel off Chaneph (see below).

[40] *QL* 43, p. 699. Ironically enough, the 'veze' has been stolen from the king, so that Ruach is, once again, afflicted by an absence of wind (or of *esprit*?). Note that while 'veze' means bladder (modern French *vessie*), the word is also reminiscent of *vesse* ('silent fart'), particularly as reference is made in the same sentence to farting ('un pet virginal').

gratuitously with itself. This is the dead centre or anti-centre of discourse, where the opposition between counterfeit and true model has been subverted.

Here the importance of Ruach is extreme, since the (accidental) antithesis *vent–vin* is devoid of any stabilizing context. The inhabitants of the island are neither malevolent nor deluded. They are simply an obverse phenomenon, a neuter species. They are the arbitrary product of a dialectic which is ruined by their vacuous presence. The name of their island, chosen by the hazardous licence of the narrator, engenders their mode of being.[41] It signifies, indifferently, *vent* or *esprit*: an emptiness or a plenitude; the accidental wind which propels the narrative, or the (super)naturally grounded mental impulse which confers a 'sense' on the fictional project. On Ruach, there is no way of distinguishing between *copia* and *loquacitas*: they are two faces of the same coin. The question about the opening word of the *Iliad* (see above, p. 127) here takes on its full force, and its full (empty) ambiguity.

Ruach is, however, not the only example of neutrality in this sense. One of the detours of the Prologue of the *Quart Livre* concerns the dispute between Ramus and Galland, professors of the Collège Royal. The subject of the dispute was dialectic: in other words, this was a dialectical performance of dialectical theory. The topic wrestles with itself. In addition, the antagonists are both called 'Pierre'. Priapus proposes to Jupiter, who has to resolve the dispute, the same remedy as in the case of the inescapable dog chasing the uncatchable fox: to turn them both to stone (*pierre*) (pp. 573–5). Similarly, Gaster, the counterfeit of Porus who lives on a mock Rock of Virtue, generates the dialectic of civilization and warfare (*QL* 61–2), culminating in a kind of perfect balance of offensive and defensive weapons. At this point in the text, the notion of equilibrium or stasis, established by the fiction of the cannon-ball arrested in mid-air by a magnetic stone, is repeated in a series of exemplary *topoi* such as that of the remora

---

[41] Cf. above, note 2, and the 'cratylic' names of the captains in the war with the Andouilles. The device of personification, which is so prominent in the QL (Quaresmeprenant, Gaster, etc.), is thus reversed, the name being prior to that which it personifies.

fish (pp. 748–51). In such (impossible) systems, entropy is suspended; there is no loss of energy, no accident, no event or catastrophe. Except, of course, that the slippage of the text itself belies its own products: the movement of these chapters is markedly sinuous and centrifugal. One is reminded of the frozen words, which are only represented by virtue of the thawed words of the narrative.

The 'parolles dégelées' episode shares with Ruach an initial association of speech with a kind of airy emptiness, in spite of the ensuing concretion of the sounds and words as they become visible and thaw out. The table talk of the voyagers as this episode begins—their 'beaulx et cours discours'—is interrupted, echoed, and inverted by the apparent sound of 'quelques gens parlans en l'air', and the act of hearing is embodied in a figure of eating and drinking.[42] But the culminating association of the motifs of wind and *festivitas* occurs in the Chaneph episode, which will provide the topical focus for a last rehearsal of Rabelaisian problems.

This new interruption is signalled by the stasis of the whole fleet, inverting exactly the conditions of the storm episode:

Au jour subséquent, en menuz devis suyvans nostre routte, arrivasmes près l'isle de Chaneph, en laquelle abourder ne peut la nauf de Pantagruel, parce que le vent nous faillit et feut calme en mer. (QL 63, p. 751)

The rather desultory reference to the voyagers' compulsive desire to talk seems here to attract the figure of a dead calm, which in turn engenders a mood of speechless torpor:

Et restions tous pensifz, matagrabolisez, sesolfiez et faschez, sans mot dire les uns aux aultres. (p. 752)

The narrative proceeds only by the elaboration of a non-event. Pantagruel himself dozes ('sommeilloit'), holding a Heliodorus,

---

[42] QL 55, p. 729: 'à pleines aureilles humions l'air comme belles huytres en escalle . . .' The simile is ambiguous: do the ears suck in the air as if they were eating oysters, or are the ears compared (in appearance) with oysters? In either case, the companions feast on air, so that this image (which also distantly recalls the figures of Ruach) anticipates certain of the expressions used later in the episode for the progressive concretion of language ('et sembloient dragée perlée de diverses couleurs', p. 732; 'motz de gueule', p. 733).

prototype of romance fictions: novel-writing—or rather novel-reading—is here reduced to a form of somnambulism. The imperfect tense of 'sommeilloit' persists through a catalogue of the idle occupations of the rest of the company: the ship's lack of movement is compensated for by a gratuitous proliferation of bubble-blowing, tooth-picking, head-scratching, finger-tapping, and nose-picking. Another dead point or neutral place seems to have been reached, but is now enacted by the Pantagrueline company itself: hence the problem is seen as endemic in the core of the text, not simply as a product of its occasional themes.

Nevertheless, an epiphany of some kind is being prepared. Frère Jan notices that Pantagruel has woken up; the silence and the suspended time of the imperfect are broken:

Adoncques rompant cestuy tant obstiné silence, à haulte voix, en grande alaigresse d'esprit, [Frère Jan] demanda: 'Manière de haulser le temps en calme?' (loc. cit.)

An eventual movement of time and weather (wind) is envisaged; appetite re-establishes itself in a series of questions (echoing Panurge's initiatory question of the *Tiers livre*) which render evident a lack, a hunger, an emptiness that seeks to be filled. Even if the questions are idle (intellectually unproductive), they will release a positive response from Pantagruel. This scene enacts, indeed, the awakening of appetite as an unfathomable shift from inertia and absence towards the potentiality of presence. The desire for sense, for the production of an event, is represented here as a 'pure' theme, uncontaminated by any specific subject-matter.

Pantagruel's response is anti-verbal, in that he proposes for all the questions (symptoms) a single solution (cure) 'par signes, gestes et effetz' (p. 753). The sign is a banquet which, as in the *Convivium religiosum*, has evangelical associations;[43] Gaster, having

[43] See the passage quoted below ('Dont tous chantèrent . . .'), and Panurge's speech in QL 65, p. 758: 'Sans poinct de faulte nous doibvons bien louer le bon Dieu, nostre Créateur, Servateur, Conservateur, qui par ce bon pain, par ce bon vin et frays, par ces bonnes viandes nous guérist de telles perturbations, tant du corps comme de l'âme, oultre le plaisir et volupté que nous avons beuvans et mangeans'. Although the emphasis on the healing value of bread and wine, following an evangelically phrased reference to God as 'Servateur', may recall the

been fully recognized in the preceding chapter, is now given his proper place. Whereas in the Gaster episode the *topos* 'venter auribus caret' had designated a mindless materialism, here it is linked with the theme of moderation.[44] The coming banquet will not be the fulfilment of an obsessive greed; rather it will engender productive conversation, manifesting the release of an authentic abundance in which the Androgynous duality of body and soul is once more unified. The dynamic equilibrium of the episode thus suggests the possibility of relocating arbitrary, groundless linguistic signs in a 'natural' sign of conviviality. Textually speaking, little space is devoted to the description of the banquet: unlike the lists of delicate dishes in the 'Gastrolâtres' episode, or the *remplissage* of the Andouilles, this sign of presence and plenitude is strictly circumscribed. The meal is copious but apparently frugal: four enormous, thirst-provoking 'pastez de jambons', drink to match, 'dessert', and fruit. A single exclamation ('Vray Dieu, comment il y feut beu et guallé!') encapsulates the delight of the feast and is immediately followed by a narrative shift to the theme of the wind:

Ilz n'avoient encores le dessert, quand le vent Ouest-Norouest commença enfler les voiles, papefilz, morisques et trinquetz. Dont tous

sacrament in general terms, it can hardly be used as evidence that the whole episode is the allegorization of an evangelical Eucharist (see Saulnier, 'Le festin devant Chaneph'). Cf. the far more explicit sacramental references in the *Convivium religiosum* (above, pp. 104–5).

[44] *Pantagruel*, in his advice to Panurge on how to prepare for prophetic dreaming (*TL* 13), uses traditional physiological arguments in order to support the contention (itself a *topos*) that fasting produces sterile thoughts (see Screech, ed. *TL*, notes on ch. 13). Hunger calls back to earth 'cestuy esprit vaguabond, négligent du traictement de son nourrisson et hoste naturel, qui est le corps: comme si l'oizeau, sus le poing estant, voulloit en l'aër son vol prendre et incontinent par les longes seroit plus bas déprimé' (p. 416). Moderation is therefore recommended: Panurge is to eat home-grown fruit and drink fresh water (p. 417). Although this is in some sense a special case, since Panurge is preparing himself for access to supernatural knowledge, and although elsewhere the diet of moderation may be less frugal, Pantagruel follows essentially the same advice when he speaks of the possibility of mediating between Quaresmeprenant and the Andouilles (*QL* 35, p. 680). At the end of the dream episode, Panurge quotes the adage 'le ventre affamé n'a poinct d'aureilles' as justification of his refusal to listen to Pantagruel's interpretation: his excessive desire is not susceptible of Pantagrueline moderation (*TL* 15, p. 424).

chantèrent divers cantiques à la louange du très hault Dieu des Cielz.
(*QL* 64, p. 756)

The songs of praise mark this clearly as the wind of *afflatus*, rein-
stating a movement towards the metaphysical *telos* proposed by
the narrative. Frère Jan's initial question, 'Manière de haulser le
temps?', is the last to receive a reply; it allows Pantagruel to
develop the theme of the rising wind through a series of tropes
and *exempla* which culminate in the figure of a winged Bacchus:

Ne sçavez-vous que jadis les Amycléens sus tous Dieux révéroient
et adoroient le noble père Bacchus, et le nommoient *Psila* en propre
et convenante dénomination? *Psila*, en langue doricque, signifie aesles.
Car, comme les oyseaulx par ayde de leurs aesles volent hault en l'air
légièrement, ainsi par l'ayde de Bacchus (c'est le bon vin friant et
délicieux) sont hault eslevez les espritz des humains, leurs corps évidentement alaigriz, et assouply ce que en eulx estoit terrestre.   (*QL* 65, p. 760)

The rhetoric of celebration is here unambiguously affirmative.
The epithet 'noble' aligns Bacchus both with 'Amour le noble
enfant médiateur du Ciel et de la Terre' and with the positive face
of Gaster as 'noble maistre des ars'. The naming of Bacchus as
Psila asserts the value of *proprietas*: a true naming is glossed by an
etymology in which the power of signifying is fully stabilized.
Similarly, the glossing of Bacchus ('c'est le bon vin . . .') permits
the production of an ethico-physiological theme resuming the
topical direction of the episode as a whole.[45] Both movements—
the thematic and the rhetorical—are crystallized in the notion of
an evidence ('leurs corps *évidentement* alaigriz'): the whole company can *see*, immediately, the deployment of a rediscovered
dynamism.[46] Speech has become possible once again, as the
opening of the next chapter indicates: 'Continuant le bon vent et
ces joyeulx propous . . .'.

[45] The ethics and the physiology of Pantagruel's argument here are, once again,
very close to those of *TL* 13; furthermore, the use of the simile of flight to express
the liberation of the spirit from corporal constraints occurs in both chapters (see
the quotation given above, note 44).

[46] Cf. *QL* 65, p. 759: 'Reste donc à vuider ce que a Frère Jan propousé:
manière de haulser le temps. Ne l'avons-nous à soubhayt haulsé? Voyez le
guabet de la hune. Voyez les siflemens des voiles. Voyez la roiddeur des estailz,
des utacques et des scoutes.'

For a moment, this episode reorganizes and polarizes the unstable antitheses of the preceding chapters. The transcendent
movement of the winged Bacchus triumphs over the faecally
orientated mock-Bacchic procession of the Gastrolâtres;[47] the
material literality of the text has been revivified by the pneuma
of its sense. For, once again, the wind which arises from the
banquet is not the wind of flatulence or vacuity but of *esprit*:
the neutrality of the isle (and word) Ruach has been by-passed.
'Bon espoir gist au fond.' Couillatris may yet recognize his
cognée, Panurge his own will. The cornucopian codpiece retains
some at least of its erective virtue. The aporia (Penia, hunger,
quaestiones) of the company may locate a way (*poros*, quest) to
abundance (Porus, *copia*), despite all copies and counterfeits.

Such is the event which is glimpsed through the lattices of the
text, a presage of ethical and epistemological progress. Its positive
aspect is endorsed by the fictional toponymy which situates the
episode near Chaneph. This island, whose name is glossed as
'hypocrisy', will—like Tapinois—not be visited by Pantagruel, so
that its inhabitants will have to be described by Xenomanes. The
'cagotz' and 'hermites' of the island are beggars, 'paouvres gens,
vivans . . . des aulmosnes que les voyagiers leurs donnent' (QL
64, p. 754): the opposition between their *quête* and the appetite of
the Pantagrueline company seems to echo, at some distance, the
opening antithesis of the *Convivium religiosum*. Furthermore, their
false abstinence (whence the name of the island) dissimulates a

---

[47] The procession of the Gastrolâtres is led by 'un gras, jeune, puissant Ventru,
lequel sus un long baston bien doré portoit une statue de boys, mal taillée et
lourdement paincte, telle que la descrivent Plaute, Juvénal et Pomp. Festus. A
Lyon, au carneval, on l'appelle *Maschecroutte*; ilz la nommoient *Manduce*' (QL
59, p. 739). After them come 'un grand nombre de gros varletz chargez de
corbeilles, de paniers, de balles, de potz, poches et marmites. Adoncques, soubs la
conduicte de Manduce, chantans ne sçay quelz Dithyrambes, Craepalocomes,
Epaenons, offrirent à leur Dieu, ouvrans leurs corbeilles et marmites: Hippocras
blanc . . .' (p. 740). The 'Dithyrambes, Craepalocomes, Epaenons' are glossed
by the *Briefve déclaration* as 'chansons de yvroignes en l'honneur de Bacchus'
(p. 779), and the 'baston', 'corbeilles', and the rest mark this as a mock-Bacchic
procession recast in the style of a rustic carnival, just as the classical Manducus
becomes interchangeable with the native 'Maschecroutte'. At the end of QL 60,
after the distended lists of gastric *remplissage*, the Gastrolâtres are obliged to
recognize that their true *telos* is 'matière fécale' (p. 746).

promiscuity which explains their abundance ('y a *copie* de petitz hypocritillons . . .'); the anti-nature of monasticism, whose sterility should be self-eliminating, ironically flourishes by virtue of its very inauthenticity. By circumscribing, and eventually circumnavigating, this negative terrain, the Pantagrueline text demonstrates its own desire for authenticity; in this respect, it resembles the Thélème episode, which feeds on negations and exclusions.

The place of abundance and celebration is not an island, but a movement, of which the above analysis has outlined the thematic components. But a still more fundamental textual movement needs to be clarified, since it creates the very conditions in which the themes may be produced. Its character derives from the opposition between Pantagruel's insistence on the priority of non-verbal signs and the need (or desire) to verbalize.[48] Ironically, he glosses the value of signs by embarking on one of his characteristic classical *exempla*, undercutting his own emphasis on immediacy ('La response vous sera *promptement* expousée, non par longs ambages et discours de parolles') (*QL* 63, p. 753). Yet the *exemplum* ('Comme jadis en Rome Tarquin l'orgueilleux . . .') is itself accompanied by a gesture (the ringing of a bell) which produces an immediate effect ('Frere Jan *soubdain* courut à la

---

[48] Cf. Jeanneret, 'Les paroles dégelées', pp. 25–9, on the linguistic implications of this episode. He points out, for example, that Pantagruel never gives a full reply to the questions asked; like Eusebius in the *Convivium*, Pantagruel defers the issue for discussion on some subsequent occasion: 'Puis (dist Pantagruel) que de ceste légière solution des doubtes propousez vous contentez, aussi foys-je. Ailleurs et en aultre temps nous en dirons dadventaige, si bon vous semble' (*QL* 65, p. 759). Thus, too, the continuation of the voyage depends on the intrinsic mobility of language. Although—as my own analysis suggests—Pantagruel's provisional answer might be said to consist in the feast (a non-linguistic sign of presence), nevertheless it emerges equally, at the textual level, from the repetition and re-reading of a proverbial phrase: the accepted figurative sense of 'haulser le temps' ('to pass the time drinking') is displaced by its literal application (the rising of the wind): 'Reste donc à vuider ce que a Frère Jan proposé: manière de haulser le temps. Ne l'avons-nous à soubhayt haulsé?' This re-reading evades the problem by means of a kind of tautology (cf. Priapus' advice to change Pierre into *pierre*). As in other episodes, a quasi-cratylist invocation of the 'natural' sense becomes a device by which the narrative may be extended: 'Nous haulsans et vuidans les tasses, s'est pareillement le temps haulsé par occulte sympathie de nature' (p. 759).

cuisine'). The theme of immediacy is thus performed by means of a controversion which is inevitable since the text cannot but operate as a mediation. The location of presence, or rather of a movement towards presence, amid the detours of topical and narrative discourse entails a more intricate set of self-exploding strategies than at any other point in the whole of the Rabelaisian fiction. One of these is the counterpointing of tenses: in this particular speech, the promise of a solution in the immediate future is overtaken by an exemplary fragment from (and in) the past. Between them, in parentheses, the 'wordless' gesture of bell-ringing is introduced by an expression of simultaneity: 'ce disant . . .'. Such tense-shifts are specific examples of the pheno- menon of interruption, which reveals here with particular clarity the double function (deflection and expansion) which makes it characteristic of the voyage as a whole. The banquet is deferred— not only by the Tarquin *topos*, but also by the discussion of Chaneph, initiated by Pantagruel himself—until a time comes ('Neuf et d'aventaige') the precision of which is tied, as a sign, to the natural fruition of appetite (*QL* 64, p. 755). But yet again, time seems to be on the point of defeating itself by provoking a gloss and thus by deferring the required immediacy of the meal: it is only when the 'officiers de gueule' interrupt Pantagruel ('Ce mot n'estoit achevé . . .') in order to lay the tables that the banquet begins (p. 756). The topic of temporal harmony has all but swamped the *festivitas* to which it pointed. But not quite. How- ever self-parodying Pantagruel's glosses may seem to be, his filling out of the time between the questions and the meal serves to lay bare, by the double movement of text and theme, the problem within which the whole episode, as a pure fictional 'event', may be seen to operate. Similarly, the table-talk which begins to proliferate as the fruit is served is therapeutically reflexive, and not only (as is evident) in the concluding glosses of Pantagruel. When Eusthenes enunciates his alphabetical list of venomous creatures (pp. 756–7), he is performing *tuber* in the mode of *uber*, a procedure which encapsulates the central strategy and mode of survival of Rabelais's work as a whole.

Hence this place of celebration can only develop in the text if and because its grounding is constantly undermined and its presence systematically placed in question. The wind which, according to epic convention, assures the continuation of the narrative, also operates as disruption, interruption, inversion, obversion. The filling of the sails is germane to the filling of hypocritical codpieces, or the bellies and wind-bags of Ruach. The textual voyage which seeks (or originates in) inspiration, the immediate word, breath divinely filled, is congenitally subject to flatulence, inflation, deflation, deflection, mediacy, and perpetual deferment. Its presence signifies or carries the absence of what it seeks. Indeed the wind, it might be said, figures the ineradicable gap between word and gloss, that hiatus or interruption which interminably forestalls the integrality proper to the ideal text. Each new accretion of the Rabelaisian book is a kind of gloss on what precedes, shifting the perspective and inaugurating a new 'reading'; consequently it also destabilizes or pluralizes the reading, inviting yet further episodes. In spite of Chaneph, the *Quart Livre* remains the book of the deferred or interrupted feast: the 'mot de la Dive Bouteille' is beyond its fictional reach. After the banquet, the experience of Ganabin and the laxative fear of Panurge enact an evident non-closure, followed by a hiatus which is in turn followed (posthumously) by a (perhaps inauthentic) fifth book which 'concludes' with an instruction to reread (see above . . .)—or, perhaps, to supplement the text by means of the endless episodes of critical commentary.

And so the circle described and prescribed by Rabelais's fiction, measuring its distance from the ideal encyclopedic text, accepts imperfection, fragmentation, plurality, as a condition of its existence. Fruitfulness can only arise, in such a self-consciously fallen and deviant text, from a performance in which the conjurer reveals and mocks both the mechanisms and the products of his magic horn, inviting the audience to participate in his act and to rehearse—at an ever-increasing distance—his inimitable sleight-of-hand.

3

Ronsard

THE problems of writing and of reading posed by Ronsard's poetry may, in the most general terms, be ascribed to its proliferation. Like Rabelais's fictions, it opens up the perspective of an ideally completed work; but the process of writing constantly (and at times quite expressly) postpones completion, exploring instead the pleasures of repetition and fragmentation. From a critical point of view, the difficulties inherent in any reading of the 'complete works' of an author are thus presented in their most acute form. The text and its reader are caught up in a pursuit of integration which, if not fruitless, is none the less bound to be frustrated. Procedures of reduction like distinction of genre or style prove to be wholly inadequate. Unlike the Virgilian model, elevated by medieval rhetoric to a paradigm of the three estates of poetry, Ronsard's writing flows over all generic boundaries: hymns, odes, elegies, eclogues refuse to separate themselves into reassuring categories and often shift their position in subsequent collective editions. Attempts to organize the poems into historically meaningful phases forming a consistent pattern of evolution also tend to break down once the level of broad generalities has been passed. Early poems on old age and the emptiness of experience, late poems asserting youthful vigour, can only be made to fit even a fictional biography by means of *a priori* decisions about what is acceptable as characteristic of this or that phase. The study of thematic motifs is subject to similar objections. How far is it legitimate to compare, say, a mythological figure in a love-sonnet with its counterpart in a cosmic hymn? Thematic integration is achieved at the expense of levelling down the local intricacies and refractions which are essential to the functioning of the text. This textual resistance ought, in any critical account, to be made manifest, but if it is, the consequence must be accepted: namely, that no commentary will ever be more than a study of selected singularities whose claims to priority are by no means self-evident.

The possibility remains, however, of making capital out of this difficulty by exploiting it as a critical theme. Thus this chapter will first outline the recurrence of non-integration as a problem in Ronsard's writing, indicate the ways in which it emerges as a theme, and isolate some of the textual features which are characteristic of it. Subsequently, a handful of poems will be considered in detail in an attempt not to illustrate some 'essentially Ronsardian' quality, but to display the more extreme consequences of the dialogue between integration and fragmentation. In other words, these instances of close analysis are offered expressly as a special case, showing what is possible in a sixteenth-century poetic text rather than what is characteristic.

Ronsard's first major publication, the 1550 *Odes*, concludes with the Horatian claim of *A sa Muse*: 'Plus dur que fer, j'ai fini mon ouvrage' (*L* II, p. 152). In retrospect, the irony of such a claim is evident: a fifth book of odes and other supplementary pieces will shortly appear; and in any case, the collection looks more like a preliminary exercise than a monument. It is characterized by extreme diversity of theme and of style—even of genre, since it contains both 'Pindaric' and 'Horatian' odes; indeed, its preface, in self-defence, makes diversity a claim to poetic superiority.[1] Exactly the same story will be repeated with the *Amours*. The 1552 collection opens with a sonnet of dedication which represents the book as a completed whole being offered up to the Muses,

---

[1] 'Je ne fai point de doute que ma Poësie tant varie ne semble facheuse aus oreilles de nos rimeurs, et principalement des courtizans . . . je m'assure qu'ils ne me sçauroient accuser, sans condamner premierement Pindare auteur de telle copieuse diversité et oultre que c'est la sauce, à laquelle on doit gouster l'Ode. Je suis de cette opinion que nulle Poësie se doit louer pour acomplie, si elle ne ressemble la nature, laquelle ne fut estimée belle des anciens, que pour estre inconstante, et variable en ses perfections' (*L* I, p. 47). Cf. the quotation from Erasmus's *De copia*, above, p. 22. Ronsard's reference to the inconstancy of nature compounds the primary notion of diversity, adding a sense of unpredictability.

but it ends (not unlike *Pantagruel*) with the promise of more to come: 'Je congnoy bien qu'encor' je ne suis pas, / Pour trop aymer, à la fin de ma ryme' (*L* IV, p. 171). In 1553 the cycle will be duly expanded by internal additions, and in 1555 and 1556 will follow the *Continuation* and *Nouvelle continuation des amours*, justifying in prologues and epilogues their right to make a new beginning. Later, the two books of *Sonnets pour Hélène* may seem to impose a kind of finality, sealed by the gesture of abdication in the concluding sonnets: 'C'est trop chanté d'Amour sans nulle recompense'; 'Je m'enfuy du combat, ma bataille est desfaite' (*L* XVII, pp. 293, 294). But, alongside and after them, the *Amours diverses* proliferate. They form a continuous supplement which contaminates the closure of the Hélène cycle as sonnets are moved from one collection to another. Thus Petrarch's exemplary sequence, its unity consecrated by the intervening centuries, is broken open, beyond any possibility of integration, by the insatiable desire to write and rewrite.

These symptoms are local examples of the problems of organization apparent in the successive editions, from 1560 onwards, of the collected works. Not only are the individual sections—*Amours*, *Odes*, *Hymnes*, and so on—subject to Protean changes and to the tensions set up by a constant influx of new materials; they are already, in 1560, shown to be indeterminate by the presence of the *Poëmes*. This motley collection seems principally designed to absorb texts which will not fit in elsewhere. Since it partakes in some measure of all the other genres, it comes near to being at once a sub-category and an inclusive category, thus undermining the etiquette of the collection as a whole. As one might expect of such a permissive genre, it allows a high degree of transmigration across its borders; it is both the parasite and the supplier of the orthodox genres.[2] Furthermore, in a late verse preface to the book, Ronsard distinguishes between 'poësie', a unified collection of different 'arguments' like the epic of

---

[2] I should like here to acknowledge a debt to Mrs. Jean Braybrook, who, in her as yet unpublished doctoral work on Ronsard's epic fragments, has supplied evidence both for these remarks on the *poëme* and for my sketch (below) of structural aspects of Ronsard's epic writing.

Homer, and the 'poëme', which represents an isolated episode.[3] The *poëme* is by definition a fragment.

Although Ronsard succeeds, in the 1584 folio, in achieving some kind of correspondence between the totality of his writing and the physical unity of the book, the pervasive uncertainty exemplified by the fragment-poem makes the exercise a precarious one. No less precarious is the choice of that edition—whether by Ronsard himself or by modern editors—as superior to the others. After all, it excludes a large number of texts which appear in earlier (and later) editions. What is more, it outlaws many different states of the texts which it does include. Ronsard's poetry proliferates (to this extent like the *Essais*) not only by the writing of new poems but also by the rewriting of old ones. These variants, instead of conferring a classical perfection and finality on the end-product, ironically multiply the Ronsardian text and make it literally impossible to recover a universally recognized 'complete works': each poem demands to be reread according to its own rewritings and according to its shifting place in the various editions.

Ronsard's composition of a monumental *œuvre*, a book containing 'all' the poems, is in any case undertaken *faute de mieux*. For the true work is a *poësie*, the finished epic which his writing unsuccessfully pursues from the earliest years.[4] The epic project often takes thematic form as the announcement of its future realization: in such cases, it relegates the text in which it appears to a preliminary or accessory status. This is true, for example, of the 1550 *A sa lyre* (*L* I, p. 164), or of certain passages in the *Ode à Michel de L'Hospital*. Elsewhere, a foretaste of the epic itself is given. The 1550 *Ode de la paix* swells to accommodate a condensed epic, a parasite which explicitly disrupts the structure of the host-poem;[5] on the other hand, the two 'Argonaut' fragments

[3] *L* XVIII, pp. 283–4. This definition does not cover all the types of poem placed by Ronsard among the *Poëmes*, but it serves to characterize their essentially centrifugal nature.

[4] The history of the project is conveniently summarized by Laumonier in *L* XVI, Introduction.

[5] Cf. *L* III, pp. 22–3: 'Muse, repren l'aviron . . . / Sans estre ainsi vagabonde. / Tousjours un propos desplaist / Aus oreilles attendantes, / Si plein outre reigle il

published in the 1556 *Hymnes* monopolize the space of their poems at the expense of any superior coherence. Taken together, they form a variation exercise. Each concerns the exploits of a legendary pair of twins; and in the *Hymne de Castor et de Pollux* the reduplication operates still more overtly as a repetition in that each hero in turn is presented in combat with a monstrous opponent.[6] That these poems are only rehearsals for an always deferred full performance is advertised in the prelude to the same hymn:

> Il faut sonder ma force, et m'esprouver un peu
> Mener un petit bruit, luire d'un petit feu,
> Faisant mon coup d'essay sur des patrons estranges,
> Avant que de tonner hautement voz louanges
> D'un son digne de vous . . .

(L VIII, p. 294)

This remark goes much further than the conventional depreciation of *juvenilia* as *coups d'essai*. It does not, in reality, mark any distinction between the lesser and the greater achievements of the writer. Since no ideally complete text will materialize to impose a hierarchy, every poem in the corpus comes to appear as an *essai*. The *poëme* or preliminary text instals itself permanently, so that even the *Franciade* will be both unfinished and internally fragmented. This, of course, does not in itself explain the failure of the *Franciade* project, in which the conditions of patronage and other external problems also play an essential part. But such problems, as will shortly be argued, erupt internally within Ronsard's work both as themes and as recurrent self-questionings, and these inner disturbances are virtually inseparable from the phenomenon of non-completion discussed here.

est / De parolles abondantes . . .'. The self-corrective movement is transposed from Pindar, together with its images. By discounting in advance the reader's potential objection, it gives licence, in effect, to the foregoing passage; the rest of this epode (and the first word of the ensuing strophe: 'Diversement') constitutes a defence of diversity, provided that it is sufficiently concentrated ('Celui qui en peu de vers / Etraint un sujet divers, / Se mét au chef la couronne'). Here, as for Erasmus, *copia* and *brevitas* counterbalance one another.

[6] It is perhaps precisely because they are so transparently similar and repetitious that, in all editions from 1560 to 1584, they are placed in separate books of the *Hymnes*. A similar reduplicated structure is apparent in the *Orphée* (L XII).

The 'internal fragmentation' referred to above as characteristic of the *Franciade* can be traced through many levels of Ronsard's texts. The epic examples illustrate most clearly procedures such as multiplication of narrative strata (in which the narration is chronically interrupted by the insertion of secondary narratives), digressions, temporal dislocations, and so on. Sometimes an allegorization or moral gloss is proposed by the text, but proves to be only partially applicable, so that a tension is set up between the poem and its own gloss.[7] But similar phenomena also occur in the rhetorical fabric: figures of displacement like metonymy and periphrasis—not to mention metaphor itself, and extended epic similes—tend to monopolize the surface of the text. *Enargeia*, invited by the desire to give narration the function of an eye-witness account and thus lend it *vraisemblance*,[8] proliferates at a tangent to the narrative, evolving its own micro-legends: fabulous cloaks and shields testify to the status of gods or heroes, but at the same time disguise them as complex rhetorical figures. These characteristics will be examined in greater detail below, although not in the context of epic poems as such. For the present, it will be enough simply to have pointed to further ways in which a Ronsardian poem undermines its own chances of completion and coherence.[9]

The problems posed by textual proliferation at these aesthetic levels have their counterpart in certain thematic motifs. These may be isolated if the object is to show, not that a given set of themes presides over and orders the whole of Ronsard's output, but that a number of texts draw attention to their own difficulties, illustrating them, attempting to transcend them, and perhaps in

[7] See, for example, the *Hymne de Calaïs et de Zetes* (L VIII, pp. 291–2, lines 709–17), where two alternative interpretations are briefly suggested.

[8] I refer here to Ronsard's epic theory as outlined in the prefaces to the *Franciade*. The notion of *vraisemblance* appears specifically in the 1572 preface (L XVI, pp. 3–5); but it is the posthumous preface (L XVI, pp. 331 ff.) which lays particular stress on mimetic techniques as a means of authenticating the narrative.

[9] This remark (and others like it elsewhere) does not in any sense represent a pejorative judgement. Disaggregation is no less productive a phenomenon in Ronsard's poetry than it is (*mutatis mutandis*) in Pascal's *Pensées*. The same problem is considered from the standpoint of normative evaluation in Silver, *Ronsard and the Greek Epic*, especially chs. xxiii–xxiv.

the end only exacerbating them. I have attempted elsewhere to indicate the recurrence of themes of abundance—and of its inverse —in Ronsard's poetry;[10] broadly, they might be summarized as constituting a dialogue between, on the one hand, the figures of plenitude embodied in natural or national fertility, Bacchic mythologies, or the neoplatonist ascent, and, on the other, the threat of emptiness or impotence. Thus, for example, the *Amours* insistently assert the productivity of their author in counterpoint to the frustrations of the lover. The text proliferates gratuitously, producing nothing but flowers of rhetoric and dreams of con-summation. Likewise, the themes of patronage conjure up frescoes of god-like monarchs and nobles, at whose feast the poet sings and whose victories he celebrates, assuring himself as well as them a place in history. But their lack of generosity rapidly emerges as a counter-theme, notably in a series of court poems, to the Cardi-nal of Lorraine and others, published between 1556 and 1565. The poet, financially as well as erotically unrequited, is left with the fragments of his own devalued mythologies.

Such figures suggest the problems of a writer deprived of an adequate reader: since the poems masquerade as messages addressed to a woman or a patron, the failure of the circuit to complete itself causes tensions and disruptions in the medium of communication. To this predicament one may add, finally, that of the writer who knows that his text depends on other texts. Pindar and Horace, Petrarch, Homer and Virgil, and many others, determine his topics and his rhetoric. He can exploit them vic-toriously, claiming to have naturalized them:

> Sus donque Muse emporte au ciel la gloire
> Que j'ai gaignée annonçant la victoire
> Dont à bon droit je me voi jouissant . . .
>   (*A sa Muse*; L II, p. 153)

Multiple imitation in the Erasmian (rather than the Ciceronian) manner also offers him a virtually limitless field of textual pos-sibilities. But this intertextual proliferation defies the imposition

---

[10] See in particular the article 'Mythes de l'abondance et de la privation'. Cf. McFarlane, 'Aspects of Ronsard's poetic vision', where a broad range of thematic motifs are shown to be grouped around these polarities.

of an order which would integrate it into a single, all-inclusive
poësie. The epic itinerary is subject to endless deviations from the
route.

The pleasures of such deviation are conveniently illustrated by the
first strophe of the *Ode à Michel de L'Hospital*. It represents the
poet, as his text begins, wandering amid colourful and copious
fragments of classical text:

> Errant par les champs de la Grace
> Qui peint mes vers de ses couleurs,
> Sus les bords Dirceans j'amasse
> Le tesor des plus riches fleurs,
> Affin qu'en pillant je façonne
> D'une laborieuse main,
> La rondeur de ceste couronne
> Trois fois torce d'un ply Thebain:
> Pour orner le hault de la gloire
> Du plus heureux Mignon des Dieux,
> Qui çà bas r'amena des Cieux
> Les filles qu'enfanta Memoire.[11]

Like *A sa Muse* (see above, pp. 153–4), this strophe both imitates
and speaks of imitation: the Grace, the flowers, the crown, the
folds of the triadic structure, are all displaced from Pindar into the
fabric of a new ode. But at the same time, the very possibility
of *imitatio* depends on *elocutio*. Both the richness of the materials
and the complexity of the weaving are illustrated by the rhetoric;
in this respect, the composition of a poetic text designated as a
'crown' for an illustrious contemporary is analogous to the fabrication, by means of *enargeia* and its satellite figures, of periphrastic

---

[11] *L* III, pp. 118–19. A close parallel is provided by a passage from Du Bellay's
Musagnœomachie. Between an enumeration of royal names and another of writers'
names, a reflexive stanza—again quoting the *topos* of the poet as a bee gathering
honey from many flowers—stresses the bewildering excess of materials available
to poetic discourse, and its consequent randomness: 'Les scadrons avantureux / Des
abeilles fremissantes / Forment leur miel savoureux / Des fleurs sans ordre nais-
santes / Par les plaines verdissantes. / Tel est le vol de mes vers, / Qui portent ces
noms divers, / Discourant parmi le monde / D'une trace vagabonde. / Mais rien
choisir je ne puis / Au grand thesor qui m'abonde, / Tant riche pauvre je suis' (ed.
Chamard, vol. 4, p. 12).

cloaks and microcosmic shields for the heroes of legend. Thus, in a single syntactical movement, the initial metaphor of flower-gathering (the figure of how the poem is to be made) is elaborated by successive layers of metonymy and periphrasis, introducing by allusion first the model-poet and then the patron. Neither is named. Pindar is displaced so that the poetic *je* can appropriate his *topoi*; and the addressee himself only appears here as a circumlocution. L'Hospital is the pretext, an empty place to be skirted by myths, narrations, and the incrustations of *elocutio*. In this way, the poem generates its folds from within by a constant process of inbreeding: flight from *proprietas* guarantees the fabulous extension of the lyric text. This is true in the larger design of the *Ode*, as well as in the rhetorical detail of individual strophes. The poem both advertises and disguises the powers of poetry by means of a series of interrelated but non-linear episodes, leading back eventually, after many detours, to the deferred figure of the patron.[12]

Together with the celebration of a poetic epiphany, this poem heralds the opening of a new age of national greatness to be brought about by culture. Indeed, the two topics are essentially linked. What one might call the 'liminary stance' of the *Ode*—and of many other similar poems—points towards the inauguration of a Golden Age which it must itself, as a privileged mode of culture, bring into being. Thus the *Ode* contains an epic fragment on the topic of royal victory (the Gigantomachy sung by the Muses) and alludes to a future epic on the historically fruitful wanderings of Francus. The *Deffence et illustration* and the official

---

[12] Even at the last moment, his place in the ode seems to be challenged by an encomium of Marguerite (*L* III, pp. 162–3). Two further points may be added here. (i) The juxtaposition of model-poet (Pindar) and patron in the opening strophe is no accidental alignment. Both are prestigious figures, who threaten the poet as well as offering him sustenance; his poem exists in an uneasy relationship to both simultaneously. 'Patron', after all, also means 'model' (as, for example, in the quotation given above, p. 227). (ii) The 'weaving' motif which is present from the beginning of the ode is recalled towards the end in a passage where the Fates are seen 'weaving' L'Hospital himself (strophe 20). The patron, like the ode itself, is a text (even a textile). Cf. also the references to Ronsard's own poetic activity as weaving at the end of the poem (lines 727 and 809–10), based on the Pindaric image of the textual 'fold'.

entry of Henri II into Paris in 1549 (on which Ronsard and Du Bellay both wrote substantial poems) repeat, in their different ways, the same gesture: future tenses, prophetic motifs, metaphors of beginning hint at a fulfilment as yet unrealized. Poetry inhabits a region in which no decision—how to begin, how to continue—is fully engaged. Meanwhile, it indulges and reflects on its own proliferation, substituting rhetorical elaboration for the plenitude which it seeks eventually to reveal. This liminary stance will be re-enacted many times in Ronsard's poetry: in the 1550s, for example, the exploration of new genres, styles, or models provides the motive power for its production, so that each volume published appears as an initiation. In one sense, indeed, every poem in the corpus takes on this character in the absence of a completed epic. Each poetic experiment may be read as an exercise in view of a performance which will never take place, as a variation (or variant) constantly renewing the cornucopian movement with its proliferation of flowers and its uncertainty of fruition.

In certain contexts—those where the dialogue with history is most apparent—the inaugural game played while waiting for a reward assumes a literally material form. Patronage appears as an exchange system in which the poem itself, like the names which circulate within it or in its margin, is a currency seeking its titular value: each ode bears in its title or in its text the effigy of its would-be guarantor (*Au roi*, *A Madame Marguerite*, *A Michel de L'Hospital*, and so on). Similarly, the lyric text which locates itself amid a superabundance of materials already evokes the image of wealth and luxury; it appears explicitly as a form of excess, to be justified by an appeal to the culture it mirrors and replenishes. Thus the *Ode à Michel de L'Hospital* offers itself as a crown, an object woven of precious materials, to a patron who is to create the conditions within which further—and still more elaborate—poems may be written. And inversely, it weaves this figure of a patron both through the 'copieuse diversité' of its own folds (since, as an artefact, it proposes a style to be adopted by its consumer) and more literally by the inclusion of the passage evoking the fabrication of L'Hospital by the Fates. The gratuitous elaboration of the ode is in this manner counterpoised by the myth of a predestined patron who will redeem it at its true value.

Among the many poems of Ronsard which are presented self-consciously as luxurious 'gifts' to friends and patrons, the 1555 *Hymne de l'Or* (*L* VIII, pp. 179 ff.) provides a model which deserves extended consideration, since the theme of wealth, and of poetry as part of (or even, in one sense, as *wholly*) a system of exchange, is there made fully explicit; the poem in this instance discloses its own self-endorsing character, and reacts symptomatically with tactics of evasion and irony. Technically, it is an exercise in demonstrative rhetoric, belonging to the category of the 'mock encomium', a device much exploited in the Renaissance to explore problematic areas of experience. The praise of gold as presented here is both arbitrary and provocative: an alternative poem in praise of Poverty is envisaged as a possibility from the outset (lines 53–8), and subsequently an alternative ethic which would predictably and conventionally stress such themes as the transient nature of material riches and the need for philosophers to remain uncontaminated by the desire for gain (lines 335 ff.). Like the *Praise of Folly* and Panurge's praise of debt, Ronsard's poem purports to defend what might seem to be morally indefensible; and it shares with them the mechanism of the paradox, in which an unresolved dialectic is proposed between an ethic and its ironic inversion.[13] Ronsard's specious argument is indeed the more unresolved in that there is no superior voice or text to

[13] See in particular Margolin, ' "L'Hymne de l'Or" et son ambiguïté'; also Verdier, 'A propos d'une controverse sur l'*Hymne de l'Or*'. Verdier summarizes a debate between Frappier and Weinberg and intervenes on the side of Frappier; both sides attempt to resolve the ambiguity of the text in order to discover whether Ronsard was 'really' praising or attacking gold (cf. Verdier, p. 18: 'le moi profond finalement transparaît'). Margolin's masterly reading, which preserves the full value of the paradox, goes much further in relating the hymn both to current socio-economic values and to the genre of the mock encomium. Cf. also Demerson, *La Mythologie classique*, pp. 408–12. On Renaissance paradox in general (of which the mock encomium is a specific instance), see Colie, *Paradoxia Epidemica*. It is important to distinguish between two types of paradox (although they may of course converge): one is the provocative reversal of a commonly accepted proposition; the other, a rhetorical form closely related to oxymoron, is a proposition containing an apparent contradiction.

anchor the shifting sense. Erasmus ends by elaborating Plato and
St. Paul on Christian folly; Pantagruel, too, reverses the sense of
Panurge's speech by means of a Pauline injunction; although
neither gesture wholly eliminates the foregoing ambiguity, each
at least appears, strategically, to polarize the ethical argument.
The *Hymne de l'Or*, by contrast, absorbs and discounts the answer-
ing voice; for example, the evangelical law of charity becomes
yet another pretext for praising gold (143–6), just as it had served
Panurge's defence of debt.

In Ronsard's hymn, gold or 'Richesse' becomes the horn of
plenty, the origin of all goods:

> Il nous donne la grace, et si nous donne encor
> Sçavoir, honneur, beauté, parentez, mariages,
> Et seul, il nous transforme en cent mille visages.
>
> (154–6)

> Et bref, la Richesse est la corne d'Amalthée,
> Qui tout donne à foison, c'est le joyau d'honneur,
> C'est la perle de prix, c'est le souvrain bon heur . . .
>
> (168–70)

The equivalence of the cornucopia with material riches was no
doubt, as Laumonier indicates, prompted by a fragment in
Stobaeus. There are also many sixteenth-century examples:
Fortuna is depicted with a cornucopia both in Alciat's emblems
and Ripa's *Iconologia*. But Ronsard goes further by making riches
the source of 'le souvrain bon heur', a phrase provocatively close
to the *souverain bien* of philosophers. This development is indeed
reminiscent, in certain respects, of the stoic paradox according to
which the sage has access to all goods, external as well as internal.[14]
The relationship between wealth and virtue is different here, in that
Ronsard makes gold the source of moral qualities rather than their
reward (or a figure of it). But the structure of the paradox is the
same in each case: the two supposedly incompatible notions of

[14] Cf. Cicero, *Paradoxa stoicorum* VI, and *De natura deorum* II. lxvi. In his adage
Copiae cornu (*Adages* I. vi. 2), Erasmus quotes Plutarch's phrase 'the stoic Amaltheia' as 'mocking the paradoxes of the stoics, who attribute all things to their
wise man: riches, freedom, health, power'. The reference is to Plutarch's *Stoicos
absurdiora poetis dicere*, 5 (1058 C). Cf. also Horace, *Satires* I, 3.

material and moral riches are made interdependent, so that the
reader is invited to reassess their relationship.[15] Thus, too, Ronsard
cites Aristotle on the value of wealth as a mediator of virtue:

> Chacun la veut avoir, chacun l'estime et prise,
> Pource, entre les Vertus Aristote l'a mise,
> Non pas comme Vertu, mais comme l'instrument
> Par lequel la Vertu se monstre clairement,
> Qui manque est de soimesme, et jamais ne se monstre
> En lumiere, si l'OR pour guide ne rencontre.[16]

Gold is thus, in what is given as a morally positive sense, a mode of
ostentation, a means by which virtue may 'show itself' publicly
(the same theme will be developed later in the poem). Virtue is in
itself an absence, a lack ('la simple Vertu n'a jamais bonne bourse',
line 160); its constant association with poverty throughout the
hymn contaminates it, exactly inverting the conventional ethic
according to which it is contaminated by riches. Virtue can only
achieve presence by becoming evident in the tangible plenitude
of wealth: the ethical abstraction must move towards, be material-
ized in, the surface of a precious metal.

Like other objects of *encomia*—debt, Pantagruélion, Gaster,
Ronsard's own Bacchus—gold is also presented as the origin of
civilization, of war and peace, of economic life:

> O gentil OR, par tout tes forces tu decœuvres
> Plus claires que le jour, tu es utile aux œuvres
> Soit de guerre ou de paix, par toy les sainctes Loix
> Fleurissent és Citez, par toy les grands Bourgeois,
> Les Palais, les Marchez pompeusement fleurissent,
> Et par toy jusqu'au Ciel les Temples se batissent.
> L'avare Laboureur, l'Artizan, le Marchant
> Transforme en ton metal l'usure de son champ,
> Car trop plus que Ceres tu luy sembles utile . . .
>   (243–51)

[15] Culler, 'Paradox and the language of morals in La Rochefoucauld', has much
that is pertinent to say about the way in which paradox operates.

[16] Lines 211–16. This quotation from Aristotle, like the other quotations used
by Ronsard in the hymn, is taken from the Florilege of Stobaeus (see Laumonier's
notes, *passim*).

It is essential to a fallen world, in which nature no longer nourishes man of its own accord as in the Golden Age; it mediates productive labour, and its absence (like the absence of Couillatris's axe) is equivalent to hunger or exposure to the elements (181–6, 196–8). Indeed, in a sense, gold fabricates its own Golden Age, its own cornucopia, imitating and displacing those of nature (173 ff.); indeed, Ronsard's praise of gold converges with Panurge's praise of the codpiece by alluding to man's need to remedy his natural vulnerability by means of protective clothing (187 ff.). Gold thus assumes the character of an economic *copula mundi*, a universal principle translating nature into human coinage: in this world, nature—like virtue—is 'manque de soymesme' and must be commuted into property, buildings, artefacts of all kinds.[17] Above all, the encomium 'demonstrates' that man's *contentement* can only be enacted in the material décor afforded by gold:

> Sçauroit-on devenir expert en la peinture,
> Expert en la musicque, ou en l'architecture,
> Si l'on n'a point d'argent pour avoir des outilz?
> Voirroit-on en tant d'artz tant de Maistres subtilz,
> S'ils n'avoient par argent payé l'apprentisage
> De leurs mestiers venduz? ô bon DIEU, que l'usage
> De ce metal est grand! ô qu'il est precieux!
> L'homme ne vit pas tant de l'air tiré des Cieux,
> De pain, de vin, de feu, comme il se laisse vivre
> De cent mille plaisirs que cét OR luy delivre:
> Sans luy, chacun languist en paresseux sejour,
> Sans luy, l'on ne sçauroit, ny pratiquer l'amour,
> Ny prodiguer festins, ny demener la dance,
> Ny au son des hauxbois marcher à la cadance . . .
>
> (123–36)

Avarice is rejected in the culminating argument of the poem because, by making the medium of exchange an end in itself, it arrests the dynamics of desire. If gold is to bring satisfaction, it

---

[17] Cf. lines 249–51 (quoted above; 'usure' here means 'yield'); also lines 181–2. Ceres is, of course, a figure of purely natural production.

must be displayed and expended, not hoarded.[18] Avarice thus creates a place of emptiness in which the image of plenitude hangs tantalizingly close but can never be grasped (585 ff.). The hymn praises repeatedly the 'force' of gold, its cornucopian power of movement from absence to presence, its capacity for making evident its own qualities as well as those of virtue or nature: thus, in the fable invented to demonstrate the supremacy and origins of gold, the Earth, mother of all the gods, opens herself up to reveal the precious metal with which the gods will hasten to adorn themselves (267–316).

The *Hymne de l'Or* is central to the two books of hymns in that it manifests an overt complicity with the system of patronage for which it is written. In its first edition, the double collection of 1555–6 is emblazoned with the names of royal and noble figures who together form the Olympic fresco of the opening hymn: Henri II, his sister Marguerite, the Châtillon brothers, the Lorraine brothers. Demonstrative rhetoric here serves the power and exemplary status of Ronsard's patrons or potential patrons, who take priority over the cosmic and mythological themes with which the hymn as an antique genre is most closely associated. Thus two motifs run side by side: the affluence of the court, expended on war and ostentatious construction, and the poet's desire to participate in it. The poetic edifice in massive *alexandrins* dedicated to Henri II, or the imaginary 'temple' in which the Châtillons are deified, are designed to provoke the release of *largesse*—money, benefices—and thus betray the anxiety of a discourse whose precarious existence depends entirely on the exchange value of the couplets it can generate.[19] If the ostentation of certain fifteenth-century Italian patrons was exhibited in the gold and gilt applied at their behest,[20] that of Henri II's court,

---

[18] Lines 552 ff. This argument is given ethical (and rhetorical) support by the preceding attack on prodigality (lines 507–50).

[19] For other passages associating poetry with architecture, see *Odes* (1550) II. i (*L* I, p. 167), and *La Lyre*, lines 335–50 (*L* XV, pp. 31–2). For Ronsard's jaundiced view of the favour given to architects at Henri II's court, see *Complainte contre fortune*, lines 331–6 (*L* X, p. 32).

[20] See Baxandall, *Painting and Experience* I. 2–4. Baxandall here outlines a shift from preoccupation with expensive materials such as gold and ultramarine to

already mirrored in the décor of Fontainebleau, is echoed in the
dedications and themes of Ronsard's poems. But in this instance
the coinage is not guaranteed by the rarity of the metal: consequently, the encomium may designate the absence of plenitude
even while purporting to celebrate its presence. The themes of a
gift yet to be given, of an always future generosity, surface again
and again in this collection and in ensuing ones; the liminary
stance continues to be repeated.

It is true that the *Hymne de l'Or* disguises its commitment to the
Establishment by the tactic of naming Dorat as its addressee:
the pun apart, one might have expected one of the cosmic
hymns, rather than this perilous exercise in praising money, to
be addressed to a scholar and a pedagogue. Within the poem
itself, the references to Homer's poverty and later to the impossibility of studying without buying books evoke again the
image of the poet as a non-aulic figure. But the disguise may of
course be read as a further manifestation of the ironic *divertisse-
ment* in which the poem as a whole is engaged: an emblem of
learning and of dedication to the Muses is offered as a guarantee
of the 'seriousness' of the argument. Moreover, two central
features of the text link it with patronage. In the first place, the
imaginary interlocutor who evokes the transience of wealth is
silenced by a lengthy reference to the hereditary establishment of
kingdoms, and in particular of the French monarchy ('Nostre
Prince Henry donne assez cognoissance / Que les biens temporels
long temps demeurent seurs') (lines 361–72). Thereafter, the
positive value of riches is repeatedly demonstrated by their
association with a royalty which guarantees their ethical status:
kings and princes are naturally inclined to valour and virtue, and
their riches are the necessary means of expression of such qualities
(379–88, 437–44, 469–76). Poverty, on the other hand, is excluded
from the presence of kings ('Jamais pour sa parente un Prince ne

emphasis on the painter's skill; however, for reasons discussed by Margolin, the
prestige of gold—as a currency and as a metaphor of value, if not as a material for
artefacts—was again at a peak in the mid sixteenth century. Cf. the exuberant
list of attributes to which the gods apply gold decoration in the *Hymne de l'Or*
(lines 295–316).

l'advoüe, / Jamais pres des grans Roys on ne la voit assoir') (484–5). In the second place, this set of arguments, in which the monarchy is explicitly presented as a place of abundance, is paralleled by the over-all thematic stratagem which makes avarice, not riches, the object of attack, and thus stresses the importance of expenditure or *largesse*. The text, it is true, refers to the royal payment of poets only in passing and in the third person (83–5). Yet it places before the reader, in its opening and closing lines, the image of the impoverished poet, thus creating an absence which the text itself will seek to fill, both by the empty celebration of a theme and by the reciprocal gesture of material reward which that celebration invites. Although Calliope is said not to favour poets who seek gain for its own sake (27 ff.), the *telos* of the poem, in both the rhetorical and the material sense, is the demonstration of gold.

Gold is one of the many figures of abundance in Ronsard's poetry. It has particular interest, not only because it pervades the network of allusions to patronage which recur throughout his work, but also because of its ambivalence. It is both the figure of an authentic, original value or productivity (as in the 'Age of Gold' myths), and a conventional sign which proliferates in the absence of any such value. While seeming to point towards the mirage of a natural plenitude, the dynamics of wealth and the only fruitfulness it can achieve depend on dissipation. As a topic of poetic texts, its functioning reflects the game of *elocutio*, the extension of the poem's surface by the expenditure of figures such as periphrasis, *enargeia*, adynaton; or, at a higher level of organization, by the recycling of imitated materials, traces of a lost age of golden letters. When, in the pastoral genre, imaginary shepherds representing poets or court figures vie with one another in wagering (and in describing) precious objects, their contest is the mechanism which allows the poem to proceed;[21] cosmic hymns, like artificial

---

[21] See the *Chant pastoral sur les nopces* (1559), *L* IX, pp. 84 ff.; the 1563 *Eglogue*, *L* XII, pp. 147 ff.; the 1565 *Bergerie*, *L* XIII, pp. 82 ff. This motif is a *topos* of pastoral poetry in the Alexandrian mode.

globes of the earth and heavens, appear as painted objects offered
to patrons;[22] and a poem purportedly exchanged for a glass or
a lyre becomes itself a fragile decorated surface whose shape is
delineated by an emptiness.[23]

Such examples make it clear that the cornucopian movement
rehearsed in the *Hymne de l'Or* and in other poems concerning
patronage is by no means trivialized by the mercenary associations of the pursuit of material gain. The set of topics involved
here is in many respects similar to—and certainly as fundamental
as—those to which studies of Ronsard have traditionally given
priority, namely, the themes of love and of poetic inspiration.
As has already been suggested, the unrequited, self-nourishing
desire for wealth has its counterpart in the erotic domain, where
the indefinite repetition of the poetic act occurs in the absence of
consummation. The paper currency of the text, destined for the
figure of a mistress which it fabricates *de toutes pièces*, becomes
a surrogate for the exchange of love; its own insufficiency to
purchase 'real' goods generates a verbal effusion, a prodigal self-
expenditure of *elocutio*. This process is demonstrated in many of
Ronsard's love-poems: in the images of cosmic and mythological
sexuality from which the poet is excluded, in the poems of dream
and metamorphosis, or in the emblematic figure of an Apollo
who charms the flowers and streams of his *copia*-landscape, but
whose song is powerless to move Cassandra.[24] As in the fables
of Ajax and Hyacinth, where the dying lover is transmuted into

---

[22] See Keller, *Palingène, Ronsard, Du Bartas*, pp. 62–5 (with reference in particular to the *Hymne du Ciel* and the *Hymne de la Philosophie*). These instances are
analogous to the Homeric *topos* of Achilles' shield as a microcosm.

[23] See the *Elegie du verre* (L VI), and McFarlane, 'Ronsard's poems to Jean
Brinon', pp. 58–62. The figure of the glass (and its shaping by the breath) is a
particularly striking thematic expression of the precarious nature of *elocutio*,
dependent as it is on the *vide*, and on an ambivalent 'inflation'. On *La Lyre*, see
below.

[24] *Amours* (1552), sonnet XXXVI (*L* IV, p. 39). A detailed analysis of this and
related texts is given in my article 'Ronsard as Apollo'. On the thematic representation of desire and its obstacles in Ronsard's poetry, see Gendre, *Ronsard poète de
la conquête amoureuse*. Cf. the close of sonnet XCVII in Du Bellay's *Olive*: 'Helas!
on veult la mienne [sc. rose] devorer: / Et je ne puis, que de loing, l'adorer / Par
humbles vers (sans fruit) ingenieux.'

a flower inscribed with his name,[25] the poet-lover disintegrates to become the texture of the verbal flora which bear his signature.

The mythology of poetic inspiration, as its analogy in the neo-platonist schema to the erotic *fureur* might suggest, has many similar features, although it is somewhat differently structured. The notion of a divine breath—or, in the dithyrambic texts, of a Bacchic energy—informing the folds of the poem offers a guarantee for the productive accidents of poetic language and thus permits, once again, the movement towards presence to be adumbrated. But here too, the circular, self-endorsing character of the situation is not hard to discern. Just as the coin bears the sign of its value (must indeed be taken at 'face value'), so too the *Ode à Michel de L'Hospital* carries its theory of divine fury as part of a mythological narrative, that is to say, of a complex instance of *enargeia* and prosopopeia; the theory is itself one of the poem's *plis*, the fold in a fabulous mantle, while at the same time it represents in its figurative décor the wind which is (said) to 'afflate' the fold. Likewise, the Muses open their mouths and endow the poem with a copious periphrasis, the figure of that plenitude which the lines of an errant text can never fully (by definition, as it were) unfold:

> Elles ouvrant leur bouche pleine
> D'une doulce Arabe moisson,
> Par l'esprit d'une vive haleine
> Donnerent l'ame à leur chanson . . .[26]

For here, the exemplary song of the Muses is represented at one remove; the Ronsardian ode is its copy, though necessarily a spurious one, since the mythological fiction it generates is the only sign of an original.

[25] Laumonier remarks that Ronsard 'a rappelé ces légendes à satiété' (*L* X, pp. 130–1, note 4), and provides a list of references. For a transposition of the *topos* to the poet himself, see *Amours* (1552), sonnet XVI (*L* IV, p. 20).

[26] Lines 171–4. The 'fullness' of the Muses' breath is translated, appropriately, into a periphrasis. Richelet's interpretation of 'une doulce Arabe moisson' as 'moisson riche et heureuse' is rejected by Laumonier, who takes it as a metaphor for the perfumed breath of the Muses (see *L* III, p. 128, note 2). But the Ceres-like image of natural plenty is in both cases associated with the poetic product of the breath.

It hardly needs to be said that the question whether Ronsard 'really believed in' the neoplatonist theory of inspiration has little pertinence in such a situation. (It is much less important, for example, than the question whether Rabelais was an evangelical, or an atheist, etc., since the Rabelaisian text, unlike the Ronsardian, seems always to envisage an ideological or at least a moral product which would be beyond or outside itself.) The *fureur* is a topic which polarizes the materials of a poem; by testing its power as an organizing theme, it also illuminates the constraints to which the writing of poetry is subject, and above all its self-constituting character, its inability to escape its own space. In many poems, this inbreeding provokes complex thematic and rhetorical structures comparable with that of the *Hymne de l'Or* or the *Ode à Michel de L'Hospital*. The four hymns of the seasons (*L* XII) will provide a central example, since they represent the most fundamentally 'natural' movement of all, that of the generative cycle. Taken as a group, they delineate the transition from absence to presence, from chaos to organization—but also from presence to absence and from integration to disintegration.

One might well assume that the mime of the four seasons would be enacted symmetrically, in four symphonic movements. This supposition is belied by the accidents of composition, which have left behind a threefold irregularity never erased or even attenuated in subsequent editions. The four hymns vary markedly in length (*Printemps*: 130 lines; *Esté*: 232 lines; *Autonne*: 470 lines; *Hyver*: 398 lines); they are distinguished topically by the intrusion into *Autonne* and *Hyver* of long introductory sections of a quasi-theoretical type, wholly unrelated (in narrative terms at least) to the ensuing fable; while *Printemps* and *Esté* each contain (different) accounts of the origin of all four seasons. This last feature has provoked the argument that *Printemps* was written first as an independent piece, the notion of a fourfold cycle being an afterthought; and the counter-argument that *Esté* was written first.[27] If this debate over the historical sequence of com-

[27] The first hypothesis is Chamard's, the second Laumonier's. See *L* XII, pp. 35-6, note 4, and p. 41, note 1.

position is at best an accessory one, it does lay bare a central aspect
of how the texts function; the reduplication of a fable of origin
points to the uncertainty of the origin or 'order' of the cycle itself.

In its simplest form, this asymmetry is a consequence of the
decision to make of each hymn not merely a *tableau* of seasonal
characteristics and activities (a familiar enough *topos*) but the
account of the genesis or maturation of a mythological figure. For
the epiphany of any one season necessarily presupposes the whole
scheme: a season is constituted by its relationship with others,
having no sense as a separate entity. Thus the birth of the seasons
must be simultaneous, as the two accounts in *Printemps* and *Esté*
specify.[28] The project of a seasonal cycle of poems must consequently have an inherent problem of organization: each poem
will be a retelling of the myth of origin from a different angle,
not simply an equal instalment in a sequential narrative. The point
is confirmed by the fact that the remaining two hymns contain
partially disguised versions of the same simultaneity: Autumn
steals attributes from her brothers Spring and Summer and participates in the negative, destructive characteristics of Winter,
while Winter himself monopolizes the space of the year until he
is 'bound' by Jupiter. The four examples taken together suggest
something like the neoplatonist 'Chinese box' system, according
to which an original principle multiplies itself from within (as in
the equivalence between Apollo, the three Graces, and the nine
Muses); except that the Ronsardian myths, being fictionally
incompatible, cannot be reduced to a homologous pattern, so that
they substitute aesthetic plurality for metaphysical unity.[29]

[28] The two versions are as follows: (i) Jupiter, jealous of Spring's union with
his own consort the Earth, takes the knife 'Dont n'aguere il avoit entamé son
cerveau, / Quand il conceut Pallas la Deesse guerriere, / Detrancha le Printemps, et
sa saison entiere / En trois pars divisa . . .' (*Printemps*, lines 66–9); this version also
refers to the violent binding and imprisonment of Winter (91–4) which is developed at greater length in *Hyver* itself; (ii) Nature, having been 'embraced' by
the Sun, gives birth to all four seasons (*Esté*, lines 107–22). A further difference
between the two accounts resides in the fact that, in *Printemps*, the myth of Spring
precedes the fourfold division which assigns to him, *post hoc*, his specific domain.
[29] The triumph of Vertumnus and Pomona in the *Songe de Poliphile* (a plato-
nizing allegory) embodies both a separate mythological characterization of each
season and a synthesis of the cycle in the triumph itself.

Reduplication, then, is a congenital aspect of the seasonal hymns; each poem partially replaces the others, causing involutions which disrupt the apparently simple line of the mythological fresco. This process may also be considered in terms of the constant displacement of a plenitude envisaged as the *telos* or product of the generative cycle. In *Printemps*, the Sun—'Par sa vertu'—makes the Earth 'de toutes choses Mere', Spring having acted as a kind of go-between. In *Esté*, the Sun becomes the lover of Nature and the father of all four seasons; subsequently, by means of a transparent reduplication within the poem's structure,[30] Summer is coupled with Ceres and is said thus to 'perfect' the sterile union of Spring and Earth. But in *Autonne*, the marriage of Autumn with Bacchus makes the horn of plenty subject to Autumn's control (the same passage emphasizes her 'participation' in both Spring and Summer); and in *Hyver*, the rehabilitation of Winter—which is celebrated at a feast of the gods—attributes to him the indispensable power of germination (lines 382–4). Although it might be claimed that the outcome of these successive rewritings is a fairly straightforward allegory of the complementary nature of the seasons (each eventually claiming its proper place), the movement towards fulfilment in each poem none the less dislocates the myths of fulfilment in all the others. In other words, the cyclical scheme undermines the individual poems, and is in turn undermined by them, an effect which is exacerbated not only by the narrative revisions but also the unequal lengths and the differing *entrées en matière*. The textual seasons constantly escape the constraints of symmetry; they trace out a series of detours which belie the heliotropic perfection of a would-be seasonal circle.

The internecine conflict of the myths carries with it a further major consequence: each seasonal personification appears as ambiguous, as both constructive and destructive. Spring is both a mediator of fruition and sterile (producing flowers without

---

[30] The speech in which Nature makes a sexual approach to the Sun, justifying her transgression of conventional morals (*Esté*, 61–90), is closely imitated by Ceres in her wooing of Summer, son of the Sun (187–210). On this and related aspects of the seasonal hymns, see Stone, *Ronsard's Sonnet Cycles*, pp. 108–18.

fruit); Summer both ripens and ravages; Autumn is associated with sickness and decay, but also with ripeness; Winter kills and germinates. This scheme reverts, it is true, to a traditional conception of the dynamics of generation according to which life and death, decay and ripeness, presence and absence are necessarily interdependent. Distinct echoes of the parallel schemes of the elements, the humours, and the 'ages of man' are also apparent here.[31] But Ronsard inserts another kind of ambiguity which disturbs the wholesome *discordia concors* of the seasons. The vigour attributed to Spring in the (brief) space of his own hymn is displaced by the heliocentric account in *Esté* of the four children of Nature and the Sun:

> De quatre embrassemens que Nature receut
> D'un amy si ardant feconde, elle conceut
> Quatre enfans en un coup: l'un fut Hermaphrodite,
> (Le Printemps est son nom) de puissance petite,
> Entre masle et femelle, inconstant, incertain,
> Variable en effet du soir au lendemain.
> L'Esté fut masle entier, ardant, roux et collere,
> Estincelant et chault, ressemblant à son pere,
> Guerrier, prompt, et hardy, toujours en action,
> Vigoreux, genereux, plain de perfection,
> Enemy de repos . . .   (107–17)

Again, the ambivalent sexuality of Spring is contrasted with the male *vertu* of Summer in the speech of Ceres:

> Depuis que le Printemps, cette garse virille,
> Ayme la Terre en vain, la Terre est inutile,
> Qui ne porte que fleurs, et l'humeur qui l'espoinct,
> Languist toujours en sceve, et ne se meurist point:
> Dequoy servent les fleurs, si les fruicts ne meurissent?
> Dequoy servent les bleds, si les grains ne jaunissent?
> Toute chose a sa fin, et tend à quelque but,
> Le destin l'a voulu, lors que ce Monde fut
> En ordre comme il est . . .   (193–201)

---

[31] See *Printemps*, line 129; *Esté*, 113 and 224; *Autonne*, 457–8. Cf. also my article 'Ronsard's Bacchic poetry', pp. 112–16.

A toy fils du Soleil est la perfection:
Tu soustiens et nourris la generation,
Car rien sans ta vertu au monde ne peut estre,
Comme estant des saisons le seigneur et le maistre.

(207–10)

At one level, this motif seems to restore a symmetry threatened
by the decision to personify the seasons according to the gender
of the French *words* for the seasons (as if the conventions or accidents
of a particular language retained the evidence of some proto-
myth):[32] Spring's effeminate nature makes him the counterpart
of the female Autumn (*Esté*, lines 117–18: 'l'Autonne fut femelle,
/ Qui n'eut rien de vertu ny de puissance en elle'), so that the two
figures mediate between the male polarities of Summer and
Winter. Yet the symmetry is also undermined by this bisexuality,
which introduces another reduplication into the thematic texture
of the cycle: both because Spring is not simply female,[33] and
because his sexual slippage from one poem to the next is one of the
unerased inconsistencies of the four hymns.

The association of the hermaphrodite figure with non-fruition
distinguishes him sharply from the androgynous model of a perfectly resolved duality. The two faces of the figure regard one
another in useless, unfulfilled desire, producing a superficial
abundance, an empty flowering of the surface. This convergence
of the hermaphrodite with the theme of 'flowers without fruit'
might well invite an investigation of how the two threads are
interwoven elsewhere in the Ronsardian corpus. One could, for
example, juxtapose a 1552 sonnet, in which Cassandre disguises
herself as Adonis, with the 1564 *Adonis*, where the idyll of Venus'
passion for the barely-mature Adonis is set within a moralizing framework stressing ephemerality and fruitlessness;[34] or one

---

[32] Folengo's account of the four seasons (which appears to have been known
to Ronsard) makes Spring and Summer female, Autumn and Winter male, in
accordance with their Italian genders.

[33] Autumn also participates in this ambiguity: see *Autonne*, line 237 ('Ainsi
dist cet hommace'), and lines 221–2, where her gender varies ('cet Autonne';
'elle parla'), as it does in the French language.

[34] See *Amours* (1552), sonnet LXXVI (*L* IV, pp. 77–8): 'Quand d'un bonet son
chef elle adonize, / Et qu'on ne sçait (tant bien elle desguise / Son chef doubteux)
s'elle est fille ou garçon?' (note that in the first tercet of this sonnet she imitates

could enumerate variants of the Adonis type (Hylas, or certain images of Bacchus), pursue the intrications of castration-myths (Atys in *Le Pin* being the central example), and dwell on the function of the hermaphrodite Cœnée as *voyeur* in *Le Baing de Callirée*.[35] The integration of such instances into a single interpretative scheme would prove difficult if not impossible, since the most fundamental feature of the fruitless hermaphrodite—the feature which allows his appearances to be 'integrated'—is precisely his irreducible non-integration. He is, for example, often associated with change or metamorphosis: Cassandre-Venus becomes an Adonis; Adonis (like Narcissus, Ajax, Hyacinth) becomes a flower. Following this figurative chain, one remarks that the loss of manhood which accompanies the metamorphosis is essential to the rhetorical flowering of the poetic text; and that the erotic fantasy of *Le Baing* is generated by the intervention of a figure which abdicates sexual unity in order to explore the decorative verbal surfaces of Callirée's body. Ronsard's hermaphrodite is a form-changer ('inconstant, incertain, / variable en effet . . .') who permits the text to pluralize itself; he is a trope, the trope *par excellence*, trope of a trope and figure of a figure in his gratuitous fabrication of flowers and his surreptitious shifting of the thematic ground.

The contrast of devious Spring with phallic Summer thus appears in a new light. The Sun and his non-accidental Son display the energy of a discourse which asserts its own rightness or propriety: Helios-Logos describing a perfect, masterly circle to rejoin the *présence à soi* of the solstice. Summer is action and immediacy; his ejaculation suffers no deferment, no fruitless languishing 'en sceve' ('Ainsi disoit Ceres, et l'Esté tout soudain, / De sa vive challeur luy eschaufa le sein') (211–12). The direct speech of Nature, inviting the reciprocation of the Sun in explicit transgression of conventional restraints and values, has

Venus); *L'Adonis* (L XII), lines 15–28 (description of Adonis), and 365–8 (ephemeral character of woman's love).

[35] For the *Hylas*, see L XV (e.g. p. 245, lines 259–60, and p. 246, lines 285–8; the contrast between Hylas and the aggressively masculine Hercules accentuates his quasi-feminine beauty); on *Le Pin* (L XV), see my article 'Mythes de l'abondance', pp. 251 ff.; for *Le Baing de Callirée*, see L XVII, pp. 155–8.

the propriety of a nature which seeks to mirror itself in a seamless coupling; an androgynous union which is then exactly mimed by Ceres and Summer amid the sensible evidence of plenitude. The second hymn is the hymn of tautologies, seeking to conserve its tropical energy in a circular structure. But this desire entails the rewriting of the seasonal pattern and the disfigurement of Spring. In consequence, the natural propriety of *Esté* fabricates a figure of impropriety whose detours are both essential to the heliotropic pattern and a parody of its circularity. The heliotrope, after all, is itself one of the flowers born from the blood of a dying hero: it bespeaks a death and an absence. *Esté* cannot escape its destiny as the figure of a textual season, written out—in the absence of authentic nature—as the fold in a discontinuous fabric.

On the margin of the poem, lying in the shade to escape the heat of summer, the poet adopts a liminary position. As the verses pair to form couplets, and the couplets redouble to form alternating masculine and feminine pairs (a convention still fresh enough perhaps, at this date, to retain a resonance of its metaphorical sexuality), the poet-figure interposes a brief reflection on his project. First he rejects imitation and marks a fundamental difference between the 'sentier nouveau' he is beginning to trace and 'les traces du vulgaire': this recurrent Ronsardian gesture, often associated with the most general, the most commonplace topics (it introduces, *inter alia*, the *Hymne de la Mort*), announces the deflection or rewriting of a given set of materials, which will now bear a new and distinctive signature (and the name of an addressee: Fleurimont Robertet, Seigneur de Fresne, whose botanical echoes are evoked in this same prelude, line 20). This difference will be authenticated by means of a transcendence, an Apolline *fureur*:

> Nouveau Cygne emplumé je veux voller bien hault,
> Et veux comme l'Esté avoir l'estomaq chault
> Des chaleurs d'Apollon, courant par la carriere
> Des Muses, et getter une obscure poussiere
> Aux yeux de mes suyvans . . .
>
> (11–15)

The movement which reunites the two faces of Apollo—

poet-god and sun-god—at once opens up the possibility of a double reading of the ensuing fable: the Sun and his progeny mime the powers of poetry as well as forming the décor of a calendar. Consequently, it creates a further involution by announcing the (always liminary) desire of a 'subject' for integration into his own poetic predicates. Since, in the thematic system of the myth, fire will be identified with sexual vigour, the double reference here to heat ('veux comme l'Esté avoir l'estomaq chault / Des chaleurs d'Apollon') already poses the *je* as a *voyeur* whose desires will be enacted, as he lies hidden in the shade, by the luminous personae of his fiction.[36] The fable with its consummations of sexual desire displaces the figure of the poet, and his *afflatus*-topic, much as it displaces the figure of Spring. The *je* is always outside the androgynous unions of the solstice. On the other hand, by circumscribing their space, the pronoun and the topics attached to it assert from the threshold that the heliocentric circle is a figure of desire, rather than some pure enunciation of presence. And if the flowering of a figure takes place in the absence of its designated fruition, the *je* as producer of figures must always resemble Spring as Ceres describes him, undoing in advance her bid for the perfecting of nature.

The questions raised here may be recapitulated in terms of the *Hymne de l'Autonne*, where both the liminary section and the fable are greatly extended. The correction by Summer of Spring's fruitless deviation has its counterpart in the marriage of Autumn with Bacchus: the god presents himself with the most reassuring credentials, and subsequently—by means of another instant union —redeems the impotence of Autumn. This is a variant of the myth of Penia and Porus, celebrating the dynamics of a mediation between sterile matter and a principle of divine fullness; different, it would seem, from the couplings of Nature-Ceres with Sun-Summer only in the heavily pejorative development of the female component. But the exclusion of pejorative notations in

---

36 Cf. *Amours* (1552), sonnet CXXVII (*L* IV, pp. 123–4), or sonnet XX (pp. 23–4), in which the optative mood is still more evident: 'Je vouldroy' is the motif which articulates the structure of the sonnet and its references to mythical consummations.

Esté was the condition of its transparent (even monotonous) circularity; in *Autonne*, by contrast, the deviant nature of Autumn produces much of the poem's extension by inserting her detours into the topical and rhetorical trajectory.

The narrative sequence is composed of a group of loosely connected episodes; the relative lack of transition between them creates an air of disjunction which perhaps echoes (or is echoed in) the shiftiness, the essential unreliability of Autumn. And the *narratio* is itself extended by means of rich interweavings of tropes and *enargeia*, each serving the other and productively deferring the resolution of the myth. Thus a multiple periphrasis for the coming of dawn marks the moment of the wind Auton's flight bearing Autumn to her father:

> C'estoit au mesme poinct que l'estoille du jour
> Avoit desja chassé les astres d'alentour
> Des pastures du Ciel, et les contant par nombre,
> Pour la crainte du chaut les alloit mettre à l'ombre.
>   Ja la Lune argentée alloit voir son amy,
> Son bel Endymion sur le mont endormy,
> Et ja la belle Aurore au visage de roses
> Les barrieres du ciel par tout avoit decloses:
> Et desja le Soleil son front avoit huilé
> De fard, à celle fin qu'il ne fust point haslé,
> Et assis dans son char desja tenoit la bride
> A ses coursiers tirés hors de l'estable vuide,
> Quand tout à l'impourveu l'Autonne arriva là.
> Adoncques le Soleil retif se reculla
> Arriere de sa fille, et tournant son visage
> (De peur de ne la voir) fist un autre voyage.
>
>   (239–54)

The intrication of *topoi* follows the sinuous course of an anticipatory clause articulated by anaphora: the figures appear to differentiate segments of the same topical moment in view of the epiphany of the Sun. For what were at first gratuitous flowers of rhetoric (the morning star counting her sheep, the reunion of Endymion and the Moon, the floral aspect of the Dawn, the Sun's cosmetic gesture) give way imperceptibly to the resumption of narrative as Autumn's appearance recalls that, within the system of the fable, the Sun must be read not as a figure but, *au propre*, as her father. Yet—appropriately enough perhaps—the Sun, who had emerged from a cluster of figures (as if he had been hidden inside them), disappears as soon as *narratio* is restored: Helios is deleted by Autumn from the heliotropic movement, leaving only the tropes to occupy the space of her poem.[37]

Or again, in the Palace of Spring, an extended simile embroiders the weaving by Zephyr of a net to catch Flora ('Ainsi qu'en nos jardins on voit embesongnée / Des la pointe du jour la ventreuse Arignée . . .') (289–90). The amorous Zephyr hides like a spider (or like a poet?) at the centre of the fabric in which the figure of flowers herself will be implicated.

As already indicated, Autumn in her turn rewrites the seasonal myths in her own manner by her surreptitious invasion of their territory. She profits from the absence of her brothers, despoils their plenitude, and thus attracts into the poem representations of their *topoi*: the *locus amoenus* of Spring (276–82), the harvest implements of Summer (312–20). From her 'thefts', she weaves in each instance a crown:

> [Autonne] à son frere ravit
> Ses bouquets et ses fleurs, et comme une larronne
> (Apres l'avoir pillé) s'en fist une couronne.
>
> (300–2)

> Elle prist finement deux rayons de son frere
> Pour emparer son chef, puis alla voir sa mere.
>
> (325–6)

The crown of flowers merges with the crown of sunlight to become the property of a season whose craft is both a weaving and a wasting, a reunification and a dissipation. The scene in Nature's palace has the same implied structure. Nature is the source of all things, the universal seed-bed; here is conserved, without loss of energy, the transformational principle of the generative cycle:

> Là sont dedans des pots sur des tables, encloses
> Avecq' leurs escriteaux, les semences des choses,

---

[37] Autumn subsequently hides among her own zodiacal signs to escape the fury of the other monstrous figures of the zodiac (lines 255–62).

Que ces jeunes garsons gardent, à celle fin
Que ce grand Univers ne preigne jamais fin,
Les semans tous les ans d'un mutuel office,
Affin qu'en vieillissant le Monde rajeunisse . . .

(349–54)

But this sustained and sustaining emission, to which Autumn—
as Nature's daughter—is heir, is threatened by Autumn herself.
She is a prodigal daughter, a waster, a principle of loss or *écoulement* destroying its own origin:

Si tost que la Nature eut aperceu sa fille:
Fuy (dit-elle) d'icy, tu perdras ma famille,
Fuy t'en de ma maison: tu seras en tes ans
La perte et le malheur de mes autres enfans.
Tu perdras tout cela que la bonne froidure
De l'Hyver germera, tout ce que la verdure
Du Printemps produira, et tout ce qui croistra
De mur et de parfait quand l'Esté paroistra,
Tu feras écouler les cheveux des bocages,
Chauves seront les boys, sans herbes les rivages
Par ta main, Phtinopore, et sur les humains
Maligne respendras mille maux de tes mains.

(357–68)

Autumn's malignity is perhaps most clearly—and obscurely—
encapsulated in the word 'Phtinopore'. An archaic epithet,
imitated, despoiled, transferred (without translation) from a rare
Greek original, an alien compound unsure even of its grammatical
function, a coined term, a patch of darkness in the verbose
prosopopeia of Nature; and yet, at the same time, a rich invention,
pregnant with its borrowed sound and sense, a densely allusive
trope, a splash of superimposed colour in the folds of *elocutio*.[38]

---

[38] In transcribing line 367, I have used the punctuation of all editions from
1564 to 1578 (in 1584, the first comma was dropped, but the capital 'P' retained).
Laumonier omits the first comma and substitutes lower-case 'p' on the grounds that
Ronsard is here echoing Pindar (*Pyth.* V, 121), who uses the adjective *phthinoporis*
to describe the wind (cf. lines 365–6 in Ronsard's text). However, since the
noun *phthinoporon* is used by Herodotus and Thucydides in the sense 'late autumn'
(see Liddell and Scott), the original seems plausible also. The question then arises
of the metaphorical connotations of the word. Even for the Pindaric epithet,

It is at precisely this moment that Bacchus erupts into the narrative, converting *tuber* into *uber*; 'Phtinopore', waster of fruits, will govern the cornucopia; the mistress of entropy will become 'Maitresse du vaisseau que l'Abondance tient, / Par qui en sa beauté Pomone se maintient'. Thus, in its themes and its dissemination of tropical energies, the fable of Autumn rephrases the cornucopian movement, in which the release of abundance depends on (is the alternative face of) a principle of dissipation. Likewise, the trajectory of the four hymns, despite their recurrently centripetal themes, is in essence centrifugal. The figure of sickness and inflation carried by the wind Auton (Autumn's masculine homonym) seems to mime the unstable flight of a poetic fantasy set free from all constraints. It is true that the Apolline ascent of the poem's opening lines appears to guarantee the divine origin of this fantasy,[39] just as the numinous Bacchus of the fable itself enacts its triumphant fruition. Yet the *phtinopore* wind and his protégée delimit their own terrain, displacing the Sun (and Summer) and generating their own ambivalent figures of authentication. Furthermore, the demonic activity of the opening and the close might itself be seen, in another perspective, to endorse the devious liberty of the poetic text, since *daimons* are by their nature ambivalent, Janus-faced beings.

At this point the question of allegory deserves some attention, if only because it appears in theoretical formulations in the prologues of both *Autonne* and *Hyver*. In both passages, Ronsard's references to the hiding of meaning appear in the most general terms as the *topos* 'allegorical theory', without determining a specific mode of reading for the fables themselves. Thus in

Liddell and Scott give 'autumnal', whereas Laumonier interprets it as meaning 'qui détruit les fruits', or 'waster of fruits'. The first meaning of *opora* is 'autumn', and it only comes to mean 'fruit' by metaphorical extension, so that in the Greek texts, the figurative sense may be residual. However, one could well argue that a sixteenth-century student of Greek would be conscious of the etymological colouring of such a word, and that Ronsard's striking use of it as a neologism invests it with the fullest possible semantic value.

[39] The poem begins with a reference to 'le Daimon qui preside / Aux Muses', who acts as the poet's *genius*; in 1584, 'Apollon' is substituted for 'le Daimon'. In the subsequent lines, this Apolline *daimon* is said to have conferred on the poet the divine fury.

Hyver, where the theory is given more scope, a general distinction between two types of philosophy—the celestial or metaphysical, and the terrestrial, which comprises ethics, politics, and physics— is followed by the announcement: 'Tel j'ay tracé cet hymne, imitant l'exemplaire / Des fables d'Hesiode et de celles d'Homere' (lines 79–80). 'Tel' appears to refer only to the second type, though this is not certain either grammatically or in terms of the reference to Hesiod and Homer (whose fables might well, in some allegorical systems, be made to produce 'metaphysical' allegories). At all events, the decodings suggested for *Hyver* have fallen into this humbler domain: notes in the early editions—quoted by Laumonier in *his* notes—specify a 'physical' orientation ('Par ces noms il entend les vens'; 'Il entend le Soleil', etc.), endorsed by Laumonier himself; more recently, a historico-political reading of the Gigantomachy has been defended.[40] Elsewhere the physical layer of meaning could be said to be doubled by a stratum embodying aspects of the nature and function of poetry, a hypothesis which is attractive because it integrates the long prologues of *Autonne* and *Hyver* (and the short one of *Esté*) with the fables proper.

The object of the present analysis is not so much to determine what the allegorical content or product is—what the poems are, or ever were, 'really' about—as to display the topical system implied in the structuring of the poetic materials. Thus, for example, the possibility that the seasons may hide a mime of poetry is simply the alternative aspect of the proposition that poetry here produces a mime of the seasons (that is to say, of 'nature', in the allegorical mode *physice*). The interest lies in the relationship of these two aspects, not in the debate concerning which is the correct one. Similarly, what is striking about the Gigantomachy of *Hyver* is its relative indeterminacy. It may function as a historico-political *topos* (if a given range of contemporary texts is placed alongside it), but it may also carry a psychological layer of reference (in the tradition of the 'Psychomachia'), or more generally the outline of a dialectic between order and disorder: Winter is tolerated (like the Huguenots)

[40] See Smith, 'The hidden meaning of Ronsard's *Hymne de l'Hyver*'.

provided it is contained within a prescribed space, which clarifies in turn the space of the other seasons. This last allegory,
indeed, reflects the process of allegorization itself: a prescribed
twofold, or fourfold, mode of exegesis contains the energies
of the text and inhibits its intrinsic movement towards indeterminacy or excess. For the demonstration hardly needs to be
made—is already made once attention has been drawn to the
effects of displacement referred to above—that these are plural
texts. Their *narrationes*, as a set of discontinuous episodes akin to
the epyllion, trace out a pursuit of integration and fruition undermined from the outset by a disruption which fragments and
pluralizes the textual cycle. In this set of mythological frescoes,
the field of potential significance is continually re-opened, and
blocked, by the shifts of the textual fabric. Something always
remains hidden in the folds of the fabulous mantle.

Finally, one may return to the two different accounts of the
origin of the seasons as an emblem of how the poems function.
Their incompatibility may be resolved by stressing the allusion
to the birth of Pallas: physical and mental generation are twin
variants of a single process.[41] According to this homology, both
versions might represent the poet's own partition or parturition
of his materials. Yet the dismemberment of Spring (which recalls
the myths of Dionysus-Osiris and of Orpheus) appears as the
inverse of Nature's reproductive act. The coming-into-being of
'The Seasons' is depicted both as an act of mastery, of conscious,
mental violence, the cutting of a body which is also a fabric—that
is to say, as an operation of art; and as an epiphany of nature,
grounded in the unerring immediacy of instinct claiming its
own propriety. This duplicity reappears throughout the hymns,
especially perhaps in *Autonne*, where the wayward artifices of
Autumn fructify by virtue of a divine fury, and where, inversely,
Nature's palace is a supreme artefact constructed by Vulcan.
Nature and art interpenetrate, change places, mime each other
and displace each other endlessly in this scenario. The hymns as

[41] For the two versions, see above, note 28. Images of parturition and the
myth of the birth of Pallas reappear in *La Lyre* in association with poetic activity
(see below).

textual artefacts—crowns, cloaks—carry and represent nature, but necessarily, at the same time, carry it away, eliminate it, exclude it from presence.

It must be stressed once again that this reading (or set of readings) is not the 'verité des choses' enclosed in the 'fabuleux manteau'. It is rather an unfolding or explication of the surface, displaying the figures by which the poems reflect their own complexities. The fabulous mantle of *Autonne* and the coloured veil of *Hyver* are both the product and the sign of an *elocutio* conceived not as an ornament for some pre-existing conceptual structure, but as sheer excess, pointing towards the plenitude—gilded fruits, gold leaf, the golden sun—from which they necessarily deviate.

The poem which Ronsard was eventually to call *La Lyre* (*L* XV) both supplements and modifies the model of the poetics of *copia* suggested by the hymns of the seasons. Like the *Hymne de l'Autonne*, it moves towards a set of mythological fictions via a quasi-autobiographical discourse, the testimony of a poet 'bien né' (lines 59–60). The theme of the nature of poetry, of poetry as a nature, is repeated here in the figure of a poet (this poet) cultivating the vine and being rewarded by the gift of Bacchic inspiration: the powers intrinsic to the vine are analogous to those which animate poetry by virtue of the authenticating *fureur* (lines 35–58). Like Summer, inspiration is felt as a burning (54, 70); its absence is figured as a 'fallow' period (141–2); and the complete cycle is adumbrated in a trope of seasonal flowering and withering:

> Elle [la fureur] me dure ou le cours d'un Soleil,
> Quelquefois deux, quelquefois trois, puis morte
> Elle languist en moy de telle sorte
> Que faict la fleur languissant pour un temps,
> Qui plus gaillarde aparoist au printemps,
> Par son declin prenant force et croissance,
> Et de sa mort une longue naissance.
>
> (88–94)

This complex of imagery converges in the domain of sowing

and childbirth. A first 'accidental' simile of painful birth (lines
101–3) is redeployed soon after by reference to the platonist
topos of the analogy between physical and spiritual children:

> Le grand Platon en ses œuvres nous chante
> Que nostre Esprit comme le corps enfante
> L'un, des enfans qui surmontent la mort,
> L'autre, des filz qui doibvent voir le port
> Où le Nocher tient sa gondolle ouverte
> A tous venants, riche de nostre perte.
> Ainsi les deux conçoivent, mais il fault
> Que le sang soit jeune, gaillard et chaut:
> Car si le sang une vigueur ne baille
> A leurs enfans, ilz ne font rien qui vaille.
>
> (117–26)

Fruition is dependent on the heat and vigour of the blood, and
thence of the seminal fluid: the natural, pre-established correspondence of spiritual and corporal energies here forms a conjunction of concepts and metaphors (a 'conception') according to
which the cyclical flow of authentic seed guarantees the maturation of the vine, of human children, and of poems. This flow is
apparent also in the extended simile of a flood:

> Et comme on voit ces torrens qui descendent
> Du haut des monts et flot sur flot se rendent
> A gros bouillons en la valée . . .
> Ainsi je cours de course desbridée,
> Quand la fureur en moy s'est desbordée . . . [42]

Its inverse is the sterility or exhaustion of fallow periods like the
one which is indicated as the poem begins: the movement of
La Lyre is inaugurated by an anxiety which its theory seems
designed to eliminate.[43] On one side of this interruption of the

[42] Lines 73–5, 85–6. The simile is elaborated by a metaphor associating the
river with a bull, splitting the earth with its horn (76–81). The triple reference to
the horn recalls the story of Hercules and Acheloüs, one of the myths of cornucopia (cf. above, p. 185, note 1).

[43] 'Belot, parcelle, ains le tout de ma vie, / Quand je te vy je n'avois plus envie /
De voir la Muse . . .' (lines 1–3). This development occupies the first fifty lines
of the poem; thereafter, it is counterbalanced by the theme of Bacchic *fureur*, but
recurs in the subsequent description of the periodic nature of inspiration. The

seminal flow is an image of the youthful dissemination of the poet's reputation:

> Et toutefois par changemens divers
> Je haïssois les Muses et les vers,
> Par qui j'avois conquis la renommée
> De tous costez en la France semée . . .
>
> (31–4)

On the other is the possibility opened up by this poem itself—still posing liminary questions, miming the accidental beginning of its own composition—of renewing the prodigal scattering of seed which will save a patron from obscurity and an ultimate absence:

> Par quel escrit faut-il que je commence
> Pour envoyer des Muses la semence,
> J'enten mes vers, par toute Europe, affin
> Que ton renom survive apres ta fin?
>
> (177–80)

This passage rephrases an earlier one (149 ff.) in which the encounter with Belot ('aussi tost qu'aux bords de la Garonne / Je te connu . . .') provokes an immediate access of inspiration, redeeming the sterility of the fallow period:

> Soudain au cœur il me prist une envie
> De te chanter, afin qu'apres ta vie
> Le peuple sceust que tes Graces ont eu
> Un chantre tel, amy de ta vertu . . .
>
> (153–6)

The history of an instance of textual generation thus becomes the topic of a text which is presented as the product of the generative act. A theory of performance, in which the threat of impotence asserts itself as inescapable (being a sign of authenticity), doubles itself to become the actual performance, a demonstration of seminal vigour. A quasi-theoretical one, no doubt, since the poem, at line 177, is still not certain of its beginning; and it is a hundred

---

balance between positive and negative aspects is a delicate one: for example, the very intermittence of the *fureur* is presented at one point as a sign of its authenticity (lines 59–72).

lines later still that it heralds the public celebration of Belot's munificence as the restorer of a 'lyre'. This climax, foreshadowed in a sequence of reflexive movements, is repeatedly deferred by them so that the potency of the operation may be fully displayed to the public.

The re-presentation to Belot of Belot's handsome present to Ronsard emerges from a figurative detour:

> L'un en cecy, l'autre en cela te chante:
> Mais de chacun la chanson plus frequente
> (Qui plus au cœur nous laisse l'aiguillon)
> C'est qu'en voyant le Gaulois Apollon
> Tout mal en poinct errer par nostre France,
> A qui la sotte et maligne Ignorance
> Au cœur enflé qui suit le genre humain,
> Avoit ravy la Lyre de la main,
> En sa faveur tu ne t'es montré chiche,
> Faisant ce Dieu en ton dommage riche,
> Luy consacrant par un vœu solennel
> Ta lyre courbe, un present eternel,
> D'un art cousteux, affin qu'on la contemple
> Pour le present de Belot en son Temple.
>
> (281–94)

The question whether Belot actually gave Ronsard a musical instrument decorated with mythological scenes is displaced—together with the question whether the 'Temple' may be identified with the priory of Saint-Cosme—by the fold in the text which results from this periphrastic disguise. It is as if the mythological motifs which will be described as contained within the space of the lyre's surface had insinuated themselves into the presentation scenario: on the surface of the poem, a patron is already seen replacing the stolen lyre of the Gallic Apollo, just as the same lyre will bear a picture (only visible, of course, within the poem) of Mercury making a lyre and presenting it to Apollo as compensation for a theft (425–48).

Such mirror-images reveal particularly clearly the poem's self-endorsing character. Much as the hymns of the seasons rewrite their own myths of germination and fruition, *La Lyre* repeatedly

copies and displaces its myths (as well as its theories) of abundance.
For the structural dislocation which here masquerades as a transi-
tional passage between the introductory section and the *blason* of
the lyre is only one instance of a phenomenon which affects every
part of the text. The two faces of the poem exchange materials
more evidently, more systematically, than the prologue and myth
of *Autonne*. If the theoretical section is already a performance in
that it inaugurates the poem whose genesis it describes, it also
carries—and, according to the same principle, is carried by—
a group of figures which prefigure the motifs of the lyre. For
example, the mechanism of authentic mental reproduction (of how
the *esprit* copies itself) is illustrated by a miniature mythological
narration of the birth of Pallas, supplied—as the theoretical context demands—with a ready-made allegorization (127–40). Pallas
will reappear on the lyre, though as the protagonist of another
topos. More centrally, the autobiographical fable of the poet as
servant of Bacchus, indeed the whole complex of images of sowing and abundance, will be answered by the cornucopian Bacchus
of the fresco. And at a still more general level of organization, the
blason of the lyre has the character of an exemplary representation
of poetic activity, thus reflecting the already partially fabulous
autobiography set out in the prologue.[44]

The apparently simple twofold structure of the poem is thus
complicated by a 'doubling' function which operates from beginning to end and which both facilitates and impedes the textual
desire to achieve fruition. The same principle which allows the
whole poem, and not just the *blason*, to be interpreted by an
analytic or allegorical strategy as the integrated paradigm of an
inspired utterance, also refracts it into a series of echoes amid
which no original voice can be found. The question 'where' (or
'when') the product of authentic *fureur* is realized in *La Lyre*
cannot be answered. 'Par quel escrit faut-il que je commence . . . ?'
The *blason* is still in a condition of beginning. It appears not as a

[44] With a little ingenuity, the scenes depicted on the lyre may be made to fit
phases of Ronsard's career—as court poet, as amorous and pastoral poet, as
polemical poet, and so on; but whether or not such a reading is viable, it is clear
that the fresco presents in mythological form aspects of the poet's role and of the
powers of poetry.

fulfilment, but as a supplement to a three-hundred line sequence
which, both by deferring it and by pre-empting its sole rights of
performance, has deprived it of the immediacy which is essential
to the *fureur*. The fold, once made, cannot be unfolded: the text
is always self-endorsed, self-styled, a hermaphrodite whose two
aspects oscillate endlessly without achieving simultaneous presence.

This process may be restated in terms of another duplication
discernible at the heart of the poem (its 'heart' being constitution-
ally excentric). The *blason* of Belot, as a provisional 'beginning'
which will eventually be displaced or supplemented by the *blason*
of the lyre, is founded on a simile:

> Ta face semble et tes yeux solitaires
> A ces vaisseaux de noz Apoticaires,
> Qui par dessus rudement sont portraits
> D'hommes, de Dieux à plaisir contrefaits,
> D'une Junon en l'air des vents souflée,
> D'une Pallas qui voit sa jouë enflée,
> Se courroussant contre son chalumeau
> Que par despit elle jetta souz l'eau,
> D'un Marsyas despouillé de ses veines:
> Et toutefois leurs caissettes sont pleines
> D'Ambre, Civette et de Musq odorant,
> Manne, Rubarbe, Aloës secourant
> L'estomac foible: et neanmoins il semble
> Voyant à l'œil ces Images ensemble
> Que le dedans soit semblable au dehors.
>
>   (181–95)

This surface decorated with mythological images seems to parody
in advance, by its very crudeness and gratuitousness ('rudement',
'à plaisir contrefaits') the richly worked belly of the lyre.[45] Moreover, the principle by which the container is downgraded in
favour of its contents threatens to undermine the aesthetic implied
by the fresco. Although the 'Silenes' simile is not specifically

[45] Two of the three miniature scenes are connected with music, while the
allusion to Marsyas is a direct foreshadowing of the 'Apollo and Marsyas' episode
of the *blason*. In 1584, line 188 was rewritten as 'Et d'un Bacchus assis sur un
tonneau', thus increasing the number of internal allusions (as well as recalling,
conceivably, the Rabelaisian model).

annexed to a theory of poetry (as was, for example, the myth of the birth of Pallas), it has the effect of dislocating the poem's structure of meaning, for a number of reasons. It the first place, a note of irony seems inseparable from an image which, in an age of hyperbolic eulogies, opens with a reference to the patron's unimpressive appearance: this is after all the man who, it was said, released the pent-up flow of seminal energy in the poet (part of that flow being the simile itself). But let that pass. More essential is the fact that this platonist *topos*, arriving in Ronsard's text via Rabelais,[46] introduces a problem which is not explicit elsewhere, although it is in fact immanent throughout the poem. For the classic relationship between soul and body, essence and accidence, interior and exterior is invoked in order to praise the *eloquence* of Belot (as well as allowing a comparison with Socrates); the simile is resolved as follows:

> Lors de ta voix distille l'Eloquence,
> Un vray Socrate, et ton docte parler
> Fait le doux miel de tes levres couler,
> Montrant au jour la vertu qui t'enflame,
> Ayant caché au plus profond de l'ame
> Je ne sçay quoy de rare et precieux
> Qui n'aparoist du premier coup aux yeux:
> Car dans ton vase abondant tu receles
> Dix mille odeurs estranges et nouvelles,
> Si qu'en parlant tu donnes assez foy
> Combien ton ame est genereuse en toy,
> Par la vertu de ta langue qui pousse
> Un hameçon aux cœurs, tant elle est douce.
>
> (246–58)

The movement from inside to outside, grounded in an invisible 'vertu' (and mediated by the 'vertu' of the tongue), is a movement of showing, of demonstration; and the initial simile here appropriately shifts its aspect to become a metaphor: Belot has at his

---

[46] As Lebègue points out (*L* XV, p. 25, note 1; see also his article 'Ronsard lecteur de Rabelais'), Ronsard specifically echoes the Prologue of *Gargantua* in at least three phrases which are not to be found either in Erasmus's *Sileni* adage or in the *Symposium* source-text.

disposal an exotically perfumed cornucopia of language.[47] Thus
Ronsard's figures of *evidentia*, animated according to the liminary
theory by the virtue of inspiration, enact the very gift attributed
to Belot: Ronsard's encomium, 'montrant au jour' the hidden
essence of his patron, reduplicates his eloquence and the operation
of the apothecary's box.

The pluralizing effect of this passage is due to a certain duplicity
inherent in the opposition between interior and exterior as used
here. Belot's physical appearance, like the surface of the boxes, is
given low priority in favour of his inner qualities; but these qualities take the form of a capacity which itself depends on exteriorization. Belot's eloquence, as a sensible manifestation, appears to
retain the values of essence; his *oratio*, not his face, is a mirror of
his soul. But then if the analogy between Ronsard's discourse and
Belot's holds good, the whole of *La Lyre* must be taken as an
exteriorization of essence; and it is at this point that the interchangeability of the painted boxes and the painted lyre becomes
inescapable. What in one instance is presented as a sign of empty
frivolity (mythological decoration) is in the other invested with a
value of plenitude; yet the faces of the coin are inseparable. The
Rabelaisian parallel encourages this paradoxical identification,
since the Prologue of *Gargantua* applies the 'Silenes' image to
a written text, thus undermining Ronsard's apparent restriction
of its import to the body–soul relationship (or at most to oral
discourse); furthermore, it implies equally that the pursuit of
a 'hidden' sense can only take place on the surface.

Hence the text of *La Lyre*, in order to advertise the inward
virtues of both poet and patron, relies confidently on verbal
and mythological figures which assert themselves on and as an

---

[47] The depiction of this hidden, inward source as a 'vase abondant' recalls the
seminal vases of Nature in the *Hymne de l'Autonne* (see above, pp. 251–2). Cf. also
a subsequent passage in *La Lyre* (271–4), where reference is made to the fertility of
the Nile: 'Nil dont la source aux homes n'aparoist, / Et qui sans pluye en abondance
croist / Aux plus chauds mois . . .'. This reference is in one sense simply a digression,
since the conquest of Egypt is presented as an illustration of Rome's power under
the aegis of Pollio. But, in the light of the metaphorical sequence established
earlier, the Nile becomes another of the figures of abundance associated with
Belot.

exterior; the container is consubstantial with its precious contents
('il semble . . . / Que le dedans soit semblable au dehors'); 'je' and
'tu' mingle with Pallas, Apollo, and Bacchus in the fresco which
carries and animates them.

Some of the equivalences, interweavings, and reversibilities of
this structure have already been indicated: a final one may here
be cited as an emblem of how the poem works. Next to Apollo,
whose myth-fragments dominate the décor of the lyre, Bacchus
is given a central place ('Sur l'autre ivoire où les cordes s'atta-
chent, / Vit un Bacchus . . .'). He holds a cornucopia which not only
reduplicates the figures of abundance of the introductory section
—vine, seminal flood, parturition, Silenes, Belot's 'vase abondant',[48] the Nile with its hidden source—but also constitutes a
textual fold by reflecting the character of the lyre itself with its
abundance of fictions:

> A traitz bossez vit une longue histoire
> En fictions d'arguments fabuleux,
> Dont ceste Lyre a le ventre orgueilleux.
>
> (298–300)

Thus Bacchus

> . . . tient entre ses bras
> De l'Abondance une corne qui semble
> S'enorguillir de cent fruits tous ensemble,
> Qui surpassoient les levres du vaisseau
> En gros trochets . . .
>
> (384–8)

The notation 'orgueilleux' / 's'enorguillir' marks the movement of
swelling or inflation, the movement towards display, so that a
cornucopian excess is inscribed on a lyre which is itself inscribed
in a lyre-text: the fold is double.

At the rhetorical level, this cornucopia again follows familiar

---

[48] A variant of line 385 substitutes 'Un vase plein qui tout enrichy semble' for
'De l'Abondance une corne qui semble'. The change, which may have been made
to avoid an awkward inversion, illustrates the equivalence between horn and
vase.

patterns. A simile, sign of rhetorical excess, describes the prodigal
fruition of a cherry-tree:

> . . . ainsi qu'au renouveau
> Un beau Guinier par gros trochets fait naistre
> Son fruit toffu, pour ensemble nous paistre,
> Et les oyseaux qui friandz de son fruit
> Autour de l'arbre affamez font grand bruit.
>
> (388–92)

The verbal repetitions ('gros trochets', 'fruits'–'fruit'–'fruit', even
'ensemble') reveal the degree to which the cherry-tree already
belongs to the set of figures located in the cornucopia and can thus
only become a simile by virtue of a kind of pleonasm: the point
is confirmed by the reappearance of 'la Cerise' in the ensuing list
of fruits.[49] For subsequently, the text expands itself (*s'enorgueillit*)
by means of *enumeratio*, a random taxonomy incrusted with further notations (epithets, tropes, indications of occult properties).
The discontinuity of this list is a characteristic indication of a
cornucopian economy. Variety is produced in what is essentially
a repetition-structure by means of the arbitrary kind and degree
of specification attached to each fruit: some are simply named,
some have a single epithet, some occupy a whole line or, in one
instance, a couplet. Inversely, an *enchaînement* is suggested in the
succession of discrete instances by the use of assonances and other
phonological accidents ('rencontre'–'Concombre'–'Pepon'–'separé'
–'Pavis'–'Pesche'–'Pavot'–'Corneille'–'Corme'–'Poire pepineuse';
'Fraize'–'froid'–'Framboise', etc.).[50] In such ways, Bacchus and
his horn reproduce the deployment of the fresco as a whole,

[49] At the same time, the phrase 'au renouveau' makes the cherry-tree a Spring
figure, a flower of rhetoric inserted into an autumnal ornament (cf. line 393:
'Là meinte Figue ornement de l'Autonne').

[50] The whole passage was subsequently rewritten more than once. The variants
include a re-ordering of the list, the displacement of some of the fruit, the introduction of others, and manipulations to make the rhyme-scheme symmetrical.
The 'final' (1584) version adds a resolving cadence to the arbitrary enumeration:
'Et par sur tout de Pampre une couronne / Qui du vaisseau les lèvres environne.'
As indicated earlier in this chapter, Ronsard's abundant variants might well be
considered as an aspect of the cornucopian movement of his text: the poems
proliferate, not only by means of topical and tropical extensions but also by being
rewritten incessantly until death makes an arbitrary end to the list.

with its series of self-contained myths linked by tangential echoes of theme or figure.

Enargeia makes itself evident within this scheme as both a macro-figure and a micro-figure. The crevices of *enumeratio* are filled with brilliant details, and the Bacchic episode is from the outset designated as an imitation of life ('Vit un Bacchus'; cf. 'Là meinte Figue . . . / Est peinte au vif', and 'Le Concombre au ventre enflé s'y *montre*'), as indeed is the *blason* itself ('A traitz bossez *vit* une longue histoire'; cf. also 'Au naturel', line 327, 'Vous le verriez', line 332, and many other examples). One of the most character-istic modes of *copia* abrogates the space created by the liminary self-questioning of the poem and establishes itself as the manifesta-tion *par excellence* of seminal energy. The lyre is its stage property, as are the cloaks, goblets, baskets, and other artefacts described in Ronsard's epyllia; the surface of apothecary's boxes; and, by extension, the poetics of the woven crown, the fabulous veil or mantle. For if the mime of the seasons appeared to be a reflection of nature, the triumph of art is openly celebrated in the mimetic decorations of the lyre. 'Nature' here appears by permission of an art which has taken the precaution of claiming its status as a second nature.[51]

Just after the first appearance in the poem of its dedicatee, Ron-sard uses an ethical *topos* to develop his model of reciprocation between patron and poet:

> Rien, mon Belot, n'y sert la grand despense,
> Les despensiers emboufiz de boubance
> Veulent gangner par un art somptueux
> Ou par banquets, par vins tumultueux
> La gloire humaine, et abusez se trompent,
> Et par le trop eux mesmes se corrompent,
> Sans acquerir un Chantre de renom,
> Qui sans banquetz peut celebrer leur nom

[51] Cf. the passage on the poet's viticulture: 'Je ne faisois . . . / Qu'enter, planter, et tirer à la ligne / Le cep tortu de la joyeuse vigne' (35–8); Du Bellay had spoken of 'grafting', in the context of imitation, as a mediation between nature and art (see above, pp. 64, 72–3). This description of horticultural activity reads, indeed, like a transposition of poetic activity: the joyful proliferation of the vine, with its natural twists or folds, is reformed, as it were, by the linear discipline of the text ('tirer à la ligne').

Par amitié, non, Belot, pour leur table,
Pour vin exquis, ny pour mets delectable:
Car aujourd'huy chacun sçait sagement
Que vault le chou, et vivre sobrement . . .

(161–72)

The attack on expenditure is a reversal, in thematic terms, of one of the central arguments of the *Hymne de l'Or*. There is, however, no fundamental incompatibility of the underlying strategies: the restriction of demand, attached to an ethic of frugality, allows the enhancement of the poem and its maker as purveyors of a superior form of enrichment, which in its turn is both the reward and the solicitation of *largesse*. Indeed, in one sense, the poem takes out an insurance policy against the uncertainties of the future by giving the Gallic Apollo a role in the text which almost eclipses that of Belot himself: this is apparent not only in the suggestion that the patron's fame depends on the poet's (153–6), but also of course in the space given to the mytho-biographies of the introduction and the fresco. The lyre, after all, occupies a privileged place in the Ronsardian corpus as a figure of poetry, so that the poem *La Lyre* is the praise and the performance (the demonstration) of its own functioning. The swollen expenditure of false patrons, their inauthentic display of 'art somptueux', their illusory banquets, are counterfeits of the proud swelling of the lyre, its mimed feast of the gods, and above all its 'art cousteux', which replenishes an impoverished poet-figure. The lyre is presented (and received) as true gold: 'D'or est l'Archet, les chevilles encor / Ont le bout d'or, le haut du coude est d'or' (295–6; cf. the reference in line 458 to the lyre as 'bien dorée'). Emerging, after the long deferment of the fallow period, from a hidden interior, it materializes as a golden artefact, its succulent (but painted) fruit hinting at some plenitude of the solstice. Its invisibly supported currency of *elocutio*, bearing the ideal images of both coiner and consumer, performs an operation of exchange which necessarily displaces any real traffic between patron and poet. The poem is an auto-presentation. Indelibly stamped from the outset with the marks of self-expenditure, loss and interruption, it nevertheless powerfully mimes its own desire for presence.

La Lyre is still a celebration. But, placed in sequence with the *Ode à Michel de L'Hospital* and the *Hymne de L'Autonne*, its intricate structure displays with increased clarity the mechanisms of inbreeding or auto-fabrication on which the mirage of celebration depends. The sequence may be prolonged, if not completed (such sequences being always subject to shifts, disruptions, and reversals), by recalling the pantomime of the *Discours ou dialogue entre les Muses deslogées, et Ronsard* (L XVIII, pp. 88 ff.).

If the Gallic Apollo of the *Lyre* assumed the aspect of a beggar, 'errant' and impoverished, the figurative movement of the poem nevertheless affirmed his restoration. In the *Discours ou dialogue*, there is an unredeemed disjunction between the poet-figure and the Muses. Their voice is heard in the text as an alien voice, not as the force which animates the lines; ironically, their speech invoking the powers granted to them echoes the *Ode à Michel de L'Hospital*, whose celebration of *fureur* seems in retrospect to belong to some prelapsarian Golden Age. The Muses are now permanently exiled, expropriated; the possibility of restoration is offered only in a passage added posthumously to the poem, and is undercut in advance by a pessimistic assessment of the chances of royal patronage.[52]

As indicated earlier (p. 172), Ronsard is here represented as exiled no less than the Muses. The poem begins with an image of cranes flying homeward, an epic figure displaced from the *Iliad* into a context of nostalgia.[53] The encounter or dialogue takes place on neutral territory in which 'wandering' (*errer* and *vagabond* recur in the course of the poem) is not the beginning of a movement towards fruitfulness, but rather an undirected reflection after the event. Thus, when a later speech by the Muses counters the attack of the poet by appealing to their power of dissemination ('avons ... semé ton renom par les terres estranges'), this power is located

[52] Lines 137–50. The name of the king (Henri III) is noticeably absent from these lines. Cf. other late poems in which the monarchy is presented in an unfavourable light (e.g. *Le Caprice*, L XVIII, pp. 315 ff.), or in which the theme of poetic immortality is treated negatively (e.g. the elegy *A Philippes des-Portes*, L XVIII, pp. 247 ff.).

[53] Cf. *Iliad* III, 1–14. Ronsard had used the figure in *La Franciade* (L XVI, p. 73). See Silver, *Ronsard and the Greek Epic*, pp. 175–80.

in the past. The claim of the 1550 ode *A sa Muse*—'Je volerai tout vif par l'univers'—is exactly inverted, not only in tense, but also in the transference of this desire from the self-endorsing 'je' to the fallen Muse ('T'avons fait desireux d'honneur et de louanges, / Et semé . . .'). Moreover, the impoverishment of the Muses also entails the beggaring of the poet. 'Ronsard' evokes the cornucopia as the source of an affluence which the Muses have failed to bestow:

> Je pensois qu'Amalthée eust mis entre vos mains
> L'abondance et le bien, l'autre ame des humains . . .

If 'le bien' is somewhat vague in that it might designate either material or moral goods, the 1587 variant—'l'argent' for 'le bien'—removes any ambiguity. The currency of the poems has not been supported by an adequate increase in material wealth; *fureur* appears very precisely as inflation. The self-presenting equilibrium of *La Lyre* has been replaced in this poem by a hostile and unproductive confrontation (mimed as an empty dialogue) between the figure of a poet and a figure of poetry.

In certain of its aspects, the *Discours ou dialogue* may recall another dialogue-event represented some twenty years before the appearance even of the *Ode à Michel de L'Hospital*. The exiled Muses of 1584 are virtually unrecognizable, but they carry the mark of their intrinsic nobility:

> De l'air abaissant l'œil le long d'une valée,
> Je regarday venir une troupe haslée
> Lasse de long travail, qui par mauvais desting
> Avoit fait (ce sembloit) un penible chemin.
>   Elle estoit mal en conche et pauvrement vestue:
> Son habit attaché d'une espine poinctue
> Luy pendoit à l'espaule, et son poil dédaigné
> Erroit salle et poudreux, crasseux et mal peigné.
>   Toutefois de visage elle estoit assez belle . . .
> Quelque part qu'en marchant elle tournast la face,
> La vertu la suyvoit, l'eloquence et la grace,
> Monstrant en cent façons dés son premier regard,
> Que sa race venoit d'une royale part . . .
>   (lines 29–37, 41–4)

Likewise, Mercury (as yet unnamed) 'portoit . . . dessous pauvre habit une face éveillée: / Et monstroit à son port quel sang le concevoit' (lines 50–1). And the dialogue itself is set in motion by a series of questions: 'Quel est vostre païs, vostre nom et la ville / Qui se vante de vous?' (57–8). That this scene should mirror the opening movement of the meeting between Pantagruel and Panurge in *Pantagruel* 9—Panurge being himself a Hermes-figure[54] —is not the result of some banal 'influence' of one author on the other. Rather, it reveals the persistency of a configuration which dominates the imaginative writing of the sixteenth century in France. In each instance, the writer or his personified surrogate confronts and questions the conditions of his own writing; in each instance, too, the scene is set in a fallen world. The disfigurement of any origin and the uncertainty of any *telos* ensure that the text will remain trapped in its own capacity for self-generation, constantly repeating the gesture of fall. Thus Rabelais's liminary farce of language and Ronsard's end-game rejoin one another on a stage where entrances and exits seem remarkably similar. The Ronsardian epyllia, the mythological fragments, the digressions and periphrases, the displaced allegories, the themes of metamorphosis, and the figures of inflation constitute a corpus fundamentally similar to that of the Rabelaisian text: in both, the rhetoric of *copia*, marked by a persistent reflexivity, asserts itself as the refusal of any possibility of full integration. Both, indeed, form *par excellence* a 'corpus': that is to say, a replica of a living body which may also appear as a dismembered corpse, like that of Orpheus; the lyre, as it floats downstream, continues to emit fragments of music according to the random blowing of the wind.

[54] See Schrader, *Panurge und Hermes*. It is not necessary to accept a total identification of Panurge with Hermes in order to make the parallel plausible in this instance. It is striking also that both Panurge and Ronsard's Muses have suffered at the hands of the Turks.

4

Montaigne

IN the absence of the horn of plenty itself, a cornucopian movement may be traced in many of the figures of the *Essais*. Thus, for
example, in *De l'institution des enfans*:

(c) Je n'ay dressé commerce avec aucun livre solide, sinon Plutarque
et Seneque, où je puyse comme les Danaïdes, remplissant et versant
sans cesse.   (I. xxvi, p. 146)

The fullness of two model-texts is here designated, it would seem,
as a source;[1] the labour of the Danaides would thus represent the
activity of transmission or exchange ('commerce'), by which the
textual substance of Plutarch and Seneca is displaced into a discourse bearing the signature 'Montaigne'. But this sentence is
marked from the beginning by a negation. Plutarch and Seneca
appear in a concessive phrase made possible only by the absence of
any 'livre solide': a characteristically Montaignian insistence on
the emptiness of discourse (particularly the written discourses of
pedagogy) allows provisional access to certain privileged texts
whose unsystematic, open-ended form endorses that of the
Essais themselves. The negation is not, however, limited to the
unnamed texts Montaigne claims to have neglected. The Danaides
are, after all, not a wholly reassuring figure of plenitude. Rabelais
cites them as a counter-example of cornucopian productivity, a
sign of despair, and the uselessness of their labours is made explicit in the following sentence: 'J'en attache quelque chose à ce
papier; à moy, si peu que rien.' The *locus* is closed, as it began, in
negation. The *moi*, in a place outside discourse, is scarcely touched

---

[1] See below, pp. 289–90, for another reference to the inexhaustibility of Plutarch.
In such cases, the ideal character of the model is presented as the antithesis of
Montaigne's writing; the positively cornucopian text is always outside the
Essais, and is mirrored in them in its inverted or negative form.

by the language even of Plutarch and Seneca; its integrity is preserved, as at the beginning of the passage, by a repudiation of books. Alien discourse cannot be 'attached' to the self, is external to it. Hence the gesture of transference, endlessly repeated, appears as an empty mime. The only thing to which fragments of another text may be attached is 'ce papier', a mediate domain which clearly concerns the *moi* (since the sentences inscribed on it have a habit of beginning with 'je'), but is no less clearly different from it. The paper on which the text of the *Essais* appears is, indeed, a place of difference: it allows the rewriting and naturalization of foreign texts; it thereby permits the search for the identity of a *moi* in contra-distinction from what is 'other'; but at the same time it defers any final access to the goal of the search, since the self is expressly an entity dissociated from the activity of writing.

Thus the Danaides invert the horn of Amaltheia. The figure they compose in Montaigne's text may be read as the emblem or epigraph of the present chapter, which will explore the interplay in the *Essais* between the desire for a fullness of experience said to be located outside language, and the contours (or detours) of a text which strives unremittingly to represent that fullness.

Any analysis of the *Essais* as an instance of discourse parallel, in some sense, to the Rabelaisian and Ronsardian texts must begin by taking account of the fact that they are presented not as fiction or poetry, but as a form of descriptive or representational discourse. A subject, 'Montaigne', describes the world and himself; he emits opinions, cites examples, explores moral themes, and in general behaves as if he wished to communicate his judgement on a wide range of topics, instructing himself and—however obliquely—others in the process. In this respect he is much closer to Erasmus than to his own French predecessors. Yet, far more than Erasmus's, his text is reflexive: the movement by which it seeks to define itself and its 'author', to identify itself with its author ('Icy, nous allons conformément et tout d'un trein, mon livre et moy') (III. ii, p. 806), has been the topic of many recent studies on Montaigne and needs no preparatory demonstration here.[2] In conse-

---

[2] See in particular Sayce, *The Essays of Montaigne*, ch. 4; Rider, *The Dialectic*

quence, the displacement of theory which occurs in Rabelais's prologues and Ronsard's prefatory verses is apparent also in the *Essais*. Here, the questions of style, imitation, interpretation, improvisation are integral to the text itself, which is in part constituted by their recurrence, and which can thus never transcend them (as it could if they were relegated to a realm of preliminary theory). Furthermore, a commitment to non-resolution, to the perpetual opening of a parenthesis, gives the *essai* a liminary role. Since there will be no full performance, the public are invited to a trial, a rehearsal or infinite *répétition*; or again, shifting the metaphor slightly in accordance with the 1580 preface *Au lecteur* (the only fragment of pre-liminary text), to a preview of the Montaignian project of self-portraiture.

The increasingly reflexive movement of the *Essais* has, in fact, a dual form: comments on the activities of writing and reading converge with the recurrent and equally self-endorsing theme of the self-portrait. The writing subject predicates its own activities, but also those of a being distinct from language. These two figures or personifications, whose identity is constituted by the repetition of certain privileged *loci* and rhetorical devices, are of course represented as the same, one 'je' serving for both; but their difference is none the less essential to the very notion of reflexivity as it appears in the *Essais*. The writer reflects on writing, it seems, in order better to reflect the total self; the book of *essais* separates itself like a mirror so that it may represent a living being. Yet, on the other hand, this duality is unstable because it can never be fully resolved either in unity or in antithesis; also because it is generated wholly by the writing process itself. In that the *Essais* aim to project the image of a self which conforms to the book, they are neither memoirs nor autobiography, but rather a surrogate self, an auto-performance which cannot but displace the 'real' Montaigne. This historical figure appears in his *essais* either as the father of the text (the guarantor of the first person singular), or as a man to whom writing is alien, whose physical presence bears no

of Selfhood in Montaigne; Norton, *Montaigne and the Introspective Mind*; Regosin, 'Montaigne's *Essais*: the book of the self'; and Wilden's important article 'Par divers moyens on arrive à pareille fin'.

inscription, and who is nothing less than he is a 'faiseur de livres'.[3] In one instance, the circularity by which the text produces a figure of its own author is self-evident; in the other, the divorce between text and life is such that they cannot co-exist: the presence of the text entails the absence of its author (a condition which would make any mirror inoperative). His absence is thus a constitutive aspect of the *Essais*, but is itself only conceivable from within the text. In other words, the duality described above cannot be reduced to a simple author–work relationship; it is traced within the text, as the circling movement of the subject back towards itself as object is refracted by the endless variety of topics (the chapter-titles, for example) to which it can be attached. And conversely, the topics are displaced by a syntax which, while it predicates them, seeks to turn back reflexively towards its subject.

In this manner, the *Essais* repeat some of the primary structures of Rabelais's fiction, and even of Ronsard's poetic mythologies. Productivity, as embodied in the ideal Homeric scripture, is consonant with full closure; the movement of the text, not being disrupted by any *philautie*, describes a perfect circle. But in the fallen text, writing is always an open question, seeking at once to assert itself and to efface itself in favour of representation: its possibility of fruition is continually held in suspense, as the writing extends and points towards some ultimate unfolding. The Rabelaisian quest, in which the final goal is always thus deferred, is internalized in the *Essais*; or perhaps it would be better to say that the narrator or 'subject' has now become the protagonist: in Montaigne, it is the first person singular, rather than Pantagruel or Panurge, who seeks plenitude in the realization of his own presence. Similarly, the doubts which Rabelais had transposed into narrative themes (Quaresmeprenant, the *paroles dégelées*, the *banquet au large de Chaneph*) pervade Montaigne's journey through *expérience*: the islands of the *Quart Livre* now appear as fragments of classical thought, or case-histories of personal illness and injury. Montaigne's *topoi* are the materials through which his text tests its (and his) own identity and questions its own presence.

[3] II. xxxvii, p. 784: 'Quel que je soye, je le veux estre ailleurs qu'en papier . . . Je suis moins faiseur de livres que de nulle autre besoigne.'

One might say, then, that the *Essais* participate both in the descriptive discourse of theory and in the performative mode of literature. They go beyond the kind of illustrative performance exemplified by the *De copia* or the *Ciceronianus*, but they do not invite the reader to consider them as fictions or myths: the liberty of the text to generate topics is restricted by the touchstone of experience. Once again, as in the instance of the personified author, it is necessary to insist that experience is not (for the reader) an external phenomenon providing an empirical test for the truth of the *Essais*. It is only visible within the text as a topic which, by its recurrence, traces and delimits the horizons of *egressio*. Anecdotes ('true' or 'false'), fragments of foreign texts, occasional topics such as cannibals, books, friendship, and coaches, all describe their detours in view of an epiphany of this master-topic. Its possibility is what constitutes every particularity of the text as an *essai*. The movement initiated by Erasmus's 'experiamur', the movement of *experientia* in the sense of *exercitatio*, the shift from *doctrina* to performance, finds its paradigm in the *Essais*. While avoiding the fallacy of a fixed, representational discourse, they yet retain the possibility of arriving at productive insights and even a degree of ethical adjustment; conversely, the products of the system are always considered as provisional: incessantly parenthesized, the moral themes of the *Essais* always emerge as indicators of the process which generates them.

Montaigne thus provides a particularly rich example of how the theoretical topics discussed in Part I of this study might appear in and as a practice of writing. The methods of *copia* are here naturalized into a continuous, infinitely extensible discourse which allows *verba* to proliferate in order to discover some eventual *res*. Variety is its guiding principle: the abundance of rhetorical textures and colours matches the diversity of subject-matter. But the mobility of the surface is organized, not in terms of a random enumeration of the *exempla*, *sententiae*, and figures appropriate to a given topic, but as a process of variation or transformation. The repetition of key topics underlies their rhetorical and thematic metamorphoses, very much as, in Erasmus's variation exercises, the initial formula gave rise to his expansive series of rewritings; except that, in the *Essais*, what is repeated only becomes evident progressively, rather than being given as a pretext. That the text should constantly revert to its own commonplaces is essential to its possibility of coherence and thence of meaning. Yet it also follows that *copia* may run the risk of appearing as *loquacitas* if the saying of many things hides a desire to repeat, *ad infinitum*, a 'topic' which might in the end be reduced to the structure of a reflexive sentence. Montaigne's frequent deprecation of his own discourse (itself another variation of the same structure) makes explicit this risk: in the cornucopian text, empty repetition is always the alternative face of productive proliferation.

This underlying duplicity appears as a theme in the innumerable references to the diversity of experience, the mobility and differentiation of the sensible world. Like Quintilian, Montaigne points out the singularities of even the most 'identical', repetitious objects—eggs, for example.[4] But, by means of a shift of aspect which is characteristic of the structuring of the *Essais*, he can invert the proposition:

Comme nul evenement et nulle forme ressemble entierement à une autre, aussi ne differe nulle de l'autre entierement. (c) Ingenieux meslange de nature. Si nos faces n'estoient semblables, on ne sçauroit discerner l'homme de la beste; si elles n'estoient dissemblables, on ne sçauroit discerner l'homme de l'homme. (b) Toutes choses se tiennent par quelque similitude, tout exemple cloche, et la relation qui se tire de l'experience est tousjours defaillante et imparfaicte; on joinct toutesfois les comparaisons par quelque coin.   (III. xiii, p. 1070)

According to this account, the two principles (identity and difference) are mutually disruptive. The 'similitude' or 'relation' drawn from experience is always contaminated by the centrifugal diversity of phenomena, which may in their turn always be

---

[4] III. xiii, p. 1065: 'Et les Grecs, et les Latins, et nous, pour le plus expres exemple de similitude, nous servons de celuy des œufs. Toutesfois il s'est trouvé des hommes, et notamment un en Delphes, qui recognoissoit des marques de difference entre les œufs . . . La dissimilitude s'ingere d'elle mesme en nos ouvrages; nul art peut arriver à la similitude . . . La ressemblance ne faict pas tant un comme la difference faict autre. (c) Nature s'est obligée à ne rien faire autre, qui ne fust dissemblable.'

submitted to some arbitrary conjunction. It is clear that this dialectic mirrors the way in which rhetoric operates: *similitude* and *comparaison* are tropes, transformations of one term or topic into another. Thus the text can vary and differentiate itself in the minutest particulars, only to reveal—at moments which consequently mark themselves as pivotal, determining all subsequent readings and re-readings—a face of uniformity or conformity. Indeed, both *Du repentir* and *De l'experience* exhibit this sleight-of-hand or structural trope in their exploitation of different forms of the root 'forme':[5] an instance of *annominatio* which comes near to unmasking the tendency of the text to produce, as its key topic, a kind of tautology. The joining of diverse themes in the search for an identity results in a repetition of pure *relation* or conjunction: the empty, reflexive form which sustains all the virtual themes of the *Essais*. Hence the equivalence of such themes (education and cannibals, coaches and experience):

à escrire, j'accepte plus envis les arguments battus, de peur que je les traicte aux despens d'autruy. Tout argument m'est egallement fertille . . . Que je commence par celle qu'il me plaira, car les matieres se tiennent toutes enchesnées les unes aux autres. (III. v, p. 876)

The flight from self-evidence, from the worn paths of the commonplace, leads into endless singularity; but the exotic topography thereby discovered is immediately eroded and naturalized by the mastery of a writer who can express (draw out) a relation between any of its features. And, according to the principle of equivalence, the path that he describes in this detour into foreign terrain will prove to be the same (in sense or direction) as that traced by the commonplaces he seeks to avoid.[6]

---

[5] See III. ii: 'Les autres forment l'homme . . . un particulier bien mal formé' (p. 804); 'la forme entiere de l'humaine condition' (p. 805); 'nous allons conformément' (p. 806); 'mener l'humaine vie conformément' (p. 809); 'reforment les vices de l'apparence', 'une forme sienne, une forme maistresse' (p. 811); 'et y conforme nostre entendement', 'imaginer et former' (p. 812), etc. Cf. also III. xiii, pp. 1065, 1067, 1068, 1070, 1071, 1072, 1073, 1074, etc. Many other root-words (e.g. *entier*, *lustre*) are varied in the same way.

[6] Cf. III. ix, p. 962: 'Je hay à me reconnoistre, et ne retaste jamais qu'envis ce qui m'est une fois eschappé Or je n'apporte icy rien de nouvel apprentissage. Ce sont imaginations communes: les ayant à l'avanture conceuës cent fois, j'ay

Such are the signs of *copia*, as an art of transformational rhetoric. The method of multiple imitation, of which the *De copia* offers a brief but fertile exposition, is also fundamental to the *Essais* (as indeed the first sentence of the above quotation implies). The lineage of the *Ciceronianus* and of the *Deffence et illustration* is evident both in Montaigne's overt references to the assimilation of model-texts and in his practice of redeploying a profusion of more or less identifiable 'sources', whether he acknowledges their presence and provenance or simply repeats their words as part of his own discourse. The process by which borrowed fragments are naturalized ('digested') and re-issued as members of a new corpus is described by Montaigne in terms of *topoi* similar to those of the anti-Ciceronians (the imitation of such theoretical *topoi* being an aspect of the same process), but is developed in a direction which, while anticipated by Erasmus, had not in his work revealed its full complexity. Although in the *Ciceronianus* and elsewhere the phrase *oratio speculum animi* had been attached to the constitution of a subject named 'Erasmus', the singularity of this subject had on the whole remained subordinate to the topics of a representational discourse (the discourse of humanist theory). The personification of Erasmus is intermittent; but in the *Essais*, the production of a self, the writing of a 'portrait' which will make good the absence of its subject, dominates all other activities.

The immediate consequence of this is an exacerbation of the problems of imitation. The subject of the *Essais* must prove his identity (his singular coherence) by rejecting, or at least opposing himself to, alien discourse. Thus remarks like 'Je n'ay dressé commerce avec aucun livre solide'; thus, too, the discussion of the 'art of conversation' in III. viii, where conversation is defined in terms of conflict with the speech of others, and where fools and pedants are treated with contempt. Whether Montaigne compares his own discourse negatively with 'ideal' texts or positively with the language of 'beginners' ('(c) Mon humeur n'est propre, non plus à parler qu'à escrire, pour les principians') (III. viii,

---

peur de les avoir desjà enrollées. La redicte est par tout ennuyeuse . . .' This passage links the fear of repetition with the impossible attempt to avoid the commonplace.

p. 938), the desire to achieve identity by an antithetical process is equally clear. But within the text of the *Essais*, the antithesis conceals a familiar duplicity. Borrowed language may at one moment be strictly tied down to its designated place in the text, but at the next it will appear on the side of the writing subject, who can only write because it is available. However much the rewriting of *topoi* may be ascribed to an author who, conveniently, claims to have thought of them independently (see below, p. 307), the exact convergence of what 'Montaigne' is said to think and what 'Plutarch' or 'Seneca' is said to have thought threatens to erase the signs of Montaigne's identity. Hence the fear of repeating what others have said ('les argumens battus'); hence, above all, the insistent reversion to the mechanics of a deictic discourse which, as an empty *forme*, declares its mastery over the materials it encompasses. If this apparatus were removed, the *Essais* would revert to a florilege: an untitled one, since the word *essai* is one of the thematic motifs through which the personified author *attempts* to dominate his foreign materials. Once again, *annominatio* is a key figure here: the lexical transformations of *essai* are accompanied by its semantic transformations (*exercitation, expérience; goûter, tâter; contrôler*, etc.);[7] and these, through the medium of reflexive syntax in the first person ('je m'escoute', 'je m'essaie'), form— or perform—a skeletal self. In this reductive sense, the thematic paraphernalia of personal experience (eating habits, sexual habits, anecdotes located in the Bordeaux region) are subject to the same principle of equivalence as the rest of the particular topics which the self says it generates, except in so far as they attract an especially intensive use of the grammar of self-portraiture. The self writes itself out, underwrites itself, rewrites itself inexhaustibly. The exercise is productive by definition, since a self cannot but be produced under such conditions; but, since it is exclusively textual (or intertextual), it also comes near to miming the infernal labours of the Danaides.

A particularly graphic illustration of this principle is provided by the *Apologie de Raimond Sebond*. It was once considered to represent a sceptical crisis in Montaigne's thought, as if the *Essais*

---

7 See Friedrich, *Montaigne*, pp. 419–25.

charted their author's adherence, at different times in his life, to different philosophical systems. One might rather say that here, Montaigne sets out a series of texts (taken from a variety of authors, but most importantly from Sextus Empiricus) which endorse the indefinite interrogative movement of the *Essais*, while at the same time removing all possibility of attaining any goal. The sceptical *epoche* (phrased as the question 'Que sais-je?') is inscribed in this text as a kind of self-discovery: the mobile intertextuality of the early *essais* now appears not as an accident but as the presage of a fruitful project. The 'scepticism' which erupts in the *Apologie* was already there from the beginning, or so it would seem. But this discovery creates a striking ambivalence. On the one hand, the sceptical argument is so seductive a thematic expression of the newly clarified project that it is pursued at enormous length, and—more important still—is presented as rational discourse, a textual amalgam which is 'outside' the *epoche* (since its function is precisely to describe the *epoche*). On the other hand, it is introduced as a *provisional* argument;[8] and, at the climax of the exposition, the writer suddenly separates himself from his discourse, anxiously indicating its subversive power:

Vous, pour qui j'ay pris la peine d'estendre un si long corps contre ma coustume, ne refuyrez poinct de maintenir vostre Sebond par la forme ordinaire d'argumenter . . . car ce dernier tour d'escrime icy, il ne le faut employer que comme un extreme remede. C'est un coup desesperé, auquel il faut abandonner vos armes pour faire perdre à vostre adversaire les siennes, et un tour secret, duquel il se faut servir rarement et reservéement. C'est grande temerité de vous perdre vous mesmes pour perdre un autre . . . Nous secouons icy les limites et dernieres clotures des sciences, ausquelles l'extremité est vitieuse,

---

[8] II. xii, p. 449: 'Considerons donq *pour cette heure* l'homme seul, sans secours estranger, armé seulement de ses armes, et despourveu de la grace et cognoissance divine, qui est tout son honneur, sa force et le fondement de son estre' (my italics). Note that, at a late stage in the sceptical argument, Montaigne uses as evidence of the uncertainty principle an observation which, if applied to the text he is writing, would give it a wholly provisional status: '(b) Maintes-fois . . . ayant pris pour exercice et pour esbat à maintenir une contraire opinion à la mienne, mon esprit, s'applicant et tournant de ce costé là, m'y attache si bien que je ne trouve plus la raison de mon premier advis, et m'en depars. Je m'entraine quasi où je penche, comment que ce soit, et m'emporte de mon pois' (p. 566).

comme en la vertu. Tenez vous dans la route commune . . . Toutes les voyes extravagantes me fachent.   (II. xii, pp. 557–8)

The writing subject is thus defined, once again, by a restriction, by an attempt to reject or at least externalize a text which threatens to overwhelm him, although this was precisely the text which allowed all others to be held at bay. The sheer extension of the *Apologie* ('un si long corps') goes far beyond what is required by any 'philosophical' demonstration: it is a writing performance, dominated by powerful alien texts.[9] It repeats obsessively a principle of uncertainty, undermining all possibility of establishing some criterion by which knowledge, and thus writing, could be mastered and stabilized. Although the prolixity and self-evidence of this sceptical text may compose an inflated chapter of the *Essais*, it also threatens to ruin them by monopolizing their terrain and thus destroying the incipient project of self-portraiture. Writing, under such conditions, becomes an extravagance, a vice or error.[10] The *Apologie*, in pouring itself out, demonstrates its own irreversible movement towards emptiness. And so the figure of a writer appears in the margin, nervously trying to fabricate

[9] One should recall also that the exercise was undertaken in order to defend another threatened text. The defence, as is well known, inverts some of Sebond's key themes, presenting nature as fallen and man as the lowest creature in the universe. But it would be wrong to consider this simply as an inconsistency in Montaigne's argument. Sebond's *Theologia naturalis* is presented, hypothetically, as a paradigm of the ideal or natural text, assisted by grace; Montaigne's discourse, moving away centrifugally from that text and its defence, nevertheless defines itself—again, provisionally and hypothetically—in antithetical relationship to it. In this perspective, the lapsarian themes which pervade the greater part of the *Apologie* may be read as figures of a discourse reflecting on its own original error (cf. p. 452: 'La presomption est nostre maladie naturelle et originelle': in a (c)-text placed almost immediately afterwards, reference is made to the platonist Golden Age in which man could communicate directly with animals, i.e. with nature; cf. also the appearance of the Babel *topos*, pp. 553–4). The Pelagian question becomes a question of writing.

[10] But elsewhere 'error' or 'extravagance' is seen to be essential to *essai*-writing: compare 'Tenez vous dans la route commune . . . Toutes les voyes extravagantes me fachent' with the later passage quoted above, p. 277 ('j'accepte plus envis les arguments battus . . . Tout argument m'est egallement fertille'), and the quotation in note 6; cf. also below, pp. 316–18. The book of *Essais* is elsewhere described as 'le seul livre au monde de son espèce, d'un dessein farouche et extravagant'.

some precarious *clôture* for his vacuous topic. Montaigne is a fold
in his own text.[11]

This illustration may serve also to introduce one further point,
which is of methodological importance and will close this section.
It is perfectly legitimate to speak of the 'evolution' of the *Essais*,
that is to say, to distribute their matter according to a chronology
established by internal and external evidence; to compare, thematically and rhetorically, early elements with late ones; and to
observe the process by which an unformed project emerges in
the form of the *essai* project. Modern editions which indicate the
three major layers of the text are in this respect indispensable.
Nevertheless, one should bear in mind that such indications
determine the reading of the *Essais* according to a set of critical
preconceptions which are not self-evidently valid. Even the exercise of reconstituting (say) the 1580 text by reading only the
(a)-layer is contaminated by the awareness of what is 'left out';
and it is equally arguable that the marking of layers fractures the
complete version, reminding the reader that certain passages were
inserted and thus inviting him to consider them as in some sense
a supplementation. There is of course no true reading. But it
is worth reflecting that Montaigne's supplementations are not
signalled in the 1588 text, and one assumes that they would not
have been, had other editions appeared during his lifetime. The
stratification is a modern device, not one adopted by Montaigne
as part of his project. Thus the expanded versions of the *Essais*
erase the difference between the layers of text, as if the writer were
erasing his own deferment in the book which is said to copy him,
to represent his life as uninterrupted *copia*.[12] Indeed, the whole

[11] This interruption is followed by a resumption of the sceptical argument;
furthermore, the closing movement of the chapter is provided by a passage
rewritten from Plutarch. The *Apologie* is a text in which its writer is constantly
being expropriated, despite his attempts at intervention, so that the phrase 'his own
text' used above should be read with a certain irony.

[12] A particularly striking instance is to be found in I. xx. Here, the (a)-text
contains precise chronological references (p. 84: 'Il n'y a justement que quinze
jours que j'ay franchi 39 ans') and an indication of the attitude to death which the
author is said to hold at this point in his life. Then, in a (c)-text superimposed on
this development, Montaigne continues to use the present tense: 'Je suis pour
cette heure en tel estat, Dieu mercy, que je puis desloger quand il luy plaira . . .'

process by which an enormous number of textual particularities
are amalgamated and presented as a single book bearing a single
signature points in the same direction. In such ways, the search
for coherence and continuity asserts itself momentarily over the
vision of the endless fragmentation of experience: the 'last' essay,
by its very title, suggests the desire to integrate experience as a
topic. But the urgency of this desire draws attention at the same
time to the inverse tendency of the text to deconstruct itself into
a series of discrete inscriptions (writing-fragments) suspended as it
were in a void. The deferment of a full self-portrait, the complete
work representing the complete man, is written into the *Essais*
far more deeply than any typographical markers can indicate.
Supplementation governs the whole of the writing project, from
its uncertain beginning to its inconclusive ending.[13] The *Essais*
always remain to be rewritten.

The foregoing section, which deliberately takes a theoretical
stance at some distance from the detail of the text, may be read as
a precautionary measure or critical *epoche*. It suspends any desire to accept the image of an easy-going humanist who offers
reassuring ethical insights, just as it bypasses the concern to

(p. 88). The reader who is aware of the different 'layers' will assign to these passages different values, one being seen as a relatively youthful and cerebral philo-
sophic stance, the other as the moving testimony of a man suffering acute illness
and near to death. But if the markers are removed, the text reverts to a single
present tense, eschewing the signs of autobiographical difference. The process of
supplementation and the chronological shifts are made fully explicit in *De la
vanité*: 'Mon livre est tousjours un. Sauf qu'à mesure qu'on se met à le renouveller
. . . je me donne loy d'y attacher (comme ce n'est qu'une marqueterie mal jointe),
quelque embleme supernumeraire. Ce ne sont que surpoids, qui ne condamnent
point la premiere forme . . . De là toutesfois il adviendra facilement qu'il s'y mesle
quelque transposition de chronologie, mes contes prenans place selon leur
opportunité, non tousjours selon leur aage' (III. ix, p. 964). The ensuing passage
refers also to the indeterminacy of biographical 'evolution'.

[13] The indefinite extensibility of Montaigne's writing is made explicit at the
opening of *De la vanité* in a predominantly negative context which stresses the
'vanity' of writing and the grotesque proliferation of 'babil': 'Qui ne voit que
j'ay pris une route par laquelle, sans cesse et sans travail, j'iray autant qu'il y aura
d'ancre et de papier au monde?' (p. 946; cf. also 947). The production of language
stifles the reality it was supposed to represent.

understand Montaigne as a thinker who, though expressly not a philosopher, founds a tradition of 'moralist' writing. Montaigne devises powerful means of engaging one's complicity in his enterprise of self-portraiture; but the complexity—the rigour even—of that enterprise imposes on his reader a particular obligation not to be duped. Despite appearances to the contrary, the *Essais*—in this respect not unlike La Fontaine's fables—is not a book for 'les principians'.[14] Yet the critical *epoche* may be a self-defeating weapon, and should be used sparingly. Once it has taken effect, it becomes possible to reopen the perspective of a writing deeply concerned with the processes of life, and to examine some of the thematic material in which the problems of self-awareness are inscribed. This section will bring back into play many of the theoretical topics of the preceding one, but now seen in their relation to a certain group of figures: predominantly those of sexual performance as they are displayed in *Sur des vers de Virgile* (III. v).

In this chapter, quotations are particularly abundant, and play more than an accessory role. They are often used to carry the weight of Montaigne's most explicit sexual references in a text which expressly claims the right to uninhibited self-portrayal: 'je me suis ordonné d'oser dire tout ce que j'ose faire, et me desplais des pensées mesmes impubliables' (p. 845). The transgression of a deeply entrenched linguistic convention is facilitated by—although by no means dependent on—the use of borrowed texts, written (and rewritten by Montaigne) in a foreign language. It might seem, indeed, that Latin is used as a kind of veil to hide the ultimate *pudenda*: when the writer wants to speak disparagingly of his own genitals, he does so by quoting the *Priapea* (p. 887). On the other hand, the balance between concealment and revelation is a fine one, as will shortly be indicated; furthermore, Montaigne claims that the classical poets had a special capacity for portraying the erotic. He dwells at length on the richness, vigour, and plenitude of Virgil's and Lucretius' style when they describe sexual episodes; quoting Lucretius, he meditates on the powerful

[14] This point is well made by Pouilloux in the Introduction to his *Lire les 'Essais' de Montaigne*.

vocabulary of the passage, contrasting it with the 'menues pointes et allusions verballes' of later poetry:

A ces bonnes gens, il ne falloit pas d'aigue et subtile rencontre: leur langage est tout plein et gros d'une vigueur naturelle et constante . . . (c) *'Contextus totus virilis est; non sunt circa flosculos occupati.'* (b) Ce n'est pas une eloquence molle et seulement sans offence: elle est nerveuse et solide, qui ne plaict pas tant comme elle remplit et ravit, et ravit le plus les plus forts espris. Quand je voy ces braves formes de s'expliquer, si vifves, si profondes, je ne dicts pas que c'est bien dire, je dicts que c'est bien penser. C'est la gaillardise de l'imagination qui esleve et enfle les parolles.[15]

Montaigne's own vocabulary is here explicitly sexual in character. According to a sustained metaphor of rhetorical potency, the Lucretian text is as well filled as Gargantua's *braguette*: the swelling or inflation attributed to imagination is authentic.[16]

The contrast between such textual energy and the impotent 'verbal' style of the later poets is grounded in the traditional opposition of *verba* and *res*: words are empty unless they proceed from, or move towards, fullness of thought ('les plaines conceptions'). The ensuing passage develops this *topos* in some detail, returning insistently to the antithesis of windy emptiness and corporal presence:

Plutarque dit qu'il veid le langage latin par les choses; icy de mesme: le sens esclaire et produict les parolles; non plus de vent, ains de chair et d'os. (loc. cit.)

The Lucretius passage is, in fact, an instance of *enargeia*; the rhetoric of presence imposes itself on the reader as a conjunction of rich verbal texture (*contextus*) with significance or sense. This impact is expressed and explored by Montaigne through the intuitive observations already quoted: 'Quand je voy ces braves formes . . . je ne dicts pas que c'est bien dire, je dicts que c'est bien penser.' A metaphor of seeing (echoed in the phrase 'Plutarque dit qu'il *veid* le langage latin . . .') registers the force of a discourse which is then

---

[15] p. 873. The Latin quotation is from Seneca.

[16] The use of 'ravit' in this passage constitutes a kind of pun, recalling both a sexual ravishing and the neoplatonist *raptio*. Cf. Bowen, 'Montaigne's anti-*Phaedrus*', on sex and rhetoric in III. v.

said to be 'well thought' rather than 'well said'. The distinction is formulated not as a metaphysical proposition but as a linguistic convention: 'This is the kind of thing one says about such language.' Precisely the same approach is indicated by a subsequent sentence: 'Nos gens appellent jugement, langage; et beaux mots, les plaines conceptions.' Although the phrase 'nos gens' establishes a degree of social distance, and although the sentence as a whole implies that what is called 'language' by such people is really 'judgement' or fullness of thought, the emphasis on linguistic convention is still paramount. The elliptical chiasmus, which makes it difficult at first sight to reconstitute the structure of the sentence, has the effect of suggesting an equivalence between thought and language; in speaking of 'profound' or 'superficial' language, we are only making an intuitive distinction between two types of discourse according to their impact. We do not see the thought; it is only when we 'see' language with particular vividness that we attribute it to the complexity of a mind.

Montaigne is thus deeply involved in this passage in the realm of linguistic *species*. Although he does not conceive of it in this context as presenting a risk (as is the case with 'specious' argument), his analysis brings to the surface a tissue of questions which link the fabrication of the *Essais*, once again, with the topics of *copia*.[17] Many strands converge here. For example, the figures of 'evidence' and the psychology of imagination are brought into play in a way which strongly suggests theoretical *loci* such as Quintilian's discussion of the force of extempore speech; and the (c)-text indeed adds an echo of *Institutiones* X. vii: 'Pectus est quod disertum

---

[17] Cf. the passage in this same development comparing Horace with Gallus: 'Gallus parle simplement, par ce qu'il conçoit simplement. Horace ne se contente point d'une superficielle expression, elle le trahiroit. Il voit plus cler et plus outre dans la chose; son esprit crochette et furette tout le magasin des mots et des figures pour se représenter; et les luy faut outre l'ordinaire, comme sa conception est outre l'ordinaire' (p. 873). Complexity of expression, drawing on the storehouse of words and figures, is the visible manifestation of a supposed complexity of thought represented by a visual metaphor. 'Crochette' and 'furette' are themselves, one might note, the product of a copious 'magasin' (Montaigne's own). Cf. also this subsequent remark, which rephrases the desire for 'extravagance' in terms of the resources of language: 'je n'eusse osé me fier à un Idiome [sc. Italian] que je ne pouvois plier ny contourner outre son alleure commune.'

facit.' At the same time, the fact that this intuitive principle is quoted, in Latin, via Quintilian reminds one that the whole passage depends on the play of intertextuality: imitation thus becomes, at a less explicit level, one of the theoretical topics generated by the argument. The surfacing of supplementary fragments, here and in the quotation from Seneca ('Contextus totus'), authorizes a certain topical movement within the larger framework of a dialogue between 'Lucretius' and 'Montaigne'. This primary intertextual process, by which a fragment of Latin verse is reconstituted in French prose, begins with a rewriting of privileged words: 'Quand je rumine ce *"rejicit, pascit, inhians, molli, fovet, medullas, labefacta, pendet, percurrit"*, et cette noble *"circumfusa"*, mere du gentil *"infusus"* . . .'.[18] Subsequently, the value attributed to such words is developed through a metaphor of the text as a living, natural organism. Heralded by the connotation of 'digestion' implicit in the word 'rumine', this metaphor writes itself out as a *topos* of rhetorical theory. But its development in specifically sexual terms appears as the unfolding, within the Montaignian text, of the theme of the Lucretian passage; a description of sexual activity is displaced to become a figure of the relationship between a text and its reader—hence the connotations of erection, penetration, and fertilization, and the possibility of a play on words in the phrase 'les plaines conceptions'.

This movement from mimetic representation to metaphor (which is also the movement of a metaphor back towards its 'proper sense') creates a fundamental equivalence or ambiguity which shifts the ground of the chapter as a whole. Sex and language are here so closely associated that it is difficult (and unnecessary) to decide whether language represents sex, or sex, language. Lucretius is quoted, not because he provides a convenient illustration of the sexual theme, but because his verses embody textual mastery: the scene they describe becomes an emblem of their own energies.

In the ensuing development, the contrast between such vigour

[18] p. 872. Some of these words occur in the parallel passage from Virgil (the 'vers de Virgile' of the title) quoted on p. 849. Thus a further strand of intertextuality—between Lucretius and Virgil—is indicated.

and the weak, ineffectual discourse of Montaigne's contemporaries is explored in terms of the respective potentiality for enrichment of Latin and of French. Abundance, in the vernacular, is said to arise not from pretentious innovation but from a judicious use of the whole range of the living language, including the specialized— and concrete—languages of hunting and warfare:

il n'est rien qu'on ne fit du jargon de nos chasses et de nostre guerre, qui est un genereux terrain à emprunter; et les formes de parler, comme les herbes, s'amendent et fortifient en les transplantant.   (p. 874)

This notion of a revaluing of language by means of its displace-ment is particularly crucial to Montaigne's own discourse, where rewriting must again and again be justified as a positive activity. Here, the relationship between Latin and the vernacular is a problematic one. It appears that, unlike Latin, French tends to droop under the burden of 'une puissante conception':

Je le trouve suffisamment abondant, mais non pas (c) maniant et (b) vigoureux suffisamment. Il succombe ordinairement à une puissante conception. Si vous allez tendu, vous sentez souvent qu'il languit soubs vous et fleschit, et qu'à son deffaut le Latin se presente au secours, et le Grec à d'autres.   (loc. cit.)

If the sexual metaphor is reinvoked in this context, one may say that French (the language in which Montaigne writes, and which is to constitute his self-portrait) is threatened with impotence; the use of loan-words (or the quotation of classical texts?) is thus a kind of therapy. Once again the sexual theme of the passages Montaigne has quoted is prolonged in the metaphors of a quasi-analytic discourse reflecting on its own procedures.

The wearing out of common words and figures in natural language is also located as a central problem of writing (and reading):

D'aucuns de ces mots que je viens de trier, nous en apercevons plus malaisément l'energie, d'autant que l'usage et la frequence nous en ont aucunement avily et rendu vulgaire la grace. Comme en nostre commun, il s'y rencontre des frases excellentes et des metaphores desquelles la beauté flestrit de vieillesse, et la couleur s'est ternie par maniement trop ordinaire. Mais cela n'oste rien du goust à ceux qui ont bon nez, ny ne desroge à la gloire de ces anciens autheurs qui, comme il est vraysemblable, mirent premierement ces mots en ce lustre.[19]

The awareness of such 'usage' accompanies the desire for a rehabilitation of language: the 'illustration' of the vernacular which is attributed hypothetically to some primary invention may be recognized and perhaps repeated by a modern writer acutely aware of how language works. Words and metaphors must be rewritten as if they were original: *derivatio* (the variety of *annominatio* which draws attention to an etymology) is the guarantor of displacement.

The interplay between the text of the *Essais* and that of the quotations it carries is generalized further in a passage which is remarkable for its oscillation between two alternative postures. Montaigne claims to dispense with the 'compaignie et souvenance' of books when he is writing, 'de peur qu'ils n'interrompent ma forme' (p. 874). Likewise,

il me vient aussi à propos d'escrire chez moy, en pays sauvage, ou personne ne m'ayde ny me releve, où je ne hante communéement homme qui entende le latin de son patenostre, et de françois un peu moins. Je l'eusse faict meilleur ailleurs, mais l'ouvrage eust esté moins mien; et sa fin principale et perfection, c'est d'estre exactement mien. (p. 875)

This argument culminates in a reflexive formula of conformity between book and self: 'tout le monde me reconnoit en mon livre, et mon livre en moy'. Yet the fear that his 'form' will be invaded by other texts betrays the fragility of the claim: the figure of a solitary who retreats from the world to write in his *library* stands immediately behind the artless personification of this passage; and *Sur des vers de Virgile* is steeped (as its very title suggests) in echoes of other books. Montaigne admits as much with regard to Plutarch, his favourite cornucopian text:

Mais je me puis plus malaiséement deffaire de Plutarque. Il est si universel et si plain qu'à toutes occasions, et quelque suject extravagant

---

[19] Loc. cit. The phrase 'ces mots que je viens de trier' presumably refers to Montaigne's list of words from the Lucretius passage. On the 'bilingual' aspect of this essay as a whole, see Coleman, 'Montaigne's "Sur des vers de Virgile" '.

que vous ayez pris, il s'ingere à vostre besongne et vous tend une main
liberale et inespuisable de richesses et d'embellissemens. Il m'en faict
despit d'estre si fort exposé au pillage de ceux qui le hantent.   (loc. cit.)

This passage precedes the one quoted above ('il me vient aussi à
propos . . .'), which is thus placed virtually in a parenthesis:
Plutarch can presumably penetrate the deepest solitudes, and
inserts himself surreptitiously into the fabric of a book which
Montaigne claims so thoroughly to *possess* ('sa fin . . . c'est d'estre
exactement mien'). Similarly, the formula of reciprocity ('tout le
monde me reconnoit en mon livre . . .') is immediately followed
by a long excursus on Montaigne's chameleon-like propensities:

Or j'ay une condition singeresse et imitatrice: quand je me meslois
de faire des vers (et n'en fis jamais que des Latins), ils accusoient evi-
demment le poete que je venois dernierement de lire; et, de mes
premiers essays, aucuns puent un peu à l'estranger . . . Qui que je
regarde avec attention m'imprime facilement quelque chose du sien.
(p. 875)

The 'anxiety of influence', the fear that the self will be invaded by
alien language, could hardly be more graphically illustrated. There
is no question, of course, of attempting to resolve this oscillation
or paradox. Indeed, Montaigne lists paradox (and abundance of
figures) among the congenital errors of his writing, that is to say,
as a distinctive part of his property—what makes his text exactly
his. It is only necessary, once again, to indicate that displacement is
constitutive of the personification 'Montaigne'; above all, where
the topic of displacement itself (imitation) generates a counter-
movement within the text, a fold like that in the *Apologie*.

The above *egressio* on imitation follows the wandering of
Montaigne's text. But the itinerary reflects at every point the
fundamental duplicity of *Sur des vers de Virgile*. This chapter-title
already hides the topic of sex, evoking the perspective of a textual
commentary as if the thematic content of Virgil's verses and
Lucretius' were secondary and accidental. The notion of concealment recurs at various points in the chapter. In the guise of the
convention of not talking about sex, it determines Montaigne's
strategy of transgression: he claims the right to make public even

this most secret of topics. Later, the argument abrasively surveys the various moral and religious principles which devalue sex as a shameful activity fit only to be concealed in darkness. This passage takes on the colouring of invective: its disapproval of repressive conventions is unambiguous (pp. 878–80).

But a disconcerting shift in the argument then follows. The chapter returns to its titular subject:

Les vers de ces deux poëtes, traitant ainsi reservéement et discrettement de la lasciveté comme ils font, me semblent la descouvrir et esclairer de plus pres. Les dames couvrent leur sein d'un reseu, les prestres plusieurs choses sacrées; les peintres ombragent leur ouvrage, pour luy donner plus de lustre . . .[20]

According to this account, partial concealment is a powerful means of revealing ('discovering') what is hidden. The notion of exciting desire by imposing restraints had been treated earlier in the chapter, in a commonplace development on chastity, marriage, cuckoldry, and the inexhaustible lusts of women (pp. 861–72): this development has marked affinities with Rabelais's treatment of such topics, not least when Montaigne refers slightingly to the custom of wearing codpieces and to the discrepancy between such garments and what they contain (pp. 859–60). In the passage of which an extract is quoted above, concealment is valued differently, modifying the invective against repression which immediately precedes it. Its particular interest lies in the conjunction of a procedure of writing (or painting) with an observation on sexual psychology. The rhetoric of copulation depends on a mingling of clarity and obscurity: the nudity of Venus must be seen as if through a lattice—'et l'action et la peinture doivent sentir le larrecin'. This observation leads to a long excursus on the pleasures of deferment:

Je ne sçay qui, anciennement, desiroit le gosier allongé comme le col d'une gruë pour gouster plus long temps ce qu'il avalloit. Ce souhait est mieux à propos en cette volupté viste et precipiteuse, mesmes à

---

[20] p. 880. The equivalence assigned to these three examples—sexual, religious, and aesthetic—is a particularly clear example of the way in which Montaigne's topics converge and replace one another, creating the possibility of an indefinite number of thematic permutations.

telles natures comme est la mienne, qui suis vitieux en soudaineté . . .
(p. 880)

Plus il y a de marches et degrez, plus il y a de hauteur et d'honneur au
dernier siege. Nous nous devrions plaire d'y estre conduicts, comme il se
faict aux palais magnifiques, par divers portiques et passages, longues et
plaisantes galleries, et plusieurs detours.   (p. 881)

The labyrinthine building as a figure of deferred desire echoes the
houses of Crassus and Eusebius; the pursuit of sense is now transposed into a pursuit of sex. The mutation, needless to say, operates
both ways. As was shown earlier, it is strictly impossible, in the
discourse of *Sur des vers de Virgile*, to speak of sex other than as
language, and vice versa. Thus this passage, with its productive
detours, may be read as a rewriting of an earlier one contrasting
Gallus with Horace (see above, note 17); or again, one might cite
Montaigne's *exemplum* of the Egyptian:

L'Ægyptien respondit sagement à celuy qui luy demandoit: Que porte
tu là, caché soubs ton manteau?—Il est caché soubs mon manteau affin
que tu ne sçaches pas que c'est.   (p. 880)

In a chapter which has dwelt on the concealment of *pudenda*,
such an example cannot but include a sexual reference among its
range of specifically undeclared meanings.[21] The possibility that
a *res* might be concealed in the mantle of *verba* excites curiosity,
inaugurates the pursuit of sense, and gives licence to *copia*.

  Sur des vers de Virgile may thus be said to make evident, in the
duplicity of its thematic structure, the pleasure of the text. When
Montaigne claims that love is nothing but 'le plaisir à descharger
ses vases' (p. 877), he uses 'Venus' as a metonymy for 'love': the
displacement invokes the verses he has quoted in which Venus is
seen performing in her own right (*au propre*). As will be clear
from the passages mentioned above, with their oscillation between the rejection of repressive language and the preference for
veiled discourse, this essay has an ambiguity which hinges on a
disruption of conventional categories and oppositions. Character-

---

[21] The theme of clothes as a covering for the *pudenda* recurs frequently in this
chapter. Cf. p. 888, where Montaigne speaks of 'nostre debte envers ce grand
juge qui trousse nos panneaus et haillons d'autour noz parties honteuses . . .'

istically, the notion of the absurdity of sexual behaviour appears as an ultimate subversion of the attempt to categorize human activity (and hence discourse) into two separate domains, the serious and the non-serious, wisdom and folly. Sex dissipates thought:

Nous mangeons bien et beuvons comme les bestes, mais ce ne sont pas actions qui empeschent les operations de nostre ame. En celles-là nous gardons nostre avantage sur elles; cette-cy met toute autre pensée soubs le joug, abrutit et abestit par son imperieuse authorité toute la theologie et philosophie qui est en Platon; et si il ne s'en plaint pas.[22]

This deflating activity, which goes even further than the symposium in by-passing conventional distinctions, is also intrinsically ambivalent. It is 'the most noble, useful, and agreeable of nature's operations', but also a sign of the Fall, 'une marque non seulement de nostre corruption originelle, mais aussi de nostre vanité et deformité' (p. 878). The sexual discourse of Montaigne partakes of the same ambivalence, since it both announces a healthy naturalness and lays bare its own congenital inadequacies.[23]

On the last page of the chapter, Montaigne parodies what he has written as 'ce notable commentaire, qui m'est eschappé d'un flux de caquet, flux impetueux par fois et nuisible'.[24] The image, recalling similar ones in Plutarch's De garrulitate and Erasmus's Lingua, would seem to have excremental connotations: on the

[22] p. 877. This development exploits arguments central also to the Praise of Folly and, of course, to Rabelais. Cf. the preceding sentence in the (c)-text: 'Ceux qui, parmi les jeux, refusent les opinions serieuses, font, dict quelqu'un, comme celuy qui craint d'adorer la statuë d'un sainct, si elle est sans devantiere.'

[23] See pp. 880 ('suis vitieux en soudaineté'), 887, 893–4. With regard to the thematic (and rhetorical) ambivalence of Montaigne's text, it is perhaps not irrelevant to remark that the essay closes on an assertion of the equivalence of the sexes.

[24] p. 897. This remark is immediately followed by a quotation from Catullus about an apple (given by her lover) which a girl hides under her dress and which falls out in her mother's presence, making her blush guiltily. The quotation develops the word 'eschappé' in the preceding sentence, but in a quite different metaphorical direction. It points to the quasi-accidental character of the chapter and its 'revelations', as if the text had surreptitiously gone beyond the scope of the initial claim to openness; and it brings back into play in an erotic context the themes of hiding and revealing. The ambiguous apple may also seem an appropriate figure for the close of a dubiously cornucopian text.

first page of *De la vanité*, the text of the *Essais* is described as 'des excremens d'un vieil esprit, dur tantost, tantost lache et tousjours indigeste' (III. ix, p. 946). At all events, this devaluation by Montaigne of his own discourse is placed in a temporal perspective, since the 'flux de caquet' is characterized as such in opposition to the potent model-texts it cites (Virgil, Lucretius, Plutarch). The power to signify is located in the past, just as true sexual potency is located in youth. Hence the passage on the ageing processes of language (their 'usage'), which explain the difficulty of achieving the plenitude of the classical poets: Virgil and Lucretius were writing at a time when language still had great intrinsic vigour. The sexual antithesis between youth and age is reflected in a parallel textual antithesis. In the opening pages of the chapter, Montaigne refers to the value of his topic as a way of sustaining mentally—or rather textually—the pleasures of his youth; he stresses the irony of the fact that his vision is now retrospective:

me vois amusant en la recordation des jeunesses passées,

> *animus quod perdidit optat,*
> *Atque in praeterita se totus imagine versat.*

Que l'enfance regarde devant elle, la vieillesse derriere: estoit-ce pas ce que signifioit le double visage de Janus? Les ans m'entrainent s'ils veulent, mais à reculons! Autant que mes yeux peuvent reconnoistre cette belle saison expirée, je les y destourne à secousses. Si elle eschappe de mon sang et de mes veines, aumoins n'en veus-je desraciner l'image de la memoire . . .[25]

This double movement, embodied here in the Janus image, is restated at the end of the chapter, and thus forms a frame for the whole topic. Love, says Montaigne, is appropriate to the earliest stages of youth, indeed almost to infancy; it begins to decline soon afterwards; experience and practice erode it by eliminating spontaneity:

l'amour ne me semble proprement et naturellement en sa saison qu'en l'aage voisin de l'enfance,

---

[25] pp. 841–2. The Latin quotation, from Petronius' *Satyricon*, crystallizes the theme of the desire for what is lost, linking it with a mental reconstruction of the past.

> *Quem si puellarum insereres choro,*
> *Mille sagaces falleret hospites*
> *Discrimen obscurum, solutis*
> *Crinibus ambiguóque vultu.*

. . . En la virilité, je le trouve desjà hors de son siege . . . Plus courte possession nous luy donnons sur nostre vie, mieux nous en valons . . . Qui ne sçait, en son eschole, combien on procede au rebours de tout ordre? L'estude, l'exercitation, l'usage, sont voies à l'insuffisance: les novices y regentent.[26]

In this strange passage, Janus, figure of the duplicity of life, is replaced by another two-faced emblem: the hermaphrodite, proto-sexual figure of the first season. His obscurity and ambiguity are delineated in a Latin text: Latin was, after all, Montaigne's first language, the lost discourse of his infancy.[27] We shall return to this concealed, formless origin later. For the present, it is sufficient to note that here, the values intrinsic to sex (and thus to 'natural' life itself) are seen as diametrically opposed to the values which the *Essais* exploit and indeed rely on. In particular, this devaluation appears to affect the notion of *expérience* and its correlate *essai* (since both are germane to *exercitation*): that is to say, it undermines the whole generative process which the book purports to celebrate. If *exercitation* is synonymous with *usage*, the *ordre* of the book (as of life itself) functions as the emptying out of an original plenitude. To put it another way, the *Essais*, by attempting to recover what was already lost before the writing began, proliferate at the expense of life. The hand that writes them is a 'main phtinopore', simultaneously ripening and ravaging.

The problems implicit in this thematic structure are deepened on closer examination by a complicating factor or asymmetry in the parallel between the opposition youth–age and the opposition classical texts–modern texts. However potent, Lucretius' representation of sexual activity is still a representation; it is a text, not

[26] pp. 895–6. The passage Montaigne quotes from Horace's *Odes* may also have provoked Ronsard's image of Cassandre disguising herself as Adonis (see above, p. 246, note 34).

[27] Cf. I. xxvi, pp. 173–5; also III. ii, pp. 810–11.

life. Yet at one point, ironically, Montaigne says that erotic experience is more concentrated, has greater plenitude in such passages than in life itself:

Mais de ce que je m'y entends, les forces et valeur de ce Dieu se trouvent plus vives et plus animées en la peinture de la poesie qu'en leur propre essence . . . Elle represente je ne sçay quel air plus amoureux que l'amour mesme. Venus n'est pas si belle toute nue, et vive, et hale-tante, comme elle est icy chez Virgile . . .[28]

This is indeed a pivotal point in the chapter, since it introduces the eponymous 'vers de Virgile': the Venus-text, representing the air of its erotic fury, joins the configuration of Janus and the hermaphrodite. The two paradigms of plenitude (textual and biographical), both located in an original season, are mutually disruptive. If love is undiminished only in extreme youth, the erotic text can only be a copy, produced by *étude, exercitation, expérience, art*. But then if erotic experience seems more intense in poetry than in life, if *enargeia* (like Galatea) outdoes any possible model, the status of that original youthful vigour is placed in doubt. Once again, the values of text and of life operate in contrary motion, even at the ideal or paradigmatic level;[29] consequently, it is inevitable that Montaigne's writing, which is moving progressively away from both origins (except in so far as it can carry fragments of Latin poetry), is seen as empty *écoulement*, as a 'flux de caquet'.[30]

[28] p. 849. Elsewhere, the same phenomenon is attributed to the *Essais* themselves: 'Me peignant pour autruy, je me suis peint en moy de couleurs plus nettes que n'estoyent les miennes premieres. Je n'ay pas plus faict mon livre que mon livre m'a faict, livre consubstantiel à son autheur . . .' (II. xviii, p. 665). As the text absorbs (or produces) the author's substance, the author is himself displaced in favour of the evidence of writing.

[29] Cf. the celebration of Homer as an 'ideal text' (II. xxxvi, p. 753): 'C'est contre l'ordre de nature qu'il a faict la plus excellente production qui puisse estre: car la naissance ordinaire des choses, elle est imparfaicte; elles s'augmentent, se fortifient par l'accroissance: l'enfance de la poësie et de plusieurs autres sciences, il l'a rendue meure, parfaicte et accomplie . . . Ses parolles, selon Aristote, sont les seules parolles qui ayent mouvement et action; ce sont les seuls mots substantiels.' On the Aristotelian allusion, see above, p. 144, note 24; the reference to the uniqueness of Homeric language ('seules', 'seuls') proves that Montaigne is quoting Aristotle via Plutarch; he himself has added the notion of 'substance'.

[30] A variation on this theme is provided by another passage from the same

The topics of *Sur des vers de Virgile* may be considered as local variants of that empty *forme* which is repeated throughout the *Essais*, and which is versatile enough to carry the most diverse materials. The principle of equivalence which governs the themes of the book as a whole is apparent here in the fact that personal experience, even in its most private form, is situated amid a variety of non-personal quotations, *topoi*, and *exempla* (like those on the sexual behaviour of women) which threaten to overwhelm it. Furthermore, the reciprocal action, demonstrated above, of the themes of sex and of language institutes the reversion of self-portraiture to textual self-consciousness—in this instance, to the problems of rhetorical potency, the status of the vernacular, and the pervasiveness of imitation. The axiom 'mon theme se renverse en soy' is no less applicable to *Sur des vers de Virgile* than to any other of the *essais*. Nevertheless, the reversibility of the text also allows the local colour of the topic to assert itself as part of the phenomenology of a self defined precisely by the flow of *cogitationes* which pass through it, whatever their anonymity or fragmentation.[31] This is the sense of the reduction or *epoche* applied earlier in the present chapter. Thus, in order to give a broader scope to the investigation of problems of writing as they are embodied in the *Essais*, one may pursue Montaigne's topics as topics, bearing in mind only that they do not function as representation, that they are articulated in a fundamentally indeterminate discourse.

essay, where Montaigne claims that his best 'resveries' are produced 'à l'improuveu' at times when he has no paper to which he can attach them; hence they 's'esvanouissent soudain' (p. 876). His most profound thoughts are said to be also his most elusive and fluid ones; those he commits to paper are never immediate, never a sign of presence.

[31] Cf. II. vi, p. 379: '(c) Je peins principalement mes cogitations, subject informe, qui ne peut tomber en production ouvragere. A toute peine le puis je coucher en ce corps aërée de la voix.' Although this remark stresses the insubstantiality of the 'cogitations' as *essai*-material (cf. also above, note 30), the ensuing passage speaks of writing as a complete self-anatomy: 'Je m'estalle entier: c'est un SKELETOS où, d'une veuë, les veines, les muscles, les tendons paroissent, chaque piece en son siege.' Writing thus appears as the phenomenology of a self coterminous with its thought-processes. On the identification of the text with the (figurative) body, which is implied by a large number of the essays analysed in the present chapter, see above, pp. 149–50.

The theme of the loss of an original plenitude, which is carried
by both the sexual and the textual motifs of III. v, recurs, in
various forms, throughout the entire book. In the later essays, the
discomforts and malfunctions of old age are insistently evoked in
counterpoint to images of *gaillardise*, of health and youth. Thus,
for example, in *Du repentir*, the commonplace association of age
with wisdom is inverted: old age is a falling away from the only
state in which virtue can be authentically practised.[32] The motto
'Viresque acquirit eundo' ('it gathers force as it proceeds'), which
Montaigne wrote in manuscript as an epigraph on the title-page
of the 1588 edition of the *Essais*, may therefore appear as tinged
with irony. The production of a word-self, continually growing
in size and potency, coincides with the progressive elimination
of the real or natural self—in short, with a movement towards
death. Death is, indeed, a kind of arch-topic in the *Essais*. In the
first place, it has a particularly privileged position in a moral
discourse which defines itself, according to an ancient commonplace, as a preparation for death ('philosopher, c'est apprendre à
mourir'):[33] this position is maintained whether the ethical prescription favours stoic bravado or pliant acceptance. Secondly
(and consequently), death provides the point of reference for
all other topics, whether positive (*volupté*, *tranquillité*, *sagesse*) or
negative (*flux*, *branle*, *vanité*). It both provides a measure for their
scope and value, and levels or empties them by means of its own
total neutrality, being itself neither positive nor negative but an
absence in view of which the language of life attempts to organize
itself. More specifically, it provides a point of departure, according to a certain fiction of autobiography, for the *essai*-project

[32] III. ii, pp. 815–16, in particular the following sentence: '(c) Je ne me suis pas
attendu d'attacher monstrueusement la queuë d'un philosophe à la teste et au
corps d'un homme perdu; ny que ce chetif bout eust à desadvouër et desmentir
la plus belle, entiere et longue partie de ma vie.'

[33] I. xx. Montaigne provides a double gloss for this tag. Either it means, he says,
that the contemplative activity of philosophy, in withdrawing the soul from the
body, represents 'quelque aprentissage et ressemblance de la mort'; or that the
object of all wisdom and *discours* is to teach us not to fear death (p. 81). The ambivalence is important, since it allows an interchange between prescriptive ethics
on the one hand and, on the other, a kind of performance of death: it could be
argued that Montaigne's writing turns precisely on this double function.

itself. The death of La Boëtie appears, in *De l'amitié*, as the loss of youth, wholeness, reciprocation;[34] it may plausibly be argued that the function of the *Essais* is in some measure to compensate for that loss, to provide a second and supplementary mirror in which the self may be reconstituted.[35] But as they proliferate around the space left by the absence of La Boëtie—like decorative motifs around a missing painting[36]—they can only designate with greater and greater intricacy their own condition of exile and *écoulement*, so that finally the focal absence reveals itself to be that of Montaigne himself. Suspended thus between the death of a mirror-self and that of their author, the *Essais* pursue images of life and *contentement* in infinite regression.

A similar principle governs the articulation of the nature–art opposition in Montaigne's text. To consider it as an antithesis is to over-simplify. It is certainly true that art may be defined as that which is not natural, that which is added to nature; it is also the case that nature tends to be valued positively, art negatively. But there are possibilities of mediation between the two concepts, and sixteenth-century discourse is often concerned with such mediations. One may recall, for example, the notion of the vernacular as a 'natural' language in a limited sense, together with the images of grafting, agriculture, and digestion which appear regularly in imitation theory. In a more general sense, contemporary uses of the words suggest that art, however denatured, is conceived of as originating in nature: it does not proceed from some distinct anti-nature. It is a consequence of the Fall, of that deflection of man's nature which leads him to refashion and hide the natural. The fig-leaf is its earliest emblem. Montaigne, like his contemporaries, presupposes that there is a nature, which might be

---

[34] This chapter (I. xxviii) elaborates the theme of a unity in which each partner corresponds exactly to the other (much as in the figure of the Androgyne); it also speaks of the emptiness of Montaigne's subsequent life in comparison with the four years in which he knew La Boëtie (both themes appear on p. 193).

[35] See in particular Wilden's analysis of this episode on broadly Lacanian lines, op. cit., pp. 587 ff.

[36] p. 183: 'Que sont-ce icy aussi, à la verité, que crotesques et corps monstrueux, rappiecez de divers membres, sans certaine figure, n'ayants ordre, suite ny proportion que fortuité?' The 'missing painting' was to have been provided in the form of a text by La Boëtie, but this project was never realized.

recovered (ideally) by removing the layers of disguise and deformation which man has imposed on it; and that this nature, in its
purest state, is a manifestation of the divine will and thus at times
virtually synonymous with God. In the individual, it grounds
the true self, which can be located by eliminating errors of self-
perception. Or again, in the domain of language, the opposition
between nature and art is broadly speaking parallel to that between
words and things: here, the task of words should be faithfully to
represent things, and not to conform themselves to the falsifying
art of rhetoric.[37]

But this last example already reveals the degree of equivocation
between the concepts. To move closer to nature, a distinction has
to be made within the realm of art, taken in its broadest sense,
between a greater and a lesser approximation to the natural. That
nature can never be itself located within language is evident from
the fact that, if the *Essais* could rediscover and fully exhibit it,
they would become superfluous.[38] As long as he goes on writing
in order to recover (his) nature, Montaigne is tacitly admitting
its absence. Instead, he speaks of 'naturalizing' art where others
'artialize' nature.[39] He elaborates models of a quasi-natural text; he
writes as if he were speaking; he writes as if he were improvising.[40]
He also composes an essay on the *art* of conversation: oral discourse here betrays its implication in the non-natural. Nature can
of course be discussed as a topic, personified, made the subject of

[37] The most extensive explicit discussion by Montaigne of the opposition
between words and things is to be found in I. xxvi, pp. 168–73; cf. also II. xvi,
pp. 618 ff.

[38] Cf. I. xxvi, pp. 167–8: 'Voicy mes leçons. (c) Celuy-là y a mieux proffité,
qui les fait, que qui les sçait. Si vous le voyez, vous l'oyez; si vous l'oyez, vous le
voyez . . . Le vray miroir de nos discours est le cours de nos vies.' Much as in
Pantagruel 9, the 'lesson' proves itself to be superfluous once it is understood. This
example is, of course, restricted to the domain of education; but in so far as the
Essais as a whole institute a search for self-discovery, they operate similarly as a
discourse which would eliminate itself were it not committed to mediation and
non-resolution.

[39] III. v, p. 874. On this topic, and on the related notion of the text as a body,
see Jeanneret, 'Rabelais et Montaigne', pp. 78 ff.

[40] See, for example, I. xxvi, p. 171 ('tel sur le papier qu'à la bouche'); I. x,
p. 40; II. xii, p. 546; III. ix, p. 963; cf. also the quotations in notes 30 and 31
above.

demonstrative rhetoric, attributed to ordinary people whose perception has not been distorted by learning; but it can only appear on the scene by permission of art, that is to say, of a discourse hardly less rhetorically organized, within its own register, than Cicero's.

Nature is thus always hidden. References to its virtues are regularly accompanied by the reservation that it has been obscured, travestied, disguised, relegated to invisibility.[41] In *De l'institution des enfans*, the child as a purely natural phenomenon is seen as being impossible to comprehend:

(a) La montre de leurs inclinations est si tendre en ce bas aage, et si obscure, les promesses si incertaines et fauces, qu'il est mal-aisé d'y establir aucun solide jugement. (I. xxvi, p. 149)

It is as if the infant were an obscure text, which has to be printed with human inscriptions before it can be read. A 1588 text inserted at this point compounds the problem by pointing out that human children, unlike animals, are altered and disguised by convention from the very beginning ('incontinent'):

Les petits des ours, des chiens, montrent leur inclination naturelle; mais les hommes, se jettans incontinent en des accoustumances, en des opinions, en des loix, se changent ou se deguisent facilement.

The presence of nature is thus established only by a negative inference; nature is that which disrupts the orderly processes of custom and art (here, more specifically, of *doctrina*): 'Si est-il difficile de forcer les propensions naturelles' (loc. cit., 1580 text). In *Des cannibales*, the society reflecting most closely the law of nature is itself at one remove from pure nature (it has customs, songs, religions). Moreover, Montaigne does not himself see that society: he relies on the reports of a mediator (conscious of how such mediations falsify, he chooses a maximally 'natural' eye-witness); and in his one brief meeting with two exiled cannibals,

---

[41] Cf. I. xxxi, pp. 205–6; or III. xii, pp. 1049–50: 'cette raison qui se manie à nostre poste, trouvant tousjours quelque diversité et nouvelleté, ne laisse chez nous aucune trace apparente de la nature. Et en ont faict les hommes comme les parfumiers de l'huile: ils l'ont sophistiquée de tant d'argumentations et de discours appellez du dehors, qu'elle en est devenue variable et particuliere à chacun, et a perdu son propre visage, constant et universel . . .'

he uses an interpreter who proves highly unreliable. One might add that the whole set of observations which make up this essay appear, in another perspective, as an instance of the literature of legendary voyages—a particularly important one, no doubt, but one which follows certain paths laid down (for example) by myths of the Golden Age and other *loci amoeni*. In *De la vanité*, Montaigne accepts the rule of custom, brushing aside utopian schemes as absurd products of art:

Et certes toutes ces descriptions de police, feintes par art, se trouvent ridicules et ineptes à mettre en practique . . . Telle peinture de police seroit de mise en un nouveau monde, mais nous prenons les hommes obligez desjà et formez à certaines coustumes; nous ne les engendrons pas comme Pyrrha ou comme Cadmus. (III. ix, p. 957)

The myths of natural society and of total regeneration are thus themselves seen as false products of art. Once again, man is inserted in a non-nature from the moment of birth.

Nature can clearly only become visible, then, through the lattices of art; or, more strictly, 'real' nature is always absent, so that discourse can only offer its replica or surrogate. Discourse invents nature as the personification (in the rhetorical sense) of what disrupts it and challenges it from outside. In the same way, the things (*res*) which were supposed to have priority over words emerge as products of discourse, as word-things, textual in origin, which have been naturalized (or artialized) by this particular text. The self which the *Essais* aim to portray, although a particularly privileged *res*, shares their conditioning and that of nature; the word-self is a topic which, as it draws all the other topics into its orbit, displaces the natural self presumed to be outside the text. Thus the *Essais* propose a series of referents without which writing would appear as vacuous and false; they are grounded in a desire to represent nature, reality, the self, experience. But they also repeatedly call in question the status of these referents, and thus make evident their own *vanité*.

De la phisionomie (III. xii) may at this point be examined, first as a further example of how the topics of death and of nature are interwoven to form a scenario for the problems of *essai*-writing,

and then as a transition to the topic of interpretation. The figure of
Socrates dominates the essay, providing a linking motif, if not
a principle of organization. He appears three times. First, in the
opening pages, he is cited as an exemplary figure, associated with
values that have been lost or obscured by art and learning. Later,
his speech to his judges (from the *Apology of Socrates*) is paraphrased, again as a paradigm of natural language and of a natural
ethical posture in the face of death. Finally, the *topos* of the contrast
between Socrates' grotesque appearance and his inward sublimity
initiates the titular subject:

Socrates, qui a esté un exemplaire parfaict en toutes grandes qualitez,
j'ay despit qu'il eust rencontré un corps et un visage si vilain, comme ils
disent, et disconvenable à la beauté de son ame . . .   (III. xii, p. 1057)

Each of these phases of the text is developed by references to the
experience of the *essai*-writer: the reactions of ordinary people
and of himself to the sufferings inflicted by the wars of religion;
the question whether his own discourse is borrowed or natural;
and his advantage over Socrates with regard to his *phisionomie*
(two personal anecdotes being narrated as examples of its beneficent effects).

  From the first phase arises a problem: the discrepancy between
the language of ethics, especially formal ethics, and the simplicity
of nature. Ordinary people, like animals, are seen to accept and
even welcome death; unlike the Stoics (Seneca is cited here), who
continually exacerbate their imagination by thinking and talking
about death, the 'natural man' ignores it until it arrives. In essence,
then, the problem appears to be caused by language, by superfluous articulation:

Toute cette nostre suffisance, qui est au delà de la naturelle, est à peu
pres vaine et superflue . . . (c) Fussé je mort moins allegrement avant
qu'avoir veu les Tusculanes? J'estime que non. Et quand je me trouve
au propre, je sens que ma langue s'est enrichie, mon courage de rien . . .
(p. 1039)

The language of formal ethics is thus condemned as a deviation from *le propre*, a gratuitous inflation provoked by the
tongue ('langue' here having both its senses). Nevertheless, the

essai-writer has to articulate these problems in his own writing;
a discourse on death is necessary in order to remind the reader
that death can be ignored. The refusal of the language of *doctrina*
is inevitably written into the search for a language of *natura* (as
a happy ignorance preceding *doctrina*) and of *exercitatio*.

Hence the quotation of Socrates' speech, which is characterized
as an instance of natural discourse. It is oral and spontaneous,
rendering superfluous the piece of conventional written rhetoric
offered by Lysias:

> Voylà pas un plaidoyer (c) sec et sain, mais quand et quand naïf et
> bas . . . ? Vrayement ce fut raison qu'il le preferast à celuy que ce
> grand orateur Lysias avoit mis par escrit pour luy, excellemment
> façonné au stile judiciaire, mais indigne d'un si noble criminel . . . Et
> sa riche et puissante nature eust elle commis à l'art sa défense, et en son
> plus haut essay renoncé à la verité et naïfveté, ornemens de son parler,
> pour se parer du fard des figures et feintes d'une oraison apprinse?
> (p. 1054)

This reference (added after 1588) might well recall, not only the
Gorgias, but also the *Phaedrus*, where Socrates equally rejects the
written rhetoric of Lysias, makes a spontaneous and 'inspired'
utterance himself, and then elaborates a theory of language which
denigrates writing as a malicious perversion. According to
Montaigne's account, Socrates' achievement here is rare, perhaps
unique, because he has succeeded in penetrating beneath the
façade of formal ethics and rhetoric, and even beneath the mini-
mally articulated beliefs of ordinary people ('l'opinion commune'),
to represent nature itself (pp. 1054–5). The simplest truths are the
most difficult to enunciate, owing to the universal contamination
by art and *doctrina*.

The problem of 'learned ignorance' appears, then, as that of the
authentic mediation or interpretation of nature. Socrates' speech
is introduced by a reference to the sage as one of the 'interpretes
de la simplicité naturelle' (p. 1052). Nature is so simple and self-
evident that any interpretation is likely to be a falsification, a
superfluous gloss. Only in the rarest of cases is a true account to be
found. But then one might ask whether the Socratic paradigm is
not a utopian ideal, inaccessible in practice. From a textual point

of view, the first mediation performed by Socrates is subject to further mediations which exhibit all the difficulties that the model was supposed to overcome. The opening sentences of the essay place the 'image des discours de Socrates que ses amys nous ont laissée' in a distant past, utterly unlike the present:

ils ne sont pas selon nostre usage. S'il naissoit à cette heure quelque chose de pareil, il est peu d'hommes qui le prisassent. (p. 1037)

Socrates himself, the oral man, has to be mediated to us by his friends and disciples. Montaigne attempts to offset this problem, as in *Des Cannibales*, by claiming the authenticity of the witnesses:

Il est bien advenu que le plus digne homme d'estre cogneu et d'estre presenté au monde pour exemple, ce soit celuy duquel nous ayons plus certaine cognoissance. Il a esté esclairé par les plus clair voyans hommes qui furent onques: les tesmoins que nous avons de luy sont admirables en fidelité et en suffisance. (p. 1038)

Again, when he later comes to transcribe the Socratic discourse itself, he adopts the deictic mode of direct speech. Even the suggestion that he is relying on his (avowedly defective) memory and that his version is only approximate—'de ce qu'il m'en souvient, il parle environ en ce sens' (p. 1052)—may be read as an indication that this is a translation according to the *sententia* rather than the *verba*, a *paraphrasis* rather than an *interpretatio*. The reproduction of Socrates' language is said to be effected via a living, human transmitter rather than by means of written intertextuality. Nevertheless, the distance between Montaigne's reader and the original nature articulated orally by Socrates is considerable; natural language only appears amid Montaigne's discourse by virtue of a process of multiple mediation in which writing plays a dominant role.

The opening sentence of the essay reduces all (or virtually all) ethical language to the status of borrowed materials: 'Quasi toutes les opinions que nous avons sont prinses par authorité et à credit.' This reduction includes Socrates' discourse as a supreme example of 'authority'. The ironic observation that even his insights need to be authorized by their antiquity allows Montaigne to suggest simultaneously that all opinion is conventional and second-hand, and that Socrates' ethic is natural and authentic. The ensuing development, indeed, stresses the opposition between the natural simplicity of Socrates and the windy inflation of art:

Nous n'apercevons les graces que pointues, bouffies et enflées d'artifice. Celles qui coulent soubs la nayfveté et la simplicité eschapent ayséement à une veuë grossiere comme est la nostre . . . Nostre monde n'est formé qu'à l'ostentation: les hommes ne s'enflent que de vent, et se manient à bonds, comme les balons. (p. 1037)

Elsewhere, the opposition is rephrased in terms of what belongs to an individual (is proper or natural to him) and what is alien (borrowed, external):

Nous sommes chacun plus riche que nous ne pensons; mais on nous dresse à l'emprunt et à la queste: on nous duict à nous servir plus de l'autruy que du nostre. (p. 1038)

The word *emprunter* and its synonyms form one of the most insistent sub-themes of the essay, together with the notion of foreignness—it is perhaps not wholly by chance that Montaigne's references to the wars, both in the earlier and the later parts of the essay, dwell on the invasion of France by foreigners or the invasion of his own house by would-be plunderers. As long as the opposition between nature and art can be maintained, there is no real problem, even if the natural and self-evident proves paradoxically more elusive than the prevarications of art. But the danger evoked at the outset—that *all* ethical knowledge might prove to be borrowed and alien, that nature might be strictly invisible or at least unsayable—colours the whole essay. The writer's need to borrow a speech from Socrates, although covered in part by the irony of the first paragraph, seems to prove the point: in order to articulate nature, a borrowed image of nature is necessary; so that the self may say about death what is proper to it, a borrowed first person singular is used.

This pervasive problem prepares and even determines the abrupt shift from the discussion of Socrates' speech to the theme of Montaigne's own borrowings:

Là [i.e. in speaking and living like Socrates] loge l'extreme degré de perfection et de difficulté: l'art n'y peut joindre. Or nos facultez ne sont pas ainsi dressées. Nous ne les essayons ny ne les cognoissons; nous nous investissons de celles d'autruy, et laissons chomer les nostres. Comme quelqu'un pourroit dire de moy que j'ai seulement faict icy un amas de fleurs estrangeres, n'y ayant fourny du mien que le filet à les lier.   (p. 1055)

The opposition between Socrates and 'us' (as borrowers) leads to the admission that *this* text, the proper text of Montaigne, may also appear to be simply an amalgam of foreign materials—including, presumably, the excerpt from the *Apology of Socrates*. A defensive position is rapidly established: the borrowings are a concession to contemporary fashion ('l'opinion publique', 'la fantasie du siecle'). Montaigne's real intention is the reverse:

je n'entends pas [que ces parements empruntez] me couvrent, et qu'ils me cachent; c'est le rebours de mon dessein, qui ne veux faire montre que du mien, et de ce qui est mien par nature; et si je m'en fusse creu, à tout hazard, j'eusse parlé tout fin seul.   (loc. cit.)

This is the kind of claim made wherever the question of imitation arises in the *Essais*. In *De l'institution des enfans*, borrowed materials are described as a shell or crust ('nostre incrustation empruntée'), covering the writer 'jusques à ne montrer pas seulement le bout de ses doigts' (I. xxvi, p. 148); here, the *essai*-writer rebels against his threatened displacement by the equivocal 'Je ne dis les autres, sinon pour d'autant plus me dire'. In *Sur des vers de Virgile*, as already demonstrated, invasion by alien authors is countered by a withdrawal into his own property, an imaginary *rus* where, alone, the writer fabricates a book which is exactly his. In *De la phisionomie*, the possibility of speaking 'tout fin seul' is evoked in the conditional mood; it is accompanied by an admission that his materials are second- and third-hand, and by a dismissive allusion to the thousands of books which surround him as he writes:

Tel allegue Platon et Homere, qui ne les veid onques. Et moy ay prins des lieux assez ailleurs qu'en leur source. Sans peine et sans suffisance, ayant mille volumes de livres autour de moy en ce lieu où j'escris, j'emprunteray presentement s'il me plaist d'une douzaine de tels ravaudeurs, gens que je ne feuillette guiere, de quoy esmailler le traicté de la phisionomie.   (p. 1056)

Equivocations and ironies abound here. This is the first indication of the titular subject, which has been deferred—it now seems—by a series of fragments culled from various sources, or rather non-sources: has Montaigne 'seen' Plato's account of the apology of Socrates, or borrowed it from a florilege? Or, since the word 'traicté' appears as ironic (the topic 'physiognomy' being restricted to a few observations and anecdotes tacked on at the end), perhaps the 'enamel' really does conceal what is important in this essay—the location of nature and the acceptance of death. Where is the reader to situate the writer's own physiognomy, his voice speaking 'tout fin seul'?

This is of course the kind of strategy which operates throughout the *Essais*. An ironic reflexivity intervenes to dislocate any given set of arguments and reveal their ambivalent status. There is no question of resolving the problem thus posed: the acceptance of contamination and the assertion of authorial priority are mutually dependent, so that it would be as false to argue that Montaigne really is, in the last analysis, speaking of himself as it would be to maintain that 'le filet à les lier' is merely a set of syntactical devices. It is of greater interest, in the present context, simply to observe that the underlying question of the mediation of Socrates' speech is brought to the surface by a textual transformation of ethical problems into problems of writing.

A further point may be added here. The possibility of an authentic appropriation of materials appears to depend on the writer's 'deformation' of what he uses:

(c) Parmy tant d'emprunts je suis bien aise d'en pouvoir desrober quelqu'un, les desguisant et difformant à nouveau service. Au hazard que je laisse dire que c'est par faute d'avoir entendu leur naturel usage, je luy donne quelque particuliere adresse de ma main à ce qu'ils en soient d'autant moins purement estrangers. (p. 1056)

This (c)-text coincides with the expressly approximate rendering of Socrates' speech: as in Erasmian imitation theory, identity between the writer and his model is achieved by the acknowledgement and exploitation of a fundamental difference between them. Montaigne cannot *be* Socrates; he speaks in Socrates' name, but claims to use his own voice, so that the first person singular becomes ambivalent. On the last page of the essay, in a different context (he is speaking of reactions to his own oral discourse), he remarks that 'Les paroles redictes ont, comme autre son, autre sens'. Rewriting is contaminated by, and at the same time flourishes on, difference. The only chance of rewriting Socrates, or—better still—of rewriting nature, is to accept deviation as a second nature.

Thus the shadowing of the Socrates-topics by Montaigne-topics becomes clearer. Socrates is closer to nature than any writer in a corrupt age can ever be; but he is absent from the text, and must be naturalized. That is to say, the figure of Socrates must be replaced by the figure of a writer who re-enacts his speech and his ethic. Hence the lengthy reference to the wars of religion, the domestic and local anecdotes in which Montaigne's attitude to his attackers is parallel to that of Socrates towards his judges. The speech of Socrates facing death is doubled by the writing of an author aware of his own death. The development on imitation concludes with a claim that this essay (and the *Essais* in general) is written at a time of life appropriate for ignorance, not *science* (cf. above, note 32); it is a symptom of decline and dissolution; its topics are vacuous (one recalls Flaubert's notion of a 'livre sur rien'); and death is imminent:

Si j'eusse voulu parler par science, j'eusse parlé plutost: j'eusse escript du temps plus voisin de mes estudes, que j'avois plus d'esprit et de memoire; et me fusse plus fié à la vigueur de cet aage là qu'à cettuy-icy, si j'en eusse voulu faire mestier (c) d'escrire . . . (b) . . . autant est la vieillesse incommode à cette nature de besongne qu'à toute autre. Quiconque met sa decrepitude sous la presse faict folie, s'il espere en espreindre des humeurs qui ne sentent le disgratié, le resveur et l'assopi. Nostre esprit se constipe et se croupit en vieillissant. . . . (c) . . . Et ne traicte à point nommé de rien que du rien, ny d'aucune science que de celle de l'inscience. (b) J'ay choisi le temps où ma vie, que j'ay à peindre, je l'ay toute devant moy: ce qui en reste tient plus de la mort. Et de ma mort seulement, si je la rencontrois babillarde, comme font d'autres, donrrois je encore volontiers advis au peuple en des-logeant. (p. 1056-7)

Thus the naturally 'ignorant' terminal discourse of Socrates is ironically remade as an old man's 'flux de caquet'. Unable to recapture the paradigm of an original eloquence, the *Essais* repeat and deform fragments of borrowed discourse in a mime of nature.

The topic of physiognomy is presented as a new point of departure after the passage just quoted, and is apparently unconnected with the first three-quarters of the essay. However, on the first page, the beauties of Socrates' language had been described as hidden beneath an ostensibly crude surface.[42] This antithesis between exterior and interior already recalls the Socratic *topos* cited by Erasmus, Rabelais, and Ronsard. It could also be said to be implicit in the notion that the self-evidence of Socrates' insights can only be perceived through layers of borrowed language, that the recovery of nature always contaminates nature. On the other hand, Montaigne's version of the speech, although affected by the same law, is in itself presented as a valid ethical position and as plain statement (a monologic discourse). As one might expect, the Socratic emblem makes its major impact not here, but in the 'physiognomy' section, where it appears in a new guise.

In the first place, Montaigne reduces the scope of the antithesis by affirming a belief—itself commonplace enough—in the conformity of body and soul, beauty and moral value. Socrates is only an unfortunate exception: 'Nature luy fit injustice.' It is true that superficial ugliness (like La Boëtie's) is discounted, and that there are moments when the whole question appears as reversible ('C'est une foible garantie que la mine; toutesfois elle a quelque consideration'). But in general, the claims of the surface are pressed hard: 'Je ne puis dire assez souvant combien j'estime la beauté qualité puissante et advantageuse' (p. 1058). The second fundamental shift in the emblem arises from the juxtaposition of Socrates with the writer, whose physiognomy, it seems, does not suffer from the same deformity:

[42] p. 1037: 'Socrates faict mouvoir son ame d'un mouvement naturel et commun. Ainsi dict un paysan, ainsi dict une femme . . . Ce sont inductions et similitudes tirées des plus vulgaires et cogneues actions des hommes; chacun l'entend. Soubs une si vile forme nous n'eussions jamais choisi la noblesse et splendeur de ses conceptions admirables.' Cf. also the preceding remarks about 'natural' style as having 'une beauté delicate et cachée; il faut la veuë nette et bien purgée pour descouvrir cette secrette lumiere'.

J'ai un port favorable et en forme et en interpretation . . . et qui faict une contraire montre à celuy de Socrates. Il m'est souvant advenu que, sur le simple credit de ma presence et de mon air, des personnes qui n'avoyent aucune cognoissance de moy s'y sont grandement fiées, soit pour leurs propres affaires, soit pour les miennes.[43]

This assertion is supported by the two anecdotes which all but close the essay. Once again, Socrates has been displaced, more overtly now than earlier in the text; and the convolution thus produced becomes still more evident when one takes into account the passage which, in the 1588 text, immediately precedes the one just quoted:

Je n'ay pas corrigé, comme Socrates, par force de la raison mes complexions naturelles, et n'ay aucunement troublé par art mon inclination. Je me laisse aller, comme je suis venu, je ne combats rien, mes deux maistresses pieces vivent de leur grace en pais et bon accord . . . (p. 1059)

The writer claims to belong wholly to the domain of nature; unlike Socrates, he has not used *art* and *raison* to correct his inward nature. Body and soul are in conformity with one another and with nature. A problem arises here from the notion that the virtue of Socrates, the natural man, is itself a product of art and education: nature appears to have receded completely from the field of vision, to reconstitute itself on the side of the writer. This can be explained in part as a consequence of the discrepancies inherent in the series of Socratic *topoi* cited in the essay: a (c)-text, in fact, seeks to remove the discrepancy at one point.[44] It also does not

[43] pp. 1059–60. I have omitted here two Latin quotations which remove this favourable physiognomy into the past ('Quid dixi habere? Imo habui . . .', etc.). The attractive Montaigne is a character in narrative (the anecdotes); the writer is once again composing himself retrospectively, exiled in an empty present.

[44] See p. 1058: 'Come Socrates disoit de la sienne [laideur] qu'elle en accusoit justement autant en son ame, s'il ne l'eust corrigée par institution. (c) Mais en le disant je tiens qu'il se mocquoit suivant son usage, et jamais ame si excellente ne se fit elle mesme.' Cf. the earlier passage, on the apology of Socrates, where all the references to nature have been inserted in the (c)-text: 'Voilà pas un plaidoyer (c) sec et sain, mais quand et quand naïf et bas, (b) d'une hauteur inimaginable, (c) veritable, franc et juste au delà de tout exemple (b) et employé en quelle necessité? (c) . . . sa riche et puissante nature eust elle commis à l'art sa défense, et

affect the earlier notion of Socrates, at the end of his life, as the supreme mediator between art and nature. But it does have an important function as the springboard for a rewriting of the emblem in terms of the figure of the writer. Socrates' 'plus haut essay' (p. 1054) in the face of death is replaced by a more relaxed ethic (or text), a movement of licence ('je me laisse aller . . .') endorsed by conformity with nature.

At the level of the production of *essai*-material, this *laisser-aller* is marked by a shift into narrative: as in *De l'exercitation*, the practising of death becomes an exercise in quasi-fictional writing.[45] At the emblematic level, where the relationship between body and soul implies a relationship between text and meaning, the homology of internal and external constitutes an invitation to the reader to trust the surface, a disarming gesture ('un port favorable . . . en interpretation'). The Montaignian physiognomy helps the writer, according to the anecdotes, to elude plunder and death; it evokes sympathy by its pose of frankness; it is a surface-nature. The *Essais* work in the same way: their verbal physiognomy (disembodied, like the Cheshire cat's grin) engages the complicity of the reader and thus ensures their survival. The problem of the mediation of nature is suppressed by attributing nature to a surface (*verba*) which is claimed to be identical to the hidden interior, so that these concluding pages affirm the credit of *species* as the place of presence ('le simple credit de ma presence et de mon air . . .'). They close the essay where it began ('Quasi toutes les opinions que nous avons sont prinses . . . à credit'), but with a marked shift towards optimism. The author here authorizes his writing, together with all the foreign materials he has domesticated ('naturalized'). Correspondingly, the reader receives the essay 'à credit'; as he rewrites it, he modifies and deforms it; as it is repeated, it emits a different sound: 'Les paroles redictes ont, comme autre son, autre sens.'

en son plus haut essay renoncé à la verité et naïveté . . .?' Socrates is naturalized *après la lettre*.

[45] Cf. III. ii, p. 804: 'Les autres forment l'homme; je le recite'; also p. 806: 'Je n'enseigne poinct, je raconte.' On the uncertainty of the borderline between 'true' and 'false' narrative, and on Montaigne's avowed inability to sustain a single, continuous narrative, see I. xxi, pp. 105–6.

The *Essais* clearly raise fundamental problems of interpretation. They pose as a unity, being published as a single volume under a single title; and the unity of the *essai*-project itself becomes a theme of the later parts of the text, compensating for the fragmentary and arbitrary character of the earlier essays.[46] On the other hand, the arguments are sinuous and centrifugal; intricate, asymmetrical syntax in the longer sentences is combined with a tendency towards parataxis as between sentences or sentence-groups; antitheses are either displaced or undermined so that they lose their function of imposing thematic and structural order.[47] The 'thread' which weaves the fragments together (see above, p. 307) is often hidden, with the result that different readers will reconstitute different threads. The first-person syntax, which appears to be the most distinctive integrating feature, may also prove to function, in the last analysis, as a *passe-partout*, a hold-all device: stretched to the limit by the diversity of what it organizes, it loses its particularity and becomes purely nominal (or pronominal).

Since interpretation is itself one of the topics of the text, the problem may be recapitulated in terms of what Montaigne says about it, though always with the reservation made earlier, that theory enunciated within a text cannot simply be excerpted and read as if it were a set of preliminary instructions.

[46] Metaphors of wholeness or integrality recur frequently in the later chapters; see, for example, III. ii, p. 805 ('chaque homme porte la forme entiere de l'humaine condition'), p. 816 ('(c) Je me veux presenter et faire veoir par tout uniformément'), and p. 817 ('L'homme marche entier vers son croist et son décroist'). Cf. also III. ix, p. 964 ('(c) Mon livre est tousjours un'), and the quotation given above, note 31 ('Je m'estalle entier'). On the lengthening of the chapters, see III. ix, p. 995.

[47] The *Apologie* is the most obvious and celebrated example. Two antithetical objections to Sebond are posited; the first is countered briefly, but the argument slides surreptitiously towards an answer to the second (p. 448: 'Je me suis, sans y penser, à demy desjà engagé dans la seconde objection à laquelle j'avois proposé de respondre pour Sebond'), which then extends itself indefinitely. On the question of formal organization in the *Essais*, see Sayce, op. cit., ch. 11; it could perhaps be argued that, in this account, too much emphasis is placed on the possibility of discovering unity at various levels of the text: it would be equally possible to demonstrate that the *Essais* are pervaded by discontinuities, asymmetries, and false indications of order, so that they are, in the end, strictly non-integrable. Cf. Butor, *Essais sur les Essais*.

A passage from *Des livres*, a text about other texts, will provide a starting-point. Here, the argument touches on the problems of a reader (the writer himself) whose interpretative powers are inadequate:

[mon jugement] s'en prend à soy, et se condamne, ou de s'arrester à l'escorce, ne pouvant penetrer jusques au fons, ou de regarder la chose par quelque faux lustre . . . Il pense donner juste interpretation aux apparences que sa conception luy presente; mais elles sont im-becilles et imparfaictes. La plus part des fables d'Esope ont plusieurs sens et intelligences. Ceux qui les mythologisent, en choisissent quelque visage qui quadre bien à la fable; mais pour la pluspart, ce n'est que le premier visage et superficiel; il y en a d'autres plus vifs, plus essen-tiels et internes, ausquels ils n'ont sçeu penetrer: voylà comme j'en fay. (II. x, p. 410)

A conventional duality of surface and content ('escorce' and 'fons') is assumed, and the surface seen as potentially distracting or misleading. The notion that a fable may have more than one 'sens' is also in conformity with long-established traditions. The criticism of those who use allegorical method ('ceux qui les mythologisent') may, by contrast, reasonably be aligned with the earlier sixteenth-century notion of 'allegory without allegories'. Systematic allegorization is superficial, a supplement to the sur-face of the text, ignoring its authentic inner sense. Montaigne's account, while retaining this concept of 'essential' meaning, tends to stress its indeterminate character ('plusieurs sens', 'il y en a d'autres . . .'): the authentic sense is multiple and open-ended.

A far more complex and ambivalent treatment of the question occurs in the opening pages of *De l'experience*: as the 'final' text of experience begins, it develops the pejorative view of interpre-tation as excess. The intrinsic diversity of nature is, according to the introductory argument, mimicked and perverted by systems designed to fix and enclose it: the artificial proliferation of legal codes and of glosses supplants the productivity of nature. There is an assumption here that 'original' texts—in particular the Bible—are equivalent to nature, the gloss being a supplement contrived by art. At the same time, an equivalence is established, early in the argument, between reading and writing:

ceux là se moquent, qui pensent appetisser nos debats et les arrester
en nous r'appellant à l'expresse parolle de la Bible. D'autant que nostre
esprit ne trouve pas le champ moins spatieux à contreroller le sens
d'autruy qu'à representer le sien, et comme s'il y avoit moins d'ani-
mosité et d'aspreté à gloser qu'à inventer.   (III. xiii, pp. 1065–6)

The licence of the reader is no less unrestricted than that of the
writer; the production and the reproduction of sense are essentially
the same activity. If this is so, then the original, natural text becomes invisible or inaccessible like nature itself. The 'expresse
parolle' of the Bible is contaminated and pluralized, from the very
outset, by its potential glosses. Returning a little later to this
displacement of the sacred text, Montaigne avers that Luther's
opinions generated more debate than his reading of the Bible
(p. 1069): in other words, his glossing of Scripture is itself displaced by glosses on his glosses. The same may be said of Aristotelian commentary:

Aristote a escrit pour estre entendu; s'il ne l'a peu, moins le fera un
moins habile et un tiers que celuy qui traite sa propre imagination.
Nous ouvrons la matiere et l'espandons en la destrempant; d'un
subject nous en faisons mille, et retombons, en multipliant et sub-
divisant, à l'infinité des atomes d'Epicurus.   (p. 1067)

A centrifugal movement is established. Interpretation is destruction and dissipation: the murdered text reverts to its anonymous
particles.

   This analysis leaves little room for a positive view of interpretation.[48] Furthermore, if interpretation is a form of rewriting,
it is also true that most if not all writing is interpretation: '(c) Tout
fourmille de commentaires; d'auteurs, il en est grand cherté'
(p. 1069). The fact that the Montaignian text so frequently refers
to its own engagement in intertextuality may here be recalled in
order to show that imitation and interpretation are two aspects of

   [48] It is true that, when Montaigne says 'il se sent par experience que tant d'in-
terprétations dissipent la verité et la rompent' (p. 1067), the intuitive criterion
according to which the negative judgement is made implies a positive alternative:
the reader's own sense of meaning is at least as valid as erudite glosses. But its
status cannot of course be guaranteed; the text becomes a blank cheque which the
reader fills in for himself and its supposed 'truth' remains hidden.

the same problem of writing. Unless Montaigne speaks 'tout fin seul', he must inevitably commit himself to the process of glossing, even if in an indirect or disguised form, and thus destroy his status as 'author'. Although the early part of *De l'experience* is primarily phrased as an attack on abuses perpetrated by others, the interposition of one sentence (in the 1588 text) makes it clear that *essai*-writing is implicated in the problem of the gloss. The first published version reads as follows:

Il y a plus affaire à interpreter les interpretations qu'à interpreter les choses, et plus de livres sur les livres que sur autre subject: nous ne faisons que nous entregloser. Combien souvent et sottement à l'aventure ay-je estandu mon livre à parler de soy? (p. 1069)

The last sentence quoted is the only overtly reflexive observation in this part of the essay, but the progression from impersonal to first person plural to first person singular, and the juxtaposition of the notions of glossing and self-glossing, make the predicament clear. The *Essais* extend themselves not only by 'glossing' other texts, but also by glossing themselves. The text is not merely reflexive here; it reflects on its own reflexivity and, at the same time, on the movement of supplementation, excess, or infinite regression which allows it to proliferate.[49]

The passage which culminates in this self-exposure describes an oblique and ambiguous itinerary. It begins with a restatement of the Danaid-like labour of interpretation:

il ne se voit livre, soit humain, soit divin, auquel le monde s'embesongne, duquel l'interpretation face tarir la difficulté[.] Le centiesme commentaire le renvoye à son suivant, plus espineux et plus scabreux que le premier ne l'avoit trouvé. Quand est-il convenu entre nous: ce livre en a assez, il n'y a meshuy plus que dire? (p. 1067)

[49] The (c)-text adds, appropriately enough, a further supplement or auto-interpretation at this point. It is generated by the word 'sottement', which is repeated as the introduction to a gloss on the affected self-consciousness which might be imputed to the *Essais*. This excursus completes the tautology by circling back to reflexivity as a topic: 'j'escry de moy et de mes escrits comme de mes autres actions . . . mon theme se renverse en soy' (loc. cit.). This is the *degré zéro* of Montaigne's writing, the principle which reveals the self-evidence of the text and of its desire to be written (the reflexive construction in the last phrase quoted is attributed to the text, not to its writer).

Glossing obscures the text, as art disguises nature; it is a sickness so
deeply rooted that it is itself natural: 'les hommes mescognoissent
la maladie naturelle de leur esprit: il ne faict que fureter et
quester . . .' (p. 1068). This reference to a fallen nature recalls a
sentence from the *Apologie* ('La presomption est nostre maladie
naturelle et originelle') (II. xii, p. 452) where the notion of an
original deviation is quite explicit; but it also recalls the first
sentence of *De l'experience* ('Il n'est desir plus naturel que le desir
de connoissance'), itself an echo of the opening of Aristotle's
Metaphysics. Everything written is inscribed into the desire, or
quest, for knowledge. The *Essais* cannot escape this destiny; all
that they can do is to recognize what others ignore ('mecognois-
sent').

The image of the quest is subsequently developed by means of
a metaphor of deferred or even illusory truth:

[l'esprit] pense remarquer de loing je ne sçay quelle apparence de
clarté et verité imaginaire; mais, pendant qu'il y court, tant de diffi-
cultez luy traversent la voye, d'empeschemens et de nouvelles questes,
qu'elles l'esgarent et l'enyvrent.   (p. 1068)

This sentence, with its pejorative formulation, deconstructs one
of the metaphors which Montaigne exploits in order to convey the
'groping' or 'wandering' movement of the *Essais* themselves.[50]
There is no path which leads out of this blindness, only an indeterminate sequence of tropes and syntactical diversions. The
1588 text pursues the same theme through further metaphors of
pursuit and deviation ('il y a tousjours . . . route par ailleurs'); all
quests are unresolvable: 'Il n'y a point de fin en nos inquisitions;
nostre fin est en l'autre monde.' According to this first version,
ambiguity and the absence of any goal may appear as purely
negative features of writing. But the (c)-text shifts the emphasis
by writing into the argument a positive perspective:

nostre fin est en l'autre monde. (c) C'est signe de racourciment d'esprit
quand il se contente, ou de lasseté. Nul esprit genereux ne s'arreste

---

[50] Cf. I. xxvi, p. 146: 'Mes conceptions et mon jugement ne marche qu'à
tastons, chancelant, bronchant et chopant; et, quand je suis allé le plus avant que
je puis, si ne me suis-je aucunement satisfaict: je voy encore du païs au delà, mais
d'une veuë trouble et en nuage, que je ne puis desmeler.'

en soy: il pretend tousjours et va outre ses forces; il a des eslans au delà de ses effects; s'il ne s'avance et ne se presse et ne s'accule et ne se choque, il n'est vif qu'à demy . . . (loc. cit.)

The movement of self-extension is now represented, not as a disease, but as a sign of nobility; it is associated with vigour and life.

The two strands—the 1588 text and its auto-gloss—converge in a reference to Apollo Loxias, who had made his entry also into the interpretative episodes of Rabelais's *Tiers Livre*:[51]

il n'est vif qu'à demy; (b) ses poursuites sont sans terme, et sans forme; son aliment c'est (c) admiration, chasse, (b) ambiguité. Ce que declaroit assez Appollo, parlant tousjours à nous doublement, obscurement et obliquement, ne nous repaissant pas, mais nous amusant et embesongnant. C'est un mouvement irregulier, perpetuel, sans patron, et sans but. Ses inventions s'eschauffent, se suyvent, et s'entre-produisent l'une l'autre. (loc. cit.)

This renders precisely the movement of the Montaignian text itself, a movement without end or origin, committed to irregularity and to indeterminacy of meaning. It is here that, after a quotation from a poem on *écoulement* by La Boëtie, the argument is recapitulated as indicated above ('Il y a plus affaire . . .') and that reference is made to the self-glossing of the *Essais*. The passage as a whole, in its shift from descriptive to reflexive discourse, enacts the most fundamental problem of writing: namely, its inability to separate itself from what it represents. Discourse can never be a transparent vehicle for a given content. Asserting its own presence, it contaminates, obscures, and renders invisible its referent; the resolution of meaning is deferred to some future articulation which will never occur, because it is 'en l'autre monde'. Yet the supplementary text (the deviation inserted after 1588) confers a kind of grace on this diseased nature: like the physical sicknesses which *De l'experience* will soon describe, this one may be understood, accepted, and indeed exploited as a source of energy and *volupté*. Sickness and health, *uber* and *tuber*, are no less inseparable in language than in life.

[51] See *TL* 19, p. 437; cf. also the references to oblique discourse and to concealment in *Sur des vers de Virgile*.

In the *Apologie*, Montaigne juxtaposes the two hypothetical extremes of interpretation as, once again, two faces of the same coin:

Sur ce mesme fondement qu'avoit Heraclitus et cette sienne sentence, que toutes choses avoient en elles les visages qu'on y trouvoit, Democritus en tiroit une toute contraire conclusion, c'est que les subjects n'avoient du tout rien de ce que nous y trouvions . . .[52]

This might be taken as an instruction for the would-be reader of the *Essais* (the more legitimately, perhaps, because it is not issued as such). According to one reading, the *Essais* are a lengthy digression, beginning and ending nowhere in particular, threading together a motley collection of disguised commonplaces. The book is empty of meaning; all its apparent propositions are provisional and reversible; the reader can learn nothing from what Montaigne writes; the project of self-portraiture is reducible to a set of syntactic and rhetorical devices conferring a spurious impression of coherence. The interest of the *Essais* in this light is that such a text could be written in the sixteenth century; and that it itself makes manifest its own emptiness—it turns itself inside out, ironizes itself infinitely, blocking the reader's attempt to make it into a moral handbook. According to the inverse reading, the *Essais* are an extraordinarily rich compendium of the epistemological and moral arguments available to a secular writer in the later sixteenth century. Their vernacular form gives them particular importance, disseminating such arguments amid a

[52] II. xii, p. 587. The whole of the preceding passage (pp. 585–7) deals with the indeterminacy of interpretation, and includes a development on Homer's intentions ('Est-il possible qu'Homere aye voulu dire tout ce qu'on luy faict dire . . .?') which comes very close to the question about Homer in the Prologue to *Gargantua*. Rabelais's characters, too, cite Heraclitus in connection with the problems of interpretation (*Pantagruel* 18, p. 291; *TL* 36, p. 500). Ironically enough, they attribute to Heraclitus the Democritan image of the 'puis inespuisable' at the bottom of which truth lies hidden. Moreover, in the first example, Pantagruel uses it with apparent optimism in anticipating his debate with Thaumaste; in the second, Panurge claims (after talking to Trouillogan the pyrrhonist philosopher) that he has been down into the well and emerged seeing and hearing nothing. Such highly reversible metaphors show that the possibility of fruitful interpretation is dependent on what might equally appear as the emptiness of a text.

potentially enormous range of readers. The meanings discovered
in them by, for example, Pascal, Gide, Villey, Friedrich, Wilden,
and Sayce (not to mention the present study) were always already
in the text, together with an indeterminate number of other
'visages' or physiognomies constituted by other readers.

It is important to insist here that these two aspects, the 'negative'
and the 'positive', are not incompatible. Indeed, the possibility of
a positively productive reading depends on its own deconstruction:
if this were not so, it would be legitimate to attempt to iron out
the inconsistencies, to take the provisional arguments for real
beliefs, in short to reduce the text to a botched instance of monologic discourse. The enigma of the Montaignian physiognomy
may best be approached by giving full play to its duplicity.

The chapter might well end at this point. However, it seems
preferable to conclude by activating, once again, the tropical
movement which undermines any theoretical formulation such
as that given above. There is a passage towards the end of *De
l'experience* in which Montaigne is speaking of the pleasures of the
table. The success of a banquet, he says, depends on the spontaneous capacity for enjoyment of the individual guest. Three times
in his life he went to a banquet when he was in perfect form for
enjoying it; but, of course, these occasions are in the distant past.
'Mon estat present', he says, 'm'en forclost' (III. xiii, p. 1106). As
in *Sur des vers de Virgile*, the evocation of past pleasure and plenitude reveals, simultaneously, the decline of old age: the *essai*,
which had seemed the epitome of the liminary text, has now
become a postscript. The same passage develops the moral theme
of the emptiness of sensual pleasures. The ostensible argument is
that we should not allow our minds to anticipate and exacerbate
this emptiness; but the subterranean weight of the tropes leads to
an elaborate metaphor of windy vacuity which embraces the
whole of the human condition:

nostre esprit maladif, rabat-joye . . . traitte et soy et tout ce qu'il
reçoit tantost avant tantost arriere, selon son estre insatiable, vagabond
et versatile. *Sincerum est nisi vas, quodcunque infundis, acescit.* Moy qui
me vente d'embrasser si curieusement les commoditez de la vie,

et si particulierement, n'y trouve, quand j'y regarde ainsi finement, à peu pres que du vent. Mais quoy, nous sommes par tout vent. Et le vent encore, plus sagement que nous, s'ayme à bruire, à s'agiter, et se contente en ses propres offices, sans desirer la stabilité, la solidité, qualitez non siennes.   (pp. 1106–7)

The banquet, as a paradigm of plenitude enjoyed in youth, gives way to an inverse paradigm of self-sufficient, unconscious emptiness, which might well be read as the emblem of pure textuality. Between the two, the 'esprit maladif' pursues its role as waster of fruits: the Horatian *sententia* denounces the contamination by the anti-cornucopian vessel of what fills it.

Full experience is always absent; presence is unattainable.[53] All that the *Essais* can do, with their ineradicable self-consciousness, is to posit paradigms of wholeness as features of a discourse which, as it pours itself out, celebrates its own inanity. The Montaignian text represents the emptying of the cornucopia by the very gesture of extending itself indefinitely until the moment of ultimate *egressio* or elimination: the figures of abundance play a prominent part in the closing pages of *De l'experience*. Whatever plenitude seems to have been proper to the past, whatever festivity is assigned to these terminal moments, Montaigne's writing is both the only place in which they can be designated, and a place from which they remain inexhaustibly absent.

[53] The most extended development on the theme of 'non-presence' occurs in the Plutarchan discourse at the end of the *Apologie* (II. xii, pp. 601–3); it is perhaps ironically appropriate that a manifestly borrowed discourse mediates for Montaigne the anxiety of absence.

CONCLUSION

*On ne peut pas à la fois tuer Zeus et conserver
la corne d'abondance* (Michel Serres, *Hermès IV:
la distribution*, p. 164)

THE various analytic paths followed by this book do not lead to
a single conclusion. Its materials are intrinsically centrifugal, not
only because they are drawn from different contexts and genres,
but also because the principal texts are themselves overtly fragmentary and unresolved, to the point of insisting—and indeed
thriving—on their own open-endedness. This very fact, however,
offers a means of reintegration or synthesis at its own level, and
the following pages, presented as a (necessarily provisional) conclusion, will be primarily concerned with the family resemblance
of a group of fundamentally inconclusive texts.

That such a family resemblance exists is an inductive observation on which the whole of the book depends, together with its
chance of achieving a synthesis. As the Introduction made clear,
the relationship between Part I and Part II is not one of historical
cause and effect. The theories analysed in the first part do not in
any strict sense determine the modes of writing examined in the
second. To take but one example, the specific influence of the *De
copia* on Rabelais or on Montaigne cannot really be proved, partly
because explicit evidence is lacking, but more centrally because
the interest of the *De copia* lies in the extent to which it transcends
traceable techniques and points towards a general theory of writing.
Thus the word *copia* as I have used it—extending the metaphorical
implications opened up by Erasmus—is not the label for a codified
method (as might be the case for, say, 'Ramist rhetoric') but the
emblem of a group of theories all concerned, in their various ways,
with elusive and at least partially unquantifiable aspects of the
writing process. Much useful work has been done, in recent years,

on the ways in which Renaissance writers were dependent on the methodologies of rhetoric and dialectic; and there is no doubt more to be said on that subject. My concern has been rather to provide examples of a sixteenth-century awareness of fundamental problems of writing, problems which often involve rhetoric but are not reducible to its procedures. Part I reviews explicit and, for the most part, conceptualized responses to such problems; Part II illustrates some of the ways in which imaginative literature of the same period may enact its own problematic nature. It is essential also to stress once again that there is a constant interchange or transfer between the two parts in the sense that the writing of Erasmus is no less 'literary' than that of the vernacular writers is 'theoretical' or 'representational'. Thus, from this converging analysis, there should arise a detailed, though highly selective, picture of what one might call the possibilities of writing—its potentialities and constraints—in the sixteenth century.

Clearly, the choice of four major writers consecrated by critical tradition predisposes the treatment of the question. One might well ask whether such an analysis is relevant to other writers of the period, whether the idiosyncrasies and sophistication of these four do not place them in a class of their own. Doubtless, what makes them critically productive is also, in some measure at least, what separates them from their contemporaries. Yet it is also true that the *cas-limite* of what is possible in a given period as a theory or practice of writing, reveals with particular clarity the constraints operative at that time. Erasmus, Rabelais, Ronsard, and Montaigne are working both within and against the predominant conventions of their period, and in the process creating new conventions, new constraints and possibilities (some of which may of course be wholly neglected by succeeding generations and only become visible once more in a much later period). The choice of Budé, Scève, d'Aubigné, and Bodin as representatives of their age would have produced different results; but such results could never contradict the arguments of this book: they would simply open further horizons. Even if someone proved that no other French vernacular text of the sixteenth century was overtly reflexive, that no other contemporary writer was preoccupied with the problems of language (and neither of these propositions is in fact tenable), only marginal adjustments to the foregoing demonstration would be necessary. With these reservations, the outlines of a potential synthesis may now be indicated.

Modern critical theory stresses the extent to which all writing is rewriting: the existence of any text depends primarily on the pre-existence of other texts rather than on phenomena external to writing. This predicament is recognized by sixteenth-century writers, both in their theories of imitation and in the visible intertextuality of their own writings. Allusion is perhaps the single most important procedure they adopt. Ronsard claims to imitate nature by imitating the ancients:

> Ainsy courant et fueilletant mes livres,
> J'amasse, trie et choisis le plus beau,
> Qu'en cent couleurs je peints en un tableau,
> Tantost en l'autre: et maistre en ma peinture,
> Sans me forcer j'imite la Nature . . .
> (L XV, 252)

The possibility of achieving mimesis is here seen to be indissolubly linked with the rewriting of materials from texts which themselves are presumed, ideally, to embody 'nature'; while, at another level, the possibility of writing out this piece of poetic theory is dependent on *topoi* derived from Pindar, Horace, Aristotle, and others. The freedom of the rewriter arises from the multiplicity of his materials, which are the fragments of an enormous dismantled corpus; and also from the difference of languages, which is thus a source both of anxiety (because the vernacular may seem ill-equipped and unstable by comparison with the great embalmed languages of antiquity) and of productivity. Hence the equilibrium of Pléiade theory, which insists on use of the vernacular and, simultaneously, rejects imitation of vernacular texts. Hence also Montaigne's constant use of borrowed materials as a spring-board for a discourse which purports to be 'exactly his'. But an acute awareness of intertextuality as the necessary condition of writing tends to defer the achievement of an integral 'new' text:

the writer and his text are always suspended between an original wholeness (illusory, no doubt, but imaginatively potent) and a future reintegration. The fragment asserts itself; multiplicity induces centrifugality. For more than twenty years, Ronsard writes poetic *essais* in view of an authentic performance which he will finally have to renounce; in Montaigne, the *essai*, an outgrowth of the *leçon* or 'reading', is accepted as the only viable procedure. In this respect, the *Essais* rephrase Rabelais's ironic dislocation of narrative (which presupposes conventions of structure and resolution, as well as a whole series of given narrative motifs) and his comic overload of precise or quasi-precise references. All three vernacular writers, no less than Erasmus, revert insistently to past texts, both by explicit reference and by implicit allusion, and constitute their own identity by a perpetual confrontation with alien writing. All three evoke images of a lost past, of a Golden Age in which textual integration was enacted; all three entertain the possibility of a future in which the *devenir* of their text will be resolved, even if, for the *Essais*, that resolution can only be the death of their author. Between past and future, the texts inhabit a fragile and ambivalent present, in which images of youthful exuberance (the sexual or Bacchic mythologies of Rabelais and Ronsard) alternate with images of old age and exhaustion (the 'isle des Macraeons', the *Sonnets pour Hélène*); in the third book of the *Essais*, the alternation is endemic.

The notion of intertextuality as an essentially insoluble problem necessarily carries with it a questioning of the text as a mediator of meaning. The rewriting of a textual fragment presupposes a repetition of its capacity to generate meaning; but, on the one hand, its removal from an original context dislocates the basis of its significance, while, on the other, *mere* repetition will appear as gratuitous, an emptying out of meaning. These difficulties provoke a characteristic response in the three vernacular writers and in certain Erasmian texts of which the *Convivium religiosum* is the most striking example. Themes or topics are presented as provisional and unstable. They are undermined by irony, placed in inverted commas, attributed to characters or speakers whose voice is not identifiable with the author's; in Ronsard, the sporadic and partial allegorization of myths is a symptom of the same uncertainty. In every instance, the possibility of a full integration of meaning is constantly disrupted by the shifting ground of the writing process itself, by the awareness that a text can only be closed by the arbitrary withdrawal of the author. Again and again, in different scenarios, significance is enacted: the appetite for meaning is aroused and the pursuit of meaning undertaken. But the topical landscape in which this pursuit takes place is, in consequence, never definitive; it can never become the *locus amoenus* where meaning resides in the guise of an inexhaustible fount or bottle. Exile is the condition of the dislocated *topos*, eternally seeking reintegration.

In this perspective, the uncertain fortunes of Erasmus, Rabelais, Montaigne, and even Ronsard in succeeding generations of readers become easier to understand. Erasmus was, in his own day, accused of being two-faced and two-tongued, and his image has remained equivocal ever since. Likewise, the *Essais* were considered subversive by seventeenth-century orthodoxy, and the question whether Montaigne was *really* a conservative or a radical thinker (or both) is still being debated.[1] Rabelais's work certainly meant different things to different sixteenth-century readers; in the twentieth century, he has been classed as an atheist or rationalist, an evangelical, and a proto-Marxist. Ronsard was a pagan according to his Calvinist contemporaries; modern Ronsardian critics have juxtaposed (for example) his neoplatonism, his role as mouthpiece of the Establishment, and his insistence on the physical and sensual, and have found that no coherent conceptual system can be extracted from his poetry. Of course, the same could be said, in some measure, for all literary texts: multiplicity of meaning is a fundamental element in the definition of 'literature'. But it is significant that the three prose writers at least (poetry enjoying in this respect a diplomatic

---

[1] Sayce, in ch. 10 of *The Essays of Montaigne*, cautiously attempts to resolve the issue. Among approaches designed to bypass this dilemma, one may cite Glauser's *Montaigne paradoxal*, Floyd Gray's 'Montaigne and Sebond: the rhetoric of paradox', and Margaret McGowan's *Montaigne's Deceits*.

immunity) have been considered as subversive. Versatility, in both the English and the French senses of the word, is a constituent aspect of their texts. Whereas other texts (Homer's epics, Racine's tragedies, Balzac's novels) are capable of more than one internally coherent interpretation, these operate in such a way as to block any coherent interpretation. Meaning can only be assigned to them provisionally and partially; the deviations of the text undo meaning as fast as it is produced. Once again, the only solution to this problem, for the critic, is to suspend his own judgement, to ironize his own analysis in order to exhibit the plurality of the discourse it questions. Once this is done, it becomes legitimate and indeed necessary to discuss the themes of a text and even to assign meaning to it, since to empty it of all possibility of meaning would be as fallacious as to attempt to reduce it to a single meaning. Plural texts like those of Rabelais and Montaigne, by drawing attention to the problem of how they should be read, give licence to an interpretative approach which is itself self-conscious and which stresses the indeterminate character of its products.

A kind of reintegration can also be brought about by proposing, as the thematic constant of a text, its own operations. The foregoing summary of the ways in which theory is inserted into practice in the sixteenth century already illustrates this phenomenon: writing institutes itself as the dominant topic, displacing all the others. It is here that the theory which performs as it enunciates converges with the performance which theorizes. Whichever way the formula is viewed, the fundamental mechanism is one of compensation. Conceptual constraints are loosened by metaphors; the dangerous liberties of writing are supervised by quasi-theoretical themes. The *Convivium*, the prologue of *Gargantua*, Ronsard's *Ode à Michel de L'Hospital*, and most of the later *Essais* depend on this compensation procedure. When broken down into more specific themes, it can be analysed as a series of reactions to an anxiety about the status of discourse. The evangelical logocentrism of Erasmus is an attempt to compensate for the imperfections of fallen language by relating it to a divine origin or model. Elsewhere in Erasmus, in Rabelais, and most strikingly in Montaigne, the acceptance of the non-transcendent humanity of discourse reveals itself in the model of a textual body, a replica of life, endowed with breath (both voice and spirit). This particular strategy is one major instance of the attempt to disguise art as nature, to reverse the necessary order according to which nature, in a fallen world, can only be enunciated within the perspective of art. Imitation theory exploits metaphors of digestion and of grafting; interpretation theory has recourse to notions of consanguinity or of mutual good will, constituting a bond of affection between writer and reader. Writing represents itself as speech, as a dialogue with an absent (and perhaps dead) friend: Montaigne's *De l'amitié* here provides the clearest instance of an assumption implicit in epistolary writing (including letter-poems) and dialogues of all kinds. The figure of the writer asserts itself as the guarantor of a text which might otherwise appear as wholly anonymous.

It will be clear that such compensations bespeak both a confidence in the potentialities of language and a deep disquiet about its congenital defects. On the one hand, the compulsion to use language, to exploit its inexhaustible richness, reasserts itself incessantly. On the other, the possibility of acceding to a natural (as opposed to conventional) language is excluded in this period from virtually all theories of discourse; hieroglyphs and cabalistic investigations provide marginal counter-examples. 'Cratylism'—if by that term one means the supposition of a natural bond between word and thing—is retained as a hypothetical *locus* (a utopia) which clarifies, *ex contrario*, the conditions of a discourse exiled from the nature it is supposed to imitate.[2] Nature and the Logos are given; human language is an addition or supplementation which usurps their authority, Satan disguising himself as an angel of light. Thus the texts considered above exhibit the uncertainties of the very models they themselves attempt to elaborate. Erasmus's ironies and authorial withdrawal, his insertion of written into oral language, and of oral into written; Rabelais's grotesque linguistic anti-bodies; Ronsard's equivocations on

---

[2] Cf. Rigolot's 'Cratylisme et Pantagruélisme', and, in a broader perspective, Genette's *Mimologiques*.

inspiration and the radical asymmetries of his poems; Montaigne's representation of the text as a flux or emission (a disintegrating body)—such more or less explicit indications invite an analysis which would deconstruct the metaphors and other rhetorical devices on which the models are based.

Indeed, the principal topic of the second part of this book is the notion that these texts simultaneously construct and deconstruct themselves. The cornucopian movement generates endless possibilities of extension and signification. But in doing so, it reveals, and at times makes explicit, the precariousness of the whole exercise. Hence the identity of *uber* and *tuber*; hence the homeopathy by means of which the *logos* seeks to cure the *logos*; hence also the heraclitan–democritan duality of the Prologue to *Gargantua* or of the *Apologie*. An *epoche* affects the whole of the writing process, allowing it to be viewed now as a rich thesaurus of meaningful topics, now as an empty or even a malignant proliferation. And although this hypothesis governs more specifically Part II, it is nevertheless prepared by the duplicities exposed in Part I. The desire for *copia* releases the cornucopian movement.

Although this study has not been primarily a historical one, its materials may nevertheless be considered to constitute a chapter in a history of the problems of writing. Or part of a chapter, since a comprehensive history would include grammatical theories, a more detailed account of the relationship between rhetoric and dialectic, and so forth. The emergence of the word *copia* as the focus for attempts to understand the nature of writing is itself a historical phenomenon, and was treated as such in the opening chapter; the question of imitation, as posed by Erasmus and his contemporaries, is linked to a localized event (the revival of rhetoric as a discipline grounded in classical style); interpretation theory is given a critical status by the reassessment of classical texts, and above all by the desire to establish an authentic text of Scripture. In each area, it is true, earlier cultural presuppositions are subsumed. *Copia* rewrites the *amplificatio* of earlier handbooks; intertextuality—as Curtius and others have shown—is an inherent characteristic of medieval writing; and the history of biblical exegesis continues unbroken (though of course with new emphases) from the Church Fathers to the sixteenth century and beyond. On a broader level, this 'chapter of history' repeats a predicament which was already apparent in Plato's linguistic theory and which is still very much with us. The notion that logocentrism—or what Barthes calls the *discours classique*— remained intact until Mallarmé and his heirs is no longer tenable. Every phase in the history of discourse renews the same problem, the same fundamental ambivalence of language. The differences arise from the changing methods and materials which carry the problem. In the later Middle Ages, scholastic philosophy placed great conceptual pressure on language and its operations, while French vernacular literature generally ignored or disguised such problems (the same could not be said of Dante or Petrarch).[3] The striking feature of sixteenth-century French literature is the eruption of explicit self-awareness at the very heart of major texts. The possibility of this transference of pressure from philosophy to literature is opened up by the humanist attempt to discredit scholastic philosophy and to locate the pursuit of truth in 'eloquence', and it is here that Erasmus plays a central role in elaborating more sophisticated accounts of how discourse operates, and in providing paradigms of the written word enacting its own problems.

Many contributing factors determine the thematization of language problems in the sixteenth century. One of them, undoubtedly, is the growth of national consciousness. But perhaps the most interesting—since it involves, in the end, all of the central issues—is the displacement of theological problems into imaginative literature. Anthony Levi has cogently argued that the theo-

[3] This generalization is subject to many restrictions. Recent work on literary texts of the French Middle Ages has claimed many instances, both overt and covert, of reflexivity and related procedures: see, for example, Todorov, *Poétique de la prose*, ch. 10, and Zumthor, *Essai de poétique médiévale* and *Langue, texte, énigme*. Karl Uitti and Eugene Vance have drawn my attention to similar aspects of medieval literature. However, I would argue that the phenomenon is more widespread, more immediately apparent, and above all more disruptive in six-teenth-century writing: there is a certain reassuring equilibrium in the relation-ship between narrative and gloss in the *Quête du Graal* as analysed by Todorov.

logians of the earlier sixteenth century, whether the professionals
of the Sorbonne or 'amateurs' like Erasmus, were unable to
find a satisfactory solution to the problem of the relationship of
grace and nature. Reacting against an orthodox 'Pelagianism'
of external observance, Erasmian evangelicals emphasized the
individual's inward power of moral self-determination, and thus
moved towards a different kind of Pelagianism, characterized
by extreme admiration for pagan wisdom ('Saint Socrates, pray
for us'). Since no one had as yet devised a formula according to
which a rehabilitated nature could be made compatible with the
acknowledged necessity of grace and faith, the Erasmian—and
Rabelaisian—alternative is to exploit the realm of dialogue and of
fiction, where incompatibilities may be left unresolved, and may
indeed be highly fruitful.[4]

This hypothesis, summarized thus, will inevitably seem schematic if not reductive; it does, however, clearly provide a further
illustration of the pressures to which literature was subject in
this period. Furthermore, with a slight transposition of context,
it can be seen to mirror exactly the problems facing the writer.
All one needs to do is to substitute the fall of language at Babel
for the fall of man at Eden. The desire to rehabilitate discourse,
to relocate it in a redeemed nature, then appears as a variant of
Pelagianism; it is embodied in the utopian images of language
to which the texts of Rabelais, Ronsard, and Montaigne (not to
mention Erasmus himself) incessantly revert. At the same time,
such images tend to imply, according to the dialectic described
above, an anxiety in the discourse which generates them. The
garrulous Panurge is far removed from the platonist heaven
whence, according to Pantagruel, the thawing words might have
descended; as a walking Babel and a master of specious argument,
he would also hardly have qualified as a Thelemite.[5]

In more general terms, it is now widely accepted that the

[4] Levi develops this argument in 'The neoplatonist calculus' and in 'Pagan
virtue and the humanism of the northern Renaissance'.

[5] As Rigolot notes (*Les Langages de Rabelais*, pp. 94–5), Thélème is a silent place;
the episode contains no dialogue, and the speaking characters of the main narrative sequence are absent from it.

multiplicity of arguments (neoplatonist, stoic, sceptic, and so on) available in the sixteenth century, coupled with the absence of a powerful philosophical tradition, is a determining factor in the intensive use of literary and other informal modes of writing. The encyclopedia, which in theory constitutes a coherent circle of knowledge mediated by eloquent discourse, tends in practice to become centrifugal, to revert to the fragments of which it is composed. It is not, perhaps, until Descartes that a rigorous philosophical method will attempt a full integration.[6] But this example clarifies the quite different emphasis of the sixteenth century. Descartes suppresses eloquence, which had been crucial to the humanist encyclopedia; one might indeed say that he suppresses *copia*, the desire to give rein to the liberties of writing. The writers discussed in the present study attempt to perform the encyclopedia in the mode of *copia*. Of course, as already indicated, the performance is often ironic or incomplete, expressly revealing the impossibility of enclosing the universe of knowledge within the perimeters of a single work. But this acceptance of non-resolution is affirmative, since it originates in the renunciation of any foreclosed system and locates productivity in the discovery of an inward release-mechanism which one might loosely call 'intuition'. It is around this intuitive centre that all the theories surveyed in Part I organize themselves; and moments of intuitive recognition (or the absence of such recognition) become thematic and structural elements of the literary texts. Couillatris discovers this principle, as applied to ethics; Pantagruel conjures up a whole series of scenarios in which his companions may be taught to grasp it (the high point being perhaps the Pantagrueline feast off Chaneph); Ronsard's figures of abundance—Bacchus and the cornucopia—are its emblems; while the *Essais* generate the 'nouvelle figure' of a 'philosophe impremedité et fortuite'. Here *copia*, as the metaphor for an intuitive theory of writing, once more converges with the cornucopian figure: proliferation of materials is affirmed by virtue of the unity of the hidden source from which they are presumed to spring—always with the reservation that its invisibility, the possibility of its

[6] Cf. Levi, 'Ethics and the encyclopedia in the sixteenth century.'

absence, continually threatens to invert (and reveal as gratuitous) the whole process.

The same issue may be placed in a somewhat different perspective by saying that this group of sixteenth-century texts attempt, in their various ways, to reduce or even abolish the distance between the two modes of discourse whose uneasy relationship dominates Western thought. Ever since the Greeks invented philosophy, attempting to separate a language of truth from the tropical languages of myth and of rhetoric, rational discourse has continued to impose constraints on its supposedly non-serious twin. But literature, in its turn, continually reasserts its liberty by rewriting itself. Like Proteus, it always seeks to evade the moment when allegorization or equivalent procedures force it to reveal 'the truth'. Conversely, philosophy is a kind of purification rite designed to remove from language its insidious asymmetries and imperfections, to purge discourse of myth. A classic example of its inevitable failure is provided by Descartes himself: his *tabula rasa* disguises a plethora of presuppositions and half-eroded metaphors. For a while, in the sixteenth century, the polarization is diminished, and texts appear which cannot be wholly assigned to one or other category: this is no doubt another reason why they have resisted analytic methods which themselves polarize literature and critical discourse. Thus, for example, Montaigne's tightrope walk between moral philosophy and literature makes him unacceptable to philosophers and difficult of access for literary critics. In the seventeenth century, Descartes's purism coincides with a hierarchical separation of genres, with the result that literature and philosophy find themselves once more hygienically segregated. Literary texts show their subordination and domestication by surrounding themselves with claims that they are designed for profit as well as for pleasure; furthermore, it is symptomatic that such claims are normally made only in prefaces or independent theoretical tracts, so that the two kinds of discourse—theory and practice—tend to remain separate.

Yet the possibility of ambivalent discourse, of philosophy as literature, is developed by Pascal and lesser moralists and will be exploited again, in counterpoint now to a powerful philosophical tradition, in the eighteenth century. It is precisely in that century that certain modern critical theories find a model for their own operation. Perhaps the most significant development in recent Continental theory is the attempt to devise a discourse which will perform the functions of rational argument while at the same time unmasking and exploiting its hidden devices of rhetoric. Literary criticism, which has so long sought recognition as a science, is now mythologizing itself again.[7] For such a venture, Erasmus and his vernacular contemporaries provide a no less suggestive group of models than Rousseau or Diderot. It is true that Renaissance humanism, with its concern for linguistic clarity and accessibility, has dominated European educational methods, in the modern arts subjects at least; it has thus founded the belief in a supposedly universal language of common sense, together with a deep suspicion of 'jargon'. Often, indeed, the complexities of recent Continental (and particularly Parisian) theory have been derided and outlawed precisely in the name of humanism, allowing the word some elasticity. But the sophistication of the texts examined in this book might give them a very different status. Aware of their own limits, exploiting their own duplicity, they outwit any attempt to domesticate them according to the conventions of orthodox criticism, and invite from their readers a reciprocal writing exercise.

[7] This does not imply that criticism can or should ever be simply a branch of literature itself. On the contrary: the interplay between complicity with and opposition to a given text must constantly be maintained. Besides, critical discourse demands of the reader a set of reading conventions different from those he would adopt if he were faced with a novel or a poem: this is true even of texts as disconcertingly 'mixed' as those of Michel Serres.

TRANSLATIONS FROM FRENCH

THE following translations are provided in order to assist the reading of passages in French quoted above.

For passages from Rabelais, I have used *The Histories of Gargantua and Pantagruel*, trans. J. M. Cohen (Harmondsworth, Penguin Books, 1970). For passages from Montaigne, I have used the translation by Donald M. Frame in *The Complete Works of Montaigne* (London, Hamish Hamilton, 1958). Since quotations from Montaigne are often difficult to trace, I have supplied the page numbers of this translation. I have preferred modern translations to the more colourful renderings of Urquhart's Rabelais and Florio's Montaigne, since my sole aim here is to help the reader, not to present materials for stylistic and linguistic comparison. In a few instances, I have made minor changes to these versions, usually in order to maintain consistency with my analysis of the text.

All other translations are my own; like my translations from Latin, they are literal and utilitarian. I have not rendered quotations inserted in a context which supplies their general sense; nor have I translated brief quotations which appear as supplementary evidence, especially in parts of the text not primarily concerned with the vernacular.

Passages are identified by page number and *incipit* following the order of my text.

p. ix **L'escrivaillerie**   Scribbling seems to be a sort of symptom of an unruly age. (p. 721)

Qui ne voit   Who does not see that I have taken a road along which I shall go, without stopping and without effort, as long as there is ink and paper in the world? (loc. cit.)

p. 25 (note 34) **Qu'il ne luy demande**   Let him be asked for an account not merely of the words of his lesson, but of its sense and substance, and let him judge the profit he has made by the testimony not of his memory, but of his life. Let him be made to show what he has just learned in a hundred aspects, and apply it to as many different subjects, to see if he has yet properly grasped it and made it his own. (pp. 110–11)

p. 56 **quand a ceux**   as for those who devote themselves wholly to an alien language (I mean 'alien' in respect of the native language), it seems to me that it is no more possible for them to attain to the natural perfection of the ancients than for art to express Nature, whatever resemblance it may claim to achieve.

j'ai translaté   I have translated this book entitled The Art of Poetry, and have tried to adapt it to our own French poetry in so far as I have been able to preserve its authentic sense.

p. 57 **ne jure**   do not stick so religiously to the words of your author that you are afraid to depart from them in order to preserve their content, following more closely the phrasing and propriety of your own language than the diction of the foreign language. Nevertheless, as much of the dignity of the author, and of the carefully expressed vividness of his discourse, should be shown in your work as would be represented in a mirror, since it is not possible actually to represent the face itself.

La plus vręę   The truest kind of imitation is translation, for to imitate is nothing other than to want to do what another does. This is what the translator does who submits himself not only to the invention of another, but also to his disposition, and even to his style as far as he can, and as far as the character of the language into which he is translating will allow. For the power of a text often consists in the propriety of words and expressions; if this is omitted, the elegance of the author is removed and his meaning corrupted.

p. 58 **le Traducteur**   the translator will be able to introduce into French a beautiful Greek or Latin expression, and import into his city, together with the weight of ideas, the majesty of the rhythm and style of the foreign language.

les Traduccions   word-for-word translations have no grace. Not that they are contrary to the law of translation, but only because two languages are never uniform in phrasing. Conceptions are common to the understanding of all men: but words and ways of speaking are particular to nations. And let no one come and cite to me the example of Cicero, who gives no praise to the conscientious translator. For no more do I. And I do not understand this in any other way than that the translator should preserve the propriety and the character of the language into which he is translating. But I do say that, in so far as the two languages are in accord, he must lose nothing of the expressions, nor even of the particularity of the words of the author, whose wit and subtlety often consists precisely in that. Whoever could translate the whole of Virgil into French verse, sentence for sentence and word for word, would be worthy of infinite praise. For how could a translator better perform his duty than by always approaching as close as possible to the author to whom he is subject? Moreover, think how magnificent it would be to see a second language responding to all the elegance of the first, and yet retaining its own. But, as I have said, it cannot be done.

p. 60 premierement been the first to restore all the good arts and sciences to their former dignity, and has made our language, which previously was rough and uncouth, elegant and—if not as copious as it might be—at least the faithful interpreter of all the others. And so that this should be so, the Greek and Latin philosophers, historians, doctors, poets, and orators have learnt to speak French. And, I must add, the Hebrews: holy Scripture bears ample witness of what I say.

Tout ce que All that I have said to defend our language and to give it lustre pertains principally to those whose profession it is to speak well, such as poets and orators. As for the other parts of literature, and the circle of sciences that the Greeks have called 'encyclopedia', I indicated some of my thoughts about that at the beginning: namely, that the labour of faithful translators is in this respect most useful and necessary.

Encores Yet, in my opinion, the learned translator should rather perform the service of a paraphrast than of a word-for-word translator, attempting to give to all the sciences he wishes to treat the adornment and brilliance of his language, as Cicero boasts of having done in the realm of philosophy.

p. 61 Mais quand But as for style, certainly the most difficult part of rhetoric, without which everything else remains useless, like a sword still covered by its sheath; as for style, on account of which above all an orator is judged most excellent, being a manner of speaking better than any other, and the origin of the word 'eloquence' itself; whose virtue lies in propriety of terms, in words which are customary and not alien to common usage, in metaphors, allegories, comparisons, similes, descriptions, and many other figures and ornaments, without which all oratory and poetry is bare, deficient, and feeble: I shall never believe that one can learn all this from translators, since it is impossible to render it with the same grace as the author, in so much as each language has some elusive quality proper to it alone. If you try to express the true nature of this quality in another language, observing the law of translation, which is to remain within the limits of the author, your style will be forced, cold, and graceless.

p. 62 vostre diction your style will be forced, cold, and graceless. And to prove it, let someone read out a Latin Demosthenes and Homer, a French Cicero and Virgil, to see if they will engender in you such feelings—nay, like a Proteus, transform you in various different ways—as you will feel when you read these authors in their languages. You will seem to pass from the burning mountain of Etna to the cold summit of the Caucasus.

p. 63 se prennent tackle poets, a kind of author to which, if I could or would translate, I would certainly address myself least of all, because of that divinity of invention which they possess more than other writers, that magnificence of style, verbal splendour, gravity of thoughts, boldness and variety of figures, and many other adornments of poetry: in short, that energy, and indefinable spirit in their writing, which the Latins call 'genius'. All these things can no more be expressed in translation than a painter can represent the soul together with the body of the person he undertakes to portray from life.

(note 37) **la vraye pierre**   the true touchstone, by which you must test all poems, in all languages.

p. 64 **par quelz moyens**   by what means then have the Romans been able thus to enrich their language, to the point of making it more or less equal to Greek? By imitating the best Greek authors, transforming themselves into them, devouring them, and, having properly digested them, converting them into blood and nourishment. Each, according to his own nature and the topic he wished to choose, took as his model the best author, diligently examined all of his rarest and most exquisite virtues, and grafted them, as I said earlier, and adapted them to their own language. In this way . . . the Romans constructed all their fine writings which we so greatly praise and admire.

p. 65 **entende celuy**   he who would imitate must understand that it is no easy thing faithfully to follow the virtues of a good author, and as it were to transform himself into him, seeing that Nature, even in things which seem greatly alike, has not managed to prevent them being distinguished by some mark or difference. I say this because there are many in all languages who, without penetrating into the most hidden and inward parts of the author whom they have chosen, adapt themselves only to the surface, and, lingering over the beauty of the words, lose the force of the subject-matter.

p. 68 **Las et combien**   Alas, how much better it would be if there were a single natural language in the world, rather than spending so many years learning words!

Les ecritures   writing and languages were invented, not for the preservation of Nature, which—being divine—has no need of our help, but solely for our welfare and utility, so that in presence or in absence, in life or in death, we might make known to one another the secrets of our hearts, and thus attain more easily to our true happiness, which lies in the understanding of the sciences, not in the sound of words.

si vous esperez   if you hope that by these reassembled fragments the Greek and Latin languages may be resuscitated, you deceive yourself, forgetting that after the fall of those proud edifices, together with the predestined ruin of those two powerful monarchies, part of them became dust, and the rest must be in many pieces, which it would be impossible to reunify. Moreover, many other parts remained in the foundations of old walls, or were lost over the long centuries and can no longer be found. Thus, when you come to rebuild this structure, you will be far from restoring it to its original grandeur if you put the bedrooms in the place where the hall used to be, or the stables in the kitchen, confusing doors with windows: in short, changing the whole form of the building.

p. 69 **Finablement** Finally, I should consider that Art could express the living energy of Nature if you could make this restored building resemble the ancient one, since the Idea, from which the model would have to be drawn in order to rebuild it, would be lacking.

les Anciens the ancients used languages which they had sucked with the milk of their nurse, and the ignorant spoke as well as the learned, except that the latter learnt the methods and the art of oratory, thus becoming more eloquent than the others.

p. 70 **paroles** words which are living and commonly fly through the lips of men.

Mais que But I will not say that, by long and diligent imitation of those who first took possession of what Nature has none the less not denied to others, we may not follow them as successfully in this as we have already done in the greater part of the mechanical arts, and sometimes in their mode of government; for this would not only be an insult to the minds of men, but against God, who gave as an inviolable law to all things created that they should not last for ever, but incessantly pass from one state to another, the end and corruption of one being the beginning and generation of the other.

(note 45) **la curiosité** human curiosity is impressed by things which are rare and difficult to find, like perfumes and jewels, although they are not so useful for daily life, far more than by common and necessary things like bread and wine.

(note 46) **an cetẹ façon** in this way, art itself has its own nature: as when one speaks of natural order and natural speech.

(note 47) **nostre Langue** our language, which is still beginning to flower without bearing fruit, or rather, like a seedling or little shoot, has not yet flowered, far from yielding all the fruit which it might well produce.

p. 71 **Qui veut voler** He who would fly through the hands and lips of men must long remain in his room; and he who desires to live in the memory of posterity must often sweat and tremble as if inwardly dead; and, however much our court poets drink, eat, and sleep at their ease, he must endure equally great hunger, thirst, and long vigils. These are the wings on which the writings of men fly to the heavens.

p. 72 **Mais eux**   But the ancient Romans, like good farmers, first transposed their language from a wild place to a domestic one; then, so that it might bear fruit sooner and better, they pruned its useless branches, and in place of these restored it with pure native branches, taken in masterly fashion from the Greek language, which immediately became so well grafted, and resembled the trunk so closely, that they no longer appear adoptive, but natural. Thence were born in the Latin language the flowers and richly coloured fruits of its great eloquence, together with its rhythms and skilful blending of sounds, all of which is customarily produced in a language not so much by its own nature as by art.

p. 73 (note 50) **Tout le commencement**   All the beginning of the chapter is incorrect and inconsistent in its metaphors, beginning with 'eating', continuing with 'planting', and finishing with 'building', while speaking all the time about the same things. This vice is common in those who always want to use metaphors where there is no need, and to apply figures where plain language would be more appropriate, thinking that a discourse which is figurative throughout is more beautiful than one which is simple and consistent and rarely interspersed with ornaments.

p. 76 (note 53) **danger y a**   there is a danger that someone will give you the nickname that Bartolommeo Scala the Florentine gave to Angelo Poliziano, calling him 'artificial Hercules', because he himself forged monsters made specially so that he could easily defeat them.

p. 95 (note 30) **Semblablement**   Likewise, if we did not dig deeper than the bark of the literal sense, we should only have the pleasure of the fables and stories without obtaining the special advantage of the pneumatic marrow, that is to say the moral understanding which comes to us by the inspiration of the holy spirit.

p. 96 **Le divin philosophe**   The divine philosopher Plato, being sick and seeing his life drawing to its close, ordered the works of Sophron, the writer of mimes, to be given to him as a pillow; considering poetry to be profound philosophy covered by the curtain of unceasing delight, and knowing that the life of man is only a fable, he wanted to die with his head on this book. Similarly, Alexander the Great used to sleep on his copy of Homer's *Iliad*, which moved him to chivalry and high deeds.

digne que   worthy that such a book be read in it [sc. French] according to the intrinsic character of the book, without allegories.

p. 97 **lesquelles**   which are treated better than elsewhere by Fulgentius in his Mythologies, who, if heaven be willing, will soon speak French. Thus each author will have the praise to which he is entitled.

Poesie mere   Poetry, mother of subtle and joyful invention, has, beneath a covering of elegant myth, so truly expressed moral and human doctrine that if the understanding of the reader is not wholly effaced by ignorance, he will draw from it honest teaching and the manner of right living: for it is nothing other than pure hidden philosophy.

p. 98 **ce nest que**   it is nothing other than pure hidden philosophy, to which Augustine in Book II of his Christian teaching prohibits the addition of allegories, since it is sufficiently self-allegorizing. For this reason, they are omitted in this *Grand Olympe*, preserving the true nature of the author as far as possible, as is the duty of every man.

p. 109 (note 44) **L'ame de lhomme**   Since the soul of man has its origin in the infinite, it is infinite also in these two acts of will and understanding which are proper to it. Thus by no power or possession, however great, can the desire of the will be fully accomplished, without there being something more to desire; and by hearing and learning, the understanding cannot be so perfectly satisfied that there does not come before the mind something more to understand and know, which it has never known or understood . . . This soul, being infinite in these two powers and acts, is not content with the simple and bare declaration of things; going beyond, it has wished to seek out another more secret sense, and attain to a higher understanding. Either it recognized this sense to be hidden and lofty; or, if such a sense appeared not to be there, it has sought to adapt one to the subject-matter.

une fiction   a marvellous fiction, an improbable narration of elegant and joyful fables.

p. 111 **beau de stature**   of handsome build, elegant in all his features, but pitifully wounded in various places.

Voyez-vous   Do you see that man coming along the road from the Charenton bridge? On my faith, he is only poor in fortune. His physiognomy tells me for certain that he comes of some rich and noble stock. It must be the misfortunes which always befall the inquisitive that have reduced him to his present ragged and penurious state.

p. 112 **Qui estes-vous**   Tell me who you are, where you come from, where you are going, what you are looking for, and what your name is.

p. 113 **A quoy respondit**   To which Epistemon replied: 'This time I did understand him. That was the Hebrew language most beautifully pronounced.'

—Quoy!   'Why!' exclaimed Pantagruel's lackey Carpalim. 'It's Greek, I understood him. But how is that? Have you lived in Greece?'

—**J'entends**   'I seem to understand,' said Pantagruel. 'For either it is the language of my native Utopia, or else it has a very similar sound.'

p. 114 —**Si faictz**   'Yes, very well, my lord,' replied the fellow. 'Heaven be praised, it's my natural mother-tongue. For I was born and brought up as a child in Touraine, which is the garden of France.'

p. 116 **[Pantagruel] nous dist**   'Can you hear something, comrades?' Pantagruel asked. 'I seem to hear people talking in the air. But I can't see anything. Listen.' We all obeyed his command, and listened attentively, sucking in the air in great earfuls, like good oysters in the shell, to hear if any voice or other snatches of sound could be picked up . . . But, notwithstanding, we protested that we could hear no voice whatever. Pantagruel, however, continued to affirm that he could hear several voices on the air, both male and female; and then we decided that either we could hear them too, or else there was a ringing in our ears. Indeed, the more keenly we listened, the more clearly we made out voices, till in the end we could hear whole words.

le manoir   the abode of truth [which is inhabited by] the names and forms, the ideas and images of all things past and future.

réservée   laid up for the future, awaiting the end of Time.

Nous serions   Shouldn't we be greatly startled if it proved to be the head and the lyre of Orpheus? After the Thracian women had torn him to pieces, they threw his head and lyre into the river Hebrus, down which they floated to the Black Sea, and from there to the island of Lesbos, still riding together on the waters. And all the time there issued from the head a melancholy song, as if in mourning for Orpheus' death, while the lyre, as the moving winds strummed it, played a harmonious accompaniment to this lament. Let's look if we can see them hereabouts.

p. 117 **Mais en pourrions-nous**   But could we see just one of them? I remember reading that, as they stood around the edges of the mountain on which Moses received the Laws of the Jews, the people palpably saw the voices.

p. 118 **O Bouteille**   O Bottle full of mystery, with a single ear I hark to thee. Do not delay, but that one word say for which with all my heart I long.

p. 119 **'Voicy,'**   'That was a notable chapter,' said Panurge, 'and a most authentic gloss. Is that all that the verdict of the thrice-great bottle intended to convey? I like it very well indeed.'

p. 120 **soyez vous mesmes**   You must be your own interpreters in this matter.

Autant   I told you that much when you first spoke to me on the subject.

p. 144 (note 24) **Me souvient**   I remember, too, that Aristotle maintains Homer's words to be bounding, flying, and moving, and consequently alive [animated].

p. 147 **ne creignent**   do not fear these changes, and with wonderful grace they let themselves thus be tossed in the wind, or seem to. The titles of my chapters do not always embrace their matter; often they only denote it by some sign... Lord, what beauty there is in these lusty sallies and this variation, and more so the more casual and accidental they seem... I seek out change indiscriminately and tumultuously. My style and my mind alike go roaming... the best ancient prose—and I scatter it here indiscriminately as verse—shines throughout with the vigour and boldness of poetry, and gives the effect of its frenzy... The poet, says Plato, seated on the tripos of the Muses, pours out in a frenzy whatever comes into his mouth, like the spout of a fountain, without ruminating and weighing it; and from him escape things of different colours and contradictory substance in an intermittent flow. He himself is utterly poetic, and the old theology is poetry, the scholars say, and the first philosophy. It is the original language of the Gods. (p. 761)

p. 151 (note 31) **ceulx qui**   those who had studied and were men of letters...   **car monseigneur**   for his Highness the Dauphin did not wish their art to be brought in; also, lest the beauty of rhetoric was detrimental in some respect to the truth of the story.

p. 153 **Quand ce viendra**   When the time comes for me to fall at last into the iron sleep of death, then all of Ronsard will not go beneath the tombstone: the better part of him will remain. Ever living, never dying, I shall fly through the universe, eternalizing the fields where I dwell, which are rich and fertile with my renown: for I have wedded in the sweet babbling of my ivory lyre those two harpists [Pindar and Horace] who in my verses find they have become Vendômois.

p. 154 **Apres qu'ilz**   When, at the two corners of the door, they had paid their respects to Pallas who bears the image of the Gorgon, and to Bacchus too, from whose marble fingers hangs a branch loaded with grapes, they wash three times in the water of the spring, three times adorn themselves with a threefold garland of verbena, walk three times round the Grotto, and three times softly call upon the Nymphs of Meudon, the Fauns, the Sylvans, and all the untamed Gods of the nearby forests, hills, and groves; then, taking courage, they entered the sacred horror of the Grotto, and, as if they were set on fire with an excess of divinity, felt their minds being filled with the holy madness of new inspiration. They were amazed to see the arrangement of such a magnificent building in such a forsaken spot: the design, the façade, and the rustic pillars, outdoing the glory of antique columns; to see that nature had decorated the walls with such fine arabesques in such hard rocks, to see the closets, chambers, and halls, the terraces, festoons, guilloches, and ovals, and the many-hued enamel which is like the colours of the meadows when spring dapples them with flowers, or like the rainbow that at its coming paints the underside of the clouds with a thousand colours.

p. 161 **gardez-vous**   take care you do not, as does the spider, turn all good meat into poison. I warn you, too, that it is dangerous to cite Scripture without reason or necessity.

Vous voulez   You mean to say, then, that when in speaking to you unbelievers we call upon God to aid us, we take his name in vain; but if there is sin in this, you alone must bear the punishment for it, for your unbelief constrains us to seek out all the oaths we can muster. And even so we cannot light the fire of charity in your icy hearts.

Mais il y a   But there is a danger that the daughters of Eve may be too ready to believe this serpent.

p. 163 **Vrayement**   Indeed, I remember that the Cabalists and Massoretes, interpreters of Holy Writ, in explaining how one can make sure of the genuineness of an angelic apparition—for often Satan's angels take the form of angels of light—say that the difference between the two lies in this: that when the good and consoling angel appears to man, he alarms him at first, but comforts him in the end, and leaves him happy and contented; whereas the wicked and corrupting angel rejoices a man at the beginning, but in the end leaves him troubled, angry, and perplexed.

p. 164 (note 7) **Je vous voy**   I can see you very well, but I can't hear you at all, and I don't know what you're saying. The hungry stomach has no ears.

p. 171 **Et paour**   Have no fear that the wine will give out, as it did at the marriage at Cana in Galilee. As much as I draw out for you at the tap, I will pour in at the bung. In this way the cask will remain inexhaustible, endowed with a living spring and a perpetual flow. So my liquor shall be like that within the cup of Tantalus, which the Brahmin sages represented figuratively; like the mountain of salt in Iberia, so celebrated by Cato; like the sacred golden bough, dedicated to the goddess of the underworld, so celebrated by Virgil. It is a true cornucopia of ridicule and fun; and if at times it seems to you to be emptied to the lees, still it will not be dry. As in Pandora's jug, good hope lies at the bottom, not despair, as in the Danaides' tub.

p. 172 **Je pensois**   I thought that Amaltheia had placed in your hands abundance and wealth, that second soul of mankind; now I realize, seeing you starving, that you only nourish the mind with idle vapours, with a windy nobility, ancient and mouldering, which you have vainly preferred to solid goods. Of what use to you is Jupiter, whose daughters you are? What use are your songs, your temples, your cities? They are only a show, a counterfeit honour, rich in fantasy, not in reality.

p. 175 **Or est il** Now it is a fact that, of all Latin poetry, there is none so ample, so rich, so diverse, and so universal as the *Metamorphoses* of Ovid, which contains in fifteen books composed in elegant heroic metre all (or nearly all) the stories of the ancient poets and writers, bound to one another, and so well linked by sustained narrative and by skilful transitions, that each seems to arise from and to depend on the other in succession, without sudden breaks, although they are extraordinarily unalike in their characters, times, and places. By means of all these myths Ovid's sole intention is to teach us that, in the nature of things, forms are continually changing, while matter never dies, as he himself shows in the fifteenth and last book through the character and the opinion of Pythagoras.

p. 176 (note 10) **Toutefois** Nevertheless, one should follow the excellent advice given by Melanchthon in his notes on Hesiod: namely, that it is not always necessary to seek assiduously for a reason, a continuity, and an appropriate and consistent coherence in every detail of poetic fables; it is sufficient to have to some extent discovered and shown what the poets wanted in general to signify in the fable as a whole.

(note 11) **Combien** Although I do not share the opinion of those who consider that most fables are delightful in their external appearance [literally 'clothed in delight'], rather than filled with either natural or moral secrets, nevertheless I do not think it is necessary to rack one's brains over this kind of painstaking inquiry; so if I have already given you a few allegories, I could not promise you, however, to continue with all the other myths.

p. 178 **Car, comme jadis** For as of old the great seer Proteus, while disguised and transformed into fire, water, a tiger, a dragon, and other strange shapes, could not foretell events to come and, therefore, in order to foretell them had to be restored to his own native shape, so man cannot receive the divine art of prophecy except when that part of him which is most divine—to wit his *Nous* or *Mens*—is quiet, tranquil, peaceable, and neither occupied nor distracted by extraneous passions or affections.

p. 180 **Donques** Therefore, if it is true that in our time the stars, as with one accord, have conspired to produce by their happy influence the honour and increase of our tongue, who among our scholars will not wish to contribute to it, pouring out into the French language a wealth of flowers and fruits from the rich Greek and Latin horns of plenty?

p. 181 (note 18) **Les philosophes**   Natural and moral philosophers may learn from it, theologians, astrologers, geometricians, alchemists, makers of mirrors, painters, and others born under the constellation and influence of benevolent stars shining upon the mentally gifted and others who desire to know all manner of arts and sciences.

p. 183 **Mais, voyans**   But if you had seen the fine wire-thread embroidery, and the charming plaiting in gold-work, set with rich diamonds, precious rubies, rare turquoises, magnificent emeralds, and Persian pearls, you would have compared it to one of those grand Horns of Plenty that you see on ancient monuments, one such as Rhea gave to the two nymphs Adrastea and Ida, the nurses of Jupiter. For it was always brave, sappy, and moist, always green, always flourishing, always fructifying, full of humours, full of flowers, full of fruit, full of every delight. I swear to God it was a pleasure to look at! But I will tell you a good deal more about it in the book that I have written, *On the Dignity of Codpieces*.

p. 186 **D'un cas**   On one point I will inform you now, however, that not only was it long and capacious, but well furnished within and well victualled, having no resemblance to the fraudulent codpieces of so many young gentlemen which contain nothing but wind, to the great disappointment of the female sex.

p. 188 **quand**   when . . . my soul shall leave this mortal habitation, I shall not now account myself to be absolutely dying, but to be passing from one place to another, since in you, and by you, I shall remain in visible form here in this world, visiting and conversing with men of honour and my friends as I used to do.

   ainsi   Indeed, I have helped you . . . as if I treasured nothing else in this world but to see you, in my lifetime, a perfect model . . .

p. 189 **Chose si précieuse**   Such precious stuff should not be foolishly wasted. Besides, he might beget a boy, and then he'd die without regret, leaving a man for a man.

p. 191 **En tel estat**   In this condition he presented himself before Pantagruel, who found the disguise strange, especially as he missed that fine and magnificent codpiece on which Panurge had once relied, as on the master-anchor, as his last resort in all the shipwrecks of adversity.

p. 192 **naufrage**   shipwreck of my past in the Straits of Misfortune.

p. 194 maintient 'maintains further that a great part of the material of reproduction springs from the brain and the spinal column. Fifthly, by the venereal act. . . .' 'I was waiting for that,' said Panurge. 'That's the one for me. Anyone's welcome to the rest.'

p. 195 J'ay cestuy I put my trust in God, that he will hear our prayers, in view of the firm faith in which we offer them, and that he will grant this wish of ours, seeing that it is a modest one.

Et, pour And since you've been moderate in your wishes and chosen wisely, by the will of Jupiter I give you the two others into the bargain.

voylà qu'advient you see what good fortune attends those whose wishes are simple, and who choose in moderation.

Soubhaitez So wish in moderation. What you ask will come to you, and better things too, if you toil hard at your own work in the meantime.

p. 196 de sa coignée on his hatchet depended his life and his livelihood. By his hatchet he lived respected and honoured by all the rich wood merchants. Without his hatchet he would die of starvation. If death had met him without his hatchet a week later, he would have mown him down with his scythe and weeded him out of the world.

Adoncques So they all lost their hatchets. There wasn't a devil among them that kept a hatchet! There wasn't a mother's son in the district who didn't lose his hatchet. No more trees were felled, no more wood was split throughout the whole country, through lack of hatchets.

p. 197 En Chinon At Chinon he exchanged his silver hatchet for good testers and other silver money; and his golden hatchet he turned into fine angels, beautiful Agnus Dei crowns, good Dutch ritters, honest reals, and gleaming sun-crowns as well. With these he bought several farms, lands, houses, cottages, huts, and summer-houses; several fields, vineyards, woods, ploughlands, pastures, ponds, mills, gardens, and willow plantations; a number of oxen, cows, ewes, sheep, goats, sows, hogs, donkeys, horses, hens, cocks, capons, pullets, geese, ganders, drakes, ducks, and small fowl.

p. 198 petitz Romipètes little pilgrims to Rome, who sell all they have and borrow from others to buy piles of indulgences from a newly elected Pope.

p. 199 Or donné Gold freely given, a man's freely shriven.

p. 200 Roy Juppiter King Jupiter, in the days when, by your ordinance and special favour, I was keeper of the gardens on earth, I noted that this word 'hatchet' was in several ways equivocal. It signifies a certain instrument used for cutting down and splitting timber. It also signifies—at least it did so of old—a female frequently, soundly, and unceremoniously laid on her back. In fact every good fellow called the girl who gave him his pleasures, 'my hatchet'.

p. 201 **il reguarde**   he looked hard at the wooden helve, and recognized his mark on it; upon which he bounded with joy, like a fox who has found some hens astray, and his face split in a grin: 'God's turds!' said he. 'This one's mine.'

p. 202 **Le serpens**   The serpent who tempted Eve was a Chitterling; yet, for all that, it is written of him that he was slyer and more subtle than any beast of the field. So are the Chitterlings. Furthermore, it is maintained in many academies that this tempter was the Chitterling named Ithyphallus, into whose shape good Master Priapus was transformed. He was a great tempter of women in the old days, in Paradise, as it was called in Greek, which in French means the pleasure gardens.

p. 207 **icy est**   this island is one of the Sporades . . . They were once fertile, much visited, wealthy, and populous, and a centre of trade subject to the power of Britain. Now, in the course of time and with the world's decay, they have become poor and desolate, as you see.

Et par   In the shady and unfrequented forest, Macrobe pointed out several old ruined temples, several obelisks, pyramids, monuments, and ancient tombs, with different inscriptions and epitaphs. Some were in hieroglyphics, others in the Ionic tongue, others in Arabic, Hagarene, Slavonic, and other tongues, which Epistemon carefully copied down.

le noble enfant   that noble child and the mediator between Heaven and Earth.

(note 29) **Au lendemain**   Next morning we touched at the Island of the Popefigs, who had once been rich and free, and were then known as Jollyboys. But now they were poor and miserable, and subject to the Papimaniacs.

p. 208 **Les naufz**   When the ships of the jovial company were refitted and repaired, and their victuals had been replenished, the Macraeons were left thoroughly satisfied and contented with Pantagruel's expenditure on their island. Our men, too, were more jovial than usual when we set sail on the following day, in high spirits, with a sweet and pleasant wind behind us.

travailloit   while doing nothing he worked, and while working did nothing. He kept his eyes open when sleeping, and slept with his eyes open . . . When he fasted, he ate nothing, and when he ate nothing he fasted.

p. 209 (note 31) **Ainsi**   So, basing her argument on evidence drawn from the brute creation, she attracted every fool and madman to her side, and won the admiration of every brainless idiot, of everyone, indeed, who lacked sound judgement and common sense. Since that time, she has brought forth the pious apes, holy hypocrites, and popemongers . . . and other deformed monsters, forged in Nature's despite.

p. 210 **[Pantagruel] condescendit** Pantagruel agreed, however, to go ashore on Savage Island, so that some of his men who had been drenched and fouled by the spouter could dry and refresh themselves. They landed at a small deserted harbour on the south side, which lay in the shelter of a pleasant little wood of fine tall trees, from which there flowed a delicious stream of sweet, clear, silvery water. There they set up their kitchen in grand tents, and they did not spare the fuel. Everyone changed whatever clothes he thought fit. Friar John rang the bell, and at that signal the tables were set up and a meal promptly served. As Pantagruel was gaily dining with his men and the second course was being brought in, he noticed a few tame little Chitterlings.

p. 212 **Quant ilz font** When they hold a feast or a banquet they set up their tables under one or two windmills, and feast there as gaily as at a wedding, discussing during their meal the goodness and excellence, the rare and salubrious qualities of winds, as you, my fellow drinkers, philosophize at your banquets on the subject of wines.

(note 37) **troys ou quatre** three or four lents a year, not counting certain special rogations and orisons.

p. 213 **une veze** a bladder full of the original wind which that old snorer Aeolus had given to Ulysses of old, to propel his ship in the calm.

p. 215 **Au jour** We pursued our journey, gossiping the while, and on the following day came off Chaneph or Hypocrisy Island, where Pantagruel's ship could not put in because the wind failed us and there was a calm at sea.

Et restions So we were all thoughtful and depressed, down in the dumps and worried, and did not exchange a word together.

p. 216 **Adoncques** Then, breaking this obstinate silence, he asked in a loud voice and in the gayest of spirits: 'What's the best way to raise fine weather [i.e. pass the time] in the doldrums?'

(note 43) **Sans poinct** We ought undoubtedly to give great praise to the good God, our Creator, Saviour, and Preserver, for this excellent bread, for this grand fresh wine, and for these splendid meats. For over and above the pleasure and delight we get from eating and drinking, we are healed by our victuals of certain disorders both of the body and the mind.

p. 217 **Ilz n'avoient** And they had not come to the dessert when the northwest wind began to fill the sails—mainsail, mizzen, topsails, and all. Then they all sang various hymns in praise of the High God of Heaven.

(note 44) **cestuy esprit** The spirit then neglects to look after its nourisher and natural host, the body; as when a hawk upon the fist, striving to fly up into the air, is suddenly pulled downwards by the leash.

p. 218 **Ne sçavez-vous** You know, do you not, that the Amycleans of old, who revered and worshipped Bacchus above all the other gods, gave him the most fitting title of *Psila*? *Psila* in Doric means wings. For as, by the help of their wings, birds fly lightly aloft into the air, so with the aid of Bacchus—of good, tasty, and delicious wine, that is to say—the spirits of humankind are raised on high, their bodies manifestly made nimbler, and what was earthy in them becomes pliant.

(note 46) **Reste donc** It remains then to deal with the problem put forward by Friar John: how to raise good weather? But haven't we raised it, as fine as you like? Look at the wind-gauge on the scuttle. Listen to the whistling of the wind. Look at how taut the stays, the ties, and the sheets are.

p. 219 (note 47) **un gras** a stout and powerful young Pauncher, who carried a wooden statue on a tall, brightly-gilt pole. It was badly carved and clumsily painted; and such as had been described by Plautus, Juvenal, and Pomponius Festus. At Lyons, in carnival time, they call it the Chewcrust. But these people called it Manduce. **un grand nombre** a great crowd of clumpish servants carrying baskets, punnets, panniers, pots, ladles, and kettles. Then, with Manduce conducting them, and singing some unknown dithyrambs, bacchic anthems, and paeans of praise, they opened their pots and baskets and made sacrifice to their god of white Hippocras. . . .'

p. 220 (note 48) **Nous haulsans** As we raised and emptied our glasses, good weather has been raised likewise, by an occult sympathy of Nature.

p. 224 (note 1) **Je ne fai** I don't doubt that my poetry, being so diverse, will seem tiresome to the ears of our rhymesters, and particularly of those at court . . . I am satisfied that they could not accuse me without first condemning Pindar, the originator of this copious diversity; moreover, it is the sauce with which the ode must be tasted. I am of the opinion that no poetry may be praised as being perfect if it does not resemble nature, which was considered beautiful by the ancients precisely because it is inconstant, and variable in its perfections.

p. 226 (note 5) **Muse, repren** Muse, take up the oars again, cease your wanderings. A speech always displeases listening ears if it is unduly full of abundant words. **Celui qui** He who compresses a varied subject into few verses wins the crown.

p. 227 **Il faut**   I must try my strength, test myself a little, quietly and modestly, practising with foreign models, before thundering aloud your praises with a sound worthy of you.

p. 229 **Sus donque**   Up then, Muse, carry to the heavens the fame I have won, announcing the victory which I am legitimately celebrating.

p. 230 **Errant**   Wandering through the fields of the Grace who paints my verses with her colours, I amass on the Dircean banks the treasure of the richest flowers, so that from my plunder I may arduously fashion the circle of this crown thrice twisted in a Theban fold: to adorn the highest fame of the happiest favourite of the gods, who brought back from heaven to earth the daughters of Memory.

(note 11) **Les scadrons**   The adventurous swarms of the fluttering bees form their tasty honey from flowers blooming at random in the green meadows. Such is the flight of my verses, which carry these various names, following a wandering path around the world. But I can choose nothing from the great treasure in which I abound, so rich-poor am I.

p. 234 **Il nous donne**   It gives us grace, and then again knowledge, honour, beauty, kin, marriages, and it alone transforms us into a hundred thousand different appearances.

Et bref   In short, Wealth is the horn of Amaltheia, which gives everything in plenty, it is the jewel of honour, the priceless pearl, the summit of good fortune.

p. 235 **Chacun la veut**   Everyone wants it, everyone values and prizes it; for that reason, Aristotle placed it among the virtues, not as a virtue itself, but as the instrument by which virtue shows itself clearly; for virtue is deficient in itself, and never shows itself in the light of day unless it has gold as a guide.

O gentil OR   O noble Gold, everywhere you reveal your powers, brighter than daylight; you are useful to works both of war and of peace; thanks to you, sacred laws flourish in the cities; great burghers, palaces, markets flourish in pomp; and thanks to you temples are built as high as the heavens. The thrifty farmer, the craftsman, the merchant transforms into your metal the yield of his land, for to him you seem far more useful than Ceres.

p. 236 **Sçauroit-on**   Could one become expert in painting, in music, or in architecture, if one had no money to buy tools? Would one see so many skilled masters of so many arts if they had not paid money for their apprenticeship in the trades they ply? O God, how great is the use of this metal! how precious it is! Man's life depends less on the air he breathes from the heavens, on bread, wine, or fire, than on the myriad pleasures with which Gold supplies him: without it, everyone would languish in idleness; without it, one could neither practise love, nor give lavish feasts, nor strike up the dance, nor pace in rhythm to the sound of oboes.

p. 241 **Elles ouvrant**   Opening their mouths full of a sweet Arabian harvest, they animated their song with the spirit of a living breath.

p. 243 (note 28) **Dont n'aguere**   with which he once had pierced his brain when he conceived Pallas the warrior goddess, cut up Spring and divided his whole season into three parts.

p. 245 **De quatre**   From four embraces which Nature received from such an ardently fertile consort, she conceived four children at once. One was a hermaphrodite (Spring is his name), of little potency, between male and female, inconstant, uncertain, variable in effect from one day to the next. Summer was wholly male, ardent, ruddy, and choleric, sparkling and hot, resembling his father, warlike, hasty, and bold, always in action, vigorous, noble, full of perfection, hostile to idleness.

Depuis que   Since Spring, that manly girl, has loved the Earth in vain, the Earth is useless, bearing only flowers, and the humour that pricks her still languishes in the sap and fails to ripen. Of what use are flowers if the fruits never ripen? Of what use are crops, if the grain never turns to gold? Everything has its end, and tends towards some goal; fate willed it thus, when the world was given the order it still has.

p. 246 **A toy**   To you, son of the Sun, belongs perfection: you sustain and nourish the power of generation, for without your virtue nothing in the world can exist, being as you are the lord and master of the seasons.

(note 34)   **Quand d'un bonet**   when she adonizes her head [i.e. makes it resemble Adonis'] with a cap, and when one cannot tell (so well does she disguise her ambiguous appearance) whether she is a girl or a boy.

p. 248 **Nouveau Cygne**   Feathered like some new swan, I want to fly high up; I want my breast, like Summer's, to be full of the heat of Apollo as I run in the track of the Muses, and to throw thick dust in the eyes of those who follow me.

p. 250 **C'estoit**   It was just when the morning star had already chased the surrounding stars from the pastures of the sky and, counting them up, was about to put them in the shade for fear of the heat. Already the silvery Moon was going to see her beloved, her handsome Endymion asleep on the hill; already beautiful rosy-faced Dawn had opened all the gates of the sky; already the Sun had oiled his brow with make-up so that he would not become tanned and, seated in his chariot, was already holding the reins of his steeds, which had been brought out of the empty stable: when quite unexpectedly Autumn arrived. Then the Sun sullenly withdrew behind his daughter, and averting his face lest he should see her, took a different route.

p. 251 **[Autonne] à son frere**   Autumn stole from her brother his garlands and his flowers, and like a thief (after plundering him) made herself a crown with them.

Elle prist   She subtly took two of her brother's rays to adorn her head, then went to see her mother.

Là sont   There, in jars on tables, are enclosed the seeds of all things, each with its label, guarded by young boys who, so that this great universe may never end, sow them every year in mutual service, that the world, as it grows old, may grow young again.

p. 252 **Si tost**   As soon as Nature had caught sight of her daughter, 'Get you gone,' she said. 'You will destroy my family; leave my house: you will in your time be the ruin and misfortune of my other children. You will destroy everything that the beneficent cold of Winter germinates, all that the green of Spring produces, and everything ripe and perfect that grows when Summer appears; you will make the hair fall from the groves, the woods will be bald and the banks shorn of plants by your hand, Phthinoporon, and you will maliciously spread among men a host of evils.'

p. 253 **Maitresse**   Mistress of the vessel that Abundance holds, through whom Pomona's beauty is maintained.

p. 254 **Tel j'ay tracé**   Thus have I traced out this hymn, imitating the model of Hesiod's fables and of Homer's.

p. 256 **Elle [la fureur]**   This divine fury remains with me for a day, sometimes two, sometimes three, then it dies and withers away in me as the flower withers for a while, and then appears in the spring more vigorous than before, taking strength and increase from its decline, and from its death a long birth.

p. 257 **Le grand Platon**   Great Plato tells us in his works that our spirit is like the body: one generates children which overcome death, the other produces sons who must see the port where the Boatman keeps his ferry open to all comers, growing rich from our loss. Thus both conceive, but the blood must be young, vigorous, and warm; for if the blood gives no strength to their children, they will do nothing of value.

Et comme on voit   And as one sees those torrents that rush down from high up in the hills and gush, wave upon wave, into the valley . . . so too I run in unbridled flight when the fury floods into me.

(note 43) **Belot, parcelle**   Belot, you who are a fragment of my life, or rather my whole life: when I saw you, I no longer desired to see the Muse . . .

p. 258 **Et toutefois**   And yet, as a result of divers changes, I hated the Muses and poetry, through which I had conquered renown and disseminated it throughout France.

Par quel escrit   With what writing must I begin in order to scatter the seed of the Muses—I mean my verses—throughout Europe, so that your renown will survive after your death?

Soudain au cœur   Immediately, my heart felt a desire to sing of you, so that after your lifetime the people should know that your Graces had such a poet to praise your virtue.

p. 259 **L'un en cecy**   One sings your praises for this, another for that; but the song most frequently sung by all (and the one which most stirs our hearts) tells how, seeing the Gallic Apollo wandering in a sorry state through our France, his lyre torn from his hand by foolish, malicious and vain Ignorance who pursues mankind—how, seeing this, you did not show yourself to be miserly towards him, but made this God rich to your own loss, offering up to him with a solemn vow your curved lyre, an eternal gift of costly art, so that it may be beheld as the gift of Belot in his Temple.

p. 261 **Ta face semble**   Your face and your solitary expression resemble those apothecary's jars, which are crudely painted on the surface with men and gods simulated according to the artist's whim—a Juno blown through the air by the winds; a Pallas looking at her puffed-out cheeks and growing angry with her reed-pipe, which in vexation she threw into the water; a Marsyas stripped of his skin. Yet these little boxes are full of amber, civet, and sweet-smelling musk, manna, rhubarb, aloes (a remedy for a weak stomach). Nevertheless, when you look at these pictures all together, you might think that the inside is similar to the outside.

p. 262 **Lors de ta voix**   Then eloquence exudes from your voice, so that you are truly a Socrates, and your learned speech makes sweet honey flow from your lips, revealing the virtue that burns within you, since in the depths of your soul is hidden something rare and precious (I know not what) which is not apparent at first sight: for in your overflowing vase you conceal ten thousand perfumes, strange and new, so that when you speak you give ample proof of the nobility of your soul by means of the power of your tongue which, so sweet is it, fastens a baited hook in the hearts of all who hear it.

p. 263 (note 47)   **Nil dont la source**   Nile, whose source is hidden from men, and which, without rain, swells abundantly in the hottest months.

p. 264 **A traitz**   There is depicted in living relief a long story composed of mythological fictions, covering the proud belly of the lyre.

   tient entre ses bras   holds in his arms a horn of plenty which seems to swell proudly with a hundred fruits at once, overflowing the rim of the vessel in great clusters.

p. 265 **ainsi qu'au renouveau**   as in the spring a fine cherry-tree brings forth its thick fruit in great clusters, to feed both us and the birds which, avid for its fruit, clamour hungrily about the tree.

p. 266 **Rien, mon Belot**   Great expense, Belot my friend, is of no use here. The spendthrifts, swollen with pride and feasting, try to earn human fame by sumptuous craft or by banquets and disorderly drinking, but they are deceived, and themselves become corrupt by excess, without acquiring a poet of renown who, without banquets, can celebrate their name for friendship's sake and not, Belot, for their table, for choice wine or delicious fare: for today everyone is wise enough to know what things are really worth, and the value of sober living.

   (note 51) **Je ne faisois**   I spent my time . . . grafting, planting, and pulling into line the crooked stock of the joyful vine.

p. 269 **Je pensois**   *see above*, pp. 344–5.

   De l'air   Lowering my eyes from the sky and looking down a valley, I saw coming towards me a company tanned and weary from long labours, who through adverse destiny, as it seemed to me, had followed a hard road. They were ragged and poorly clad; their dress, fastened with a pointed thorn, hung awry from their shoulders, and their dishevelled hair was dirty and dusty, filthy and ill-combed. And yet their faces were beautiful enough . . . Whichever way they turned their heads as they walked, virtue, eloquence, and grace followed them, showing in a hundred ways from their first glance that their lineage was of royal birth.

p. 270 **portoit**   wore beneath a poor coat a lively countenance, and showed by his bearing what blood had conceived him.

   Quel est   What is your country, your name, and the town that boasts of you?

p. 271 **Je n'ay dressé**   I have not had any regular dealings with any solid book, except Plutarch and Seneca, from whom I draw like the Danaides, incessantly filling up and pouring out. (p. 107)

J'en attache   Some of this sticks to this paper; to myself, little or nothing. (loc. cit.)

p. 274 (note 3) **Quel que je soye**   Whatever I may be, I want to be elsewhere than on paper . . . I am less a maker of books than of anything else. (p. 596)

p. 276 **Comme nul**   As no event and no shape is entirely like another, so none is entirely different from another. An ingenious mixture on the part of nature. If our faces were not similar, we could not distinguish man from beast; if they were not dissimilar, we could not distinguish man from man. All things hold together by some similarity; every example is lame, and the comparison that is drawn from experience is always faulty and imperfect; however, we fasten together our comparisons by some corner. (p. 819)

(note 4) **Et les Grecs**   Both the Greeks and the Latins, and we ourselves, use eggs for the most express example of similarity. However, there have been men, and notably one at Delphi, who recognized marks of difference between eggs . . . Dissimilarity necessarily intrudes into our works; no art can attain similarity . . . Resemblance does not make things so much alike as difference makes them unalike. Nature has committed herself to make nothing separate that was not different. (p. 815)

p. 277 **à escrire**   in writing I am the more unwilling to accept the well-worn topics, for fear I may treat them at someone else's expense. Any topic is equally fertile for me . . . Let me begin with whatever subject I please, for all subjects are linked with one another. (p. 668)

(note 6) **Je hay**   I hate to recognize myself, and never reread, if I can help it, what has once escaped me. Now I am bringing in here nothing newly learned. These are common ideas; having perhaps thought of them a hundred times, I am afraid I have already set them down. Repetition is boring anywhere . . . (p. 734)

p. 280 **Vous, pour qui**   You, for whom I have taken the pains to extend so long a work contrary to my custom, will not shrink from upholding your Sebond by the ordinary form of argument . . . For this final fencer's trick must not be employed except as an extreme remedy. It is a desperate stroke, in which you must abandon your weapons to make your adversary lose his, and a secret trick that must be used rarely and reservedly. It is great rashness to ruin yourself in order to ruin another . . . Here we are shaking the barriers and last fences of knowledge, in which extremity is a vice, as in virtue. Stay on the highroad . . . All eccentric ways irritate me. (pp. 418–19)

(note 8) **Considerons**   Let us then consider for the moment man alone, without outside assistance, armed solely with his own weapons, and deprived of divine grace and knowledge, which is his whole honour, his strength, and the foundation of his being. (p. 328)

Maintes-fois   Many times . . . having undertaken as exercise and sport to maintain an opinion contrary to my own, my mind, applying itself and turning in that direction, attaches me to it so firmly that I can no longer find the reason for my former opinion, and I abandon it. I draw myself along in almost any direction I lean, whatever it may be, and carry myself away by my own weight. (p. 426)

p. 282 (note 12) **Je suis**   I am at this moment in such a condition, thank God, that I can move out when he chooses. (p. 61)

Mon livre   My book is always one. Except that at each new edition . . . I allow myself to add, since it is only an ill-fitted patchwork, some extra ornaments. These are only overweights, which do not condemn the original form . . . Thence, however, it will easily happen that some transposition of chronology may slip in, for my stories take their place according to their timeliness, not always according to their age. (p. 736)

p. 283 (note 13) **Qui ne voit**   Who does not see that I have taken a road along which I shall go, without stopping and without effort, as long as there is ink and paper in the world? (p. 721)

p. 284 **je me suis**   I have ordered myself to dare to say all that I dare to do, and I dislike even thoughts that are unpublishable. (p. 642)

p. 285 **A ces bonnes gens**   These good people needed no sharp and subtle play on words; their language is all full and copious with a natural and constant vigour . . . 'Their whole contexture is manly; they are not concerned with pretty little flowers.' This is not a soft and merely inoffensive eloquence; it is sinewy and solid, and does not so much please as fill and ravish; and it ravishes the strongest minds most. When I see these brave forms of expression, so alive, so profound, I do not say 'This is well said,' I say 'This is well thought.' It is the sprightly vigour of the imagination that elevates and swells the words. (pp. 664–5)

Plutarque   Plutarch says that he saw the Latin language through things. It is the same here: the sense illuminates and brings out the words, which are no longer wind, but flesh and bone. (p. 665)

p. 286 (note 17) **Gallus**   Gallus speaks simply, because he conceives simply. Horace is not content with a superficial expression; it would betray him. He sees more clearly and deeply into the thing. His mind unlocks and ransacks the whole storehouse of words and figures in order to express itself; and he needs them to be beyond the commonplace, as his conception is beyond the commonplace.   **je n'eusse**   I would not have dared trust myself to an idiom that I could neither bend nor turn out of its ordinary course. (loc. cit.)

p. 288 **il n'est rien**   For there is nothing that might not be done with our jargon of hunting and war, which is a generous soil to borrow from. And forms of speech, like plants, improve and grow stronger by being transplanted. (loc. cit.)

Je le trouve   I find it sufficiently abundant, but not sufficiently pliable and vigorous. It ordinarily succumbs under a powerful conception. If your pace is tense, you often feel it growing limp and giving way under you, and that when it fails you Latin comes to your aid, and Greek to others. (pp. 665–6)

D'aucuns   Of some of those words that I have just picked out it is harder for us to perceive the energy, because the frequent use of them has somewhat debased and vulgarized their grace for us; as in our vernacular we encounter excellent phrases and metaphors whose beauty is withering with age and whose colour has been tarnished by too common handling. But that takes away nothing of their savour to those who have a good nose, nor does it detract from the glory of those ancient authors who, as is likely, first brought these words into this lustre. (p. 666)

p. 289 **il me vient**   For this purpose of mine it is also appropriate for me to write at home, in a backward region, where no one helps me or corrects me, where I usually have no contact with any man who understands the Latin of his Paternoster and who does not know even less French. I would have done it better elsewhere, but the work would have been less my own; and its principal end and perfection is to be precisely my own. (pp. 666–7)

tout le monde   Everyone recognizes me in my book, and my book in me. (p. 667)

Mais je me puis   But it is harder for me to do without Plutarch. He is so universal and so full that on all occasions, and however eccentric the subject you have taken up, he makes his way into your work and offers you a liberal hand, inexhaustible in riches and embellishments. It vexes me that I am so greatly exposed to pillage by those who frequent him. (p. 666)

p. 290 **Or j'ay**   Now I have an aping and imitative nature. When I used to dabble in composing verse (and I never did any but Latin), it clearly revealed the poet I had last been reading. And of my first essays, some smell a bit foreign . . . Anyone I regard with attention easily imprints on me something of himself. (p. 667)

p. 291 **Les vers**   The verses of these two poets, treating of lasciviousness as reservedly and discreetly as they do, seem to me to reveal it and illuminate it more closely. The ladies cover their bosoms with a veil, the priests many sacred things; painters put shadows in their work to bring out the light more. (p. 671)

Je ne sçay   I don't know who it was in ancient times who wanted his throat as long as a crane's neck so as to relish longer what he swallowed. That wish is more appropriate in this quick and precipitate pleasure, especially for natures such as mine, for I have the failing of being too sudden. (loc. cit.)

p. 292 **Plus il y a**   The more steps and degrees there are, the more height and honour there is in the topmost seat. We should take pleasure in being led there, as is done in magnificent palaces, by divers porticoes and passages, long and pleasant galleries, and many windings. (loc. cit.)

L'Ægyptien   An Egyptian made a wise answer to the man who asked him: 'What are you carrying there hidden under your cloak?' 'It is hidden under my cloak so that you won't know what it is.' (loc. cit.)

(note 21) **nostre debte**   our debt to that great Judge who tucks up our rags and tatters from around our shameful parts. (p. 677)

p. 293 **Nous mangeons**   We eat and drink as the animals do, but these are not actions that hinder the operations of our mind. In these we keep our advantage over them. But this other puts every other thought beneath its yoke and by its imperious authority brutifies and bestializes all the theology and philosophy there is in Plato: and yet he does not complain of it. (p. 669)

ce notable commentaire   this notable commentary, which has escaped from me in a flow of babble, a flow sometimes impetuous and harmful. (p. 684)

(note 22) **Ceux qui**   Those who will not allow serious ideas in the midst of games act, as someone says, like a man who is afraid to worship the statue of a saint if it is undraped. (p. 669)

p. 294 **des excremens**   some excrements of an aged mind, now hard, now loose, and always undigested. (p. 721)

me vois amusant   I amuse myself in the remembrance of my past youth: 'The soul craves what it has lost, and wholly throws itself into the past.' Let childhood look ahead, old age backward: was not this the meaning of the double face of Janus? Let the years drag me along if they will, but backward.

As long as my eyes can discern that lovely season now expired, I turn them in that direction at intervals. If youth is escaping from my blood and veins, at least I want not to uproot the picture of it from my memory. (p. 639)

l'amour   Love does not seem to me properly and naturally in its season except in the age next to childhood: 'If you should place him in a troop of girls, with his ambiguous face and flowing curls, a thousand sharp onlookers could be wrong and fail to pick him out amid the throng.' . . . In manhood I find it already out of place . . . The shorter the possession we give Love over our life, the better we are . . . Who does not know how in his school they proceed contrary to all order? Study, exercise, practice, are ways leading to incapacity; the novices there give the lessons. (pp. 683-4)

p. 296 **Mais de ce que**   But from what I understand of it, the powers and worth of this god are more alive and animated in the painting of poetry than in their own reality . . . Poetry represents some indefinable air that is more amorous than love itself. Venus is not so beautiful all naked, alive, and panting, as she is here in Virgil. (p. 645)

(note 28) **Me peignant**   Painting myself for others, I have painted my inward self with colours clearer than my original ones. I have no more made my book than my book has made me—a book consubstantial with its author. (p. 504)

(note 29) **C'est contre**   It was against the order of nature that he created the most excellent production that can be. For things at birth are ordinarily imperfect; they gain in size and strength as they grow. He made the infancy of poetry and of several other sciences mature, perfect, and accomplished . . . His words, according to Aristotle, are the only words that have movement and action; they are the only substantial words. (p. 570)

p. 297 (note 31) **Je peins**   What I chiefly portray is my cogitations, a shapeless subject that does not lend itself to expression in actions. It is all I can do to couch my thoughts in this airy medium of words.   **Je m'estalle**   I expose myself entire: my portrait is a cadaver on which the veins, the muscles, and the tendons appear at a glance, each part in its place. (p. 274)

p. 298 (note 32) **Je ne me suis**   I have made no effort to attach, monstrously, the tail of a philosopher to the head and body of a dissipated man; or that this sickly remainder of my life should disavow and belie its fairest, longest, and most complete part. (p. 620)

p. 299 (note 36) **Que sont-ce**   And what are these things of mine, in truth, but grotesques and monstrous bodies, pieced together of divers members, without definite shape, having no order, sequence, or proportion other than accidental? (p. 135)

p. 300 (note 38) **Voicy mes leçons**   These are my lessons. He whose conduct shows them has profited by them better than he who merely knows them. If you see him, you hear him; if you hear him, you see him . . . The true mirror of our discourse is the course of our lives. (p. 124)

p. 301 **La montre**   The manifestation of their inclinations is so slight and so obscure at that early age, the promises so uncertain and misleading, that it is hard to base any solid judgement on them. (p. 109)

Les petits   The young of bears and dogs show their natural inclination, but men, plunging headlong into certain habits, opinions, and laws, easily change or disguise themselves. (loc. cit.)

Si est-il   Still it is difficult to force natural propensities. (loc. cit.)

(note 41) **cette raison**   this reason of ours that we handle as we will, always finding some diversity and novelty, leaves in us no apparent trace of Nature. And men have done with Nature as perfumers do with oil: they have sophisticated her with so many arguments and farfetched reasonings that she has become variable and particular for each man, and has lost her own constant and universal countenance. (p. 803)

p. 302 **Et certes**   And indeed all those imaginary, artificial descriptions of a government prove ridiculous and unfit to put into practice . . . Such a description of a government would be applicable in a new world, but we take men already bound and formed to certain customs; we do not create them, like Pyrrha or Cadmus. (p. 730)

p. 303 **Socrates**   About Socrates, who was a perfect model in all great qualities, it vexes me that he hit on a body and face so ugly as they say he had, and so incongruous with the beauty of his soul. (p. 809)

Toute cette   All this ability of ours that is beyond the natural is as good as vain and superfluous . . . Should I have died less cheerfully before having read the *Tusculans*? I think not. And now that I find myself close to death, I feel that my tongue has grown richer, my courage not at all. (pp. 794-5)

p. 304 **Voylà pas**   Is that not a sober, sane plea, but at the same time natural and lowly . . . ? Truly he was right to prefer it to the one that the great orator Lysias had put in writing for him, excellently fashioned in the forensic style, but unworthy of so noble a criminal . . . And should his rich and powerful nature have committed his defence to art, and, in its loftiest test, renounced truth and sincerity, the ornaments of his speech, to bedeck itself with the make-up of the figures and fictions of a memorized oration? (pp. 806-7)

p. 305 **ils ne sont pas**   They [sc. the sayings of Socrates] are beyond our experience. If anything of the kind were brought forth at this time, there are few men who would prize it. (p. 792)

Il est bien   It happened fortunately that the man most worthy to be known and to be presented to the world as an example should be the one of whom we have most certain knowledge. We have light on him from the most clear-sighted men who ever lived: the witnesses we have of him are wonderful in fidelity and competence. (p. 793)

Quasi   Almost all the opinions we have are taken on authority and on credit. (p. 792)

p. 306 **Nous n'apercevons**   We perceive no charms that are not sharpened, puffed out, and inflated by artifice. Those which glide along naturally and simply easily escape a sight so gross as ours . . . Our world is formed only for ostentation; men inflate themselves only with wind, and go bouncing around like balls. (p. 793)

Nous sommes   We are each richer than we think, but we are trained to borrow and beg; we are taught to use the resources of others more than our own. (p. 794)

Là . . . loge   There lies the extreme degree of perfection and difficulty; art cannot reach it. Now our faculties are not so trained. We neither essay them nor know them. We invest ourselves with those of others, and let our own lie idle. As for example someone might say of me that I have here only made a bunch of other people's flowers, having furnished nothing of my own but the thread to tie them. (p. 808)

p. 307 **je n'entends**   I do not intend that these borrowed ornaments should cover and hide me; that is the opposite of my design, I who wish to make a show only of what is my own, and what is naturally my own; and if I had taken my own advice I would at all hazards have spoken absolutely all alone. (loc. cit.)

Je ne dis   I do not speak the minds of others except to speak my own mind better. (p. 108)

Tel allegue   Some people quote Plato and Homer who have never looked at them. And I myself have taken enough passages elsewhere than at their source. Without trouble and without competence, having a library of a thousand volumes around me in this place where I write, I will presently borrow, if I please, from a dozen such patch-makers, people whom I do not often leaf through, enough to bedeck this treatise on physiognomy. (p. 808)

p. 308 **Parmy tant d'emprunts**   I, among so many borrowings of mine, am very glad to be able to hide one now and then, disguising and altering it for a new service. At the risk of letting it be said that I do so through failure to understand its original use, I give it some particular application with my own hand, so that it may be less purely someone else's. (p. 809)

p. 309 **Les paroles**   Words when reported have a different sense, as they have a different sound. (p. 814)

Si j'eusse   If I had wanted to speak from knowledge, I would have spoken earlier. I would have written at a time nearer to my studies, when I had more wit and memory, and would have trusted myself more to the vigour of that age than of this one, if I had wanted to make a profession of writing ... old age is as unsuited to this sort of work as to all others. Whoever puts his decrepitude into print [literally 'in the press'] plays the fool, if he hopes to squeeze out of it humours that do not smell of ungraciousness, dreaminess, and drowsiness. Our mind grows constipated and sluggish as it grows old ... And there is nothing I treat specifically except nothing, and no knowledge except that of the lack of knowledge. I have chosen the time when my life, which I have to portray, lies all before my eyes; what is left is more related to death. And even of my death, if I should find it garrulous, as others do, I would willingly give an account to the public on the way out. (p. 809)

p. 310 **Je ne puis**   I cannot say often enough how much I consider beauty a powerful and advantageous quality. (p. 810)

(note 42) **Socrates faict**   Socrates makes his soul move with a natural and common motion. So speaks a peasant, so speaks a woman ... His are inductions and similes drawn from the commonest and best-known actions of men; everyone understands him. Under so mean a form we should never have picked out the nobility and splendour of his admirable ideas.   **une beauté**   a delicate and hidden beauty; we need a clear and well-purged sight to discover their secret light. (p. 793)

p. 311 **J'ai un port**   I have a favourable bearing, both in itself and in others' interpretation ... —one very unlike that of Socrates. It has often happened that on the mere credit of my presence and manner, persons who had no knowledge of me have placed great trust in me, both for their own affairs and for mine. (pp. 811–12)

Je n'ay pas   I have not, like Socrates, corrected my natural disposition by force of reason, and have not troubled my inclination at all by art. I let myself go as I have come. I combat nothing. My two ruling parts, of their own volition, live in peace and good accord. (p. 811)

(note 44) **Come Socrates**   So Socrates said of his ugliness that it betrayed what would have been just as much ugliness in his soul, if he had not corrected it by training. But in saying this I hold that he was jesting according to his wont. So excellent a soul was never self-made. (p. 810)

p. 312 (note 45) **Les autres**   Others form man; I tell of him. (p. 610)
Je n'enseigne   I do not teach, I tell. (p. 612)

p. 314 **[mon jugement] s'en prend**   my judgement blames and condemns itself either for stopping at the outer bark, not being able to penetrate to the heart, or for looking at the thing by some false light . . . It thinks it gives a correct interpretation to the appearances that its conception presents to it; but these are weak and imperfect. Most of Aesop's Fables have many meanings and interpretations. Those who take them allegorically choose some aspect that squares with the fable, but for the most part this is only the first and superficial aspect; there are others more living, more essential and internal, to which they have not known how to penetrate; this is how I read them. (p. 298)

p. 315 **ceux là**   those people must be jesting who think they can diminish and stop our disputes by recalling us to the express words of the Bible. For our mind finds the field no less spacious in registering the meaning of others than in presenting its own. As if there were less animosity and bitterness in commenting than in inventing! (p. 815)

Aristote   Aristotle wrote to be understood; if he did not succeed, still less will another man, less able, and not treating his own ideas. By diluting the substance we allow it to escape and spill it all over the place; of one subject we make a thousand, and, multiplying and subdividing, fall back into Epicurus' infinity of atoms. (p. 817)

Tout fourmille   The world is swarming with commentaries; of authors there is a great scarcity. (p. 818)

(note 48) **il se sent**   it is evident from experience that so many interpretations disperse the truth and shatter it. (p. 817)

p. 316 **Il y a plus**   It is more of a job to interpret the interpretations than to interpret the things, and there are more books about books than about any other subject: we do nothing but write glosses about each other. How often and perhaps how stupidly have I extended my book to make it speak of itself! (p. 818)

il ne se voit   there is no book to be found, whether human or divine, with which the world busies itself, whose difficulties are cleared up by interpretation[.] The hundredth commentator hands it on to his successor thornier and rougher than the first one had found it. When do we agree and say, 'There has been enough about this book; henceforth there is nothing more to say about it'? (p. 817)

(note 49) **j'escry**   I write of myself and my writings as of my other actions
. . . my theme turns in upon itself. (p. 818)

p. 317 **les hommes**   Men do not know the natural infirmity of their mind:
it does nothing but ferret and quest. (p. 817)

[l'esprit] pense   The mind thinks it notices from a distance some sort of
glimmer of imaginary light and truth; but while running toward it, it is
crossed by so many difficulties and obstacles, and diverted by so many new
quests, that it strays from the road, bewildered. (loc. cit.)

il n'y a point   There is no end to our researches; our end is in the other
world. (loc. cit.)

C'est signe   It is a sign of contraction of the mind when it is content, or of
weariness. A spirited mind never stops within itself; it is always aspiring and
going beyond its strength; it has impulses beyond its powers of achievement.
If it does not advance and press forward and stand at bay and clash, it is only
half alive. (pp. 817–18)

(note 50) **Mes conceptions**   My conceptions and my judgement move
only by groping, staggering, stumbling, and blundering; and when I have
gone ahead as far as I can, still I am not at all satisfied: I can still see country
beyond, but with a dim and clouded vision, so that I cannot clearly distinguish
it (p. 107)

p. 318 **ses poursuites**   Its pursuits are boundless and without form; its food
is wonder, the chase, ambiguity. Apollo revealed this clearly enough, always
speaking to us equivocally, obscurely, and obliquely, not satisfying us, but
keeping our minds interested and busy. It is an irregular perpetual motion, without model and without aim. Its inventions excite, pursue, and produce one
another. (p. 818)

p. 319 **Sur ce mesme**   From the same foundation that Heraclitus had, and
that maxim of his that all things had in them the aspects that were found in
them, Democritus derived a wholly opposite conclusion, that things had in
them nothing at all of what we found in them. (p. 443)

p. 320 **nostre esprit**   our sickly, kill-joy mind . . . treats both itself and all
that it takes in, now one way, now the other, according to its insatiable, erratic,
and versatile nature. 'Unless the vessel's pure, all you pour in turns sour.'
I, who boast of embracing the pleasures of life so assiduously and so particularly,
find in them, when I look at them thus minutely, virtually nothing but wind.
But what of it? We are all wind. And even the wind, more wisely than we,
loves to make a noise and move about, and is content with its own functions,

without wishing for stability and solidity, qualities that do not belong to it.
(p. 849)

p. 324 **Ainsy courant** Thus, leafing rapidly through my books, I pick out, select, and gather together the very best, which I paint with a hundred colours, now in one picture, now in another; and being master of my painting, I imitate Nature without forcing myself.

BIBLIOGRAPHY

Classical Latin and Greek works are omitted from the list of primary sources, except where a sixteenth-century edition or translation has been consulted. Otherwise, I have included all works cited, both primary and secondary, together with a small number of others which I consulted but had no specific occasion to mention in text or notes. The list of secondary sources is necessarily highly selective, given the wide range of areas touched upon in this study.

The editions listed, of both early and modern works, are in all cases those I have used; where the date of the first edition is relevant to my argument, it is given in the text or notes. Where information concerning the date and place of publication of a work is not to be found on the title-page but appears elsewhere in the work, it has been placed in parentheses. Copies of all the early editions listed are to be found in one or more of the following libraries: Bibliothèque Nationale, Paris; British Library, London; Bodleian Library, Oxford; Library of the Taylor Institution, Oxford.

Where no place of publication is indicated, all works whose title is in English were published in London, all French titles in Paris.

The following abbreviations have been used:

BHR	*Bibliothèque d'Humanisme et Renaissance*
EC	*L'Esprit Créateur*
ER	*Études Rabelaisiennes*
FS	*French Studies*
JMRS	*Journal of Medieval and Renaissance Studies*
PMLA	*Publications of the Modern Language Association of America*
Ren. and Ref.	*Renaissance and Reformation*
RF	*Romanische Forschungen*
RR	*Romanic Review*
SF	*Studi Francesi*
THR	*Travaux d'Humanisme et Renaissance*

PRIMARY SOURCES

AGRICOLA, Rudolphus, *De ratione studii epistola Rodolphi Agricolae* (= *De formando studio*), n.p., n.d. (*c.* 1520).

—— *De inventione dialectica libri tres*, Paris, Simon Colin, 1538.

ALCIAT, Andreas, *Les Emblemes de Maistre Andre Alciat, puis nagueres augmentez par ledict Alciat, et mis in [sic] francois, avec curieuse correction*, Chrestien Wechel, 1542.

AUGUSTINE, St., (Works), in *Patrologiae cursus completus . . . series latina prior*, ed. J.-P. Migne, vols. xxxii–xlvii, Paris, 1861.

—— (Works), in *Corpus Christianorum series latina*, vols. xxix–l, Turnhout (various dates; not yet complete).

—— *Writings of St. Augustine*, vol. iv, *Christian Instruction*, trans. J. J. Gavigan, Washington, D.C., 1966.

BERALDUS, Nicolaus (Nicolas Bérault), *Nicolai Beraldi Aurelii Dialogus. Quo rationes quaedam explicantur, quibus dicendi ex tempore facultas parari possit: deque ipsa dicendi ex tempore facultate: ad reverendiss. Cardinalem Oddonem Castellionensem . . .* , Lyons, S. Gryphius, 1534.

BOCCACCIO, Giovanni, *Genealogie deorum gentilium libri*, 2 vols., ed. V. Romano, Bari, 1951.

—— *Boccaccio on Poetry: being the Preface and the Fourteenth and Fifteenth Books of Boccaccio's 'Genealogia Deorum Gentilium'*, ed. and trans. C. G. Osgood, Indianapolis and New York, 1956.

BOVILLUS, Carolus, *Liber de differentia vulgarium linguarum et Gallici sermonis varietate*, Paris, Robert Estienne, 1533.

BUDÉ, Guillaume, *Omnia opera*, 4 vols., ed. C. S. Curiol (facsimile of the 1557 Basle edition), Farnborough, 1966.

—— *De transitu hellenismi ad christianismum: le passage de l'hellénisme au christianisme*, facsimile and trans. M. Lebel, Sherbrooke, 1973.

DES PÉRIERS, Bonaventure, *Cymbalum mundi*, ed. P. H. Nurse, Manchester, 1958.

Dictionarium poeticum, Lyons, Haeredes Iacobi Iuntae, 1556.

DOLET, Étienne, *L'Erasmianus sive Ciceronianus d'Étienne Dolet (1535)* (facsimile of the *De imitatione ciceroniana*), ed. E. V. Telle, Geneva, 1974 (*THR* cxxxviii).

—— *La Maniere de bien traduire d'une langue en autre. D'advantage de la punctuation de la langue francoyse, plus des accents d'ycelle*, n.d. (an 1830 reprint of the 1540 Lyons edition).

DU BELLAY, Joachim, *Œuvres poétiques*, 6 vols., ed. H. Chamard, 1908–31.

—— *La Deffence et illustration de la langue françoyse*, ed. H. Chamard, 1948.

ERASMUS, Desiderius, *Omnia opera*, 9 vols., Basle, Froben, 1540 (Fr.).

—— *Desiderii Erasmi Roterodami opera omnia, emendatiora et auctiora, doctorumque virorum notis illustrata*, 10 tomes in 11 vols. (facsimile of the ed. by J. Le Clerc, Leyden, 1703–6), London, 1961–2 (LB).

—— *Opera omnia*, vol. I– , Amsterdam, 1969– (Am.).

—— *The Collected Works of Erasmus*, trans., vol. I– , Toronto, 1974– .

—— *Declamatio de pueris statim ac liberaliter instituendis*, ed. and trans. J.-C. Margolin, Geneva, 1966 (*THR* lxxvii).

—— *In D. Erasmi libros de duplici copia, verborum ac rerum, commentarius non minus utilis quam eruditus M. Veltkirchii, oratoriae professoris in schola Wittenbergensi*, Paris, Chrestien Wechel, 1539.

—— *Opus epistolarum*, 12 vols., ed. P. S. Allen, Oxford, 1906–58 (Allen).

—— *La Philosophie chrétienne* (selected works), ed. and trans. P. Mesnard, 1970.

—— *Adages*, see Secondary Sources, Phillips, M.M.

—— *The Colloquies of Erasmus*, trans. C. R. Thompson, Chicago and London, 1965.

—— *La Correspondance d'Érasme et de Guillaume Budé*, ed. and trans. M.-M. de La Garanderie, 1967.

—— *On Copia of Words and Ideas* (*De utraque verborum ac rerum copia*), ed. and trans. D. B. King and H. D. Rix, Milwaukee, 1963.

—— *Erasme Roterodame De la declamation des louenges de follie / stille facessieux et profitable pour congnoistre les erreurs et abuz du monde*, Pierre Vidoue for Galliot Du Pré, 1520.

—— *Praise of Folly, and Letter to Martin Dorp*, trans. B. Radice, ed. A. H. T. Levi, Harmondsworth, 1971.

ESTIENNE, Robert, *Dictionarium, seu Latinae linguae thesaurus . . . cum gallica fere interpretatione*, 2 vols., Paris, R. Estienne, 1531.

—— *Dictionarium latinogallicum multo locupletius Thesauro nostro recens excuso*, Paris, R. Estienne, 1546.

FABRI, Pierre, *Le Grant et vray art de pleine rethorique: util: proffitable et necessaire a toutes gens qui desirent a bien elegantement parler et escripre . . . Par lequel ung chuscun [sic] en le lysant pourra facilement et aornement composer et faire toutes descriptions en prose: comme oraisons: lettres missives: epistres: sermons recitz: collations et requestes*, Pierre Sergent, 1534.

FLISCUS, Stephanus, *Synonima excellentissimi rhetoris Ciceronis Victurii viri disertissimi: una cum Stephani Flisci synonimis utriusque linguae consumatissimi: ex omnibus partibus grammaticae orationis secundum ordinem alphabeti constructis: quae in humanum usum: aut commodum evenire possunt: noviter impressa* (Venice, Melchior Sessa and Petrus de Ravanis, 1525).

HOMER, *Copiae cornu sive Oceanus enarrationum homericarum, ex Eustathii in eundem commentariis concinnatarum, Hadriano Iunio autore*, Basle, Froben, 1558.

—— *Les Iliades d'Homere prince des poetes, traduict de Grec en vers françoys*, trans. Hugues Salel, Claude Gautier, 1570.

Hypnerotomachia, see *Le Songe de Poliphile*.

LE CARON, Louis, *Les Dialogues*, Vincent Sertenas, 1556.

LEFÈVRE D'ÉTAPLES, Jacques, *The Prefatory Epistles of Jacques Lefèvre d'Étaples and Related Texts*, ed. E. F. Rice, New York and London, 1972.

LORRIS, Guillaume de, and MEUN, Jean de, *Cy est le Romant de la roze Ou tout lart damour est enclose . . .* , Galliot Du Pré (1526).

LUTHER, Martin, *Werke*, 58 vols., with supplements, etc., Weimar, 1883– .

MACROBIUS, Ambrosius Theodosius, *Saturnalia* and *Commentarii in Somnium Scipionis*, 2 vols., ed. J. Willis, Leipzig, 1963.

MARGUERITE DE NAVARRE, *Les Dernières poésies*, ed. A. Lefranc, 1896.

—— *L'Heptaméron*, ed. M. François (1960).

MELANCHTHON, Philip, *Opera quae supersunt omnia*, ed. C. G. Bretschneider and H. E. Bindseil, in *Corpus Reformatorum*, Braunschweig, 1834–60, vols. i–xxviii.

—— *In Erasmi Rot. Libellum de duplici copia* (printed with other works, beginning: *Tabulae de schematibus et tropis, Petri Mosellani. In rhetorica Philippi Melanchthonis . . .*), Strasburg, Christianus Regenolphus, 1529.

—— *Elementorum rhetorices libri duo*, Paris, Simon Colin, 1532.

—— *Liber selectarum declamationum Philippi Melanthonis, quas conscripsit, et partim ipse in schola Vitebergensi recitavit, partim aliis recitandas exhibuit. Omnia recens in lucem aedita. Adiectae sunt eiusdem Praefationes in aliquot illustres Autores*, Strasburg, Crato Mylius, 1541.

—— *In Hesiodi libros de Opere et Die Enarrationes, una cum elegantissima authoris praefatione*, Paris, Jacques Bogard, 1543.

MONTAIGNE, Michel de, *Les Essais*, ed. P. Villey and V.-L. Saulnier, 1965.

MORELLUS, Theodoricus (Thierry Morel), *Enchiridion ad verborum copiam multiplici auctario locupletatum*, Paris, 1535.

OVID, *La Bible des Poetes de Ovide Methamorphose. Translatee de latin en Francoys. Nouvellement Imprimee a Paris*, Philippe Le Noir, 1531.

—— *Le Grand Olympe des Hystoires Poetiques du prince de poesie Ovide Naso en sa Metamorphose / Œuvre authentique / et de hault artifice / plaine de honneste recreation. Traduict de Latin en Francoys / et imprime Nouvellement* (Estienne Laveiller), 1537.

—— *Six livres de la Metamorphose d'Ovide, traduictz selon la Phrase Latine en Rime Françoise, sçavoir le III. IIII. V. VI. XIII. et XIIII.*, trans. François Habert, Michel Fezandat, 1549.

—— (*XV livres de la Metamorphose d'Ovide*), trans. François Habert (Rouen, George l'Oyselet), n.d.

—— *Trois premiers livres de la Metamorphose d'Ovide, Traduictz en vers François. Le premier et second, par Cl. Marot. Le tiers par B. Aneau. Mythologizez par Allegories Historiales, Naturelles et Moralles recueillies des bons autheurs Grecz, et Latins, sur toutes les fables, et sentences. Illustrez de figures et images convenantes.*

Avec une preparation de voie à la lecture et intelligence des Poëtes fabuleux (by Barthélemy Aneau), Lyons, Guillaume Rouille, 1556.

PELETIER DU MANS, Jacques, *L'Art poëtique*, ed. A. Boulanger, 1930.

PEROTTUS, Nicolaus, *Cornucopiae, sive linguae latinae commentarii*, Venice, Aldus, 1513.

PETRARCH, Francesco, *Francisci Petrarchae Florentini . . . Opera quae extant omnia*, Basle, Henricus Petri, 1554 (facsimile reprint in 3 vols., Ridgewood, N.J., 1965).

PICCOLOMINI, Aeneas Sylvius (Pius II), *Aeneae Sylvii Piccolominei . . . opera quae extant omnia*, Basle, Henricus Petri, 1571.

POLITIAN, Angelo (Poliziano), *Omnium Angeli Politiani operum (quae quidem extare novimus) Tomus prior . . . Caetera eiusdem opera et opuscula in posteriore indicabunt Tomo seu particula*, Paris, Badius Ascensius (1519).

RABELAIS, François, *Œuvres*, ed. A. Lefranc and others, vol. I– , 1913– .

—— *Œuvres complètes*, ed. G. Demerson and others, 1973.

—— *Gargantua*, ed. R. Calder and M. A. Screech, Geneva and Paris, 1970.

—— *Le Tiers Livre*, ed. M. A. Screech, Geneva and Paris, 1964.

—— *Le Quart Livre*, ed. R. Marichal, Geneva, 1947.

RAMUS, Petrus (Pierre de La Ramée), *Dialecticae institutiones*, Paris, Jacques Bogard, 1543.

RIPA, Cesare, *Iconologia*, Padua, Pietro Paolo Tosti, 1611.

RONSARD, Pierre de, *Œuvres complètes*, 20 vols., ed. P. Laumonier, I. Silver, and R. Lebègue, 1914–75.

SEBILLET, Thomas, *Art poétique françoys*, ed. F. Gaiffe, 1932.

SPERONI, Sperone, *Dialogi di Messer Speron Sperone*, Venice, Aldus, 1542.

Le Songe de Poliphile, preface by A.-M. Schmidt, facsimile of the first French edition of the *Hypnerotomachia Poliphili* (ed. J. Martin; J. Kerver, 1546), 1963.

TALON, Omer (Audomarus Talaeus), *Institutiones oratoriae, ad celeberrimam et illustrissimam Lutetiae Parisiorum Academiam*, Paris, Jacques Bogard, 1545.

TELIN, Guillaume, *Bref sommaire des sept vertus / sept ars liberaux / sept ars de Poesie / sept ars mechaniques / des Philosophies / des quinze Ars magicques . . .* , Nicolas Cousteau for Galliot Du Pré (1533 o.s.).

TORY, Geoffroy, *Champ fleury. Au quel est contenu Lart et Science de la deue et vraye Proportion des Lettres Attiques, quon dit autrement Lettres Antiques, et vulgairement Lettres Romaines proportionnees selon le Corps et Visage humain*, G. Tory and G. Gourmont (1529).

TYARD, Pontus de, *Œuvres: Solitaire premier*, ed. S. F. Baridon, Geneva and Lille, 1950.

VALLA, Lorenzo, *Laurentii Vallae Opera, nunc primo non mediocribus vigiliis et iudicio quorundam eruditiss. virorum in unum volumen collecta* . . . , Basle, Henricus Petri, 1540.

SECONDARY SOURCES

I. Works of Reference

ABBOTT, K. M., OLDFATHER, W. A., and CANTER, H. V., *Index verborum in Ciceronis Rhetorica necnon incerti auctoris libros ad Herennium*, Urbana, Ill., 1964.

BLAISE, A., *Dictionnaire latin-français des auteurs chrétiens*, Turnhout, 1954.

BLOCH, O., and VON WARTBURG, W., *Dictionnaire étymologique de la langue française*, 1968.

COTGRAVE, R., *A Dictionarie of the French and English Tongues*, facsimile of the first edition (1611), New York, 1950.

DU CANGE, D., *Glossarium mediae et infimae latinitatis*, 7 vols., Paris, 1840–50.

GODEFROY, F., *Dictionnaire de l'ancienne langue française et de tous ses dialectes du IXe au XVe siècle*, 10 vols., 1881–1902.

HENKEL, A., and SCHÖNE, A., *Emblemata: Handbuch zur Sinnbildkunst des XVI. und XVII. Jahrhunderts*, 2 vols., Stuttgart, 1967, 1976.

HUGUET, E., *Dictionnaire de la langue française du seizième siècle*, 7 vols., 1925–67.

LAUSBERG, H., *Handbuch der literarischen Rhetorik*, 2 vols., Munich, 1973.

LEWIS, C. T., and SHORT, C., *A Latin Dictionary*, Oxford (many editions).

LIDDELL, H. G., and SCOTT, M. A., *A Greek–English Lexicon*, Oxford (many editions).

MURRAY, J. A. H., *A New English Dictionary on Historical Principles*, 11 vols., Oxford, 1888–1933.

Oxford Latin Dictionary, 6 fascicles pub. to date, Oxford, 1968– .

TERVARENT, G. de, *Attributs et symboles dans l'art profane, 1450–1600*, Geneva, 1958–9 (*THR* xxix).

Thesaurus linguae latinae, vol. I– , Leipzig, 1900– .

II. General

ALLEN, D. Cameron, *Mysteriously Meant: the rediscovery of pagan symbolism and allegorical interpretation in the Renaissance*, Baltimore and London, 1970.

ARBUSOW, L., *Colores rhetorici: eine Auswahl rhetorischer Figuren und Gemeinplätze*, Göttingen, 1948.

ARMSTRONG, E., *Ronsard and the Age of Gold*, Cambridge, 1968.

AUGUSTIJN, G., 'Hyperaspistes I: la doctrine d'Érasme et de Luther sur la "claritas scripturae"', in *Colloquia Erasmiana Turonensia* (q.v.), vol. ii, 737–48.

BAKHTIN, M., *Rabelais and his World*, trans. H. Iswolsky, Cambridge, Mass., and London, 1968.

BARTHES, R., *Le Degré zéro de l'écriture*, 1953.

—— *Essais critiques*, 1964.

—— *Sade, Fourier, Loyola*, 1971.

—— *Le Plaisir du texte*, 1973.

BAXANDALL, M., *Giotto and the Orators: humanist observers of painting in Italy and the discovery of pictorial composition 1350–1450*, Oxford, 1971.

—— *Painting and Experience in Fifteenth Century Italy*, Oxford, 1972.

BEAUJOUR, M., *Le Jeu de Rabelais*, 1970.

BÉNÉ, C., *Érasme et saint Augustin*, Geneva, 1969 (*THR* ciii).

BERRY, A. F., 'Rabelais: Homo Logos', *JMRS*, iii (1973), 51–67.

BLOOM, H. I., *The Anxiety of Influence: a theory of poetry*, New York, 1973.

BOLGAR, R. R., *The Classical Heritage and its Beneficiaries*, Cambridge, 1973.

—— (ed.) *Classical Influences on European Culture A.D. 1500–1700*, Cambridge, 1976.

BORST, A., *Der Turmbau von Babel: Geschichte der Meinungen über Ursprung und Vielfalt der Sprachen und Völker*, 6 vols., Stuttgart, 1957–63.

BOWEN, B. C., *The Age of Bluff: paradox and ambiguity in Rabelais and Montaigne*, Urbana, Ill., 1972.

—— 'Montaigne's anti-*Phaedrus*: "Sur des vers de Virgile" (*Essais*, III. v)', *JMRS*, v (1975), 107–21.

—— (ed.) *The French Renaissance Mind: studies presented to W. G. Moore, EC*, xvi (1976).

BREEN, Q., 'The terms "loci communes" and "loci" in Melanchthon', *Church History*, xvi (1947), 197–209.

—— 'The subordination to rhetoric in Melanchthon', *Archiv für Reformationsgeschichte*, xliii (1952), 13–28.

BROWN, F. S., (ed.) *Renaissance Studies in Honor of Isidore Silver, Kentucky Romance Quarterly*, xxi (1974), supplement no. 2.

BUFFIÈRE, F., *Les Mythes d'Homère et la pensée grecque*, 1956.

BURKE, K. D., *The Rhetoric of Religion: studies in logology*, Boston, Mass., 1961.

BUTOR, M., *Essais sur les Essais*, 1968.

—— and HOLLIER, D., *Rabelais: ou c'était pour rire*, 1972.

CASTOR, G., *Pléiade Poetics: a study in sixteenth-century thought and terminology*, Cambridge, 1964.

CAVE, T. C., 'Ronsard's Bacchic poetry: from the *Bacchanales* to the *Hymne de l'autonne*', *EC*, x (1970), 104–16.

CAVE, T. C., 'Ronsard as Apollo: myth, poetry and experience in a Renaissance sonnet-cycle', *Yale French Studies*, xlvii (1972), 76–89.

—— 'Mythes de l'abondance et de la privation chez Ronsard', *Cahiers de l'Association Internationale des Études Françaises*, xxv (1973), 247–60.

—— 'Ronsard's mythological universe', in *Ronsard the Poet* (see below), 159–208.

—— 'Copia and cornucopia', in *French Renaissance Studies*, ed. Sharratt (q.v.), 52–69.

—— '*Enargeia*: Erasmus and the rhetoric of presence in the sixteenth century', in *The French Renaissance Mind*, ed. Bowen (q.v.), 5–19.

—— (ed.) *Ronsard the Poet*, 1973.

CHRISTIE, R. Copley, *Étienne Dolet: the martyr of the Renaissance 1508–1546*, 1899.

COLEMAN, D. G., *Rabelais: a critical study in prose fiction*. Cambridge, 1971.

—— 'Montaigne's "Sur des vers de Virgile": taboo subject, taboo author', in *Classical Influences*, ed. Bolgar (q.v.), 135–40.

COLIE, R., *Paradoxia Epidemica: the Renaissance tradition of paradox*, Princeton, 1966.

COLISH, M. L., *The Mirror of Language: a study in the medieval theory of knowledge*, New Haven and London, 1968.

Colloquia Erasmiana Turonensia (Douzième stage international d'études human-istes, Tours, 1969), 2 vols., Paris, 1972.

COPPENS, J., (ed.) *Scrinium Erasmianum*, 2 vols., Leyden, 1969.

CULLER, J., *Structuralist Poetics: structuralism, linguistics, and the study of literature*, 1975.

—— 'Paradox and the language of morals in La Rochefoucauld', *Modern Language Review*, lxviii (1973), 28–39.

—— 'Beyond interpretation: the prospects of contemporary criticism', *Comparative Literature*, xxviii (1976), 244–56.

CURTIUS, E. R., *European Literature and the Latin Middle Ages*, trans. W. R. Trask, New York, 1953.

DÄLLENBACH, L., *Le Récit spéculaire: essai sur la mise en abyme*, 1977.

DEFAUX, G., *Pantagruel et les sophistes: contribution à l'histoire de l'humanisme chrétien au XVIe siècle*, The Hague, 1973.

DEMERSON, G., *La Mythologie classique dans l'œuvre lyrique de la 'Pléiade'*, Geneva, 1972 (*THR* cxix).

DERRIDA, J., *De la grammatologie*, 1967.

—— *La Voix et le phénomène*, 1967.

—— *La Dissémination*, 1972.

—— *Marges de la philosophie*, 1975.

DETIENNE, M., *Les Jardins d'Adonis*, 1972.

DUBOIS, C.-G., *Mythe et langage au seizième siècle*, Bordeaux, 1970.

EBELING, G., *Evangelische Evangelienauslegung: eine Untersuchung zu Luthers Hermeneutik*, Darmstadt, 1962.

ENGELHARDT, G. J., 'Medieval vestiges in the rhetoric of Erasmus', *PMLA*, lxiii (1948), 739–44.

FOUCAULT, M., *Les Mots et les choses*, 1966.

FOULET, A., ' "Les adventures des gens curieulx" ', *RR*, liv (1963), 3–5.

François Rabelais : ouvrage publié pour le quatrième centenaire de sa mort (1553–1953), Geneva and Lille, 1953 (*THR* vii).

FRIEDRICH, H., *Montaigne*, Berne and Munich, 1967 (Fr. trans. Rovini, Paris, 1968).

GADOFFRE, G., *Ronsard par lui-même*, 1960.

—— 'Ronsard et le thème solaire', in *Le Soleil à la Renaissance: science et mythes* (colloque international, 1963), Brussels and Paris, 1965, 501–18.

GARRETT, C. H., *The Marian Exiles: a study in the origins of Elizabethan Puritanism*, Cambridge, 1938.

GENDRE, A., *Ronsard poète de la conquête amoureuse*, Neuchâtel, 1970.

GENETTE, G., *Figures I, II,* and *III*, 1966–72.

—— *Mimologiques: voyage en Cratylie*, 1976.

GILSON, E., *Les Idées et les lettres*, 1932.

GLAUSER, A., *Rabelais créateur*, 1964.

—— *Montaigne paradoxal*, 1972.

—— *Le Faux Rabelais, ou de l'inauthenticité du Cinquième Livre*, 1975.

GMELIN, H., 'Das Prinzip der Imitatio in den Romanischen Literaturen der Renaissance', *RF*, xlvi (1932), 83–360.

GOEBEL, G., 'Zwei Versuche zur Architekturbeschreibung in der Dichtung der Renaissance', *RF*, lxxviii (1966), 280–313.

GORDON, A. L., *Ronsard et la rhétorique*, Geneva, 1970 (*THR* cxi).

GRAY, F., *Rabelais et l'écriture*, 1974.

—— 'Ambiguity and point of view in the Prologue to *Gargantua*', *RR*, lvi (1965), 12–21.

—— 'Montaigne and Sebond: the rhetoric of paradox', *FS*, xxviii (1974), 134–45.

GRIFFIN, R., *Coronation of the Poet: Joachim Du Bellay's debt to the trivium*, Berkeley and Los Angeles, 1969.

GUITON, J., 'Le mythe des Paroles gelées', *RR*, xxxi (1940), 3–15.

HELGERSON, R., *The Elizabethan Prodigals*, Berkeley and Los Angeles, 1977.

HIGMAN, F. M., 'Calvin and the art of translation', *Western Canadian Studies in Modern Languages and Literature*, ii (1970), 5–27.

JEANNERET, M., *Poésie et tradition biblique au XVIe siècle: recherches stylistiques sur les paraphrases des psaumes de Marot à Malherbe*, 1969.

—— 'Les paroles dégelées: Rabelais, "Quart Livre" ', *Littérature*, xvii (1975), 14–30.

—— 'Rabelais et Montaigne: l'écriture comme parole', in *The French Renaissance Mind*, ed. Bowen (q.v.), 78–94.

KAISER, W., *Praisers of Folly: Erasmus, Rabelais, Shakespeare*, 1964.

KELLER, L., *Palingène, Ronsard, Du Bartas: trois études sur la poésie cosmologique de la Renaissance*, Berne, 1974.

KERMODE, F., *The Sense of an Ending: studies in the theory of fiction*, Oxford, 1967.

KRAILSHEIMER, A. J., *Rabelais and the Franciscans*, Oxford, 1963.

—— 'The Andouilles of the "Quart Livre" ', in *François Rabelais* (q.v.), 226–32.

KRISTEVA, J., 'Une poétique ruinée', preface to Bakhtin, *La Poétique de Dostoievski*, 1970.

LA CHARITÉ, R. C., 'The unity of Rabelais's *Pantagruel*', *FS*, xxvi (1972), 257–65.

—— '*Mundus inversus*: the fictional world of Rabelais's *Pantagruel*', *Stanford French Review*, i (1977), 95–105.

—— (ed.) *O un amy! Essays on Montaigne in honor of Donald M. Frame*, Lexington, Ky., 1977.

LANHAM, R. A., *The Motives of Eloquence: literary rhetoric in the Renaissance*, New Haven and London, 1976.

LEBÈGUE, R., 'Ronsard lecteur de Rabelais', *BHR*, xvi (1954), 82–5.

LEFRANC, A., *Grands Écrivains français de la Renaissance*, 1914.

LEVI, A. H. T., 'The neoplatonist calculus', in *Humanism in France* (see below), 229–48.

—— 'Pagan virtue and the humanism of the northern Renaissance' (The Society for Renaissance Studies, occasional papers, no. ii), 1974.

—— 'Ethics and the encyclopedia in the sixteenth century', in *French Renaissance Studies*, ed. Sharratt (q.v.), 170–84.

—— 'Erasmus, the early Jesuits and the classics', in *Classical Influences*, ed. Bolgar (q.v.), 223–38.

—— (ed.) *Humanism in France at the End of the Middle Ages and in the Early Renaissance*, Manchester, 1970.

LUBAC, H. de, *Exégèse médiévale: les quatre sens de l'Écriture*, 2 parts in 3 vols., 1959–64.

McFARLANE, I. D., 'Aspects of Ronsard's poetic vision', in *Ronsard the Poet*, ed. Cave (q.v.), 13–78.

—— 'Ronsard's poems to Jean Brinon', in *Renaissance Studies*, ed. Brown (q.v.), 53–67.

McGOWAN, M., *Montaigne's Deceits: the art of persuasion in the 'Essais'*, 1974.

McKEON, R., 'Rhetoric in the Middle Ages', *Speculum*, xvii (1942), 1–32.

MARGOLIN, J.-C., *Recherches érasmiennes*, Geneva, 1969 (*THR* cv).

—— 'L' "Hymne de l'Or" et son ambiguïté', *BHR*, xxviii (1966), 271–93.

—— 'Érasme et le verbe: de la rhétorique à l'herméneutique', in *Érasme, l'Alsace, et son temps* (catalogue and proceedings of colloquium), Strasburg, 1971, 87–110.

MARICHAL, R., 'L'attitude de Rabelais devant le néoplatonisme et l'italianisme', in *François Rabelais* (q.v.), 181–209.

—— '*Quart Livre*: commentaires', *ER*, i (1956), 151–202 and v (1964), 65–162.

MASTERS, G. Mallary, *Rabelaisian Dialectic and the Platonic-Hermetic Tradition*, Albany, N.Y., 1969.

MAYER, C. A., 'Rabelais's satirical eulogy: the praise of borrowing', in *François Rabelais* (q.v.), 147–55.

MICHEL, A., *Rhétorique et philosophie chez Cicéron*, 1960.

MOORE, W. G., 'Montaigne's notion of experience', in *The French Mind: studies in honour of Gustave Rudler*, ed. W. G. Moore, Oxford, 1952, 34–52.

MORTIER, R., *La Poétique des ruines en France: ses origines, ses variations de la Renaissance à Victor Hugo*, Geneva, 1974.

MURPHY, J. J., *Rhetoric in the Middle Ages: a history of rhetorical theory from Saint Augustine to the Renaissance*, Berkeley, 1974.

NORTON, G. P., *Montaigne and the Introspective Mind*, The Hague, 1975.

—— 'Translation theory in Renaissance France: Étienne Dolet and the rhetorical tradition,' *Ren. and Ref.*, x (1974), 1–13.

—— 'Translation theory in Renaissance France: the poetic controversy', *Ren. and Ref.*, xi (1975), 30–44.

NYKROG, P., 'Thélème, Panurge, et la dive bouteille', *Revue d'Histoire Littéraire de la France*, lxv (1965), 385–97.

ONG, W. J., *Ramus: Method, and the Decay of Dialogue*, Cambridge, Mass., 1958.

—— *The Presence of the Word: some prolegomena for cultural and religious history*, New York, 1970.

—— *Rhetoric, Romance, and Technology: studies in the interaction of expression and culture*, Ithaca, N.Y., 1971.

—— 'Commonplace rhapsody: Ravisius Textor, Zwinger and Shakespeare', in *Classical Influences*, ed. Bolgar (q.v.), 91–126.

PADLEY, G. A., *Grammatical Theory in Western Europe 1500–1700*, Cambridge, 1976.

PARIS, J., *Rabelais au futur*, 1970.

PAYNE, J. B., 'Towards the hermeneutics of Erasmus', in *Scrinium Erasmianum*, ed. Coppens (q.v.), vol. ii, 13–49.

PÉPIN, J., *Mythe et allégorie: les origines grecques et les contestations judéo-chrétiennes*, 1958.

—— 'A propos de l'histoire de l'exégèse allégorique: l'absurdité, signe de l'allégorie', in *Studia Patristica, I, Texte und Untersuchungen*, lxiii (1957), 395–413.

—— 'L'herméneutique ancienne: les mots et les idées', *Poétique*, xxiii (1975), 291–300.

PHILLIPS, M. Mann, *The 'Adages' of Erasmus: a study with translations*, Cambridge, 1964.

—— 'Erasmus in France in the later sixteenth century', *Journal of the Warburg and Courtauld Institutes*, xxxiv (1971), 246–61.

—— 'Erasmus and the art of writing', in *Scrinium Erasmianum*, ed. Coppens (q.v.), vol. i, 335–50.

—— 'Érasme et Montaigne', in *Colloquia Erasmiana Turonensia* (q.v.), vol. i, 479–501.

—— 'From the *Ciceronianus* to Montaigne', in *Classical Influences*, ed. Bolgar (q.v.), 191–7.

PONS, E., 'Les "jargons" de Panurge dans Rabelais', *Revue de Littérature Comparée*, xi (1931), 185–218.

POPE-HENNESSY, J., *The Portrait in the Renaissance*, New York and London, 1966.

POPKIN, R., *The History of Scepticism from Erasmus to Descartes*, Assen, 1964.

POUILLOUX, J.-Y., *Lire les 'Essais' de Montaigne*, 1969.

RAIBLE, W., 'Der Prolog zu *Gargantua* und der Pantagruelismus', *RF*, lxxviii (1966), 253–79.

RAYMOND, M., and STEELE, A. J. (ed), *La Poésie française et le maniérisme 1546–1610(?)*, Geneva and Paris, 1971.

RECHTIEN, J. G., 'A 1520 French translation of the *Moriae Encomium*', *Renaissance Quarterly*, xxvii (1974), 23–35.

REGOSIN, R., 'Montaigne's *Essais*: the book of the self', *EC*, xv (1975), 39–48.

RICE, E. F., *The Renaissance Idea of Wisdom*, Cambridge, Mass., 1958.

—— *The Prefatory Epistles*, see Primary Sources, Lefèvre d'Étaples.

RICHMOND, H. M., 'Personal identity and literary personae: a study in historical psychology', *PMLA*, xc (1975), 209–21.

RICŒUR, P., *La Métaphore vive*, 1975.

RIDER, F., *The Dialectic of Selfhood in Montaigne*, Stanford, 1973.

RIGOLOT, F., *Les Langages de Rabelais*, Geneva, 1972 (*ER* x).

—— 'Cratylisme et Pantagruélisme: Rabelais et le statut du signe', *ER*, xiii (1976), 115–32.

RIX, H., 'The editions of Erasmus's *De copia*', *Studies in Philology* (University of North Carolina), xliii (1946), 595–605.

ROUSSET, J., *Anthologie de la poésie baroque française*, 2 vols., 1961.

RUEGG, W., *Cicero und der Humanismus*, Zurich, 1946.

SACRÉ, J., 'Les métamorphoses d'une braguette', *Littérature*, xxvi (1977), 72–93.

SAULNIER, V.-L., *Le Dessein de Rabelais*, 1957.

—— 'Le festin devant Chaneph ou la confiance dernière de Rabelais', *Mercure de France*, cccxx (1954), 649–66.

—— 'Le silence de Rabelais et le mythe des paroles gelées', in *François Rabelais* (q.v.), 233–47.

SAYCE, R. A., *The Essays of Montaigne: a critical exploration*, 1972.

SCHRADER, L., *Panurge und Hermes: zum Ursprung eines Charakters bei Rabelais*, Bonn, 1958.

SCREECH, M. A., *The Rabelaisian Marriage: aspects of Rabelais's religion, ethics and comic philosophy*, 1958.

—— *L'Évangélisme de Rabelais: aspects de la satire religieuse au XVIe siècle*, Geneva, 1959 (*ER* ii).

—— 'The sense of Rabelais's *Énigme en prophétie*', *BHR*, xviii (1956), 392–404.

—— 'Commonplaces of law, proverbial wisdom and philosophy: their importance in Renaissance scholarship (Rabelais, Joachim Du Bellay, Montaigne)', in *Classical Influences*, ed. Bolgar (q.v.), 127–34.

—— and CALDER, R., 'Some Renaissance attitudes to laughter', in *Humanism in France*, ed. Levi (q.v.), 216–28.

SERRES, M., *Hermès III: la traduction*, 1974.

—— *Hermès IV: la distribution*, 1977.

SEZNEC, J., *The Survival of the Pagan Gods*, New York, 1961.

SHARRATT, P. (ed.), *French Renaissance Studies 1540–70: humanism and the encyclopedia*, Edinburgh, 1976.

SILVER, I., *Ronsard and the Hellenic Renaissance in France*, vol. i: *Ronsard and the Greek Epic*, St. Louis, 1961.

SIMONE, F., 'La notion d'encyclopédie: élément caractéristique de la Renaissance française', in *French Renaissance Studies*, ed. Sharratt (q.v.), 234–62.

SMALLEY, B., *The Study of the Bible in the Middle Ages*, Oxford, 1952.

SMITH, M. C., 'The hidden meaning of Ronsard's *Hymne de l'Hyver*', in *Renaissance Studies*, ed. Brown (q.v.), 85–97.

SOWARDS, J. K., 'Erasmus and the apologetic textbook', *Studies in Philology* (University of North Carolina), lv (1958), 122–35.

SPITZER, L., 'Rabelais et les "rabelaisants"', *SF*, xii (1960), 401–23.

—— 'Ancora sul prologo al Gargantua', *SF*, xxvii (1965), 423–34.

STEINER, G., *After Babel: aspects of language and translation*, 1975.

STONE, D., *Ronsard's Sonnet Cycles: a study in tone and vision*, New Haven and London, 1966.

TELLE, E. V., 'A propos de la lettre de Gargantua à son fils (*Pantagruel*, chap. VIII)', *BHR*, xix (1957), 208–33.

—— 'Dolet et Érasme', in *Colloquia Erasmiana Turonensia* (q.v.), vol. i, 407–39.

TODOROV, T., *La Poétique de la prose*, 1971.

VALLESE, G., 'Érasme et le *De duplici copia verborum ac rerum*', in *Colloquia Erasmiana Turonensia* (q.v.), vol. i, 233–9.

VASOLI, C., *La dialettica e la retorica dell'umanesimo: 'invenzione' e 'metodo' nella cultura del XV e XVI secolo*, Milan, 1968.

VERDIER, M. F., 'A propos d'une controverse sur l'*Hymne de l'Or* de Pierre de Ronsard', *BHR*, xxxv (1973), 7–18.

VILLEY, P., *Les Sources et l'évolution des Essais de Montaigne*, 2 vols., 1933.

WALKER, D. P., *The Ancient Theology: studies in Christian Platonism from the fifteenth to the eighteenth century*, 1972.

WEINBERG, F. M., *The Wine and the Will: Rabelais's Bacchic Christianity*, Detroit, 1972.

—— ' "La parolle faict le jeu": Mercury in the *Cymbalum mundi*', in *The French Renaissance Mind*, ed. Bowen (q.v.), 48–62.

WILDEN, A., 'Par divers moyens on arrive à pareille fin: a reading of Montaigne', *Modern Language Notes*, lxxxiii (1968), 577–97.

WIND, E., *Pagan Mysteries in the Renaissance*, 1968.

YATES, F. A., *Giordano Bruno and the Hermetic Tradition*, 1964.

—— *The Art of Memory*, 1966.

ZUMTHOR, P., *Essai de poétique médiévale*, 1972.

—— *Langue, texte, énigme*, 1975.

INDEX OF NAMES

Characters in fictional works, dialogues, etc., are not listed separately, but have been subsumed (together with names of works) in the entries for the relevant authors.